The Political Crisis of the 1850s

The
Political Crisis
of the 1850s

MICHAEL F. HOLT
The University of Virginia

W · W · NORTON & COMPANY

New York · London

Copyright © 1978 by John Wiley & Sons, Inc.

Published simultaneously in Canada by George J. McLeod Limited, Toronto.

Printed in the United States of America

First published as a Norton paperback 1983

Library of Congress Cataloging in Publication Data

Holt, Michael F. (Michael Fitzgibbon)
    The political crisis of the 1850s.

    Originally published: New York: Wiley, © 1978.
    Bibliography: p.
    Includes index.
    1. United States—Politics and government—1845-1861.
2. Slavery—United States—History.   3. Compromise of
1850.   I. Title.
E415.7.H74   1983   973.6   83–13499

W. W. Norton & Company, Inc.
500 Fifth Avenue, New York, N.Y. 10110
W. W. Norton & Company Ltd.
37 Great Russell Street, London WC1B 3NU

ISBN 0-393-95370-X

1 2 3 4 5 6 7 8 9 0

Foreword

The resurgence of political history is one of the most intriguing developments in recent American historical scholarship. In the years immediately following World War II, scholars tended to dismiss the study of past politics as mundane and old-fashioned as they focused on cultural, psychological, ethnic, and intellectual approaches to the American experience. But the enduring importance of political events, brought home to scholars as well as journalists by the tumultuous events of the 1960s and the devastating Watergate scandal, led historians to reexamine the political past. Many borrowed ideas and techniques from social scientists to probe into new areas such as voting behavior, party fluctuations, and the role of ethnocultural factors in politics. Others relied on more traditional studies of campaign rhetoric and the impact of charismatic leaders on the political process. The result was a new flowering of political history.

Critical Episodes in American Politics is a series of interpretive volumes designed to bring the new scholarship to bear on eight major episodes, from the origins of the first party system in the 1790s to the trauma of Vietnam and Watergate. Each author examines the political process at a critical time in the American past to demonstrate how the democratic system functioned under great stress. Employing different techniques and approaches, each author seeks to explain the distinctive events in his period to give the reader an insight into both the strengths and weaknesses of the American political tradition.

In this volume, Professor Michael F. Holt offers a new and provocative explanation for the breakdown of the Second American Party System and the coming of the Civil War. Disagreeing with the historians who focus their concern primarily on the issue of slavery, Holt sees the disintegration of the Whig-Democratic party structure as a major cause of the political crisis of the 1850s instead of as the result of growing sectional discord. Holt contends that for nearly three decades, the contest between two national parties had kept the antagonism between the North and the South within the realm of political compromise. Only when the Whigs and Democrats failed to offer voters distinctive and attractive alternatives in the early 1850s did the sectional conflict achieve the dangerous level that finally led to the Civil War in 1861. By focusing on party dynamics on the state level and on the national level, Holt offers a new and arresting analysis of the most celebrated breakdown of American democracy.

Robert A. Divine

Preface

This is not the book I set out to write. Several years ago when I agreed to contribute to the Wiley series on Critical Episodes in American Politics, I had determined to define the crisis of the 1850s in terms of the political reorganization and voter realignment of that decade. I was then starting a long-term study of the demise of the Whig party, and I viewed this book as an opportunity for testing some ideas about the reasons for, and consequences of, the collapse of the Second American Party System. My theory rested on a behavioral model of the way two-party systems operate and why they fail, and I had tentatively settled on an alliterative title that reflected the thrust of my hypothesis: *Conflict, Consensus, and the Coming of the Civil War.*

As the following pages will reveal, I have not abandoned that theory, but I have felt the need to change the title so that it more accurately represents the end product. While researching and writing, I discovered that a purely behavioral model was inadequate to explain either the politics of the 1850s or their relation to the coming of the Civil War. More important, I became convinced that the notion of a political crisis in the 1850s was not simply an artificial construct that a historian blessed with hindsight could impose on the period. Abundant evidence suggested that a genuine sense of crisis troubled Americans living in that decade. Many feared that the existence of republican self-government itself stood in danger, and I am now persuaded that only if one recognizes that sense of crisis and the responses to it can the political origins of the Civil War be understood.

The political crisis of the 1850s was rooted in ideology as well as in behavior. Unlike other historians who have found conflicting sectional ideologies based on fundamentally different economic and social structures in the North and South at the core of Civil War causation, however, I believe that the ideological values that were central were basically political, not social, moral, or economic, and that they were shared by Americans in both sections. This ideology has been described brilliantly by historians of the Revolutionary era, and has been called republicanism. It was both a set of premises about the kind of government and society necessary to secure individual freedom and equality and a framework of perception through which the American public in the antebellum period judged the significance of political events. Always nervous that republican society might be undermined or corrupted, Americans were determined to protect self-government, liberty, and equality for whites from anything that threatened those most cherished possessions. It was that obsession, I maintain, that drove Americans to the point of killing each other in 1861.

why?

To understand the political crisis of the 1850s, in sum, I have found it necessary to take political ideas just as seriously as political behavior. By embracing both the ideological and behavioral approaches to political history, I reject the notion that those modes of analysis are necessarily at odds and mutually exclusive—an impression one might easily get from the conflicting accounts of American political history written in the last twenty-five years. Instead, this study posits an integral relationship between the dynamics of party interaction, which did indeed have a mechanistic dimension seemingly impervious to the content of ideas, and popular republican values. It argues that this relationship had existed since the 1820s, if not before, and that the same dynamics and ideology that sparked the breakup of the nation in the winter of 1860 to 1861 had shaped what we consider normal party political development since the Jacksonian and Whig parties began to emerge. Put another way, it argues that the same reasons that explain why the political system could contain the smoldering sectional conflict for over thirty years before 1854 also explain why, after that date, the political system helped to fan that fire until it exploded into open warfare in April 1861. Whether this merger of behavioral and ideological analysis represents a blessed union based on authentic affinity or only an unsuccessful marriage of convenience is for the reader to determine.

Some other warnings are in order. This book is about politics and political parties. It tries to show how the workings of the party system and the ideology that had been basic to it contributed to the disruption of the Union. Its primary concern is not with the intensification of sectional conflict between North and South. Thus I have not included certain staples found in other books about the coming of the Civil War, such as the nature of Negro slavery or the rise of abolitionism. I have omitted these, not because they were unimportant to the development of the sectional conflict, but because I believe other things were more important to political evolution. This, then, does not pretend to be a full-fledged account of the reasons Northerners and Southerners disliked each other. Instead, its focus is on the political developments that caused that animosity to explode into civil war.

Nor, obviously, is it a complete account of the politics of the 1840s and 1850s. For one thing, limitations of space have kept me from bringing all the evidence I have on certain aspects of the story to bear. More important, my own research on the period from 1844 to 1856 is incomplete. As I will argue strenuously below, I believe that the state level of politics was beyond doubt the most important in the nineteenth century, and any complete account of prewar politics must analyze each individual state. Even if I had the space to provide such an analysis, I have not yet done the research on all states that would allow it. Nevertheless, I have no reason to believe now that additional research would fundamentally alter the outlines of the following argument. The reader should beware, however, that my present lack of information on Southern state politics in the 1850s may distort my discussion of the secession crisis in Chapter VIII. Secession is beyond the scope of the research in which I am engaged, and I have had to rely largely on the work of others. Moreover, I do not think that any successful explanation of secession—or more particularly of the different responses of Southern states to Abraham Lincoln's election— has yet been given. Undeterred by that dearth, I have ventured a theory of my own, but it is more speculative than any other part of the book.

Finally, a caveat about my discussion of political decision making is necessary. My concern has been more with the impact of the party system on leadership decisions than with the morality of particular decisions themselves. Because I believe that political leaders in the nineteenth century fully understood how the system worked and what was necessary to maintain voter loyalty to their organizations, I have interpreted their actions primarily in that regard. To some this tack will seem overly cynical and one-dimensional, but I do not mean to imply that seeking political advantage was the only motive that stirred politicians. They may well have believed that the programs they advocated and the strategies they pursued were good for the nation. Certainly they felt constrained by and shared the popular insistence that republican government be perpetuated by their policies. Most leaders undoubtedly saw no discrepancy between the advocacy of principle and the pursuit of partisan goals. I have focused on the latter only because I believe that in the reasons why popular faith in political parties first waxed, then waned, and then was restored in most of the country lie the answers to the vexing problem of why a sectional conflict of long duration disrupted the nation in 1861.

Michael F. Holt

Charlottesville
May 1977

Acknowledgments

Although this is a short book, I have accumulated a long list of obligations during its preparation. During the summers of 1975 and 1976, Wilson-Gee Research Fellowships from the University of Virginia allowed me to devote full time to writing. During the academic year 1976 to 1977, moreover, I have been the recipient of a Senior Fellowship from the National Endowment for the Humanities. That grant has been used to fund research on my larger study of the Whig party, but between research trips I have incorporated some of my findings into this work.

The *Journal of American History* has kindly allowed me to reproduce here much of my article, "The Politics of Impatience: The Origins of Know Nothingism," *Journal of American History, 60* (1973), 309–331.

I hope my indebtedness to other scholars who have worked on this period is evident from my footnotes, but two debts merit special acknowledgment. Although I disagree with much in the writings of Professor Eric Foner, his exciting work has greatly stimulated my own thinking. In some ways, indeed, this whole book is an extended dialog with Foner's work. In a book that is aimed primarily at undergraduates, moreover, I am happy to note how dependent I have been on the work of my former students at Yale University and the University of Virginia. I have cited their research amply in my footnotes, but I want to emphasize here that most of these young men and women were undergraduates when they wrote their excellent papers for me. Their work stands as a testimonial to the high quality that undergraduates are capable of achieving.

Professor Robert A. Divine has been an exemplary editor, and I am especially obliged to him for allowing me to exceed both the length and the amount of documentation originally established for books in this series.

Professors Robert F. Dalzell, Jr., of Williams College and William J. Cooper, Jr., of Louisiana State University read parts of the manuscript, and I have benefited from their suggestions. I owe Professor Cooper much more, however. He generously allowed me to read in draft form and to cite copiously from his manuscript on the Second Party System in the South, *The Politics of Slavery,* which is to be published by the Louisiana State University Press. Although I often use his evidence to make a different point than he does, I could not have written the book without it.

My colleagues at the University of Virginia, Robert J. Brugger and Joseph F. Kett, as well as James C. Mohr of the University of Maryland, Baltimore County, and Joel H. Silbey of Cornell University, took time from their own work to read the entire manuscript. Professor Richard H. Sewell of the University of Wisconsin, who served as outside reader of the manuscript for John Wiley & Sons, very kindly sent me a list of valuable suggestions privately. All of these men have helped to root obscurities from my prose and sharpen my thinking. None has agreed with everything I say, and each has tried to save me from blunders. Indeed, although it is customary to end acknowledgments such as these by exempting others from the author's own errors, I want to emphasize that here that pardon is not perfunctory. These men have made me well aware that what I say is controversial. If it remains wrongheaded, it is because of my own stubbornness.

M. F. H.

Contents

List of Tables   xv

Quotations   xvii

1. Party Dynamics and the Coming of the Civil War   1

2. The Second Party System in Operation   17

3. Slavery Extension and the Second Party System, 1843-1848   39

4. Dynamics of the Party System and the Compromise of 1850   67

5. The Second Party System Undermined, 1849-1853   101

6. Realignment, Reorganization, and Reform, 1854-1856   139

7. Slavery, Republicanism, and the Triumph of the Republican Party   183

8. Politics, Slavery, and Southern Secession   219

Selected Bibliography   261

Footnotes   281

Index   319

List of Tables

Table 1   Indexes of Party Disagreement on Selected Roll-Call Votes in Seven State Legislatures during the Jacksonian Period   26

Table 2   Partisan Dimensions of State Legislative Votes on Texas Annexation   45

Table 3   Average Indexes of Party Disagreement on State Legislative Roll-Call Votes on Various Issues, 1847-1854   116

Table 4   Slaves and Slaveholders in the South in 1860   229

Table 5   Indexes of Interparty Competition Between the Democrats and Their Opponents in Presidential Elections, 1848-1860   232

Table 6   Margins Between the Parties in State Elections, 1850-1860   234

Table 7   Aggregate Indexes of Interparty Competition in State Elections in the Upper and Lower South   236

"That Union should so long have been preserved in a confederacy which contains an element of discord of such magnitude and of so disturbing a nature as that of Slavery is a wonder more surprising than its dissolution would be. This has been owing to the fact, I firmly believe, the single fact that there have always been neutralizing considerations of sufficient force to maintain party cohesions between men of the free and slave states. Slavery questions have from the beginning had more or less to do with our political contests but have never before had the effect of dissolving old Party connections and sympathies. . . ."

Martin Van Buren to Moses Y. Tilden, September 1, 1856, Samuel J. Tilden MSS (New York Public Library)

"But what new combinations will grow out of this it is difficult to foresee, as national parties can only be formed by the action of the general government. Parties are broken up by local causes and that centrifugal force which throws individuals and masses beyond the attraction of the central power; but new parties of a national character can only be gathered from these fragmentary *nebula* of dissolving systems by the magnet of some great national and centripetal force at Washington. Will any question present such a magnet at the ensuing session of Congress?"

Millard Fillmore to John Pendleton Kennedy, October 14, 1853, John Pendleton Kennedy MSS (George Peabody Division of the Enoch Pratt Free Library, Baltimore). Reprinted by permission.

"There is no other way to carry out in practice the theory of our Republican Government but openly and clearly to declare principles and measures and for men and parties to divide upon them as they are for them or against them. . . . Our whole theory of Government stands upon the idea that the electors of the whole country can and will understand and choose the right."

Preston King to Francis P. Blair, Sr., November 21, 1855, Blair-Lee Papers (Princeton University Library)

Party Dynamics and the Coming of the Civil War

The Civil War represented an utter and unique breakdown of the normal democratic political process. When one section of the country refused to accept the decision of a presidential election, secession and the ensuing war became the great exception to the American political tradition of compromise. The rending of the nation was the one time that conflict seemed too irrepressible, too fundamental, to be contained within common consensual boundaries. Because the war was such an anomaly, both participants and later historians have been fascinated with its causes since the shooting started.

The literature on the causation of the Civil War is vast and requires no detailed review here. Basically historians have been divided into two camps, although there have been a number of variations in each. Because the war pitted one section against another, many insist that a fundamental and intensifying conflict between the North and South brought it on. Members of this group have differed about the sources of sectional division, but most have argued that irreconcilable differences over Negro slavery inexorably ruptured one national institution after another between 1830 and 1860 until those differences produced war in 1861. In reply revisionist historians have minimized the internal solidarity of both the North and the South and the seriousness of the disputes between them. They have blamed the war instead on the mistakes of political leaders and the efforts of agitators such as the abolitionists and Southern fire-eaters. Despite the variations of the debate, the central issue has always been the role of slavery in causing the war, and recently the fundamentalists have won the larger audience. Historians like Eugene Genovese and Eric Foner have established beyond cavil the reality and gravity of ideological, economic, and political conflict between the free labor society of the North and the slave-based plantation society of the South.[1] Slavery and irreconcilable views about the desirability of slavery's expansion lay at the base of that sectional clash, they argue, and the unwillingness of either section to tolerate the triumph of the other's values produced the war. Thus we have returned to an older view that sectional conflict over Negro slavery caused the Civil War.

Without disputing the reality of sectional conflict between North and South, one can still point out that the sectional conflict interpretation leaves certain crucial questions about the breakup of the nation unanswered. For one thing, to delineate the factors that divided North from South does not by itself explain why the slave states behaved so differently from each other during the secession crisis. When secession first occurred and the Confederacy was formed, only seven states in the Deep South withdrew, yet eight other slave states chose to remain in the Union. True, four more states joined the Confederacy once Abraham Lincoln called up troops after the firing on Fort Sumter, but resistance to overt federal coercion was far different from secession in anticipation of a Republican administration. If a desire to protect or extend black slavery caused Southerners to break up the nation, why didn't all the slave states react the same way in the initial crisis?

More important, the argument that an escalating sectional conflict between North and South before April 1861 produced war between them after that date does not really explain why a conflict of long duration produced war then and not at some other time. The problem is how a basic conflict between sectional interests and values that had long been carried on in peaceful channels such as politics abruptly became a shooting war after smoldering for decades, and why it did so at one time instead of at another. What produced the sectional hostility, in other words, was not necessarily what caused armed conflict in 1861. Ideological differences, after all, do not always produce wars.

2

One could argue, for example, that in the years following World War II many Americans saw a fundamental, irrepressible conflict between democratic capitalism and totalitarian communism, yet that conflict by itself has yet to produce a shooting war between the United States and the Soviet Union. To be more concrete, there most certainly was sectional conflict between North and South over slavery-related matters, yet that conflict, or cold war, had existed at least since the Constitutional Convention of 1787. Can a conflict that lasted almost three-fourths of a century explain why war broke out in 1861 and not earlier? If slavery or even the slavery extension issue caused the war, for example, why not in 1820 or 1832 or 1846 or 1850 or 1854? The basic problem concerning the war, in short, has less to do with the sources of sectional conflict than with the war's timing. The important question is not what divided North from South, but how the nation could contain or control that division for so long and then allow it suddenly to erupt into war.

This book argues that the answers to these questions about varying Southern behavior and the timing of the Civil War lie in the political crisis of the 1850s. The key to Civil War causation is to be found in the reasons why the American political system could no longer contain the sectional conflict, not in the conflict itself. The book differs from those of the fundamentalists by focusing less on the intensifying conflict than on the capacity of politicians and political structures to confine it to normal political channels. It argues that the change in that capacity had less to do with the explosiveness of the slavery issue *per se* than with a whole range of political developments, some of which created and others of which were responses to a crisis of confidence in the normal political process. Moreover, while I agree with revisionists that the individual decisions of politicians were important in exacerbating the situation, my emphasis is less on their ineptitude or the fanaticism of agitators than it is on the mechanics or dynamics of the political system itself.

The political crisis of the 1850s had two interrelated dimensions. The first was a fundamental reshaping of the nature of party competition. A national two-party system of Whigs and Democrats, which had functioned superbly for twenty years in all parts of the country and had helped contain the sectional conflict, collapsed. A realignment of voters followed between 1853 and 1856 in which a Democratic majority was replaced by an anti-Democratic majority in the North, even as the Democrats assumed an unassailable position in the South. Finally, new parties were organized, and out of the turmoil of the late 1850s the anti-Southern Republican party emerged triumphant. Because Southern secession was a direct response to the victory of the Republican party in the presidential election of 1860, there was a direct causal link between those political developments and the outbreak of war. One cannot account for Southern secession without accounting for the political events in the North that drove the South out of the Union. The political reorganization and realignment that replaced the national competition between Whigs and Democrats with a sectional competition between the Northern Republican party and a predominantly Southern Democracy was a major factor in the disruption of the Union.

More was involved in the collapse of the old two-party system, however, than merely the disappearance of national parties with affiliations across sectional lines. An equally crucial development took place at the state and local level. There, in the political arenas closest to the people, older frameworks of competition also dissolved. Voters with local needs and grievances that were every bit as important, if not more important, to them than national issues no longer had familiar party alternatives through which to seek political action. In this vacuum they tried to form new parties to meet their immediate needs, and much of the story of the political reorganization of the 1850s that led to civil war is to be found in those efforts. Local and state politics were just as crucial as national developments in shaping the political crisis of the 1850s.

The second aspect of the political crisis of the 1850s has received far less notice from historians, but it was just as critical as the first. This volume will attempt to demonstrate that the collapse of the old framework of two-party rivalry aggravated and in part reflected a loss of popular faith in the normal party political process to meet the needs of voters, to redress personal, group, and sectional grievances. Malignant distrust of politicians as self-centered and corrupt wirepullers out of touch with the people spread like an epidemic during the 1850s. So, too, did dissatisfaction with political parties as unresponsive and beyond popular control. Americans grew impatient with the inefficacy of traditional political methods and institutions. Widespread disgust with politics as usual engendered cries for reform that helped to destroy the old parties, propel voters to new affiliations, and shape new parties as ways were sought to return power to the people.

Underlying and intensifying the sense of crisis in the 1850s was a deep-seated republican ideology that had suffused American politics since the time of the Revolution. To Americans of the antebellum period, republicanism meant a number of things, and different Americans emphasized different parts of the creed. But to most white Americans who perceived political developments through the framework of republicanism, it meant, in Lincoln's words, government by and for the people, a government whose power over the people was restrained by law, and whose basic function was to protect the equality and liberty of individuals from aristocratic privilege and concentrations of arbitrary or tyrannical power. When Americans differed with each other politically, it was not so much over the desirability of republican government as over their perceptions of what most threatened its survival.

Since the 1820s, much vitality had been given to interparty combat by the ability of opposing parties to identify some menace to republicanism and to provide a way to nullify that threat by voting. The mass parties formed in the Jacksonian era were viewed as instruments with which the people could control government, and because each party offered a different way to secure equal rights and protect liberty from power and privilege, voters believed in the legitimacy of a political process that manifestly preserved republicanism. When voters lost faith in the responsiveness of that system in the 1850s, when they thought that political parties no longer offered the governed access to their governors, many feared that republicanism itself was endangered. This apocalyptic sense of crisis was national, not sectional, and men in all parts of the country sought explanations for what had gone wrong. In this situation it was only natural for ambitious politicians who hoped to build new parties to follow the traditional practice of identifying and crusading against antirepublican monsters. They charged and men believed that powerful conspiracies, contemptuous of the law and abetted by corrupt politicians, had usurped government from the people and were menacing the most cherished values of Americans, their liberty and sense of equality.

Most Americans, North and South, therefore, were concerned with the same thing in the 1850s: the need to reform the political process in order to preserve republicanism and return political power to the people. Where they differed was in the way they defined the antirepublican plot and in the steps they took to combat it. Some saw the political pretensions of the hierarchical Catholic Church, directed by the Pope, as the major subverter of the American republic, and they formed a new political organization that promised to restore government to the people and to purify the corrupt political process by insisting that native-born Protestant Americans rule America. Others claimed with justice that this new anti-Catholic organization was itself a menace to republicanism. Yet the somewhat paradoxical result was that those on opposing sides regained confidence that they could do battle for republicanism within the party political process.

The common fear for the republic also fed the fire of sectional antagonism. Northerners and Southerners both identified powerful and hostile groups in the other section who would destroy their liberty and reduce them to an unequal status. This was made politically possible, even likely, because the collapse of the old two-party system in the early 1850s had been accompanied by a resurgence and exacerbation of naked sectional conflict between North and South. One of the reasons that conflict became so emotional, in turn, was that each section began to view the other as the subverter of republicanism, as a lawless and usurping tyrant bent on perverting the traditional basis of society and government. Hence the secessionist impulse in the Deep South was another manifestation of the national sense of crisis, of disgust with politicians and the old political process, and of the search for reform to save republicanism. Whatever else secession represented, it was a rejection of the normal political process that other Americans by 1860 were still content to work through, a refusal not only to tolerate the election of Lincoln but also to believe that the system could neutralize whatever threats he represented.

Like other Americans in the 1850s, Southerners had lost faith in politics as usual. Unlike Americans elsewhere, however, men from the Deep South never regained their faith in the efficacy of party politics. Thus they proved more receptive to the message that secession itself was necessary to restore republicanism. I will argue, in other words, that sectional extremism flourished in the Deep South precisely because no new framework of two-party competition had appeared there—as it had in the North and upper South—to help restore public confidence that republicanism could once again be secured by normal political methods.

Since 1787 there had been a suggestive relationship between sectional extremism and political structure. Sectional antagonism was most marked, powerful, and dangerous precisely at those times when or in those places where two-party competition did not exist. On the other hand, when two parties were present, sharp sectional lines often dis-

6

appeared, sectional antagonism was moderated, or, when it persisted, party loyalties neutralized it so far as shaping political behavior. As many politicans recognized, in short, interparty competition was an alternative to naked sectional conflict. Before the Federalist and Jeffersonian parties formed in the 1790s to contest matters of economic and foreign policy, for example, Congress had divided into sectional blocs.[2] Sectional lines disappeared during the height of interparty conflict in the late 1790s, but they reappeared after 1800 when the Federalist party was too weak to provide anything but token opposition to the dominant Jeffersonians.[3] In the absence of interparty competition, sharp sectional polarization developed over Missouri's admission as a slave state between 1819 and 1821. Astute political observers then foresaw the possibility of a dangerous sectional alignment of politics in the absence of competing parties, and Martin Van Buren helped form the Jacksonian Democratic party in the 1820s specifically to revive a two-party system as a substitute for sectionalism. "Party attachment in former times," he wrote, "furnished a complete antidote for sectional prejudices by producing counteracting feelings."[4]

Similarly, the nullification crisis of 1832 to 1833 produced dangerous sectional extremism, but radicalism in defense of slavery and state rights was confined to South Carolina alone, the one state in the country without recent experience in party politics. Other slave states that had political parties and often incipient two-party competition at the state level spurned South Carolina's call for aid and maintained faith in Andrew Jackson, the Democratic party, and the normal political process to protect their rights. South Carolina looked to an extrapolitical, constitutional solution for its grievances, whereas other slave states kept faith with elected politicians and the normal give and take of politics. By the winter of 1860-1861, the seven slave states that seceded had developed the same distrust of parties, politicians, and the political process that characterized South Carolina in 1832, and, as South Carolina had earlier, they turned to a final solution beyond the reach of party politicians to protect Southern rights.[5]

To identify the inverse relationship between the strength of two-party competition and of sectional extremism is not, of course, to explain precisely how it operated. Yet one can suggest at least three interrelated ways in which party strife worked to moderate sectional extremism. First, as Van Buren recognized, the existence of national parties with wings in both sections often caused party politicians and voters to put party loyalty ahead of sectional loyalty. Northerners would aid Southerners of the same party before joining Northerners of the opposition party in an attack on the South. Two-party competition thus helped to prevent either section from forming a solid phalanx in hostility to the other section. Second, within each section the presence of an opposition party often prevented ambitious politicians from taking too extreme a stand on sectional matters. To adopt such a stance was to give the opposing party the moderate side of the issue. Its champions could accuse extermists of endangering the Union, that unrivaled guarantor of republican liberty and equality. The lack of an opposition party in certain states, conversely, removed this check on politicians who wished to agitate sectional animosity for political gain.

Finally, popular faith in the efficacy of the entire political process seems to have depended largely on the presence of competing parties, each with a real chance of winning, to give voters options for political action and an opportunity to remove an unpopular regime from power. For a variety of reasons, dating back to the 1820s and 1830s, Americans had looked to political parties to forge governmental policies that would protect their interests and preserve the republic. Because most issues, whether they were economic, ethnic, religious, ideological, or regional, had at least two sides, interparty rivalry was necessary to assure divergent groups in society that they had a political voice, a political vehicle through which they could carry on conflict with rival social groups, if only vicariously. Political conflict in the 1840s and 1850s was often a surrogate for social conflict, but the faith of various groups in that political surrogate required the presence of identifiable party alternatives. Experience with two-party politics that dealt with local, state, and national issues caused men to view most questions in normal political terms of one party versus another. Defeat on an issue required nothing more than greater effort at the next election to oust the offending party and replace it with the more reliable alternative. Without experience in two-party politics, without the availability of party alternatives, however, men tended to view opposition to their interests in nonpolitical terms, as an external alien threat that required fundamental, nonpolitical solutions.

Because the presence of two-party competition seems to have been the key in restraining sectional conflict to peaceful channels, explanation of the ultimate breakdown of the political system requires analysis of how the so-called Second American Party System of Whigs and

Democrats operated, why it broke down when it did, what happened once it did, why a sectionally oriented party emerged from the disarray in the North, and why two-party competition was restored within certain Southern states and not others. Only by doing so can one explain how the sectional conflict was contained for so long, why it became unmanageable when it did, and why Southern states responded so differently to the secession crisis.

Historians have long looked to politics for the origins of the Civil War, and they have offered two major interpretations of political developments between 1845 and 1860. Both are primarily concerned with the breakdown of the old party system and the rise of the Republicans and not with the second aspect of the crisis—the loss of faith in politicians, the desire for reform, and their relationship to republican ideology. By spelling out my reservations about and disagreements with these interpretations, the assumptions behind and, I hope, the logic of my own approach to the political crisis of the 1850s will become clearer.

The standard interpretation maintains that intensifying sectional disagreements over slavery inevitably burst into the political arena, smashed the old national parties, and forced the formation of new, sectionally oriented ones. The Second Party System was artificial, some historians contend, since it could survive only by avoiding divisive sectional issues and by confining political debate to sectionally neutral economic questions on which the national parties had coherent stands. Once sectional pressure was reaggravated by the events of the late 1840s and early 1850s, those fragile structures shattered and were replaced. "On the level of politics," writes Eric Foner, "the coming of the Civil War is the intrusion of sectional ideology into the political system, despite the efforts of political leaders of both parties [Whigs and Democrats] to keep it out. Once this happened, political competition worked to exacerbate, rather than to solve, social and sectional conflicts."[6]

There is much to be said for this interpretation. The Republican party did rise to dominance in the North largely because of an increase of Northern hostility toward the South, and its ascendance worsened relations between the sections. Attributing the political developments prior to its rise to the same sectional force that caused the rise has the virtue of simplicity. But that argument distorts a rapidly changing and very complex political situation between 1845 and 1860. There were

9

three discrete, sequential political developments in those years that shaped the political crisis that led to war—the disappearance of the Whig party and with it of the old framework of two-party competition, a realignment of voters as they switched party affiliation, and a shift from a <u>nationally balanced party system where both major parties competed on fairly even terms in all parts of the nation to a sectionally polarized one with Republicans dominant in the North and Democrats in the South.</u> Although related, these were distinct phases, occurring with some exceptions in that order, and they were caused by different things. Although the inflammation of sectional antagonism between 1855 and 1860 helped to account for the new sectional alignment of parties, sectional conflict by itself caused neither the voter realignment of middecade nor the most crucial event of the period—the death of the Whig party, especially its death at the state level. It bears repeating that the demise of the Whig party, and with it of the traditional framework of two-party competition at the local, state, and national levels, was the most critical development in this sequence. Its disappearance helped foster popular doubts about the legitimacy of politics as usual, raised fears that powerful conspiracies were undermining republicanism, allowed the rise of the Republican party in the North, and created the situation in the lower South that produced secession there and not elsewhere.

The theory that the Second Party System was artificial and was shattered once the slavery issue arose, like the larger theory of the war's causation it reflects, founders on the problem of timing. There is considerable evidence that sectional conflict over slavery characterized the Second Party System throughout its history. Slavery was not swept under the rug; it was often the stuff of political debate. Proponents of the traditional interpretation, indeed, have often confused internal divisions within the national parties with their demise. Although they point to different dates when the rupture was fatal, they have assumed that once the national parties were split into Northern and Southern wings over slavery, the parties were finished. Yet the Whig and Jacksonian parties, like almost all political organizations at any time, had frequently been divided—over slavery as well as other issues. They functioned for years in that condition. To establish the existence of sectional splits within the national parties is not to answer the vexed question of why those divisions were fatal in the 1850s and not in the 1830s and 1840s. If it was the sectional conflict that destroyed the old party system, the crucial question is why the parties were able to manage that conflict at some times and not at others. For a number of reasons, the easy reply that the volatile slavery issue simply became more explosive in the 1850s than earlier is not an adequate answer to this question.

The second major interpretation of the politics of the 1850s also has its merits and liabilities. Arguing that traditional historians have viewed events in the 1850s with the hindsight knowledge that the Civil War occurred, a new group of political historians insist that the extent to which sectionalism affected political behavior, especially popular voting behavior at the grass-roots level, has been exaggerated. Local social tensions, especially ethnic and religious tensions, motivated voters in the 1850s, they contend, not national issues like slavery, which was of so much concern to national political elites. What applies to Congress and national leaders, these new political historians say in effect, does not apply to the local level of politics. Prohibitionism, nativism, and anti-Catholicism produced the voter realignment in which the Whigs disappeared and new parties emerged in the North.

voter behavior

By focusing on voting behavior, this ethnocultural interpretation presents a compelling analysis of why an anti-Democratic majority was created in many parts of the North. Explaining why Northern voters realigned between 1853 and 1856, however, does not answer why the Republican party appeared or why party politics were sectionally polarized at the end of the decade. Prophets of the ethnocultural thesis, moreover, have done little to explain Southern politics, yet developments in Dixie where Catholics and immigrants were few were just as important as events in the North in leading to war. Nor do voting studies really explain the crucial first phase—the death of the Whig party. Party reorganization accompanied voter realignment in the 1850s, and ethnocultural tensions alone do not explain why new parties were necessary. Why didn't anti-Democratic voters simply become Whigs? This question has a particular urgency when one realizes that in the 1840s ethnocultural issues had also been present and that the Whigs and Democrats had aligned on opposite sides of them. The problem with stressing ethnocultural issues, as with stressing sectionalism, is why those issues could be contained within, indeed could invigorate, old party lines at one time yet could help to destroy them at another.

The fundamental weakness of previous interpretations of why the old two-party system broke down is their misunderstanding of how and why it worked. They have not adequately explored either the relationship between political parties and issues or the impact of the federal system with its divided responsibilities among local, state, and national governments on the parties and the party system. Whether historians stress sectionalism or ethnocultural issues, their central assumption seems to be that issues arising from the society at large caused political events. The Second Party System functioned because it dealt with "safe" economic questions, but once those issues were replaced or displaced by new disruptive matters the parties broke down and realignment followed. Yet what made the Second Party System work in the end was not issues *per se* or the presence of safe issues and absence of dangerous ones. In the end what made the two-party system operate was its ability to allow political competition on a broad range of issues that varied from time to time and place to place. If the genius of the American political system has been the peaceful resolution of conflict, what has supported two-party systems has been the conflict itself, not its resolution. As long as parties fought with each other over issues or took opposing stands even when they failed to promote opposing programs, as long as they defined alternative ways to secure republican ideals, voters perceived them as different and maintained their loyalty to them. Party health and popular faith in the political process depended on the perception of party difference, which in turn depended on the reality—or at least the appearance—of interparty conflict. As long as parties seemed different from each other, voters viewed them as viable vehicles through which to influence government.

Politicians had long recognized that group conflict was endemic to American society and that the vitality of individual parties depended on the intensity of their competition with opposing parties. Thomas Jefferson had perceived in 1798 that "in every free and deliberating society, there must, from the nature of man, be opposite parties, and violent dissensions and discords." "Seeing that we must have somebody to quarrel with," he wrote John Taylor, "I had rather keep our New England associates for that purpose, than to see our bickerings transferred to others."[7] Even more explicit in their recognition of what made parties work were the founders of New York's Albany Regency in the 1820s. They deplored the lack of internal discipline and cohesion in the Jeffersonian Republican party once the Federalists disappeared, and they moved quickly to remedy it. Although any party might suffer defeats, they realized, "it is certain to acquire additional strength . . .

by the attacks of adverse parties." A political party, indeed, was "most in jeopardy when an opposition is not sufficiently defined." During "the contest between the great rival parties [Federalists and Jeffersonians] each found in the strength of the other a powerful motive of union and vigor."[8] Significantly, those like Daniel Webster who deplored the emergence of mass parties in the 1820s and 1830s also recognized that strife was necessary to perpetuate party organization and that the best way to break it down was to cease opposition and work for consensus.[9] Politicians in the 1840s and 1850s continued to believe that interparty conflict was needed to unify their own party and maintain their voting support. Thus an Alabama Democrat confessed that his party pushed a certain measure at the beginning of the 1840 legislative session explicitly as "the best means for drawing the party lines as soon as possible" while by 1852, when opposition to that state's Democracy appeared to disintegrate, another warned perceptively, "I think the only danger to the Democratic party is that it will become too much an omnibus in this State. We have nothing to fear from either the Union, or Whig party or both combined. From their friendship and adherence much."[10] Many of the important decisions in the 1840s and 1850s reflected the search by political leaders for issues that would sharply define the lines between parties and thus reinvigorate the loyalty of party voters.

If conflict sustained the old two-party system, what destroyed it was the loss of the ability to provide interparty competition on *any* important issue at *any* level of the federal system. Because the political system's vitality and legitimacy with the voters depended on the clarity of the definition of the parties as opponents, the blurring of that definition undid the system. What destroyed the Second Party System was consensus, not conflict. The growing congruence between the parties on almost all issues by the early 1850s dulled the sense of party difference and thereby eroded voters' loyalty to the old parties. Once competing groups in society decided that the party system no longer provided them viable alternatives in which they could carry on conflict with each other, they repudiated the old system by dropping out, seeking third parties that would meet their needs, or turning to nonpartisan or extrapolitical action to achieve their goals. Because the collapse of the Second Party System was such a vital link in the war's causation, therefore, one arrives at a paradox. While the Civil War is normally viewed as the one time when conflict prevailed over consensus in American politics, the prevalence of consensus over conflict in crucial parts of the political system contributed in a very real way to the outbreak of war in the first place.

One of the reasons the Second Party System functioned for so long despite the presence of sectional antagonism was the federal system. Historians of the politics of the 1840s and 1850s, indeed, of most periods, have not adequately assessed the impact of the federal system on parties. They have assumed that forces operating at one level of political activity caused developments at all levels. Historians of the prewar period have especially been obsessed with national events. If slavery ruptured the national parties in Congress, if the speeches and correspondence of national leaders were filled with remarks about slavery, slavery must have destroyed the old parties and shaped political developments. As the new voting studies show, however, this assumption may be unwarranted.

Yet even grass-roots voting studies frequently neglect the most crucial arena of political activity in the nineteenth century—the states. Most of the legislation that affected the everyday lives of people was enacted at state capitals and not at Washington. State parties formed the core of the political system, not the flimsy national organizations that came together once every four years to contest the presidency. To voters and politicians, therefore, control of a state's government was often more important than electing men to Congress; consequently, within an individual state, the competitiveness of a party in gubernatorial and legislative elections was often more influential in determining its longevity than national affairs. Attention has been inordinately focused on Washington, but the real story of the political reorganization of the 1850s is to be found in individual states with their varying conditions. In accounting for the demise of the Second Party System, for example, one must be careful to distinguish between the sectional divisions within national parties and the death of state parties within each section. The old Whig party disintegrated, the Democratic party was reshaped, and voters realigned not in presidential elections where national party cohesion mattered, but in state and local elections where parties in each section could go their own way. Similarly, the pace at which the new Republican party arose, the nature of its coalition, and the emergence of a new two-party framework in the South varied from state to state according to conditions within them. Only by recognizing the complexity caused by the division of powers within

14

the federal system can one arrive at a more accurate portrayal of the political antecedents of war.

For a long while the federal system was a key to the health of the Second Party System. Because both parties functioned at different levels, politicians had the luxury of saying different things in different parts of the country. They could define for home audiences lines of interparty conflict that did not necessarily apply to the country as a whole. Many voters, probably the vast majority, learned of national and even state issues only what their local politicians and newspapers told them. In this situation politicians could make issues that hurt their parties at one level help them at another. Issues involving slavery that disrupted the parties along sectional lines in Congress, for example, were often debated along party lines in the states. New York Whigs and Georgia Whigs could have diametrically opposed views on a matter involving slavery, but at home they could use their divergent positions to strengthen themselves against the common Democratic foe. Before a home audience what mattered most was not that the Whigs disagreed with each other in Congress, but that they differed from the Democrats in their state. The ability of the old system to provide party alternatives on slavery-related matters at the state level, indeed, was the major reason why the Second Party System managed the sectional conflict for so long, even when national parties were divided by it.

The advantages of the federal system went beyond even this important mechanism. State parties battled over more than national issues. There was a whole range of state issues over which they could conflict, issues they could use to reinforce the image of party difference or often to divert attention from disrupting national matters. At the local level, moreover, parties could add parochial concerns to the list of state and national questions over which they contended. Although national and state parties might eschew clear party positions on temperance or religion, for example, local party newspapers could adopt opposing stands to attract voters interested in one side or the other of those issues. At some level or other of the multitiered federal government structure, almost every issue that entered the political arena could be fought on party lines. Multilevel party competition thus normally reinforced the voters' faith in existing parties as vehicles for competing ethnic, economic, religious, and regional groups in the society at large. Only when the image of party difference disappeared at all levels and when, as a result, faith in the parties waned, did the political conditions develop in the North and South that led to the breakup of the nation.

By exploring the relationship between political parties and the federal system, I will try to show that the sectional conflict alone did not cause the political crisis of the 1850s. Yet my intent is not to read the sectional conflict out of the politics of the 1850s or to dismiss it as one of the factors bringing on the Civil War. Instead, the purpose here is to relate the sectional conflict to the dynamics of the party system and to the pervasive republican ideology that did so much to create the sense of crisis and shape the responses to it—responses that led directly to Civil War. My intent, in sum, is to try to understand why an enduring sectional conflict became so unmanageable that war broke out in April 1861.

The Second Party
System in Operation

The Second American Party System was born with vitality. From the beginning the Democratic and Whig parties seemed to contend over issues or at least appealed to values that mattered a great deal to Americans. Not only did they address concrete needs, but the alternatives they provided to voters created a more generalized sense that through the party political process, men could secure republicanism: government by the people in which individual freedom and equality were safeguarded from corruption, privilege, and power. Although those parties did not crystallize until the 1830s, three developments during the previous decade had already laid the groundwork for the passionate interest voters would devote to the battles between them.

First, the Panic of 1819 and subsequent depression during the early 1820s engendered needs and grievances that raised political consciousness. Men responded to economic hardship in different ways. Some demanded relief from debt through stay laws or paper money inflation. Others pushed for additional governmental action to promote economic growth: higher tariffs to protect manufacturers and the wages of their employees, improved transportation facilities to reduce the cost of trade, and more bank credit to finance recovery. Advocates of positive steps such as these often endorsed the American System of Henry Clay which promised national action on all fronts. Many farmers and workingmen, however, blamed the Panic on excessive banking credit and overspeculation. The depression aroused in them what Alexis de Tocqueville astutely identified as a basic sentiment of materialistic Americans in the early nineteenth century—the love of equality and hatred of anything that threatened it.[1]

Specifically, the Panic fostered widespread hostility to the privilege of economic elites, especially the privileges of banking corporations that, through their ability to issue paper banknotes and with their protection of limited individual liability for stockholders, seemed both to cause the fluctuations of the economy so catastrophic to the average citizen and to suffer less from them than individuals without corporate privileges. When a farmer could not meet his debts, he normally lost all his property. In contrast, when a bank could not meet its debts (i.e., redeem in coin the face amount of the paper banknotes it had issued), it simply suspended specie payments, and its owners escaped further foreclosure on their personal property. To many Americans, privileges like these, be they economic, social, or political, were the antithesis of equality and therefore intolerable. As a result, there emerged at the state level in the 1820s efforts to replace banknotes with hard money controlled by the people's government, to substitute state-controlled banks for private ones, and even to abolish banks altogether. Those efforts, of course, stimulated opposition from men who favored easy credit, banks, and corporations. Throughout the history of the Second Party System, indeed, conflicts over banking and currency, corporate monopoly, state promotion of economic growth, and the general question of equality versus privilege would be bulwarks of two-party competition.

Economic developments in the 1820s raised many of the issues that would occupy politicians for the next thirty years, but they also shaped the remedies men seized to improve their economic situations. Whether men favored banks or opposed them, whether they wanted inflation to relieve debtors or abhorred it, whether they wanted to hasten or delay the commercialization of the economy, they turned to national and state governments to advance or protect their interests. The depression awakened men to the importance of politics to their everyday lives. Men with conflicting goals sought to control governmental policies. Those without the vote now demanded it so they could have a voice in determining who controlled government. Those who thought their section of a state underrepresented in the legislature pushed for reapportionment. Most important, men with conflicting interests learned they must have political vehicles or parties to represent them in the battles to control state governments. Hence, in New Hampshire, Pennsylvania, North Carolina, Kentucky, Ohio, Georgia, Tennessee, Alabama, and other states sharp battles developed over issues such as relief, banking, and legislative reapportionment, and around those issues emerged clearly defined factions and, in some cases full-fledged parties. Those political battles of the 1820s instilled in many voters an enduring belief that political conflict involved their vital interests and that political parties were the best vehicles to advance those interests. Many veterans of these state contests who fought against economic privilege, moreover, would vote for Andrew Jackson in 1828.

Second, another series of events in the 1820s increased Southern fears about the security of slavery. Resistance by many Northerners to the admission of Missouri as a slave state between 1819 and 1821 alarmed Southerners for a number of interrelated reasons. Full-scale Northern attacks on the economic, political, and moral evils of slavery during the Missouri debates outraged Southerners who considered slavery exclusively their own problem, one not even to be discussed by outsiders. Moreover, the attempt to prevent Missouri's entry with slavery as its residents wanted seemed a denial of the equal right of all states to determine their own domestic institutions. Most Southerners considered the United States a federated republic in which all states were equal, and they fought to protect the equality of states just as fiercely as others sought to protect the equality of individuals from corporate privileges. Indeed, the very attempt of Northerners to impose abolition on unwilling Missourians as the price of statehood seemed to augur further intolerable expansion of national power vis-à-vis the states. If Congress could prohibit slavery in a new state, Southerners feared, the next step would be congressional attacks on slavery in the old states. What made this threat compelling to thoughtful politicians of both sections was that the divisive Missouri debates, in an era without two national parties, seemed to portend a permanent realignment of politics along sectional lines. The slavery issue seemed capable of mobilizing a Northern majority in Congress, a majority that might exert force directly against slavery. Additional Northern antislavery resolutions later in the 1820s and President John Quincy Adams's ardent advocacy of a more powerful national government only increased the alarm of proslavery, strict constructionist Southerners.[2]

Like economic grievances, concern for slavery turned men to political parties for protection. Certain politicians in both sections, known as Old Republicans or Radicals, attributed the crisis to the lack of two national parties and to the abandonment by the all-inclusive Republican party of its original Jeffersonian principles of state rights and strict construction. The party had been corrupted by the nationalistic doctrines of Clay, Old Republicans like Virginia's Thomas Ritchie and New York's Martin Van Buren complained. The absence of external opposition resulting from the disappearance of the Federalist party had destroyed internal discipline within the party and allowed Northern Republicans to assail the interests of their Southern allies. Those assaults on slavery could never have occurred had there been tight party discipline across sectional lines. The way to protect slavery and the rights of Southern states, Old Republicans therefore believed, was to reconstruct two national parties that reflected the different interpretations of national power under the Constitution. Specifically, they wanted to rebuild a national party dedicated to old Jeffersonian principles that would exclude anyone who advanced heretical notions about a strong national government and would exercise such tight discipline over members from both sections that the slavery question could be smothered.

These goals were explicitly articulated in Martin Van Buren's famous letter to Ritchie in which he called party conflict an "antidote" to sectional conflict. Arguing that Jackson's nomination by Old Republicans in 1828 "would draw anew old Party lines & the subsequent contest would reestablish them," Van Buren maintained that a renewed sense of party loyalty would force Northerners "to decide between an indulgence in sectional & personal feelings with a separation from their old political friends on the one hand or acquiescence in the fairly expressed will of the party, on the other." If the old lines of party division were suppressed, "geographical divisions founded on local interests or, what is worse prejudices between free & slaveholding states will inevitably take their place." Only when the old party lines had disappeared was "the clamor ag[ains]t Southern influence and African slavery. . .made effectual in the North. Formerly, attacks upon Southern Republicans were regarded by those in the North as assaults upon their political brethren and resented accordingly. This all powerful sympathy has been much weakened. . . . It can & ought to be revived. . . ."[3] Persuaded by Van Buren, Ritchie led Old Republicans from South Atlantic states into the coalition that elected Jackson in 1828. From its inception, therefore, a major wing of the Jacksonian party was dedicated to state rights and suppression of the slavery issue. Only through a national political party committed to their principles, they believed, could the South protect its rights.

While the aroused antibanking and proslavery sentiments tended initially to benefit the Jacksonian party, the third development of the 1820s that awakened men to the necessity and potential of party political action primarily helped the foes of Jackson. Thus the Antimasonic movement that mushroomed in the late 1820s also helped instill popular faith in the new two-party system. Started in 1826 as a protest over a murder in western New York, Antimasonry evolved into a defense of republican institutions from the secrecy and power of the Masonic fraternity. The rule of law, liberty, and equality could not survive such irresponsible and privileged concentrations of power, Antimasons insisted, and they soon extended their condemnation to all privileged monopolies. As important, Antimasons insisted that people could achieve almost any social, economic, or political goal by going to the polls and voting. In an era when suffrage rights were expanding, this praise of the omnipotence of the majority had wide appeal in the North, and thousands supported the Antimasonic party who had not participated in the events that sparked its formation. Nominally a third party independent of both the Jacksonians and their early foes, the National Republicans, the Antimasons were, in fact, the major anti-Jackson party in Pennsylvania and Vermont, and they developed significant strength in other Middle Atlantic and New England states as well. Support for or opposition to the Antimasonic crusade was so frenzied that it polarized many Northern voters for more than a generation.[4]

Although Antimasons' egalitarian assault on privilege in some states did not differ from the economic egalitarianism of groups elsewhere who supported Jackson, at least three circumstances explain why most Antimasons later joined the Whig party. First, Jackson himself was a Mason who gloried in his membership instead of renouncing it, and Masonry was anathema to Antimasons. Second, in certain states the groups whose control of government and eco-

nomic privileges Antimasons opposed were the groups who supported
Jackson for president. In New York, for example, Van Buren's machine, the Albany Regency, was responsible for granting bank charters
and fostering land monopolies that the Antimasons considered intolerable. Most important, Antimasonry drew support from evangelical Protestant religious groups who were alarmed by what seemed
to be an increasing secularization of American society. The symbol
of that secularization was the failure of a Protestant campaign in the
late 1820s to prohibit mail deliveries by the federal government on
the Sabbath. Leading the successful effort to continue Sunday mail
service were prominent Jacksonians, especially Senator Richard M.
Johnson of Kentucky. That effort forever stamped the Democratic
party with the stigma of being an antireligious party in the eyes of
many evangelical Antimasons.[5] Indeed, one of the appeals of Antimasonry's promise that people could accomplish *anything* at the
polls was that evangelical groups could use control of government to
impose religious and moral reforms on society. When most Antimasons
merged with the new Whig party in the 1830s, therefore, they brought
to it a viable populistic, antiprivilege appeal of its own and a zealous
faith in the possibilities of political and governmental action.

Events in the 1820s stimulated widespread public interest in
questions of government's economic role, privilege, slavery, and moral
reform and helped to create public faith in the party political process
to channel battles over those issues, but the Second American Party
System itself took shape around the programs and charismatic personality of Andrew Jackson. Jackson was elected President in 1828
by a broad and heterogeneous coalition of men drawn by his reputa-
tion as a military hero, by his contrast to John Quincy Adams who
symbolized not only an Eastern aristocratic elite but Northern antislavery sentiment as well and, among Old Republicans, by hopes of
resurrecting around Jackson a principled state rights party to oppose
the nationalistic doctrines of Adams and Clay. It was an amorphous
Jackson coalition in 1828, not a coherent Democratic party.

Jackson's actions and rhetoric as President, however, helped to
streamline that coalition into the Democratic party, prompted the
formation of the opposition Whig party around which galvanized
the foes of Jacksonians in various states, defined the early lines of
interparty conflict, and helped to energize the attachment of voters
to the new parties. To some his ringing pronouncements of class conflict during the Bank War, his bold denunciations of monstrous and

iniquitous foes whose immense power threatened political liberty and equal economic opportunity, and his vigorous expansion of presidential power vis-à-vis established political elites in Congress and the federal bureaucracy proved that he championed the people against corrupt and privileged interests. To others, those same actions smacked of executive tyranny at the expense of the states, the people's representatives in the legislature, and the rule of law. Executive despotism, in their eyes, was just as great a threat to republican institutions as Masonic power or corporate privilege. The Whig party began simply as a collection of the disparate foes of Jackson, and the party's name symbolized its opposition to the monarchical usurpations of King Andrew I. From Jackson's presidency on, indeed, Democrats and Whigs fundamentally disagreed about the power of the executive branch versus the legislative branch of state and national governments, and Democratic platforms would continue to uphold while Whig platforms denounced executive vetoes of the legislative will.

The importance of Jackson as an individual in shaping attachments to the Democratic and Whig parties cannot be exaggerated. It was not just the substance of his policies that energized support or opposition, although many of his messages adroitly reignited antibanking, antiprivilege, and prostate-rights sentiments. Jackson as President personalized issues. It was Jackson versus the Bank, Jackson versus Clay, Jackson versus Calhoun and the Nullifiers. Not only did Jackson himself view political clashes as a kind of personal frontier shoot-out, but his various messages went over the heads of political leaders to seek popular support on personal terms. He made the issue one of supporting or opposing Jackson, and consequently he even more than his policies became the dominant issue of his presidency.

Because few could remain neutral about Jackson, even after he left office, he injected an emotional context into the new party conflict at its birth. His name alone could polarize parties and energize supporters. That the Whig party formed as an anti-Jackson coalition is not the only evidence of his impact. A Mississippi Democrat later recalled, "I found myself a democrat without being able to explain why I was of that party. . . . I began as a follower of Jackson, knowing nothing of the Force Bill, regarding 'nullification' as a heresy without knowing what it meant."[6] Even after Jackson was dead, Whigs dismissed the presidential pretensions of John McLean because McLean had been a Jackson man in the 1820s "and there are many Whigs who will never vote for one who supported Jackson."[7] From the 1830s on, then, Andrew Jackson himself was an issue that sharply divided the leaders and voters of the parties, a figure who elicited both passionate loyalty and passionate hatred. Because his personification of issues dramatized them for voters, because his rhetoric and that of his opponents appealed to basic republican values that had been aroused by events in the 1820s, Jackson and his Whig opponents grafted onto the incipient national parties the passions aroused by state-level political battles earlier. In short, one of the major contributions of Andrew Jackson to American political life was that he made people give a damn about party politics.

As long as Jackson remained in the White House, disagreement over him formed the clearest line dividing the Whig and Democratic parties. They espoused different interpretations of the constitutional powers of the national government, with the Democrats rehearsing their state rights, strict construction principles whenever possible. But in terms of specific economic issues or the performance of office-holders when voting on legislation, both were internally divided so that programmatic differences between the parties were fuzzy. It is revealing, for example, that Democratic congressmen would often protest their loyalty to Jackson personally when justifying their votes against his administration on policy matters, while Whigs tried to muster support for Henry Clay's scheme to distribute federal land revenues to the states by portraying it as a way to liberate federal funds from Jackson's personal control.[8] Party lines in the states were in even greater disarray. Just when Jacksonians in Washington were denouncing the evils of monopoly and the privileges of bankers, Democratic officeholders in states like New York, New Jersey, Pennsylvania, and Ohio were simultaneously chartering banks and other privileged corporations just as readily as the Whigs. The early 1830s were years of booming prosperity, and many Democrats were just as eager as Whigs to create the institutions and credit to stimulate economic growth[9] (see Table 1). As a result, support for or hostility to Jackson, not coherent economic policies, most clearly distinguished a Democrat from a Whig.

During his last two years in office, however, Jackson attempted to define a more specific Democratic economic program. Through a series of directives to the state banks in which federal funds were deposited after their removal from the Bank of the United States in 1833, and the Specie Circular of 1836, which banned the sale of government land for anything but hard money, he moved to prevent the national government from accepting and redistributing private banknotes, especially those of small denominations. Restricting government dealings in paper money would undermine public confidence in its value, reduce its circulability, and therefore act as a deflationary measure by decreasing the money supply. Perhaps because probanking Democrats recognized the need for an expansive currency to fuel the boom, perhaps because Jackson was a lame duck, his policies failed to unify his party. Instead, both in Congress and the states, they exacerbated divisions between the probanking (or conservative) and antibanking, hard money (or radical) wings of the party.[10]

Jackson's imminent retirement, in fact, created a dilemma for both parties as the presidential election of 1836 approached. Because Jackson himself was the issue over which the parties fought most intensely, his departure from the political scene threatened their entire *raison d'etre*. While he was in office, the opposing parties might convince the voters they offered true alternatives, that the victory of one or the other was vital to protect the people from irresponsible concentrations of power and privilege. But what would happen when Jackson was gone? The parties needed new issues to maintain and broaden their support.

Hostility to Jackson, not a positive program, was the only thing that united the Whigs. To some extent, they continued to run against him in 1836 by denouncing his record and criticizing his successful effort to handpick his successor, Martin Van Buren, as yet another example of executive tyranny.[11] This strategy, however, had its limits. To first-time voters joining the electorate, whom Whigs hoped to attract, attacking Jackson might seem an irrelevant issue after he left office. Even worse, it might offend voters in the South where Jackson himself remained immensely popular and where the Whigs most needed to broaden their base. Failing to develop a unified strategy, the Whigs ran three different candidates in 1836: Daniel Webster of Massachusetts, a prominent defender of the Bank of the United States; William Henry Harrison, an old Indian fighter who was popular in the West and with the Antimasons of the Northeast; and Hugh Lawson White of Tennessee, an erstwhile ally of Jackson who was forwarded as a true Jacksonian and who would be the major Whig standard bearer in the South.

The Democratic problem was just as great, since Jackson was the only glue holding the coalition together. The internal divisions in the party over Jackson's hard money policies revealed a lack of cohesion,

TABLE 1

Indexes of Party Disagreement on Selected Roll-Call Votes in Seven State Legislatures During the Jacksonian Period[a]

State	1833	1834	1835	1836	1837	1838	1839	1840	1841	1842	1843	1844
Business Incorporations												
New Jersey	7		44	21	86	94.5	12		62	56		
Pennsylvania			11		34	35			73.5	74		
Ohio	16	47	37	70	74							
New Hampshire					41	88	83	75.5		100		
Missouri						3		83		35		
Virginia	6						68					
Mississippi				10	32	48		14	26	43	63.5	81
Banking												
New Jersey	21		29	52	100	84			78.5			
Pennsylvania		8	32	45	79				100	47		
New Hampshire		11.5	8			77				67		
Ohio	42	34.5	49	64.5	97	40.5			92	37		
Missouri			16	6.5				80	61			
Virginia		37	29	48			70					
Mississippi				17.5	49	21	43.5	64	88	68	56	88
Paper Money												
New Jersey					93							
Pennsylvania	12	11.5			35	16				91		
New Hampshire					80	99				82		
Ohio			86	74	97	94		65	100			
Missouri						83.5				71		
Virginia				70		16				62.5		
Mississippi				45	51	58	49			47		47.5

(table continued)

Internal Improvements

Pennsylvania	6	10	53	38			49
New Hampshire							
Ohio	63.5	12.5	14	30.5	50	71	
Missouri	7.5	68	3	9	17		
Virginia	14	11	26	38	22	33	20
Mississippi							11	37

Incorporations for Internal Improvements

New Jersey	43	24.5	4
Pennsylvania	41		77	47
New Hampshire	46		77	48
Ohio		10		
Missouri			35	
Virginia	12	39	16	35
Mississippi		16	35	92

[a]The data for all the states in this table except Mississippi can be found in the tables in Herbert Ershkowitz and William G. Shade, "Consensus or Conflict? Political Behavior in the State Legislatures during the Jacksonian Era," *Journal of American History, 58* (1971), 591-622. Those for Mississippi are based on the tables in M. Philip Lucas, "The Second American Party System in Mississippi, 1836-1844" (unpublished seminar paper, University of Virginia, 1975). In all cases, the data in the original tables are listed in terms of the percentage of each party voting in favor of particular bills. I have converted those figures to a single index of party disagreement, which is simply the difference between the proportion of Whigs voting Yea and the proportion of Democrats voting Yea on a particular bill. When more than one roll call was used by the authors for a particular year, I have used the average index of party disagreement. The lower the index, the more the parties agreed with each other. The higher the index, the sharper the conflict between the parties. For example, if two-thirds of the Whigs opposed three-fourths of the Democrats, it would be 50. If three-fourths of the Whigs opposed three-fourths of the Democrats on a roll call, the index of disagreement would be 34.

and Democratic leaders tried to overcome this by transferring Jackson's personal popularity with the voters to the Democratic party as an organization. The party and its principles, not its men, were all important, they insisted, and in an address to the voters issued in the summer of 1835 they spelled out what principles the party stood for: state rights and strict construction versus the pernicious consolidating, loose construction principles of their foes; opposition to the Bank of the United States and the corrupt power it represented; and continuation of the republican policies pursued by Jackson through his heir, Van Buren, whom the party had nominated in May 1835. Good Jacksonians, the address asserted, must remain loyal to the party. This effort to wrap Van Buren and the party in the Jacksonian mantle received its sternest challenge from the Whig campaign in the South.

Jackson had swept the South by overwhelming margins in 1828 and 1832, but his staunch advocacy of national power against South Carolina's Nullifiers and his removal of federal deposits from the Bank of the United States offended a number of Southern politicians and created a leadership cadre for the Whig party in various Southern states. It is unclear, however, that either action dented Jackson's immense personal popularity with the mass of Southern voters. What is clear is that Southern Whig leaders did not rely primarily on attacking Jackson during the 1836 campaign. Instead, they seized a new issue that struck a responsive chord among Southern voters—slavery.

In the mid-1830s Southerners were more and more alarmed by the growing abolitionist petition campaign calling on Congress to abolish slavery in the District of Columbia and by the even more threatening effort to mail abolitionist literature to the South itself. Control of Congress and the federal postal service became a vital issue. Because many Southerners had been attracted to the Democratic party by the hope that its state rights, strict construction doctrines would prevent any federal interference with slavery, the Whigs' problem was to convince Southern voters that they were a more reliable proslavery party than the Democrats. Beginning in 1835, therefore, they argued that no Northern president could be trusted to resist abolitionist pressure. The Southerner White was much safer than the Yankee Van Buren. In January 1836 a Whig senator from Louisiana declared, "I think our interests imperatively require a Slaveholding President," and throughout Dixie the Whig slogan became

"The cause of Judge White is the cause of the South."[12] Southern Whigs went beyond rhetoric in their efforts to outflank the Democrats on the slavery issue. A study of roll-call voting in the House of Representatives from 1836 to 1860 found that 1836 and 1838 were the only years in which Southern Whigs took a more proslavery position than Southern Democrats.[13]

The charge that Van Buren could not be trusted to protect slavery from the abolitionist assault because he was a Yankee was, of course, absurd. The Little Magician had been the principal architect of the Old Republican plan to reconstruct a state rights party around Jackson specifically to protect slavery. But Van Buren's dealings with Southern politicans like Thomas Ritchie had been secret, and Democratic attempts to bury the slavery issue with state rights theories paled beside the Whig tactic of pushing it out into the open and insisting that only a Southern president could stand up to the abolitionists. "Judge White is cutting into our ranks," warned Ritchie himself, and Southern Democrats demanded that Van Buren and the Jackson administration do more to prove the Democratic party trustworthy on the slavery issue.[14]

In response to this Southern pressure in 1835 and 1836, the Democratic leaders in Washington adopted a much more explicit proslavery position. Jackson demanded that Congress ban incendiary abolitionist publications from the mails, and Postmaster General Amos Kendall authorized Southern postmasters to destroy abolitionist material even without such a law. Van Buren helped arrange the Gag Rule in the House of Representatives in 1836 to quash debate on abolitionist petitions, and in March 1836 he came out publicly against abolition in the District of Columbia. To assuage Southern Democrats, Northern Democratic legislatures passed resolutions denouncing the abolitionist movement. Van Buren himself persuaded William L. Marcy, the Democratic Governor of New York, to launch a vigorous assault on the abolitionists in his annual message in early 1836, and Van Buren's friend, Silas Wright of New York, made a speech in the U.S. Senate praising antiabolitionist mobs as a true expression of Northern sentiment.[15] Finally, it is likely that Jackson's appointment of three Southerners to the Supreme Court in 1835 and 1836 was also part of the administration effort to neutralize the Southern Whig campaign.[16]

All of this failed to stem a remarkable growth of the Whig party in the South. Even though Van Buren won the election, the Whigs carried Kentucky, Maryland, Tennessee, and Georgia in 1836, and they made impressive showings in other slave states that Jackson had carried almost unanimously four years earlier. One index of the new competitiveness between the two parties was a much larger turnout of voters in the South than in 1832. The election had extended the Second Party System to Dixie.

Three other aspects of the 1836 campaign merit emphasis. First, like Southern Democrats, Southern Whigs stressed the protection of slavery from outside interference from the inception of their party. They did not try to bury or avoid the sectional issue. Instead, they exploited it by arguing that their party was a better defender of the South than the Democratic party and, to some extent, this jockeying between the parties as to which offered more protection to Southern interests continued throughout the life of the Second Party System in the South. Sectional conflict, in short, did not weaken the two-party system in Southern states; from the very beginning it strengthened the two parties there by giving them an additional issue to fight about.

Second, what permitted the Whig proslavery campaign in the South was the looseness of the federal system, which allowed the Whigs to say different things in different sections. Running three candidates, of course, increased their flexibility, but until the presidential election of 1852 the Whigs would always manage the slavery issue by exploiting the possibilities of the federal system. As early as 1836, Northern and Southern Whigs were sharply polarized on slavery. If Southern Whigs that year took a more extreme proslavery line than Southern Democrats, Northern Whigs were clearly more favorable to the antislavery movement than Northern Democrats. Over 95 percent of the abolitionist petitions presented to Congress were introduced by Whigs, Northern Whig congressmen opposed the Gag Rule while Northern Democrats supported it, and in Northern state legislatures Whigs generally voted for antislavery or problack measures while Democrats opposed them.[17] Thus the Whig party could and did survive a fundamental division on the slavery question from its birth. Moreover, within each section voters could find alternative positions on the slavery question within the two-party system. If opposition to slavery or to the abolitionists was the decisive influence motivating a Northern voter, for example, he could express it by voting Whig or Democratic. The ability of the parties in the two sections to provide alternatives on the sectional issue, in turn, increased public faith in the party political process as the optimal way to influence government policy.

Third, the election failed to solve the Democratic dilemma. The victorious Democrats had continued to rely on Jackson's name to unify their divided ranks and give prestige to their party during the campaign. In his inaugural, Van Buren could continue this tactic by stressing his intimacy with Old Hickory. Such reaffirmations might retain already committed Democratic voters, but their relevance to the new voters joining the electorate was unclear. Nor did they heal the growing divisions on the currency issue between the conservative and radical wings of the party. In addition, Democrats feared further erosion of their Southern support, because the Whigs as the "out" party remained free to agitate the slavery question in different ways in different sections.

Van Buren tried to assuage the South by reiterating his pledge to veto any congressional attempt to abolish slavery in the District of Columbia and by appointing two Southerners to his Cabinet. Like some other Democrats, however, he had long believed that the best way to protect slavery and hold the Democratic party together was to keep sectional issues out of politics by promoting national two-party conflict over other matters and by holding firm to state rights, strict construction doctrines. Internal party cohesion, he was convinced, depended on the clarity and intensity of issue conflict between the parties since, as the Regency's newspaper in Albany had argued in the 1820s, an individual party was "most in jeopardy when an opposition is not sufficiently defined."[18] To unify his dividing party and make it attractive to new voters, therefore, Van Buren hoped to polarize the Whig and Democratic parties around new issues on which the contrasting positions of the opposing parties would be crystal clear. To do so, however, was difficult for a president who believed that the role of the national government should be limited and that policymakers in Washington should take no new initiatives.

The Panic of 1837 provided Van Buren with a golden opportunity. By generating demands on the government for relief and reigniting antibank, hard money sentiment, the Panic evoked visceral popular reactions and resurrected in concrete form the old conflicts between equality and privilege. Thus it had the potential to be an emotional new political issue to replace Jackson as the crux of interparty conflict. As is usual in American politics, however, events did not automatically create an issue between the parties. What was necessary to make it a partisan issue was contrasting responses from the leaders of the opposing parties. The Whigs immediately blamed the Panic on Jackson's destruction of the Bank of the United States and his subsequent hard money policies. Van Buren, on the other hand, was initially hesitant because the Panic exacerbated the divisions between the probanking and anticorporate wings of the Democracy. In most states, however, it shifted the balance of power within the party in favor of those Democrats who hated banks, paper money, and corporations in general, Thus the groundwork was laid for defining a coherent Democratic economic policy at both the national and state levels, an opportunity Van Buren built on when he took a hard money, antibank stance in response to the Panic. This achievement came at the cost of numerous defections by probusiness Democrats to Whig ranks, but it went a long way toward clarifying the programmatic differences between the parties. The Panic of 1837 and subsequent depression which lasted until 1843 thus formed a crucible in which were shaped clear, contrasting, and durable party positions about the proper role of government, both state and national, in the economy.

In September 1837 Van Buren asked Congress to create an Independent Treasury System by which federal deposits would be removed from private banks altogether. Specifically exempting Jackson's hard money policies, he blamed the Panic instead on excessive speculation encouraged by the overissue of paper banknotes. He offered no specific legislation, but he recommended that the government refuse to accept unbacked banknotes and deal only in specie. Denouncing "corporate immunities," he urged the states to reform their banks and restrict their privileges. Having outlined his own program, Van Buren pointedly contrasted it to the Whig alternative of a new national bank. The majority of voters had rejected such a bank as "a concentration of power dangerous to their liberties"; it represented "the constant desire among some of our citizens to enlarge the powers of the Government and extend its control to subjects with which it should not interfere."

Throughout the message, Van Buren harped on the renewed importance of strict construction and negative government to the welfare of the people. "The less government interferes with private pursuits the better for the general prosperity," he argued; such intervention by Congress or state legislatures inevitably produced "complaints of neglect, partiality, injustice, and oppression." Any active governmental role in the economy, in short, produced inequalities or privilege. The best way to preserve equality of opportunity was for government to do nothing. Government "was not intended to confer special favors on individuals or on any classes of them, to create systems of agriculture, manufacturers, or trade, or engage in them either separately or in connection with individual citizens or organized associations." Even demands for government relief to help people ruined by the depression should be rejected, because "it is not [government's] legimate object to make men rich or to repair by direct grants of money or legislation in favor of particular pursuits losses not incurred in the public service."[19]

Although not all Democrats agreed with Van Buren's prescription for recovery, his doctrine of the negative state became Democratic dogma until the 1850s. In platforms, in speeches, and, most important, in the voting records of legislators, the party rallied behind it. In Congress Democrats opposed relief measures, a new national bank, protective tariffs, distribution of federal revenue to the states, and most federal internal improvements. Such programs, they contended, violated strict construction principles and favored some people at the expense of others. In the states, the arena that acted on most economic legislation affecting the lives of the people, moreover, Democrats moved to restrict banking privileges or to abolish banks and paper money altogether, opposed the chartering of corporations of any kind, and often tried to restrict state activism in social areas as well—such as constructing public education systems at state expense or enacting prohibition laws. According to Democrats, any action by government fell unequally on the people by creating privileges for a few or infringing on the individual liberties of some groups to satisfy the demands of others. The best way to protect liberty and equality and thereby advance the general welfare was for the state to do nothing. Many Democrats insisted there was no common welfare since the interests of rich and poor, upper and lower classes, were sharply in conflict. Proudly accepting the epithet of Locofoco hurled at them by conservatives, they explicitly presented their economic policies as "radical" measures to help workingmen and farmers against the pro-business Whig party. Their portrait of class warfare was overdrawn, but there is no denying its impact in cementing the loyalties of some voters to the opposing Whig and Democratic parties.

The conscious Democratic swing to negative state doctrines virtually forced on the Whigs the alternative of positive governmental intervention into the economy to promote growth and recovery from the depression. Proclaiming harmony instead of conflict among the interests of classes, they argued that positive governmental action would help everyone. Specifically, Whigs and conservative Democrats were horrified by the Independent Treasury plan because, by removing government monies from circulation in the private sector, it would exacerbate deflation in an already depressed economy. The basic rationale of the entire Whig economic program, indeed, was that a dearth of private capital hindered economic growth and that government could best promote the general prosperity either by providing that capital itself or by aiding private citizens to accumulate it. Economic growth would expand opportunities for all and would strengthen the fabric of the republic. Hence, at the national level, Whigs favored federal relief, a new national bank instead of the Independent Treasury, higher tariffs to aid manufacturers, federal internal improvements, and, if these were not possible, the distribution of federal revenue from land sales to the states so that state governments could finance internal development. In the states, Whigs voted for the chartering of banks and other corporations, defended corporate privileges such as limited liability as necessary to attract investment, promoted state subsidies to internal improvements, and advanced other measures to promote public prosperity through state aid. Reflecting the Antimasonic faith in the state as agent of social change and often the moral values of evangelical Protestant groups as well, the Whigs also supported more frequently than Democrats laws to create public school systems, to prohibit activity on Sunday, and to ban liquor sales. As noted above, moreover, in Northern states Whigs were much more favorable to antislavery, pro-Negro measures than Democrats.[20]

By the early 1840s, in short, the parties presented to the voters much clearer programmatic alternatives than they had in the early 1830s, not only in their promises during elections, but in their performances in legislative halls (see Table 1). And while the depression lasted, many of the economic questions they dealt with mattered a great deal to voters. The battles over Van Buren's Independent Treasury plan and over banking in the states not only reflected different party responses to the depression; they also symbolized vastly different conceptions of how government should interact with society. Each party favored prosperity, but the Whigs clearly stressed the promotion of growth, while the Democrats emphasized the protection of individual liberty and equality, not only from privileged concentrations of economic power like corporations but from state-imposed social reform as well. In states as diverse as New York and Alabama, Pennsylvania and Mississippi, the differences between the parties were sharp and consistent: men who sought to increase the banking capital of their community versus those who opposed banking privileges; men who favored corporations versus those who resented any corporation as a monopoly; men who pushed for social reform versus those who detested reformers' efforts as self-righteous invasions of personal freedom. In most cases, in other words, the positions assumed by state parties were congruent with those assumed by parties at the national level. For the first time, state-level party conflict sharpened the image of party difference generated by combat at the national level instead of blurring that image. As a result, the Second Party System seemed more responsive to most voters' needs than it ever had before, voters developed remarkably strong attachments to the contending parties, and popular faith in the political process of party competition flourished.

Leadership conflict in legislative halls had importance beyond the intrinsic interest of voters in the issues at stake themselves. Not all voters cared about or were even aware of all the issues contested by the parties in statehouses and Congress. For many, party identity became a substitute for specific issue concern. By the early 1840s, many voters viewed themselves primarily as Democrats or Whigs, and they brought to those identities a determination to defeat the political foe similar to the present-day fans' enthusiasm for the local football team. That politics was the most popular spectator sport of the day is attested to by the large attendance at political rites such as pole raisings and parades and by the widespread betting that accompanied elections, with vote margins in particular districts given as a handicap like pointspreads on today's games. In sociological terms, Democratic and Whig voters regarded each other as negative referents, and they often saw elections primarily as a chance to score a victory over their rivals. A shrewd Mississippian captured this motivation precisely when he observed that "as a general rule about one half of those who vote look upon the privilege as worthless unless they can use it to gratify a personal hostility or religious antipathies, or to inflict injury on what they hate." Politicians could count on this mutual animosity to determine which way men would vote in elections, but they still recognized the need to provide voters with a conflict to whip up their enthusiasm and get them to the polls in the first place. Thus a Tennessee Whig editor complained in 1851, "There is I think some lukewarmness, not to say defection, among some Whigs. . . . They need warming up. If we could have a collision on the stump here, it would help us much." Politicians even welcomed the attacks of opponents because they would provoke their own followers to action. The Georgia Whig Alexander H. Stephens hailed Democrats' boasts that they would carry Georgia in the 1844 election. "The Locos seem determined to do what they can by gasconnading, and the only effect of it is I think to arouse the Whigs and make them energetic, and that is all we want."[21] Voters, in short, often cared more about party victory than about what position their party assumed on particular issues. The clashes in Congress and state legislatures, no matter how arcane or irrelevant the issue, were primarily important to them because they provided contests in which they could cheer on their respective teams.

Because party leaders realized that interparty combat enhanced their chances both to coalesce legislators into a disciplined phalanx and to march fervent legions of voters to the polls on election day, they defined the differences between the parties as sharply as possible. In 1841, for example, a Tennessee Whig legislator reported that the Democrats had "introduced a long string of Resolutions, condemning the whole Whig creed, which are regarded as the beginning of a six weeks war. This is to be an angry and stormy session."[22] Newspapers were especially crucial in outlining the battleground between the parties for the voting public, and leaders sought to establish as many as possible. Hence a North Carolina Whig complained in 1850, "The Whig party of our state suffers greatly for the want of an efficient Press in the State. . .stating clearly and concisely and in a popular manner the issues, reasons, and arguments which divide the two parties."[23] If for some reason there was a lull in the battle over substantive issues, party leaders consciously provoked conflict over artificial ones to energize their supporters. Thus Pennsylvania's Democratic legislators at the beginning of the 1846 assembly session moved to recess on January 8 to celebrate the anniversary of Jackson's victory at New Orleans, and the motion had the desired effect of polarizing the parties against each other immediately.[24] Similarly, Alabama's Democrats, who always enjoyed a majority in the legislature, normally packed the internal improvements and education committees with Whigs so that when Whigs reported bills calling for state action in these areas, the Democrats could unify in opposition and use the Whig bills as campaign fodder in the next election as well.[25]

That strength of party identity among voters and the vigor of interparty conflict were vitally important. Van Buren's maxim that interparty conflict was the optimal way to avoid naked sectional division in the country worked in several ways. It did not apply only to national parties and the subsequent unity between their Northern and Southern wings. It was a product of party combat within the individual states, as well. As long as the parties fought with each other over national and state matters, voters developed allegiances that often became their preeminent identification. Loyalty to party and the hope for party victory within states became more important than anything else. As long as this commitment remained strong, people within the states of the two sections would be internally divided politically, and the efforts of agitators to unite them into a Northern phalanx against the South or a Southern phalanx against the North proved futile. Partisan animosities and the priorities they engendered frustrated those who wished to solidify the respective sections for the defense of sectional rights. As long as men thought in old party terms, long-standing sectional differences over Negro slavery could not produce sectional disruption.

Men like John C. Calhoun, who rejected the major parties and tried to form a separate party uniting all Southerners, realized that the spirit of party was inimical to their cause. In 1847, for example, Alabama fireeater William Lowndes Yancey denounced "this foul spirit of party which thus binds and divides and distracts the South."[26] In part the reason why the allegiance of men to parties worked against sectional extremism was simply a mechanism of competing allegiances. Although most of the inhabitants of Dixie thought of themselves as Southerners and cherished Southern rights, they also had more immediate concerns. Because of the utility of parties *within* their respective states to battle over matters affecting their everyday lives, such as state spending and taxation and the presence or absence of transportation and banking facilities within their communities, Southern party members placed party victory ahead of a unified sectional defense.

More important, popular faith in the political system rested on ideology. Interparty conflict over a broad range of issues at different levels of government increased popular confidence in the ability to achieve goals through the ebb and flow of party competition and thereby increased popular reluctance to adopt drastic apolitical or constitutional remedies for sectional grievances. The party battle itself seemed to insure the protection of republicanism, of liberty and equality, which was the most fundamental goal of Americans in both the South and the North. Certainly each party in the South, as in the North, employed a rhetoric that portrayed itself as a paladin against heinous concentrations of power and privilege represented by the opposition and as a champion of the people and of the republican doctrine of government by the people. Thus Alabama Whigs in 1836 denounced the Democrats' use of nominating conventions as a menace to the republic itself. "It is due to independence, . . . it is due to liberty itself that this odious system should be spurned from the embrace of freemen. . . . let our chief officers continue to be chosen in this way, and . . . we may wear for a while longer the forms of freemen; but our spirits will be effectually enslaved." Alabama's Democrats were no less skillful in portraying their foes as enemies of the republic. Every Whig, it was charged in 1839, was "untiring in his exertions to pull down the fabric of liberty based upon the Constitution and prostrate the rights of the people, for the purpose of advancing upon the ruins thereof, Aristocratic power."[27] While belaboring the enemy, each trumpeted its own republican virtue. "The people are the only source of legitimate power," cried one Southern Democratic paper, while another echoed, *"The Sovereignty of the People* is the great fundamental principle . . . to which we adhere." In the same language the *Richmond Whig* riposted that the basis of the Whig party lay in "the simple, the plain, the old-fashioned, the recognized in all ages, Republican maxim, that *the majority,* and *the majority only,* have a right to rule."[28]

Freedom, equality, and self-government, it seemed to Southerners, could best be defended through political parties. Until men ceased to think in party terms, until they lost faith in the efficacy of parties to protect the republican principles and institutions they cherished, the attempts of secessionists to convince them that they must reject parties and the national government itself in order to secure true equality and liberty would fail. So, too, in the North the cries of antislavery zealots that the major parties be rejected in order to forge a crusade against Negro slavery would prove vain. The tenacity of the parties' grip on the allegiance of voters and the futility of extremists while that grip was maintained would become clear when the slavery extension issue first emerged in the 1840s.

☆ THREE

Slavery Extension and the Second Party System, 1843–1848

The issue that drove the deepest wedge between North and South in the two decades before the Civil War was not the institution of slavery itself, but the question of whether slavery should be allowed to expand westward beyond the boundaries of the slave states. Most Northerners found slavery repugnant, but the abolitionist campaign to persuade Americans to make its destruction their highest priority had failed in the North as well as the South. And although abolitionist petitioners had their champions in Congress, sectional divisions over petitions and the Gag Rule had not disrupted the national party lines that prevailed on the vast majority of business handled by Congress. Similarly, although Southerners deplored the abolitionists as fanatics, the anti-slavery crusade had been unable to weld the South into a political unit. Northern attempts to bar slavery from distant western territories, in contrast, generated much more widespread support in the North and promoted a sectional consciousness in the South that galvanized Southerners, regardless of party, into opposition to that prohibition. The slavery expansion issue, in short, indisputably polarized Northerners

expansion as main issue [handwritten marginalia]

and Southerners against each other, thereby dividing both national parties.

Because slavery expansion had this impact, many historians have concluded that its emergence doomed first the Second Party System and then the nation itself. When the issue first rose in the 1840s over Texas annexation and the Mexican Cession, however, the two major parties were able to manage it, even though their Northern and Southern wings often disagreed sharply. In part they did so because other issues that formed the basis of interparty conflict remained salient in the 1840s. Equally important, they continued to find ways to offer party alternatives on the volatile slavery extension issue itself. The end result was that party lines and the two-party system were maintained. The slavery extension issue by itself could not destroy the Second American Party System.

Until 1843 interparty conflict focused primarily on Andrew Jackson and the economic questions growing out of the depression of the late 1830s. As the Jackson presidency faded further and further into the past and as prosperity began to return in the 1840s, however, the salience and resonance of the old issues on which the party system had been founded appeared to diminish. As a result, certain influential politicians sought new issues to shift the battleground of party competition and advance their own careers by doing so.

One of these was President John Tyler, nominal leader of the Whig party. A state rights Virginian who had never adopted the nationalistic, positive economic philosophy of the Whigs, Tyler had succeeded to the presidency when William Henry Harrison, the first Whig president, died in April 1841, a month after his inauguration. Tyler quickly broke with the congressional wing of his party by vetoing its cherished economic programs—a new national bank and distribution of land revenues to the states. This rupture had two results. By distilling Tyler loyalists like Henry Wise of Virginia out of the Whig party, it purified that organization and made it all the more cohesive behind the economic programs advanced by Henry Clay. That is, the break further clarified the lines dividing the major parties on economic policy. At the same time, it left the President without a party. Because he hoped to be reelected on his own right in 1844, Tyler needed a new issue to rouse support for him personally and to shift attention from the economic matters being contested through the Democratic and Whig parties. Influenced in part by a coterie of Virginia friends who were speculating in Texas lands and who in any case wanted annexation of the proslavery Republic of Texas to strengthen slavery in the South, Tyler used his presidential control of foreign policy to initiate negotiations with Texas. In the spring of 1844 he presented a treaty of annexation to the Senate, a treaty on which he rested his hopes for reelection. Ratification of the treaty failed that summer, but what support annexation had was largely Democratic.

The reasons why Democratic senators supported Tyler's project lay as much in the condition of their own party as in any groundswell of public demand for territorial expansion. As the presidential election of 1844 approached, the Democratic party was in disarray. Ex-President Van Buren remained the party's chieftain and seemed a sure bet to obtain its nomination for the 1844 race. A significant minority of Democrats, however, wanted to jettison both the party's hard money, antibusiness program and its major proponent Van Buren who, they thought, had dragged the party down to defeat in 1840. With the end of the depression and resultant popular pressure to expand banking credit, they considered Van Buren's program suicidal. Because Van Buren still had the majority of the Democratic party behind him on economic matters, however, these probanking Democrats needed a new issue to derail his drive for renomination. Simultaneously, the small but influential band of Southern Democrats loyal to John C. Calhoun also hoped to stop Van Buren and capture the Democratic nomination for the South Carolinian. Still others opposed Van Buren's nomination simply because they thought he was a loser and because they wanted a new face. Texas annexation provided the issue these disparate anti-Van Buren Democrats needed. The Little Magician publicly opposed annexation in the spring of 1844, because he privately feared it would turn antislavery Northern voters against the Democrats. Hence, when Tyler presented his Texas treaty, the various groups of anti-Van Buren Democrats backed it, as much to gain its endorsement at the Democratic convention in May 1844 and thereby stop Van Buren as to secure its ratification.[1]

Heading the effort to thrust Texas annexation into the political arena was Democratic Senator Robert J. Walker of Mississippi. Walker played a major role in persuading the Democratic party to endorse annexation in the 1844 presidential campaign. Working behind the scenes since 1842, Walker secretly secured the support of Jackson's magical name for immediate annexation. He then undertook a strenuous but sophistical propaganda campaign to persuade reluctant Northern Democrats opposed to slavery extension and a growing black population that additional slave territory in Texas would, in fact, benefit the antislavery cause. Slaves from the Old South would be drawn to the rich lands of Texas, he argued, until the older regions were depopulated of slaves. Then, when Texas's lands lost their fertility, the slaves would naturally gravitate south to Mexico. Annexation would thus eventually rid the country of the twin problems of slavery and race adjustment.[2] Walker's activities went beyond pamphleteering. He worked ceaselessly to agitate the Texas issue in the spring of 1844 and to unite the anti-Van Buren Democrats behind it. Largely because of Walker's exertions, the Democratic national convention overthrew Van Buren, nominated James K. Polk of Tennessee, and adopted a platform, written by Walker, that forcefully committed the Democracy to expansion not only in Texas but in Oregon as well.

Precisely why Walker was so determined to impose Texas annexation on the Democratic party is unclear. He was not a member of the effort to build a new party behind Tyler. Nor was he an arch-foe of Van Buren; indeed, he appears to have favored Van Buren's nomination on a proannexation platform until Van Buren's opposition made that prospect hopeless. Although he speculated heavily in Western lands, he seems to have had no direct economic interest in Texas, as did others around Tyler. Nor was he as committed as others in the pro-Texas camp to extending slavery as an end in itself. Because Walker's major goal appears to have been endorsement of annexation by the Democratic party, his motives most likely emerged from the political situation, not from economic interest, personal loyalty, or sectional chauvinism. With the old issues of Jackson and the depression fading, Walker was probably looking for a new issue that could reunite and reinvigorate the feuding Democrats. Thomas Ritchie, for example, who reluctantly turned against Van Buren in favor of a pro-Texas man, explained before the convention, "For forty years . . . have I been Editor of a paper and never have I seen the . . . party in so much danger. . . . We are breaking up . . . we are divided by miserable contests and contemptible jealousies."[3] Similarly, Walker must have recognized that without the presence of the charismatic Jackson the Democracy was splintering and that the parameters of two-party conflict would have to be redefined to save it. Expansion into both Texas and Oregon would meet that need by diverting attention from economic disputes within the party and reuniting its Northern and Southern wings.

What was necessary to regalvanize Democratic loyalty, of course, was Whig opposition to expansion; nothing could unify Democrats like Whig attacks on them. By the early 1840s, Walker had considerable evidence that he could count on such opposition if the Democrats took up Texas. As early as November 1842, for example, the Whig *Ohio State Journal* had announced: "As a party, in the free states, the Whigs are opposed to the acquisition of Texas," and by June 1843 even Virginia's *Richmond Whig* had come out against annexation and urged other Whigs to follow suit.[4] Rumor had it, moreover, that Henry Clay, the sure Whig candidate in 1844, opposed immediate annexation, Finally, the Whigs had traditionally resisted territorial expansion because it would weaken the fabric of the republic, and they could be counted on in any case to fight any proposal by the apostate Tyler. Walker could hope with good reason, therefore, that Texas annexation, even though it involved slavery extension, would enliven and strengthen the Second Party System by polarizing the parties on a new issue, an issue, moreover, on which the Democrats would have the edge.

Whether or not Walker had these expectations, the parties quickly aligned against each other on Texas. Once the Democrats demanded the immediate "reannexation of Texas and reoccupation of Oregon" in the 1844 campaign, the Whigs opposed those measures. Party affiliation, not section, dictated the stands of newspapers and politicians on the expansion issue, and party, not section, largely determined votes on Texas in Congress and in state legislatures as well. Indeed, as Thomas Alexander has shown, once the dimension of expansion was attached to the slavery question, Whig unity on votes in the House of Representatives actually increased. Tyler's treaty with Texas was defeated in the Senate by a unified Whig party joined by a bloc of Van Buren Democrats.[5] Antislavery sentiment in part motivated Northern Whigs' opposition to annexation, and they certainly exploited that sentiment in the presidential campaign. But the important point is that proslavery Southern Whigs also opposed immediate annexation as inexpedient because it might bring on war with Mexico and because Texas would provide ruinous competition to cotton and sugar planters in older states. On the other hand, many antislavery Northern Democrats who had earlier opposed annexation now accepted and often endorsed it, while Southern Democrats argued it was in the best interest of the South.[6] Party lines among voters held at the polls in November despite the injection of the new issue into the campaign, and the closest students of that election discount the impact of the slavery-related Texas issue on its results, although Southern politicians of both parties thought it had given the Democrats an edge in Dixie.[7] Party lines remained sharp in the congressional votes on annexation by joint resolution in the session following the election, although a few more Southern Whigs joined the Democrats in supporting the measure, and postelection votes in the state legislatures of Ohio, Indiana, and Illinois also continued the pattern of dramatic party polarization on the Texas issue[8] (see Table 2). In sum, the annexation of Texas and concommitant slavery extension issue did not destroy party lines or the Second Party System. Instead, they shifted the grounds of party battle and, on the whole, invigorated the system by reinforcing the attachment of voters and most politicians to the established parties precisely because annexation became a strict party measure.

The emergence of the slavery extension issue strained the bonds of party loyalty to some extent. The abolitionist Liberty party increased its vote almost tenfold between 1840 and 1844; nevertheless, its 62,300 votes constituted less than 3 percent of the total poll. Related issues that arose during the congressional debates over Texas, moreover, fragmented both sectional and party lines.[9] Van Buren Democrats did oppose Tyler's treaty, and their anger at the ultimate annexation in 1845 increased their alienation. But they had rallied to Polk in the election, and it was only the later actions of Polk when combined with their residual bitterness over Texas that sparked their brief revolt from the Democratic party in 1848. Finally, as historians have overemphasized, the Texas issue provided the entering wedge between Cotton and Conscience Whigs in Massachusetts, a division that would later drive many Conscience Whigs to the Free Soil party.

If the fault lines beneath the surface of party unity were widened, however, one can stress with equal justice how very limited those tremors were. Some degree of intraparty tension is endemic to politics; as James L. Sundquist has brilliantly observed, parties should be conceived of as battlegrounds that contending factions constantly fight to control.[10] They have never been static monoliths. For the vast majority of voters and politicians in the 1840s, Texas was a party, not a sectional issue. The rupture of Northern Whigs was confined largely to Massachusetts, a fact that Charles Francis Adams, leader of the Massachusetts insurgents, learned to his dismay during the summer of 1845 when he made herculean but spectacularly unsuccessful efforts to recruit Democratic and Whig voters from other

TABLE 2

Partisan Dimensions of State Legislative Votes on Texas Annexation[a]

		Proportion favoring annexation, percent		Index of disagreement
		Whigs	Democrats	
Indiana House	December 1843	13	86	73
Ohio House	December 1844	0	100	100
Indiana House	December 1844	13	100	87
Illinois House	February 1845	10	97	87
Illinois Senate	February 1845	18	100	82

[a]These figures are based on the tables in Norman E. Tutorow, "Whigs in the Old North West and the Mexican War," pp. 433-440. They exclude abstentions, which varied in size from vote to vote. In each case Whigs opposed while Democrats favored annexation.

states for a new organization to continue the fight against Texas. Voters elsewhere saw no need for a new party, his correspondents made clear, because the major parties were already so sharply divided over the issue. From Hartford, Connecticut, William Ellsworth reported, "But with almost entire unanimity, the Whigs *feel* right & will do right. The Democratic party, with equal unanimity feel wrong, or at least will *act* wrong, on this subject." A Pennsylvanian provided an even shrewder analysis of how the dynamics of interparty competition prevented the formation of a new antislavery party. Because Northern Democrats now accepted annexation as a party measure, warned Julius Lemoyne, only Whigs and Liberty party members could possibly be recruited. Their opposition would automatically reinforce the determination of rank and file Democrats to achieve annexation. "The whole movement would necessarily assume a *party aspect,* and that alone would insure its defeat. For if the old parties have one principle of action, more influential than another in deciding their conduct, it is *opposition* to *each* other, right or wrong."[11] The Second Party System had incorporated the slavery extension issue into its matrix of partisan competition so completely that, in the mid-1840s, it simply could not be used to disrupt that system.

Although sectional tension over the slavery extension issue was aggravated during the presidency of James K. Polk, the net result of his term was to intensify interparty conflict and thereby strengthen partisan identification at both the national and state levels, not weaken them. A proponent of the traditional Democratic economic program, Polk vigorously pushed bills through Congress to lower the tariff and establish the Independent Treasury; with few exceptions, they passed in 1846 by strict party votes. Moreover, Polk and the Democratic party strove to keep alive the expansion issue that had divided the parties in the 1844 campaign, even though Congress made the offer of annexation to Texas before Polk was inaugurated. It was no accident that the *Democratic Review* in New York first articulated the phrase "Manifest Destiny" in the summer of 1845 after Texas had accepted annexation or that Polk called for all of Oregon and hinted that California might seek annexation as had Texas in his annual message of December 1845. Polk's thirst for continental expansion to California helped lead to the outbreak of war with Mexico in May 1846, and he quickly made the war an administration measure all good Democrats were expected to back. The expansionist zeal of the Democrats also provoked sharp party division; the Whigs on the whole opposed territorial acquisition. They soon denounced "Mr. Polk's War" as an immoral aggression on a weaker neighbor, a naked and intolerable land grab to satisfy the lust of the President, and the natural result of the Democrat's Texas policy. Polk's supposed tyranny was vilified as a threat to republican government, just as Jackson's had been. With different exceptions in each case, the final admission of Texas to statehood in December 1845, the drive for all of Oregon in 1846, and voting on the Mexican War between 1846 and 1848 reinforced party lines in Congress. True, Democratic cohesion on nationally financed internal improvements began to break down, especially in the Senate after Polk vetoed a Rivers and Harbors bill in August 1846 that Midwestern Democrats favored. But the two closest students of congressional voting in these years both conclude that party lines remained surprisingly strong.[12]

Equally important, the renewed conflict in Washington sharpened party lines in the states, both in legislatures and in state and congressional elections. The Whigs were appalled at Polk's economic program and territorial designs, but they nevertheless welcomed his actions as ammunition for the election campaigns of 1846, 1847, and 1848. As soon as Henry Clay's defeat in 1844 was certain, for example, Horace Greeley of the influential New York *Tribune* charged that the Democrats had "concealed or mystified" the vital issues of Texas and the tariff and thereby had hoodwinked Northern voters. Once in office, they would have to act, and the Whigs would reap the benefit of an angry public reaction. The passage of the low Walker Tariff in 1846 only increased the confidence of New York Whigs that they had a winning issue in upcoming elections. Elsewhere Whigs also believed that clarifying the lines of party difference would spark a Whig comeback. A Democrat warned Howell Cobb in the summer of 1846 that Georgia's Whigs anticipated Democratic action on the tariff "with the eagerness of hyenas and jackals, waiting only for the onslaught to be over to rush on to the work of mutilation." By dampening any Whig enthusiasm for the Mexican War, they confidently expected to wreak "havoc" with the tariff issue in the next congressional elections.[13]

If Georgia's Whigs initially hesitated to attack Polk's war policies, they like their counterparts in other states soon launched assaults on the war and expansion, and those issues provided campaign fodder for contending state parties until the end of the war. Even in the Northwest where enthusiasm for Oregon was bipartisan and universal, the Mexican War provoked sharp party alignments in legislatures and electoral campaigns. Roll-call votes in state assemblies again provide the most graphic evidence of this party polarization. In Ohio, Indiana, and Michigan resolutions endorsing or opposing the war produced strict party votes while a vote on prowar resolutions in the Illinois House of Representatives in 1846 saw 100 percent of the Democrats in favor and 73 percent of the Whigs opposed. In the Illinois Senate 85 percent of the Democrats opposed 83 percent of the Whigs on the same measures. Similarly, the issues of the war, the tariff, and the Independent Treasury became fodder for interparty combat in Northeastern states such as Massachusetts, Connecticut, and New Jersey.[14]

Indiana provides a splendid example of a state in which Whigs exploited Polk's programs at the national level to rejuvenate their fortunes in state and congressional elections after Clay's disappointing defeat in 1844. As early as December 1844, despondent Whigs were urged not to give up because "time will give us an opportunity to strike. The locos have a hard task before them. To reconcile the conflicting interests of North & South on the tariff & Texas questions will be no easy one." By January 1846, before Congress had acted on Polk's recommendations, Indiana's Whigs were still desperate for issues to use in the impending gubernatorial campaign, since they had no advantageous state issues to ride. One Whig predicted with marvelous foresight, however, that "Congress may kick up some deviltry out of which we can make something to put in our pipes." Democratic actions provided a great deal for the Whigs to smoke; by 1847 a Whig congressional candidate was implored to "attack the Administration at every vulnerable point—upon the Oregon question—the veto of the River & Harbor bill—the subtreasury—with a raking fire at the Mexican war. . . ."[15]

Few states offer as good an example of how the national issues growing out of Polk's term clarified the lines of interparty combat at the state level and thereby reinforced party loyalty among the rank and file as Pennsylvania. The Independent Treasury and the related drive for hard money, Oregon, and the Mexican War all provided material for partisan strife in gubernatorial messages, legislative debates, and party platforms.[16] As might be imagined, the tariff became the hottest issue in industrial Pennsylvania. In 1844 the Democrats had campaigned there as the true defenders of the Tariff of 1842, which was really a Whig measure, and many Pennsylvania Whigs blamed their defeat that year on this false claim. Even before the 29th Congress met in December 1845, a western Pennsylvania Whig urged his party to allow the Democrats to reduce the tariff so the Whigs could regain the issue the Democrats had fudged in 1844.[17] Until the Democrats acted on the tariff in Congress, however, partisan exploitation of the issue was difficult, because many Pennsylvania Democrats continued to advocate the high protective rates of 1842. In the legislative session of 1846, before the Walker Tariff passed Congress, for example, Democrats on two different occasions introduced resolutions requesting the state's congressional delegation to oppose revision of the Tariff of 1842. On these and on other Democratic resolutions endorsing a tariff reduction, the Democrats were badly divided. Only the addition of hard money, antibank amendments to the tariff resolutions produced Democratic unity and clear party polarization.[18] Until the summer of 1846, the Whigs had difficulty defining where the Democrats stood on the tariff issue and thus making the best partisan use of it to rouse their own supporters.

As soon as the Walker Tariff passed, however, the Whigs moved to exploit it, even though all but one of the state's Democratic congressmen had voted against it. The Whigs campaigned victoriously against the new duties in the fall of 1846, and the Richmond *Enquirer* astutely noted that those results showed "that the clamor against the new Tariff was not so much in behalf of 'domestic industry' as to make Whig capital for the next Presidency."[19] The Whigs, indeed, knew a good thing when they saw it, and they continued to milk the issue. In the 1847 session of the legislature they gleefully exulted that the Walker Tariff proved Democratic deception in 1844; the Democrats retorted accurately that the Whigs were simply exploiting the issue for campaign purposes. State resolutions on the national tariff, after all, had little effect in changing rates; only Congress could do that. With the Democrats committed by the action of their national party, however, party discipline tightened, and much sharper lines of conflict appeared on tariff votes in the 1847 session than in the previous year's session. Those lines extended from the legislature to the parties' state platforms in 1847 and 1848 where the Democrats defended and the Whigs denounced the Walker Tariff.[20] The tariff may have been more important in Pennsylvania than in other states, but the combined actions of the Polk administration clearly heightened the level of interparty competition in Pennsylvania and elsewhere and thereby strengthened the two-party system.

Historians of pre-Civil War politics have largely ignored this evidence that issues growing out of the Polk years reinforced the loyalty of Whigs and Democrats by sharply polarizing the parties against each other at the national and state levels. Indeed, as pointed out earlier, because of an obsession with the paramount importance of national-level politics they have sharply underestimated the importance of state-level political conflict in welding the allegiance of voters to parties in any period. Thus, what has caught their attention about the Polk years is the palpable sectional division of the national parties that emerged over the question of extending slavery to territory acquired from Mexico as a result of the war. For these historians, Polk's presidency was a transitional period that saw the shift from the old Jacksonian alignment of politics around economic issues to a period, lasting until the outbreak of the Civil War, when sectional conflict over slavery dominated political development. It was the disruption of party lines during the Polk years, not their reinforcement, that they stress. There is no denying the deep chasm that opened between North and South over slavery in the territories, but its impact on the party system, at least in the 1840s, has been exaggerated.

The problem of what to do with slavery in any new territory was crystallized in August 1846 when David Wilmot, a Democratic Congressman from Pennsylvania, introduced an amendment to an appropriation bill requested by the Polk administration for the conduct of the war. Polk's desire to acquire territory from Mexico, especially California, was well known, and many congressmen thought Polk intended the money as a down payment to the Mexicans. Northern Democrats feared that such a purchase would give weight to Northern Whig charges that the war was being fought for the benefit of slaveholders to gain more land for their slaves. To defuse this charge and enable Northern Democrats to go to the voters on the question of expansion without slavery, Wilmot's amendment, afterward known as the Wilmot Proviso, banned slavery by congressional statute from any territory to be acquired from Mexico. The House split along sharp North-South lines on the amendment; both parties were ruptured. The Proviso passed the House because the North had a majority of seats, but it was buried in the Senate. That pattern would be repeated each time the Proviso was introduced over the next four years. Eventually the legislatures of every Northern state except one would call on its congressmen to support the Proviso, while Southern states threatened to secede if it were passed and signed into law. Even though the problem it addressed—what to do with slavery in Mexican territory—was strictly hypothetical until the Treaty of Guadeloupe Hidalgo was ratified and the country actually received land from Mexico in 1848, the conflicting passions aroused by the Proviso most definitely proved a threat to the national parties and to the nation itself.

The reasons for the sharply contrasting sectional reactions to the Proviso are important to understand, because they formed the basis of the sectional conflict over slavery in the territories until the Civil War. Northern hostility to slavery expansion sprang from a number of sources. Some Northerners, undoubtedly a minority in the section, sincerely viewed black slavery as such an intolerable moral evil that it could not be allowed to expand and thus perpetuate itself. They and others, moreover, honestly believed that preventing slavery's expansion would ensure its destruction. Many more abhorred slavery as an economic system inimical to the free labor system of the North. If planters settled with their slaves in the territories, Northerners feared, nonslaveholding farmers from the North could not. Free labor and slavery could not coexist. And because many Northerners believed that the continued growth of their own economic system and with it of opportunities for upward economic mobility depended on continued expansion into new lands, they viewed the struggle over the territories as vital. More important still was a growing Northern resentment of the overweening political power of the South and the slaveholders in the national parties and the national government, a political influence and arrogance symbolized by the epithet "Slave Power," which Northern politicians of both parties used to denounce the political pretensions of slaveholders. Prohibiting slavery from the territories was the easiest way to prevent the admission of more slave states and thus to stop the growth of the political power of slaveholders. As David Wilmot himself later wrote:

> I am jealous of the **power** of the South. . . . The South holds no prerogative under the Constitution, which entitles her to wield forever the Scepter of Power in this Republic, to fix by her own arbitary edict, the principles & policy of this government, and to build up and tear down at pleasure. . . . Yet so dangerous do I believe the spirit and demands of the **Slave Power,** so insufferable its arrogance, if I saw the way open to strike an effectual and decisive blow against its domination at this time, I would do so, even at the temporary loss of other principles.

A young Massachusetts Whig expressed the same resentment of Southerners in his party and the same desire to humble them, although he put it in earthier terms in a letter to a former Yale classmate. "They have trampled on the rights and just claims of the North sufficiently long and have fairly shit upon all our Northern statesmen and are now trying to rub it in and I think now is the time and just the time for the North to take a stand and maintain it till they have brought the South to their proper level."[21]

The opprobrium inherent in the term Slave Power, indeed, applied to more than the unfair control of the national government and the political parties Northerners believed slaveholders exerted. In some Northern eyes, slavery had created an aristocratic society in the South dominated socially, economically, and politically by a small oligarchy of planters in defiance of the republican principle of majority rule. Elite control was a flagrant challenge to the American value that all men, at least all white men, were equal and should have an equal voice in government. In republican ideology, power itself was evil, the natural antagonist of the freedom and independence it had been the purpose of the Revolution to protect. To prevent the extension of slave society, therefore, was to insulate Northerners from that privileged, powerful, and antirepublican aristocracy. Opposition to slavery extension thus became a new phase in the long battle to protect liberty and equality from power and privilege, an ideological crusade to defend republicanism that had helped invigorate *interparty* conflict since the 1820s.

Finally, there was a darker side to antiextension, or free-soil, sentiment. The North, like the South, was a racist society. Blacks were discriminated against economically, legally, and politically, and several Midwestern states had passed statutes barring the entry of free Negroes. That same racist antipathy toward intermingling with blacks characterized a good deal of free-soil sentiment, thus sharply distinguishing it from the much smaller abolitionist movement that pushed for equal rights for free blacks as well as the emancipation of the slaves. Determined to preserve unsettled territory for whites only, many Northerners of both parties opposed slavery extension explicitly to keep blacks, free and slave, out of that territory. Praising the "White Man's Proviso," the foes of slavery expansion boasted that they were the real friends of Northern whites, since they would protect them from contact with the despised blacks in the territories.

None of the components of free-soil sentiment were mutually exclusive; they reinforced each other. Even racists, for example, often thought that restricting black slavery to the South would eventually doom its existence there. It seems clear, however, that the vast majority who rallied to the free-soil cause were not motivated by any humanitarian sympathy for the enslaved blacks in the South. Instead, the majority were either apathetic about the blacks' plight or actively hostile to them. Hostility to Southern slaveholders more than abolitionism or even antislavery was the emotion that held the free-soil forces together. Less altruistic or moralistic than abolitionism, free-soilism was a much more powerful and widespread sentiment in the North, and Northern politicians had to pay it heed.

The intensity of Southern hostility to the Proviso was just as evident as that of Northern opposition to slavery expansion, but the reasons for it are more difficult to decipher. Three-fourths of the Southern white population did not own any slaves, and their resistance to the Proviso especially requires explanation. To some extent, Southern motives were the mirror image of those in the North. Convinced that slavery as an economic system had to expand to survive because the cotton economy exhausted lands so quickly, some Southerners eyed the acquisition of New Mexico and especially California with the same lust as they had viewed Texas. Here was a vast new area into which slavery could expand. There is evidence as well that racist nonslaveholding whites who saw slavery primarily as a necessary system of race control feared being penned up with and eventually overwhelmed by a growing black population unless it could be continually dispersed into new areas. Robert Walker's propaganda for Texas annexation had in part been aimed at those racial fears of the South just as it was aimed at the racial fears of the North. Many Southerners, moreover, were aware that the South was becoming more and more of a minority section in the nation because the Northern population was growing much faster, and they wanted slavery expansion to increase the political power of the South just as Northerners wanted to stop it to prevent the growth of that power. Some Southerners, in short, sincerely believed slavery had to expand and genuinely expected that it would be extended into the territory won from Mexico, especially California.

Yet there is abundant evidence that other Southerners who were equally adamant in their opposition to the Proviso neither felt the need for the immediate expansion of slavery nor believed that the institution could possible exist in the territories in dispute between the sections in the late 1840s or 1850s. For one thing, when the territories of New Mexico, Utah, and even Kansas in the 1850s were eventually opened to slavery, there was no stampede of slaveholders to take their chattels there. Many planters, moreover, clearly did not feel the economic pressure to obtain new territory for slavery that some historians have seen as the basis of the expansionist drive; they were optimistic about the present and future economic prospects of slavery within the area of the existing slave states.[22] Finally, many Southerners, including Calhoun, asserted that they did not expect or even wish that slavery could be extended to the territory acquired from Mexico. Climate and terrain, many thought, made the area inhospitable to slavery. As a Georgia Democrat wrote in 1848 when arguing that Northern Democrats did not need the Proviso to keep slavery out of the Mexican Cession, "The interest of slaveholders will prevent them from wishing to cross the Rio Bravo with their slaves."[23] Certainly no Southerners expected slavery to flourish in the new Oregon territory, but as a unit they bitterly resisted congressional prohibition of slavery in that territory when it was organized in 1848. Hence what was at stake in the territorial issue was not just the hope or realistic expectation that slavery could ever enter the territories in question.

What was at stake, and what gave the Proviso issue such an emotional impact in the South, was the Southern refusal to accept the Northern denial, inherent in the Proviso, of the South's right to expand. Although that right was seemingly an abstraction of little concrete value, Southerners clung to it even when they had no intention of exercising it because it symbolized Southern equality in the nation. Over and over again Southerners affirmed that they were contending for equal rights in the nation. If a Northern majority could bar Southern institutions from common territories, then Southern citizens were no longer the equals of Northern citizens. A Democratic Justice of the Supreme Court from Virginia said that the Proviso was based on a view that "pretends to an insulting exclusiveness or superiority on the one hand, and denounces a degrading inequality or inferiority on the other; which says in effect to the Southern man, Avaunt! you are not my equal, and hence are to be excluded as carrying a moral taint with you." Calhoun introduced resolutions into the Senate in February 1847 that insisted "That Congress . . . has no right to make any law, or do any act whatever, that shall directly, or by its effects, make any discrimination between the States of this Union by which any of them shall be deprived of its full and equal right in any territory of the United States, acquired or to be acquired." Any such law was "in derogation of that perfect equality which belongs to them as members of this Union." Similarly, Calhoun's political foe, the Georgia Whig Alexander H. Stephens, protested in a public letter in August 1848, "Any legislation by Congress or by any territorial legislatures which would exclude slavery would be in direct violation of the rights of the Southern people to an equal participation in them and in open derogation of the equality between the states of the South and North which should never [be] surrendered by the South."[24] Southerners were not about to surrender that right to equal treatment; throughout the late 1840s they rallied to the cry of Southern Rights.

By making the issue the symbolic one of equality, Southern politicians struck a chord among the Southern electorate, especially among the nonslaveholders, that could not have been matched by more concrete plans actually to take slavery to the territories or even by cries, raised by some, that the Proviso was the first step by the North toward forceful abolition of slavery *within* the South. It is not that Southerners, then or later, faced the prospect of abolition with equanimity. It is simply that the threat to Southern equality was much more palpable, a threat that menaced the deepest values of all Southerners, not just the slaveholders. However undemocratic Northerners thought the South was, Southerners were just as fierce in their determination to protect equality and liberty from privilege and power as any other Americans. For years political battles within Southern states had raged over the same crusades against privilege, monopoly, and arbitrary power that had characterized state politics in the North. Rhetorical promises to protect republican freedom and equality from subversion and tyranny had pervaded presidential campaigns, too. In 1840, for example, the Whig newspaper in Richmond had urged Virginia Whigs to "strike off those manacles of a cold-blooded party despot and restore your sons to freedom. Expel from the capital the man who would subjugate them and you." Similarly a Democratic paper in Georgia insisted that Democrats were pledged "to save the South from vassalage to the North. . . . We are fighting a great battle for the maintenance of all of our liberties and institutions." By translating the territorial issue into terms of equal rights, Southern politicians exploited a republican idiom that Southern voters recognized and responded to. The Mississippi Democratic state platform in 1847 explicitly made the connection when it vowed that "all legislation not founded upon the equality of rights and privileges, irrespective of classes of the people, or geographical divisions of the country is at war with the genius of republican government."[25]

Southern whites, indeed, may have been more nervous about the vulnerability of equality and independence than other Americans. Southern whites shared a belief, labeled *herrenvolk democracy* by one historian, that all whites were equal precisely because the despised and inferior black face was enslaved.[26] White equality depended on black slavery; the status of slavery, in turn, was the antithesis of liberty and equality. To white Southerners, in short, inequality meant slavery, since that institution was the ubiquitous gauge that dramatically defined inequality throughout the South. Hence Southern politicians constantly denounced the threat of enslavement by Northern tyranny. They consistently harped on the derogatory and degrading implications of the Northern denial of equal rights for the South. To submit abjectly to Northern dictation, to accept the inequality that went with prohibition, was to be no better than a slave. Unless the South resisted Northern aggressions, protested one Alabamian, it would be "the inferior, the Bondsman in fact, of the North." "Will you submit to be bridled and saddled and rode under whip and spur" or will you affirm "the great doctrine of *Equality:* Opposition to ascendancy in any form, either of classes by way of monopoly, or of sections, by means of robbery?" the Montgomery, Alabama *Advertiser* demanded of its readers in 1851. "I should rather my State should be a grave yard of martyred patriots than the slave of Northern abolitionists," vowed South Carolina Congressman Lawrence M. Keitt in 1856.[27]

Slavery was an emotional issue to Southerners, therefore, not just because they feared the economic and racial consequences of its abolition, not just because it supported the social dominance of the planter class, but because it symbolized the absence of freedom and equality. It was the status every self-respecting white feared slipping into. The pervasive presence of black slavery was a constant reminder to whites that they must be ever vigilant in the defense of republicanism. What was at stake in congressional prohibition of slavery's extension, therefore, was not the actual need or desire to go west, but the manhood, honor, and fundamental values of Southern voters. As a result, opposition to the Proviso was universal. As in the North, politicians could not disregard public sentiment, and both Southern Whigs and Democrats felt it obligatory to denounce the Proviso whenever possible and even threaten secession should it pass.

The Wilmot Proviso, therefore, polarized the nation and not just its politicians. The issue involved more than the kind of society that would emerge in Western territories. Northern and Southern whites saw in the positions of the other threats to republican values they held in common: social democracy, equality, and freedom. If Northerners railed against the tyranny of the Slave Power, Southerners found an arbitrary Northern majority just as heinous. Although the divisions over principle were fundamental and irreconcilable, however, they were also narrow. The North was not totally wedded to the Proviso, that is, to congressional prohibition in the territories. Its main concern was that slavery not expand and that the political power of the South not grow. Most Southerners, on the other hand, did *not* demand that slavery actually expand. Instead, they insisted that their equal rights be protected, that they not be forced to submit to Northern dictation and to the inferiority such submission entailed. If the territorial issue could be shifted away from naked congressional prohibition, a complete and final rupture between the sections could be avoided.

The political parties very quickly moved to exploit this room for maneuver. Democrats from both sections were committed to the war and to territorial gains from it. As early as the winter of 1847, therefore, some Northern Democrats like Senators Lewis Cass of Michigan and Daniel S. Dickinson of New York began to back away from the Proviso, because they realized that no appropriations to buy territory could pass the Senate with the Proviso attached. By the end of 1847, many Democrats were rallying around a solution suggested by Cass, Dickinson, and Vice-President George M. Dallas that would avoid congressional prohibition. Known as popular sovereignty, this alternative would leave to the settlers of the territories themselves the decision of accepting or prohibiting slavery. Popular sovereignty had great political advantages. It would remove from Congress the whole question that had disrupted party lines, assure Southerners an equal opportunity to take their institutions to the territories until a decision was made by the settlers, and give Northern Democrats the chance to argue, correctly, that climate would bar slavery from the territories at issue, that nonslaveholders would go there in greater number than slaveholders, and that free soil would thus be achieved without the threat to the Union inherent in the Proviso.

Until the end of the war, on the other hand, Whigs could rally around their traditional opposition to any territorial expansion, and most of them supported resolutions introduced in February 1847 by Georgia Whigs John M. Berrien in the Senate and Stephens and Robert Toombs in the House that no territory be taken from Mexico as a result of the war. Whig Speaker of the House Robert C. Winthrop of Massachusetts explained his party's position in early 1848.

> My view of the Wilmot Proviso has always been that its chief value was in creating an interest North & South against extending our Territory. If the North can be prevented from uniting in such extension for fear the new territory would be slave & the South for fear it should be Free, we can put an end to all these projects of aggrandisement. [28]

Southern Whigs could argue they would protect the South from the insult of the Proviso by preventing the acquisition of any territory to which it could be applied. Northern Whigs who wished to eschew the Proviso could argue that they would stop slavery's extension by rejecting the area into which it might go. Whigs bent on holding their party together behind the "No Territory" formula denounced the Treaty of Guadeloupe Hidalgo, which ended the war and awarded the United States the Mexican Cession, as an unconscionable land grab. A few Whig senators even voted against it.

In part because of these contrasting "No Territory" and popular sovereignty formulas, party lines remained remarkably strong in Congress during 1847 and 1848. Even when Southerners began to coalesce across party lines to oppose the Proviso, many Northern Whigs and Democrats still voted differently from each other. Long-time opposition between the parties was enough to prevent the complete replacement of party lines by sectional phalanxes even on the slavery extension issue, especially since traditional party distinctions continued on other issues.[29]

However divided the national parties in Congress were by the fundamental disagreement between North and South over slavery extension, Whig and Democratic state parties within each section provided clear party alternatives on the issue during 1847 and 1848. They made slavery extension another source of interparty combat between them and thereby retained the loyalty of most of their voters. To some extent, the Proviso issue in the states developed along lines similar to those in Congress. In 1846 and early 1847, before alternatives to the Proviso had crystallized, Democrats and Whigs in Michigan, New York, and Pennsylvania joined to support resolutions endorsing the Proviso while Southerners, with equal unanimity, denounced it. When Northern Democrats began to abandon the Proviso for popular sovereignty, however, Whigs either endorsed "No Territory" or, by 1848 when it was clear some land would be annexed, once again backed the Proviso. In the legislatures of Ohio, Indiana, and Illinois clear interparty conflict emerged over resolutions concerning the Proviso by 1848. In Northeastern states, by then, Democrats tried to avoid any statement on the Proviso whatsoever, while Whigs either endorsed it or pointed to the long record of their party against slavery expansion. To neutralize the Whigs' advantage in the North, Democrats could only denounce agitation that threatened the Union. In the South the parties sometimes vied over the merits of expanding on a popular sovereignty basis as opposed to not expanding at all. Elsewhere, each tried to outdo the other in the firmness of its opposition to the Proviso. In those contests Democrats in the South-east had an advantage; Democratic state conventions in Virginia, Georgia, Florida, and Alabama pledged that they would support no Democrat for president in 1848 who was not on record against the Proviso.[30]

The approach of the presidential election in 1848 appeared to threaten not only the tenuous unity of both parties in Congress but also the ability of Northern and Southern state parties to exploit the different sectional prejudices of their constituents. Ratification of the treaty with Mexico not only rendered the Whigs' "No Territory" strategy defunct, but it made the problem of what to do with the Mexican Cession real instead of hypothetical. That Northerners and Southerners were still irreconcilably divided by the Proviso became clear in the summer when attempts were made to apply it to Oregon. If the issue had remained the Wilmot Proviso, in other words, neither major party could have effected national cooperation in the 1848 campaign. Yet such cooperation between the parties' Northern and Southern wings was vital if they were to elect a president. Nor could the major parties ignore the slavery extension issue entirely; extremists in both sections tried to form third parties on the Proviso issue precisely because it allowed the major national parties so little room for maneuver. To retain their voting support, the Whigs and Democrats had to neutralize those third-party efforts.

As early as 1846 Calhoun had seen in the Proviso the issue he needed to effect his long-cherished goal of eliminating party lines in the South and unifying the section behind a Southern Rights party. "I wish the Southern Representatives would consent to act together without regard to party," another South Carolinian wrote a prominent Georgia Democrat. "The Wilmot Proviso is paramount to all party. We are in great danger. The North is resolved to crush slavery—are we equally in the South resolved at all hazards to defend it?"[31] Scorning efforts to dodge the Proviso itself and claiming the South must abandon the national parties, boycott their national conventions, and unite to defend itself, Calhoun and his lieutenants in other states put great pressure on Whigs and especially Democrats in Dixie to hold their support. One result of this pressure was the pledge by Democratic state parties where Calhounites were strong not to support any candidate who did not oppose the Proviso.

Similarly, the most determined foes of slavery extension and the Slave Power in the North—Liberty Party members, Van Buren Democrats in New York who were called Barnburners, and Conscience

Whigs—insisted that the Proviso be adopted. They made it clear before the national conventions of both parties met that they would not accept candidates who were not explicitly pledged to the Proviso. Eventually, after the Whigs and Democrats had nominated unacceptable candidates, those groups would come together at Buffalo to form the Free Soil party and nominate Martin Van Buren as their presidential candidate. Estranged from the Polk administration and hostile to the new Democratic candidate, fearful that Southerners were imposing a proslavery orthodoxy on the national Democratic party, and engaged in a bitter fight with a rival faction for control of the state Democratic organization, the New Yorker who had tried so hard throughout his previous career to bury the slavery issue would now reluctantly accept the nomination of this avowedly antislavery party.

Whigs and Democrats, however, proved as adroit at neutralizing the menace of third parties formed on the Proviso issue as at preserving unity in Congress. Their response exemplified perfectly how the federal nature of politics gave the Second Party System marvelous flexibility and resilience. Although the differences between the North and South on the slavery extension issue were profound, both parties found ways to avoid a national commitment on the Proviso itself and to provide two-party competition on the slavery extension issue in each section within the framework of those profound sectional differences over it. The parties did not resolve the sectional conflict or even avoid it. Instead, they were able to exploit it for partisan purposes by running very different campaigns in the opposing sections.

The Democrats nominated Lewis Cass, who had publicly denounced the Proviso as unconstitutional and advocated popular sovereignty as a better solution to the problem of slavery in the territories. Their platform made no explicit statement about the territorial issue whatsoever. Cass's nomination directly sparked the creation of the Free Soil party by New York's furious Barnburners, who had long regarded him as anathema, and angered Southern extremists like Alabama's Yancey as well. Unlike those in the North, efforts to form a third party in the South after the Democratic convention fizzled, however. Most Southern Democrats rallied to their party's candidate. During the campaign, Southern Democrats stressed Cass's pledge to veto the Proviso should it pass Congress and the Democrats' achievement in gaining territory from Mexico into which slavery might expand. They chastized the Whig candidate for failing to make such an explicit pledge, attacked the Whig vice-presidential candidate Millard Fillmore as an abolitionist sympathizer, and pointed out with justice that Northern Whig congressmen were, by 1848, the most ardent supporters of the Proviso. In the North, in contrast, Democrats rehearsed the free-soil implications of popular sovereignty that they had trumpeted for over a year. It would bar slavery from the territories just as surely as the Proviso, they insisted, but without the danger to the Union. Besides, they pointed out, the Whig candidate was a slaveholder, while Cass came from a free state.

Democrats took special pains to negate the threat of third-party incursions into their ranks. That Van Buren had been a major Democratic leader for over twenty years acutely embarrassed them. Since the Free-Soil strategy was to insist that the old issues that had divided the parties were "obsolete" and that the old parties could therefore be deserted for new ones to meet the great new issue of slavery expansion head on, Democrats insisted that in fact the traditional issues of the tariff and banking were very much alive. Men should not join a single-issue crusade when so much remained to be resolved between the old parties. Men who detested privileged monopolies, banks, and tariffs should remain Democrats. In the South, as well, Democrats raised paeans to party loyalty and to the virtues of the national Democratic party. Howell Cobb of Georgia was particularly active through speeches in Congress and public letters in defending the necessity of party loyalty and in praising the reliability of Northern Democrats to protect Southern Rights.[32] First aimed at the Southern Rights movement of Calhoun, these pronouncements were later meant to prevent Democrats from being lured into defection by the Whig campaign of 1848.

The Whigs proved even more ingenious than the Democrats in meeting the threat of the Proviso, but they, too, ran a Janus-faced campaign. Even before the Mexican Cession destroyed the viability of the "No Territory" strategy, Whigs in both sections consciously planned an exploitation of the possibilities provided by the federal system. In March 1848, for example, a New York Whig congressman wrote his state's Whig boss Thurlow Weed, "The Wilmot Proviso brings some perplexity. Our Southern brethren are fractious, and they sometimes threaten to draw Mason & Dixon's line between us. I tell them they may have their way south of it, & we must manage things for ourselves on the north side."[33] In early 1848, indeed, many Democrats and Whigs expected that the Whigs would run different presidential candidates in the North and South to appeal to the opposing sentiments. Shrewder Whig politicos realized, however, that all the party required was the absence of a platform commitment on the issue and a malleable candidate who could be run different ways in different sections.

For a long while, the Whigs disagreed who that candidate should be. A few Northern Whigs and a number of Southerners led by anti-Clay Whigs in Kentucky and the Georgia duo of Toombs and Stephens boomed General Zachary Taylor as early as 1847. As the first hero of the Mexican War and a slaveholder, Taylor was enormously popular in the South. He certainly seemed malleable, moreover; his views on issues, indeed his political affiliation, were unknown. For a long while Taylor men arranged "People's," "Independent," or "No Party" rallies to present Rough and Ready as a man above party who would not run a partisan administration. In part this tactic was aimed at heading off Calhoun's third-party effort, which called on Southerners to reject the old parties. In part it was an attempt to broaden the party's support by attracting Democrats who could not stomach supporting a Whig. Taylor seemed willing to accept a nomination from any party or group, and it was not until April 1848 that he admitted in a public letter that he was a Whig, but not an "ultra-Whig." The early enthusiasm of Calhounite leaders for Taylor and the exertions of Democrats like Cobb to denounce the "No Party" tactic both indicate that Taylor had wide appeal across party lines.[34]

Other Whigs agreed that a noncommital general was the Whigs' best bet, but they feared that Taylor's Southern identification and consequent unpopularity in the North would ruin the two-faced tactic they anticipated. Thomas Corwin of Ohio, for example, preferred Winfield Scott to Taylor precisely because he feared the slaveholder Taylor would have to endorse the Proviso to reassure Northern Whigs and thereby damage his chances in the South. Scott, a nonslaveholder, could remain absolutely mum and sweep both sections.[35]

Still other Whigs were appalled by the 'No Party" strategy and opposed Taylor because of his refusal to commit himself to Whig economic principles. Taylor's acceptance of a nomination by the anti-immigrant Native American party in the spring of 1848 further alienated them. Since Clay's defeat in 1844, the Whigs had been divided over the proper strategy for the 1848 campaign. Some thought the Whigs had simply been beaten on the old issues and would have to broaden their base by alliances with the Native Americans and whoever else would support them. Others blamed Clay's defeat on an abortive alliance with the nativists in 1844 that cost more votes than it produced and on their failure in crucial states to delineate sharply enough what the issues between the Whigs and Democrats were. Only by reemphasizing Whig principles, not fudging them with an ostensibly nonpartisan candidate, they thought, could the Whigs win. Whigs such as these demanded the nomination of Clay because he was "the very soul & impersonation of those principles for which we have been battling for the last twenty years."[36]

In the end, Taylor won the Whig nomination, and the Whigs gleefully pursued the two-faced strategy on the slavery extension issue they had planned for months. Careful not to pass a national platform, they were free to take different stands in the two sections and appeal to local prejudices. Even the conservative *National Intelligencer* in Washington lauded Taylor as a *"candidate who can receive the support of the North and the South"* because he had made no commitment on the Proviso. Certain Whig congressmen like Truman Smith of Connecticut artfully orchestrated the Whig campaign to exploit Taylor's malleability by sending pro-Southern literature about Taylor to the South and pro-Northern literature about him to the North. Taylor's silence allowed Northern Whigs to endorse the Proviso openly or point to their long antislavery record. Voting Whig was the best way to prohibit slavery extension, Whig orators insisted, because Taylor was publicly committed to the Whig doctrine of not vetoing congressional legislation. To block slavery expansion, all Northerners had to do was elect Whigs to Congress. They would pass the Proviso, and Taylor would sign it into law. In the South, Whigs did not stress slavery extension so much as the broader, more emotional issue of Southern Rights. Taylor, they argued, as a Southerner and slaveholder was certain to defend the South better than a Northerner Cass. Besides, the untrustworthiness of Northern Democrats was evident. A one-time Democratic president was now heading the Free-Soil ticket pledged to bar slavery from the territories by congressional statute. Moreover, they contended, Taylor was a true national hero who would draw broad national support. As president he could rise above party and section and settle the sectional conflict once and for all. Taylor, they promised, would end Northern aggressions on Southern Rights and thereby preserve Southern equality in the nation.[37]

The Whigs, too, attempted to prevent third-party incursions into their ranks. They had neutralized Calhoun's effort in the South with their "No Party" campaign for Taylor, but they feared the Free Soil party because the most ardent antislavery men in the North, aside from abolitionists, had traditionally voted Whig. In addition to constantly iterating that the Whig party was just as opposed to slavery extension as the Free-Soilers, the Whigs, like the Democrats, also pointed out that traditional economic issues were at stake, issues on which only the Whig party could be trusted. In Pennsylvania, New York, Massachusetts, and elsewhere, therefore, Whigs stressed the baneful impact of the Walker Tariff and Independent Treasury on the economy.[38]

Thus, both major parties accommodated themselves to the fundamental sectional division over slavery extension by running different campaigns in the North and South. In the North both claimed to be friends of free soil; in the South each claimed to be the better defender of Southern Rights. Yet within each section the two parties continued to offer clear alternatives for voters interested in the issue: popular sovereignty versus the Proviso and congressional Whig support of it in the North; Cass's pledge to veto the Proviso versus Taylor's Southern identity in the South.

Because both the Whigs and Democrats were obviously divided by the sectional issue in 1848 and because an openly sectional third party that drew from both was in the field, many historians have seen the election of 1848 as the beginning of the end for the Second Party System. Slavery was clearly destroying it, they contend. The election results, however, testify to the continued strength of the system among voters. The Free Soil party captured only 10 percent of the popular vote and only 14 percent of the vote in the North. Van Buren failed to carry a single state. Free-Soilers siphoned votes from the Whigs in Ohio and gave that state to Cass, but the defection of the famous Conscience Whigs in Massachusetts failed to prevent Taylor from carrying the state, although the Whigs' long-time majority was reduced to a plurality. One Whig even rejoiced after the election there: "After all, what a real blessing to the Whig party it is to have an occasional sifting such as the Free Soil agitation has given it. We are really all the stronger for the secession of calculating, self-seeking men like [Charles] Sumner, Adáms, [John Gorham] Palfrey, *et. id genus omne.*"[39] Van Buren ran best in New York, but his support there derived largely from Barnburner loyalty to him personally and hatred of Cass. Those Democrats would soon return to the party fold.

Because new voters entered the electorate, calculating the extent of defections from the major parties is difficult to do with precision.

Observers in the South asserted that some Democrats bolted party ranks to vote for Taylor, and a number of Whigs and Democrats clearly bolted in the North. Excluding new states that entered the Union between the presidential elections of 1844 and 1848, the Democratic vote in the Northeast (New England and the Middle Atlantic States) dropped by 151,784 (24.5 percent) since 1844, but over four-fifths of that decline occurred in New York, where circumstances were special because of the wide split in the state's Democratic party. The Whig vote in the Northeast, however, declined by only 20,360 (3.3 percent) from 1844. In the Northwest, the Democratic vote actually increased by 9968 (3.2 percent) over 1844, while the Whig vote dropped 7237 (2.5 percent). In the slave states the Democrats did suffer 15,285 defections, 3.7 percent of their 1844 total. The Whigs, on the other hand, gained 37,814 (9.7 percent), over twice as much as the Democrats lost. Taylor clearly had an appeal to first-time voters in Dixie. All in all, party lines held remarkably firm. The Democrats retained roughly 84 percent of their 1844 vote in the free states and 96 percent in the South. More important was the performance of the Whigs, since it would be their disintegration that marked the end of the Second Party System. They maintained 97 percent of their vote in the free states and actually increased it in the South.[40]

By the end of 1848 fervent party loyalty and the ingrained hostility of Whigs and Democrats toward each other had continued to maintain the health of the two-party system in both the North and South. Underpinning those emotional attachments were interparty conflicts at national, state, and local levels over a number of issues: territorial expansion, the economic role of the state, ethnocultural conflict, slavery, and other widely varying matters at the state and local level. Neither party was completely united everywhere on every issue, but they were sufficiently cohesive to give the parties a coherent image in the eyes of the voters so that they appeared to provide clear alternatives on almost every issue that entered the political arena.

The presence of a number of issues in combination in the 1840s helped the Second Party System weather the storm of minor parties formed on the slavery question. The renewed salience of economic matters during Polk's administration and the ability to translate the slavery problem into the question of territorial expansion or "No Territory" had helped prevent major defections until 1848. When the disposition of slavery in the territories became a reality in the spring of that year, the parties had managed to continue to provide party alternatives to the voters of the opposing sections and to argue that nonslavery issues still required the preservation of the major parties. Popular perceptions of different party responses to the issues raised by immigration also strengthened the two-party system. After 1844, Whig leaders had divided over the advisability of pursuing the nativist vote, but Whigs in Massachusetts, Maryland, Virginia, Kentucky, and elsewhere had openly denounced the fraudulent naturalization of foreigners and called for reform, Taylor had sought and won the support of the separate Native American party, and voting patterns in Michigan, New York, Pittsburgh, and elsewhere revealed that many native-born Protestants tended to vote Whig because Catholic immigrants, whom they despised, voted Democratic.[41] Certainly the most evangelical or moralistic Protestant denominations voted Whig, and they drove opponents of Sunday laws, Bible reading in schools, and temperance into the Democratic party, which artfully wooed them.

Except for the most determined anti-Southern and pro-Southern groups, therefore, almost all contending elements in society continued to be comfortable within the confines of the Second Party System because its member parties in 1848 continued to meet their needs and to provide alternative positions on such a wide range of issues. Within only four years, however, the lines separating the parties on this gamut of issues would be erased. Whigs and Democrats would then seem to agree more than they disagreed. As a result, the hold of the Second Party System on American voters would be loosened.

FOUR

Dynamics of the Party System and the Compromise of 1850

During the presidential administrations of Zachary Taylor and Millard Fillmore, politicians in Washington made decisions that briefly but effectively removed the slavery issue as a source of partisan conflict between Whigs and Democrats. During those same years, political, social, and economic developments outside of Washington helped erode the lines between the two parties on other issues. This chapter will focus on the way in which the slavery issue was temporarily depoliticized; the next chapter will deal with the reasons why interparty conflict disappeared on other kinds of issues at the national, state, and local levels between 1848 and 1853. Although these developments are separated here for analytical clarity, it is important to remember that they were occurring simultaneously.

Two legacies of the election of 1848 shaped the political divisions over the measures that would eventually form the famous Compromise of 1850. First, the Whigs had elected as president a man who was firmly committed to the "No Party," nonpartisan appeals made on his behalf in 1847 and 1848. Believing that he had been elected by a broad coalition and not just the Whig party, Taylor was determined to preserve that heterogeneous following with both his patronage dispensation and his programmatic recommendations. His would not simply be a Whig administration. Taylor's policy for dealing with the Mexican Cession was a product of this determination, and the varying responses of congressional Whigs to his efforts to reshape the old Whig party influenced which Whigs aligned for and against his plan.

The second and more important legacy of the election was the continuing necessity of such a plan. The election had failed to provide a solution to the problem of slavery in the territories. Even though the major parties had managed through two-faced strategies to retain the bulk of their voting support, sectional tension over the possibility of applying the Wilmot Proviso to the Mexican Cession remained explosive. The problem was exacerbated in 1849 when tens of thousands of settlers rushed to California because of the discovery of gold there in 1848. Congress would have to act on the divisive territorial question, and the major parties were in danger of losing the room for maneuver they had exploited earlier.

Elected in November 1848, Taylor was not inaugurated until March 1849 and could not send Congress his own territorial policy until the new session met in December 1849. In the interim relations between the North and South deteriorated as agitation over the Proviso and other sectional issues heated up. Some Northerners renewed demands for abolition in the District of Columbia, while a few Southerners, frustrated by obstructionism in Northern states, called for a more effective fugitive slave law. This situation gave new life to the sectional extremists who wanted to jettison the old two-party system for new sectional parties—the Free Soilers in the North and the Calhounites in the South. Pressure from these dissidents forced the major parties to shift their positions from those taken earlier. Nevertheless, it appeared for a while that the basic party alignment of 1848 on the slavery extension issue would continue. Whigs and Democrats in the North and Whigs and Democrats in the South found new ways to offer alternative party positions on the problem of slavery expansion to the voters of the two sections. It was only after the territorial problem was apparently solved by the passage of the Compromise of 1850 and pressure was exerted to gain adherence to it that the slavery issue proved most dangerous to the Second American Party System.

During the second session of the 30th Congress, from December

1848 to March 1849, John C. Calhoun made his last major effort to unite the South across party lines. Fierce wrangling over the Wilmot Proviso continued, and when a few Northerners introduced bills to abolish slavery or the slave trade in the District of Columbia, the South Carolinian seized the excuse to call a caucus of all Southern members in the House and Senate to unify Southern resistance to Northern aggressions. From this caucus there emerged in January 1849 a public letter written by Calhoun known as "The Address of the Southern Delegates in Congress to Their Constituents." The importance of the Southern Address lay neither in the specific grievances listed nor in the specific remedies suggested. It did rehearse a long series of supposed aggressions including the Missouri Compromise, the abolitionist movement, and the refusal of the North to return fugitive slaves. It also demanded that slaveholders have equal access to California and New Mexico. "What then we do insist on, is, not to extend slavery," but that slaveholders not be prohibited merely because they are slaveholders. Such a denial of rights, argued Calhoun, would sink Southerners "from being equals, into a subordinate and dependent condition." More important than specifics, however, was the overall tone of the Address. It asserted that Northern aggressions were leading inevitably toward the horror of abolition, that Southerners must drop lesser matters and unite to prevent that cataclysm, and that Southerners were justified in using any method of resistance, regardless of the consequences, because everything was at stake—"your property, prosperity, equality, liberty, and safety."[1] In short, the Address implied that any Southerner who did not unite in defense of slavery was a traitor to his section and that secession itself was an appropriate, if ultimate, means to protect the South.

As an effort to disband the old parties in the South, the Southern Address failed completely. Many moderates of both parties, especially Whigs, refused even to attend the caucus, and most Whigs who did were bent on defusing Calhoun's effort. Only 48 out of the 121 Southerners in Congress signed the Address, and that figure included only 2 out of 34 Southern Whigs. Once again party loyalty had proved too strong to allow sectional consolidation across party lines. As the Charleston *Mercury* lamented, "The antipathies of Whig and Democrat are too strong in Washington and their exercise forms too much the habit of men's lives there."[2]

What the predominantly Democratic support for the Address did instead was to provide Southern Democrats with a platform for

the upcoming state and congressional elections in 1849. Not all Southern Democrats supported the Address, and some, like the Georgian
Howell Cobb even denounced it. But many Democrats blamed their
defeat in 1848 on the Whigs' ability to appear more pro-Southern
behind the candidacy of the slaveholder Taylor than they could with
the Yankee Cass. Almost as soon as the elections were over, therefore,
they tried to move to a more advanced position on the slavery extension issue by dropping popular sovereignty and demanding equal
access to the Mexican Cession. Now the Whig reluctance to sign the
Southern Address gave those Democrats who wished the chance to
vilify Whigs as unsafe on slavery, as traitors to their section.

Southern Whigs refused to sign the Southern Address because,
at the beginning of 1849, they were confident they held a winning
hand. Their party, indeed their man, was in the White House. Proclaiming Taylor a defender of the South who would end Northern
aggressions by solving the sectional crisis gave every hope of being
just as viable a campaign tactic in 1849 as it had been in 1848. Whigs,
indeed, interpreted Calhoun's caucus as an index of Democratic disarray. "The Southern Democracy are perfectly desperate," wrote
Robert Toombs. "Almost every man of the Southern Democrats
have joined Calhoun's movement. . . . The action of the Southern
Democrats is based, not on the conviction that Genl. T. can *not* settle
our sectional difficulties, but that he *can* do it. They do not wish it
settled." They have "followed his lead," wrote a North Carolina Whig,
"some from conviction, some from a fear of being left behind in a
cheap . . . method of gaining and keeping popularity & others from a
desire to . . . ruin Genl. Taylor's [administration] & the Whig party."
Southern Whigs were so confident of their strength at home that
many, including Toombs, supported efforts during that session to
resolve the territorial problem by immediately organizing the entire
Mexican Cession as a state and admitting it with or without slavery
as its constitution prescribed. Although Toombs himself expected
the state would be free, he could support the plan because the area
"cannot be a slave country" and because the scheme, by skirting
the Proviso, would uphold Southern honor.[3] The proposal failed
to pass, however, and the disposition of the Mexican Cession remained
to be solved. When the next Congress met in December 1849 and
Taylor promoted a very similar plan to bypass the territorial stage,
Toombs would lead the Southern Whigs in opposition to the plan and
the president they had supported in January.

Developments between March and December produced this about-face. Maintaining the momentum generated by the Southern Address, Democrats attempted to push strong resolutions through the legislatures of Virginia, North Carolina, and Florida, calling for resistance if the Proviso should be passed. In general Whigs tried to moderate such resolutions. Almost everywhere in the South Democrats attacked Taylor as an untrustworthy Proviso man in disguise, while they chastised Whigs for failing to sign the Southern Address. Throughout Dixie a new line of demarcation developed between the parties. Democrats began to insist that state conventions meet, with the implied threat of secession, if Congress passed unpopular laws. Whigs denounced the Democrats as disunionists. In this new competition, Democrats had the advantage. Taylor did seem to favor antislavery men in his patronage appointments in the North. Worse still for Southern Whigs, word filtered South that Taylor had pledged to a crowd in Mercer, Pennsylvania in August that "the people of the North need have no apprehension of the further extension of slavery."[4] Worst of all were the results of the elections themselves. Democrats won the gubernatorial elections in all seven states in which they were held, three of which had been carried by Taylor the previous fall. While the balance of congressional delegations remained the same in Kentucky, North Carolina, Alabama, and Louisiana, the Whigs lost a seat in both Maryland and Mississippi and three in Tennessee. Most disastrous were the results in Virginia. There the Whigs lost seven seats in the regular election but regained one later in a special poll. The only Whig to win in the regular election, moreover, ousted a Whig incumbent, not a Democrat, by charging that the incumbent had refused to sign the Southern Address.[5]

As if the election results were not menacing enough to Southern Whigs, Southern Democrats in state after state then took the lead in calling for a Southern Convention to meet at Nashville in June 1850 to decide on common measures of resistance to Northern aggressions. Whigs were forced to go along with the initial moves to choose delegates to the convention, often because they viewed it as the best option they had to delay secession. By the fall of 1849, some Southern Democrats were demanding disruption of the Union if California were admitted as a free state. By the time Congress met in December 1849, therefore, those Southern Whigs who had survived felt enormous pressure to find a more viable political position on slavery extension. Boasting of Zachary Taylor's Southern identification and presumed loyalty to the South was no longer enough. To remain competitive at home, Southern Whigs had to carve out a distinctively Whig position that promised the South some concessions on territorial matters.

In the North as well the Whigs in 1849 seemed to lose the advantages on the slavery extension issue they had enjoyed in 1848. Many things had contributed to their retention of voting support in the North, but clearly the party had benefited from the contrast of its devotion to the Proviso and its long antislavery record with the uncertainties of the Democratic popular sovereignty plan. During 1849, when Democratic state parties were no longer shackled by the Cass candidacy, however, they jettisoned popular sovereignty, announced eternal opposition to slavery extension, and often re-adopted the Proviso itself in Pennsylvania, Indiana, Massachusetts, and elsewhere. In New York the free-soil Barnburners rejoined the Democratic party and captured many local nominations. Moreover, in Vermont, Massachusetts, Connecticut, and parts of Ohio, Indiana, Illinois, and Wisconsin, the Democrats formed coalitions with the Free-Soilers which, among other results, helped elect three Democratic congressmen in Connecticut and secured control of the Ohio legislature that then sent the Free-Soiler Salmon P. Chase to the U.S. Senate. In almost all of those states some Democrats opposed the shift to explicit free-soil ground and tried to cling to popular sovereignty, but the upshot was that the Whigs had lost both their distinctive position on the territorial issue and the momentum generated in the 1848 elections. When Congress met in December 1849, Northern Whigs, too, were looking for a distinctive, winning program to use in competing against their Democratic and Free-Soil foes.

Shifting party positions on the territorial issue in 1849, however, were not the only factors that influenced reactions to the alternatives presented in the great debates of 1850. Equally important was Zachary Taylor's conception of what his administration should be. This shaped not only Taylor's program for the Mexican Cession, but also the reaction of congressional Whigs and Democrats from the different sections to it.

In 1847 and 1848 Whigs had often campaigned for Taylor as a man above party who would form a nonpartisan administration, as a national hero like Washington who could end the sectional conflict and unify the nation. Although many Whigs had obviously acquiesced in this strategy for the temporary purpose of attracting non-Whig voters in the presidential election, others, including Taylor himself, were firmly committed to this effort to remake or even replace the old Whig party permanently. Taylor was often judged by contemporaries and has been judged by later historians as a stubborn, ignorant, and hopelessly unskilled political amateur. Although he did prove to be stubbornly inflexible toward the end of his presidency, as a candidate Taylor displayed shrewd judgment and the boldness to pursue his goals. Throughout 1847 and 1848, while he publicly announced his willingness to accept presidential nominations from anybody, he privately wrote John J. Crittenden of Kentucky and other Whigs that he believed that the old Whig party, running on its old issues, was a sure loser. The traditional issues that had divided the parties, he insisted, should be "considered as settled . . . for many years to come, if not by the act of limitation at least by common consent." He deplored "the rabid politicans on both sides [who] hold on to them with greatest tenacity" and insisted on agitating them when they were "generally acknowledged to be dead." Constantly he lamented "the asperity of party feelings between the Whigs & Democrats" that endangered the country and disgusted the people. The Whig party by itself was a hopeless minority because new immigrants were flocking to the Democrats, but, as an independent, he could get the support of a "strong party of Whigs, Democrats, and Natives." If elected moreover, he would not be "a party president in the strict sense of the term" but would distribute patronage "equally . . . according to numbers among the Whigs, Democrats, and natives."[6]

The new nominal leader of the Whig party, therefore, obviously believed that he had been elected by a broad coalition, not just the Whigs, a coalition whose loyalty to him personally he meant to cement while in the White House.[7] Taylor, moreover, clearly meant to eschew the dynamics of interparty conflict that had helped sustain the Second American Party System since the presidency of Van Buren if not of Jackson—the drawing of sharp party lines on economic issues like the tariff, banking, and internal improvements. He believed that the public was fed up with party bickering over those measures and that the time was right to build a new amorphous or consensus party on new grounds.

Taylor moved immediately to effect this strategy when he constructed his cabinet. Purposely shunning "ultra Whigs" like Henry Clay and Daniel Webster who were publicly associated with traditional demands for a high tariff, grandiose schemes of federal internal improvements, and abandonment of the Independent Treasury in favor of a new national bank, he drew around him advisers unfriendly to the old Whig leadership, original boosters of the Taylor campaign, and men who were equally committed to redefining and even re-naming the party around the personage of Zachary Taylor.[8] For example, the new Secretary of State, John M. Clayton of Delaware, was the nation's chief advocate of building a new "Republican" or "Taylor Republican" party around the President. "We won our victory as Taylor men—not merely as Whigs," he was convinced.[9] As early as December 1848, to the consternation of Whig regulars like William Henry Seward of New York, he moved to form a Taylor Republican organization in Pennsylvania to cement the fusion between Native Americans and Whigs that Clayton and scores of Pennsylvanians believed had been necessary to carry the state for Taylor.[10] "If we cannot rally a new party composed of the elements which brought Taylor into power, we shall be beaten under the old name of Whig this year," he warned Crittenden before the inauguration. Taylor must commit himself to run again and iterate his all-parties policy in his inaugural. "The moment he proclaims it the work will go on rapidly & thousands will now join in who never voted for us before. *Republican* is a word of exceeding good command. Here [Washington] all I talk to (being Whigs) concur in the necessity of some demonstration on the Republican basis." For the Treasury Taylor chose William M. Meredith of Philadelphia, a little-known Whig politician who had joined the Taylor Republican movement during the campaign and who would take pains to give patronage to Native Americans to preserve it. Reverdy Johnson of Maryland, the Attorney General, was a foe of Clay and ultraism, and William Ballard Preston of Virginia had been an original Taylor backer against more established Whig chieftains.[11]

To further the effort, Taylor established his own newspaper in Washington, significantly named the *Republic,* because the regular Whig paper was too firmly wedded to the traditional "ultra" doctrines of Clay and Webster. Its publisher Albert T. Burnley wrote Crittenden in the summer of 1849 that even under Taylor's leadership the Whigs would have to discard "the old Hunker Whig politicians & the stale, chronic & unpopular doctrines of *ultra* whiggery." The administration should "improve" the Independent Treasury and Walker Tariff, but not repeal them as the ultras advocated.

Such a policy will draw to our ranks tens of thousands of Republicans, who submitted to be called democrats but who repudiate & despise Locofocoism & thus we will reconstruct the true old Republican party, out of the practical part of Whigery [sic] & honesty of democracy. The elements of this Republican party elected Genl. Taylor —they will sustain him if he acts wisely.[12]

Unless they were intimate with the new administration, regular Whig politicians of all stripes were appalled by Taylor's advisers, and they became more alienated the longer the cabinet remained in office. Southern Whigs like Toombs were angry that the cabinet seemed too pro-Northern. Although four slave states were represented in the body, only Toombs's lieutenant George W. Crawford of Georgia, the Secretary of War, seemed reliable on Southern interests to Deep South Whigs faced with the taunts of extremist Democrats. In addition, free-soil Whigs like Seward seemed alarmingly influential with Taylor and the Cabinet.[13] Especially dismayed were the Whig giants Clay and Webster and their myriad supporters. All the federal appointments were going to "the Taylor men to the exclusion of the friends of other candidates," complained Clay.[14] Nor, portentiously, were Vice-President Millard Fillmore and his New York followers happy with the prominence of Seward, their rival for control of the New York Whig party.

If the selection of the cabinet alarmed these men, the subsequent distribution of federal patronage below the cabinet level horrified them. Everywhere newcomers to the Taylor movement were appointed ahead of old Whig regulars. Native Americans won places in Pennsylvania, and the cabinet even appointed some Free-Soilers elsewhere to lure that party's support. In the South, on the other hand, the cabinet retained many Democrats in office during 1849 in hopes of preserving Taylor's broad coalition in the state and congressional elections of that year. When the Whigs lost those elections, they howled that patronage policies had angered Whig voters and kept them home. The fury reached its peak in Virginia where Whig losses were heaviest. Indeed, throughout 1849 and 1850, complaints poured into Washington from Georgia, North Carolina, Mississippi, Tennessee, Virginia, Pennsylvania, Massachusetts, Ohio, Indiana, Illinois, Kentucky, and elsewhere that Taylor and his advisers were wrecking the Whig party. Disappointment over patronage distribution has always accompanied a new administration, but these complaints seemed especially numerous and bitter.[15]

The old Whig regulars had a point. If Taylor and his men were not trying to wreck the Whig party, they were certainly trying to change it. What they envisioned was a party based on Taylor's personal prestige, not on sharply defined doctrine. "Old Zack is the Rock, politically, on which you ought to build," wrote Crittenden. "There is . . . the source of strength and popularity . . . for the Administration." Taylor would be a new Cincinnatus to save the republic from peril, another Andrew Jackson or George Washington who could attract men from all the old parties and all sections merely on the basis of his patriotic devotion to the nation. They would make loyalty or opposition to Taylor himself the main issue, just as Jackson had done twenty years earlier. Whigs could be attracted by the President's explicit deference to the legislative will while Democrats would appreciate the soft-pedaling of traditional Whig economic programs. Sectional extremists would be mollified by settling the sectional controversy without offending either side. Ideological legitimacy would be gained by pledging devotion to republican liberty and equality and especially by adopting the name "Republican." As a Connecticut Democrat wrote to Clayton after claiming that at least 4000 Democrats had voted for Taylor in the Nutmeg state, "The name of Republican is a potent engine to influence the masses—my desire is, that the Administration party shall avail themselves of its influence." All of these themes were summarized in Taylor's inaugural address, which consisted of vague patriotic platitudes, specific encomiums to the example of Washington, and pledges "to adopt as the basis of my public policy those great republican doctrines which constitute the strength of our national existence."[16]

Taylor's recommendations for resolving the territorial dispute by immediately forming state governments in California and New Mexico should be seen as part of his effort to settle all the old party and sectional questions and to build a broad national consensus party. They were the policy parallel of his patronage offensive. As early as 1847, Taylor had written that the problem of slavery in the territories was the gravest the nation had ever faced. Intransigent sectional divisions over the Proviso clearly prevented Congress from solving it.[17] Taylor recommended that the territorial stage be skirted altogether.

Thus he would eliminate the necessity of congressional action for the Mexican Cession, render superfluous the Proviso prohibition, which offended Southerners of all political persuasions, and thereby obliterate the major source of sectional tension between North and South. Taylor may have determined on this course even before the election, since the cabinet was carefully constructed of Southerners who would go along. Secretary of the Navy Preston was a former Whig congressman from Virginia who had introduced the bill in the previous session of Congress by which the entire Mexican Cession would have been formed into a single state. The Georgian Crawford was a friend of Toombs, who had backed the scheme. Johnson of Maryland had never been a proslavery zealot, and Clayton of Delaware was the only Whig senator from a slave state ever to vote for the Proviso. Clayton, moreover, was in constant contact with Kentucky's Governor Crittenden, another Taylor adviser, and the two had agreed on the desirability of such a scheme in the winter of 1848-1849. "The right to carry slaves to New Mexico or California is no very great matter, whether granted or denied," wrote the Kentuckian, "and the more especially when it seems to be agreed that no sensible man would carry his slaves there if he could."[18]

Taylor and his cabinet quickly decided to urge California and New Mexico to write constitutions and apply for statehood. All assumed they would be free, because Mexican law which had applied to the area prohibited slavery. Those who would write and ratify the constitutions in 1849, therefore, were almost all nonslaveholders. In April Taylor dispatched Thomas Butler King, a Georgia Whig, to California to prod the settlers there, although the Californians had called for a state constitutional convention before King arrived. As early as April 18, 1849, Clayton assured Crittenden, "As to California & New Mexico, I have been *wide awake*. . . . The plan I proposed to you last winter will be carried out fully. The States will be admitted —free and Whig!" California completed its constitution banning slavery in October, and it was ratified overwhelmingly in November. In his annual message to Congress in December 1849, Taylor urged Congress to approve the constitution when it arrived in Washington and admit California to statehood as soon as possible. Settlers in New Mexico would also soon write a constitution, he explained, and Congress should defer any action on that area until it too applied for statehood. "By waiting their action all causes of [sectional] uneasiness may be avoided and confidence and kind feeling preserved."[19] Taylor reiterated his plan in a special message in January, and here he added the argument that because the state of Texas claimed a large part of New Mexico, including the trading center of Santa Fe, quick statehood for New Mexico would allow the Supreme Court to settle the boundary dispute as a matter between two equal states. By the summer of 1850, indeed, the Texas-New Mexico boundary dispute would become the focal point of the sectional conflict.

Whatever the benefits or shortcomings of Taylor's plan for the nation, it had immense political advantages from his point of view. As Whigs reminded the administration, Whig initiative in boosting California statehood might make the state Whig and thus add two new U.S. Senators to the administration legions.[20] Moreover, Southern Whigs had backed a similar scheme in the previous session, as had some Northern Democrats like Stephen A. Douglas of Illinois. All could presumably support the plan now. By avoiding explicit use of the Proviso, Taylor might be able to retain the support of those Southern Democrats who had voted for him as a defender of Southern Rights. To Northern Whigs who had hitherto demanded application of the Proviso to the Mexican Cession, Taylor offered the substance of free soil in the new states. Equally important, by eliminating the territorial stage, he demolished the entire rationale of the Free Soil party whose major principle dealt with territories, not states. Indeed, in his speech at Mercer, Pennsylvania reassuring Northerners that slavery would not spread, Taylor had specifically predicted, "The necessity of a third party . . . would soon be obviated."[21] Northern Whigs who had bolted to the new party could thus come home, and the basis for the vexatious Free Soil-Democratic coalitions in Northern states would be destroyed. Finally, by skipping the territorial stage, Taylor provided a sharp alternative to those Democrats who still insisted on applying popular sovereignty to congressionally organized territorial governments. Although he aimed at a new consensus party, Taylor never envisioned the absorption of all voters in it. He expected most Democrats to continue in opposition, and, like other politicians, he recognized the importance of defining a line between the parties. But he wanted to draw this line on new grounds so that he could build a new majority party of Whigs, defecting Democrats, Native Americans, and even Free-Soilers.

Taylor's expectations may have been realistic at the beginning of 1849, but conditions had changed considerably when he presented his plan in December. Many Whig congressmen from both sections were furious about Taylor's patronage policies and his attempts to broaden the party. They were ready for revolt, and, by an accident of constitutional timing, the same session of Congress that had to deal with his California plan also had to approve or reject his appointees. The convening of Congress was the first chance regular Whigs as a group had to respond to the administration offensive. And, as Henry Clay observed of the new Congress, "There is a great and bitter complaint against the Administration from all the Whigs, or nearly all." The degree of satisfaction or dissatisfaction with Taylor's patronage distribution became inextricably mixed with reactions to his program. Men unhappy with the one might oppose the other.[22]

The Whigs who were most unhappy with Taylor's patronage and territorial policy were the Southerners who had survived the 1849 elections and who were looking for a new, viable platform on which to revive Whig fortunes in Southern states. Already 6 out of 28 Southerners had bolted the Whig caucus in December, because it refused to repudiate the Proviso, and their intransigent opposition to the Whig candidate for Speaker of the House, Robert C. Winthrop of Boston, contributed to the election instead of the Georgia Democrat Howell Cobb. Fearful that the stigma of supporting Northern free-soil Whigs would prove ruinous in the South and outraged with the patronage allocation, the bolters included original Taylor men like Toombs and Alexander H. Stephens of Georgia, Henry Hilliard of Alabama, and Florida's E. C. Cabell. They and other Southern Whigs could no longer stick with Taylor's California plan as they might have at the beginning of the year, because Southern Democrats immediately denounced it as the Wilmot Proviso in substance if not in name. Slaveholders had been shut out of California and denied a voice in its decision. California's admission as a free state, moreover, would upset the balance between free and slave states in the Senate. Hence they vowed opposition to its admission. Nor, cried the Democrats, could the South condone postponement of action on the remainder of the Mexican Cession, because, until Congress acted, Mexican law prohibiting slavery might still apply. Southerners would thus be excluded from the entire area gained in the war. The ferocity and cogency of the Democratic assault made endorsement of the Taylor plan seem suicidal to nervous Southern Whigs. They needed a solution for the territories with more concessions for the South. Yet mere opposition to Taylor's plan would not suffice, because it would not distinguish them from the Southern Democrats who led the charge against it. Southern Whig congressmen required an alternative for the Mexican Cession that would not only be politically acceptable, but also distinctively Whig.

The crosswinds whipping Whigs and Democrats from the North were only slightly less forceful. Many Northern Whig politicos, too, were dismayed by the patronage allocation, especially the friends of Clay, Webster, and Fillmore. Significantly, however, the one major bloc of Whigs satisfied with Taylor that was not a part of the "Republican" movement were the free-soil supporters of Seward and Thurlow Weed of New York, who had won the largest share of offices, not only in New York itself but also in New England and the Midwest. Although Taylor was calling on them to surrender the Proviso on which they had campaigned so successfully in 1847 and 1848, the Proviso issue had temporarily lost it utility in many states because of the Democratic shifts and coalitions with the Free-Soilers. Securing free states immediately was a new Whig platform on which they could compete.

On the other hand, Democratic regulars unhappy with the coalitions and abandonment of popular sovereignty were looking to the 31st Congress to recommit the national Democracy to the dogma of 1848 so they could regain dominance in the party. Taylor's plan was of no use to them, because it negated the need of popular sovereignty in the territories and because they wanted the political credit for settling the territorial crisis to go to the Democrats, not to the Whig administration. Democratic leaders wanted to stop their own party from splitting irreparably over slavery and, at the same time, prevent Democratic defections to the Taylor party, which the President was hoping to provoke. They needed a program, as one Illinois congressman wrote, that would "preserve the integrity of our party." What confused the situation still further was that these conservative Northern Democrats like Daniel S. Dickinson of New York held the balance of power in the Democratically controlled Senate, the body that would have to confirm all of Taylor's patronage appointees. Whigs from either section who wanted to block the Taylor appointments had to deal with these Democrats who, in turn, delayed confirmations as long as possible to gain leverage against the President.[23]

The Congress to which Zachary Taylor sent his California plan in late December, therefore, was a maelstrom. Politicians from both parties and both sections were maneuvering for political advantage vis-à-vis other factions within their own parties and vis-à-vis the opposition party at home. Still, one can discern four rough blocs in this turmoil. Proadministration Whigs tended to come primarily from the North and from Clayton's Delaware. Most Northern Whigs, who heavily outnumbered their Southern colleagues, belonged to this group. The Whigs unhappy with Taylor, on the other hand, were primarily Southern, although this group included the Northern friends of Clay, Webster, and Fillmore. Southern Democrats who had campaigned behind the Southern Address in 1849 rejected Taylor's California plan outright and insisted on admission of slaveholders at least to part of the Mexican Cession. Such a policy, of course, was difficult politically for Northern Democrats to condone. Finally, there were the moderate Democrats, who included most of the Northern wing of the party and some Southerners and who wanted a new national party policy, distinctive from Taylor's, that they could use to undercut their extremist rivals within the Democratic party in both sections.

None of these blocs was perfectly cohesive, but the political situation, despite the changes in 1849, was strikingly similar to that in 1848. Both the Whigs and Democrats were divided into Northern and Southern wings, but, within each section, most Whigs and Democrats took different positions from each other. The same dynamics of interparty conflict—the need to find distinctive party positions despite basic sectional divisions—that had shaped the 1848 campaign would influence maneuvering in 1850 until the Compromise of 1850 was passed. Contributing to those maneuvers, however, were the similar dynamics of intraparty factionalism, the need of rivals within the same party to develop alternative stands on issues so they could bid for support from different groups of voters within their parties at home.

Soon after Taylor sent his California proposal to Congress, it became apparent that his supporters were in the minority. The Democrats controlled both houses, and most Southern Whigs considered the plan politically untenable. Taylor's plan thus became less a program that politicians realistically expected to effect than a rallying point for his supporters against other proposals. Initially, they had the advantage because the President was the first to come forth with a concrete proposal for the Mexican Cession. Now it was up to the various dissident elements in Congress to present alternatives.

They were not long in coming. Several days after Taylor sent his

December message, Henry Foote, a Democratic Senator from Mississippi, insisted that Congress organize territorial governments for California, New Mexico, and Utah. Foote's rival within the Mississippi Democracy, Jefferson Davis, talked of extending the 36° 30' line to the Pacific coast so that slavery would be guaranteed admission south of it. The most comprehensive alternative, however, was offered by Henry Clay, the deposed Whig chieftain who had returned to the Senate. On January 29, 1850, Clay presented eight resolutions to resolve all the salient grievances between North and South. His proposals urged the admission of California with its antislavery constitution, the creation of territorial governments for the rest of the Mexican Cession without any condition regarding slavery, and the settlement of the Texas-New Mexico boundary dispute by which Texas would be compensated by payments from the United States in return for surrendering its claims. Pronouncing it inexpedient to abolish slavery in the District of Columbia, they called for an end to the slave trade there and balanced this concession to the North by urging a more effective fugitive slave law and by denying the power of Congress to prohibit the interstate slave trade.

Although the measures that eventually constituted the Compromise of 1850 resembled Clay's original proposals, it is important to note that Clay's resolutions differed from the final Compromise in several significant respects. Equally important, although the final Compromise did include a new Fugitive Slave Law and a law abolishing the slave trade in the District of Columbia, those matters were peripheral to the real concerns of the Compromise. There was, in fact, very little compromising on them. Overwhelming support from the South and the North, not cross-sectional coalitions, pushed the respective bills through.

The heart of the crisis of 1850 and of the eventual Compromise concerned the disposition of the Mexican Cession. Northerners insisted that California be admitted, and Southern diehards vowed to prevent it. What separated compromisers from Taylor supporters was that the latter insisted that California be admitted with no strings attached, that no concessions be given the South in exchange; compromisers would sweeten the pill for the South by organizing territories in the remainder of the Mexican Cession into which Southerners would have a chance of taking slavery. At least Southerners would not be barred from them by congressional statute, immediate free-state constitutions, or Mexican law. It must be remembered that unless and until Congress acted, most men thought, Mexican laws banning slavery still applied to the former Mexican possessions. Once territorial governments were involved, then the question of applying or not applying the Proviso was reopened. Every Northern state legislature but one had instructed its senators and requested its representatives to insist on the Proviso in any territory, while no Southerner could tolerate its adoption and many viewed that eventuality as grounds for secession. That was what the threat of the impending Nashville Convention was all about.

The crucial territorial issue and the point on which real concessions by both sections were required was the matter of the Texas-New Mexico boundary dispute. Because Texas was already a slave state, any area included within its borders was guaranteed to slavery. By the terms of Texas's admission to the Union, moreover, as many as four additional states could be carved out of its vast expanses, all of which would presumably be slave states. Although, ironically, many Texas politicians were not optimistic about the possibility, other Southerners clung to that hope. Southerners who agreed to surrender Texas's claims to part of New Mexico, therefore, seemed to be sacrificing a sure thing for the mere chance of taking slaves into New Mexico. On the other hand, Northerners who agreed to the creation of a territorial government without the Proviso were extending that opportunity in the place of the surefire prohibition of slave extension inherent in the Proviso, Mexican law, or the Taylor plan.

With these considerations in mind, Clay's initial proposals take on a new light. To be sure, they involved some compromises and concessions. California's admission was connected to other matters, territories were to be organized without the Proviso, and Texas was to forfeit its claims for compensation. In these respects, Clay's proposals differed from Taylor's. On the other hand, one should not exaggerate those differences, as most historians have. His initial resolutions entailed no ironclad *quid-pro-quo* for California's statehood. They were presented as discrete measures, to be taken up one at a time, with California first. His plan allowed the possibility that California would be admitted and then nothing else would be done—exactly what Taylor proposed. Initially, many Whigs in and outside Washington saw no dramatic differences between Clay's and Taylor's plans. Even more important, Clay's proposal for territorial governments did *not* include the Democratic formula of popular sovereignty.

He would make no provisions regarding slavery. Indeed, his original proposal explicitly stated that slavery did not exist in the area by Mexican law "and is not likely to be introduced" and that Congress should not "provide by law either for its introduction into or exclusion from any part of said territory." Clay in his speeches defending this proposal, and Daniel Webster, in the famous Seventh of March speech, argued at great length, moreover, that nature would bar slavery from the Mexican Cession. In short, the only concession Clay offered the South on the crucial territorial question was the organization of territories without the Proviso. Even without it, he asserted, climate and Mexican law would preserve that area for free soil.[24]

Without questioning the authenticity of Clay's devotion to sectional accord and preservation of the Union, therefore, one can most accurately view his scheme as intended to be a congressional Whig alternative to that offered by the administration, a proposal he hoped all Whigs could back. Resenting the way he and other regular or "ultra" Whigs had been treated by the administration, Clay hoped to regain control of the Whig party from his Senate seat just as he had a decade earlier in his fight with John Tyler. He and the regular Whigs, not Taylor and the Taylor Republicans, would appropriate credit for solving the sectional dispute. Clay clearly believed that dissident Southern Whigs would find his proposal more attractive than Taylor's, and he must have hoped that its free-soil implications would induce Northern Whigs as well to follow his leadership once again.[25] The absence of popular sovereignty, after all, attested to his plan's Whig pedigree.

Clay's hopes proved delusive. Many Southern Whigs did swing to his support, including those who had bolted the Whig caucus in December. Clay's plan, by providing some territorial concession to balance California, seemed to offer enough for them to remain competitive at home. Yet some Whigs denounced the purported compromise as too pro-Northern, while others continued initially to back the President. Response from Northern Whigs was even less enthusiastic. In the Senate only Webster and Pennsylvania's James Cooper backed Clay. Webster, too, was alienated from the administration, and he also seized on Clay's plan as an opportunity to regain leadership within the party. Still hungering for the Whig presidential nomination, he realized he had no chance of obtaining it if the sectional conflict were not resolved or if Taylor and his supporters proved successful. Cooper was battling for control of Pennsylvania Whiggery with Secretary of the Treasury Meredith and Whig Governor

William F. Johnston. Losing out in the state's patronage allotment, Cooper also harbored grievances against the administration. In the House friends of Clay and Webster as well as New York allies of Fillmore swung into line, but they were a minority. The vast majority of Northern Whigs continued to back the Taylor plan and condemned Clay's proposal as an effort to break down the administration. For them the President's plan was the distinctive, winning proposal they needed to retain their free-soil constituents. William Henry Seward admitted on the eve of his notorious "Higher Law" speech against Clay's plan, indeed, that Webster's support for it opened the way for Seward to assume command of Northern Whiggery by backing the President on strong antislavery grounds. He had nothing to gain by moderation, he wrote, because Webster's course "has rendered of little value the little moderation I can practice in regard to the other portion of the Union."[26]

Nor were the Democrats content with Clay's original plan, even though it included territorial organization. Southern extremists like Calhoun and Jefferson Davis attacked it immediately as being as bad as Taylor's proposal. Pointing out that California would still be admitted and proslavery Texas stripped of territory, they labeled it a sellout of the South, not a compromise. More moderate Democrats, in contrast, initially seemed to praise Clay's plan in newspapers and congressional speeches. This apparent support, however, probably meant that Democrats at first saw Clay's alternatives as the best available weapon with which to oppose the administration. But Democrats were no more anxious for Clay and the congressional Whigs to monopolize the political credit for resolving the territorial dispute than for Taylor to do so. On February 7, the Democratic Washington *Union* declared Clay's plan a failure. "We must now look to clearer, and more generous, and more intrepid minds to save the Union from the horrors which he so eloquently predicted."[27] If there was to be a compromise, in other words, the majority party wanted it to be a *Democratic* compromise. In concrete terms this determination meant incorporating the Democratic formula of popular sovereignty into the territorial bills.

Even while Clay's plan monopolized attention in February and March, influential Democrats headed by Stephen A. Douglas, chairman of the Senate Committee on Territories, and his counterpart in the House planned to bring forth bills delegating to territorial legislatures the power to protect or prohibit slavery in the territorial stage, although the word "slavery" itself would not be used. Cooperating with this group, significantly, were not only Speaker Cobb, a Georgia Democrat, but also Georgia's two foremost Whigs, Toombs and Stephens. Operating outside the Douglas orbit, Foote of Mississippi also sought to reshape Clay's plan. Why a Mississippi Democrat would be in the compromiser's ranks at first seems puzzling, until it is recalled that Foote was a rival of Jefferson Davis for control of the state party. Since Davis had already taken firm ground against any plan that admitted California, Foote, who needed a distinctive position, had little choice but to support some form of compromise. But he wanted one more palatable than Clay's.

As early as February, Foote moved to take control of Clay's Whig compromise plan by moving that all resolutions concerning the Mexican Cession be combined into a single "Omnibus" bill, as it was derogatorily called, and that a special committee write the detailed legislation. Both Clay and Douglas opposed this move, but Foote and other Democrats eventually prevailed in undermining Clay's initial strategy. Combining California admission in a single bill with the organization of territorial governments meant that it was impossible to vote for the one without the other. Northerners desirous of California would have to accept territories without the Proviso, while Southerners promoting territorial governments in order to replace Mexican law in the Cession had to accept California. A line was thus sharply drawn between administration supporters and compromisers.

Lack of space prevents a detailed analysis of the procedures by which the Compromise of 1850 was finally hammered out. The territorial measures were combined into an Omnibus and then separated out again at the end of July. Almost every measure was altered and realtered. What began as a congressional Whig alternative to Taylor's California plan was changed by the Democratic majority into a Democratic compromise. Popular sovereignty was written into the bills for Utah and New Mexico, although even then a loophole was left for the Supreme Court to overturn territorial action. Those Whigs already committed against the administration for personal or partisan reasons had no choice, once it was clear the Whig party as a whole would not desert Taylor, but to align with the Democratic compromisers. The final Compromise of 1850 admitted California as a free state, organized territorial governments for Utah and New Mexico with legislative power over "all rightful subjects of legislation" (i.e., slavery), denied Texas's claims to Santa Fe, but compensated Texas with $10 million, half of which was to be paid directly to the holders of Texas bonds instead of to the Texas government, enacted a stringent new Fugitive Slave Law, and abolished the slave trade in the District of Columbia. More Democrats than Whigs supported the final measures, and Democratic leadership, especially Douglas's, was critical in August and September after the Omnibus was broken up.

Still, the Compromise may not have passed if Zachary Taylor, had not died on July 9, 1850 from an illness contracted a few days earlier. The President, convinced that his plan was superior and jealous of Clay's rivalry for Whig leadership, had threatened to veto the Omnibus bill. Taylor's opposition had rallied Whig opponents of the Compromise and stalled action in Congress. His death brought to the White House Millard Fillmore of New York. An archrival of Seward and the free-soil Whigs who opposed the Compromise, Fillmore backed it. He symbolized his commitment by making Daniel Webster his new secretary of state. More to the point, congressional Whigs unhappy with Taylor's patronage appointments now swung to support Fillmore and the Compromise. Incredibly, even by the summer of 1850, the Democratic Senate had still refused to confirm men Taylor had nominated a year before. Fillmore had the chance to withdraw those nominations and name new men. Whig and Democratic Senators favoring the Compromise, moreover, used their control over confirmations as leverage against Whig congressmen who were content with Taylor's appointments and wanted them approved.[28] With the new Whig administration now backing the Compromise, defections occurred among Northern Whig representatives and senators who had steadfastly opposed the Compromise while Taylor was alive. Erosion was especially heavy in the immense Whig delegation from New York. Either by abstaining or voting directly for them they allowed the controversial laws constituting the Compromise of 1850 to pass.

The dynamics of the Second American Party System are readily apparent in the party alignments that developed over the Compromise. Even though the Omnibus that encapsulated the heart of the Compromise was broken up, one can still discern which politicians were for and against the idea of compromise. None of the final bills obtained clear favorable majorities from both sections. Neither party nor sectional lines were clear. Instead, the four blocs that had developed over the slavery extension issue in 1848 persisted. Like the Free-Soilers, most Northern Whigs opposed the Compromise even after Taylor's death. Most Northern Democrats backed it. Most Southern Whigs favored the Compromise. Most Southern Democrats opposed it. The pattern can be represented schematically.[29]

Party and Sectional Attitudes Toward the Compromise

	Whig	Democratic
North	Anti-Compromise	Pro-Compromise
South	Pro-Compromise	Anti-Compromise

Neither party was united, but within each section the parties continued to offer party alternatives to the voters on the slavery issue which, by 1850, had become the Compromise issue.

That this pattern was largely the product of the dynamics of interparty competition instead of personal preference alone is confirmed by the fact that these lines extended from Congress to state parties and state party newspapers both before and after the Compromise passed. Southern Democrats who had moved to a more intransigent position on the slavery issue in 1849 remained there in 1850. Throughout the winter and spring of that year, Southern Democratic state parties denounced the prospect of California's admission; some, like Georgia's, even called it sufficient grounds for calling state conventions to consider secession. Because compromise plans included California's admission, Southern Democrats were forced to denounce them. Southern Whigs, in turn, had moved further in a conservative direction, defending the admission of California as harmless to the South, especially when connected with concessions in the rest of the Mexican Cession, denouncing Democrats as secessionists, and balking now at the Nashville Convention. When that gathering met in June, most Whig delegates boycotted it, and the few who attended objected to the address that castigated the Compromise because it admitted California and proposed instead the extension of the $36°30'$ line to the Pacific. With Southern Democratic state parties now isolated in opposition to the Compromise, the Whigs found support for it a viable political posture, even if it included popular sovereignty. Although Southern Whigs had to desert Taylor to support the Compromise, they could claim consistency with their stand of 1848. Then they had promised that Taylor would solve the sectional conflict and end Northern aggressions on Southern rights. Now they could argue that the Compromise, introduced by the Whig Clay and backed by the new Whig administration of Millard Fillmore, did precisely that. The South, Whigs asserted, had won with the Compromise, not lost. Southern liberty and equality had been saved within the Union that Democrats threatened to destroy.

In the North Whigs were just as happy to oppose the Compromise as most Democrats were to defend it. Once again Whigs denounced the Democratic formula of popular sovereignty in the territories as less trustworthy than either the Proviso or immediate statehood. The North, they asserted, had been sold out by the Democrats. The most potent ammunition for Northern Whigs, however, came with the new Fugitive Slave Law. That law made it a crime to help fugitives or to refuse to help catch them. Northern citizens were required by the law to join posses called by U.S. marshals in pursuit of slaves. The Fugitive Slave Act, in short, could be portrayed as a direct aggression by the Slave Power on the republican rights and liberties of Northern whites. Refusing to accept the Compromise as a finality, Whigs in state after state in 1850 and 1851 vowed to work for repeal or revision of the Fugitive Slave Law and amendment of the territorial laws to ensure against the spread of slavery.[30] By writing and defending the Compromise, Northern Democrats had given Northern Whigs a powerful political weapon. Opposing the Compromise seemed a promising way once again to attract the bulk of the antislavery, anti-Southern vote in the North.

Northern Democrats, in contrast, saw much to be gained by supporting the Compromise. The men who backed it initially in Congress abhorred Democratic dealings with Free-Soilers, and they could make support of the Compromise a test of Democratic orthodoxy to regain control of their party in the states. More important, they could claim for the Democratic party the credit for saving the Union. When Northern Whigs attacked the Compromise after its passage, Democrats exultantly denounced them as agitators who would destroy the Union. By calling on all true patriots to support the Compromise by voting Democratic, Northern Democrats believed they held the winning hand. They had good reason to think they did; Whig candidates like Pennsylvania's Governor Johnston, who ran against the Fugitive Slave Law in 1851, invariably suffered defeat at the hands of pro-Compromise Democrats.

On the surface, therefore, the passage of the Compromise of 1850 did not change the party alignments that had prevailed in the 1840s.

The Compromise had temporarily become the slavery issue, but in state after Northern state Whigs and Democrats continued to vie as to which had the better plan to prevent slavery expansion. Democrats demanded absolute compliance with the popular sovereignty and fugitive slave parts of the Compromise, while Whigs insisted that New Mexico and Utah be made free states and that the Fugitive Slave Law be revised or repealed. Pennsylvania again provides an especially good example of the intertwining of state and national politics. A state law of 1847 forbade the use of jails in the state for the retention of fugitive slaves. Because that act seemed to violate the new Fugitive Slave Act, Democrats in the legislature pushed for its repeal against Whig opposition. When the Democratic majority obtained repeal in 1851, Whig Governor Johnston vetoed the bill, and Johnston's noncompliance with the spirit of the Compromise was a major issue between the parties in his campaign for reelection that fall. In 1852 the parties again polarized in the legislature over repeal of the 1847 statute. Again the Democrats prevailed, but this time a new Democratic governor signed repeal into law. Patterns were reversed in the South, where Whigs defended the Compromise and Democrats continued to denounce it.[31]

In 1850 and 1851, in short, state parties followed the same practice they had since the 1830s and 1840s. They seized on national issues concerning slavery and made them grist for interparty conflict at the state level. Parties still seemed to offer voters of the two sections alternatives on sectional issues. If that pattern had continued, the slavery issue in its Compromise form seemed no more capable of disrupting party lines and destroying the Second American Party System than it had been in the 1830s and 1840s.

Not all politicians, however, wanted to maintain the Compromise as a source of conflict between the Whig and Democratic parties. The Fillmore administration was determined to enforce the Compromise, including the Fugitive Slave Act. Publicly and privately after taking office, Fillmore had urged Congress to pass the Compromise quickly; in his annual message of December 1850 he praised it as a "final and irrevocable" settlement of sectional difficulties.[32] This anomaly of the Whig administration backing an essentially Democratic compromise did not trouble Southern Whigs, who benefited from the White House policy, but it proved embarrassing to those Northern Whigs intent on campaigning against the Compromise. Soon after Fillmore had succeeded Taylor, Seward had wondered about the impact of his stand: "If the Compromise Bill shall pass now and obtain the signature of the President, what will be the issue on which we go to the Polls?"[33] Determined to preserve that issue, the Sewardites wrote an anti-Compromise platform in the New York Whig convention in the fall of 1850; in response the supporters of Fillmore, known as Silver Grays, bolted the convention and wrote their own platform. Throughout the North, except perhaps in Webster's Massachusetts, anti-Compromise Whigs formed the majority of the party, but the presence of administration backers everywhere posed grave problems for Northern Whigs. Internal party divisions and pressure from Washington hindered the formulation of a distinctive party stand that contrasted with the Democrats' appeal.

Some politicians hoped to bury the Compromise issue by achieving consensus on its finality, but others saw a chance to build new parties on the basis of support for, or opposition to, the Compromise as a final settlement of the slavery question. The success of such a reorganization, of course, would have doomed the Second Party System. Free-Soil foes of the Compromise like Joshua R. Giddings eagerly anticipated such a reshuffling of parties, but even conservative members of the major parties worked for it because they thought the issue could be made one of union or disunion. Clay called for a new party in a speech in Kentucky in the fall of 1850, and Webster himself flirted for a while with the idea of creating a Union party from Whigs and Democrats. The apparent popularity of Taylor's nonpartisan campaign may have convinced Webster that now was the time to abandon the old parties. He was clearly impressed by the ostensibly nonpartisan Union meetings being held in Northern cities to back the Compromise, although those mass meetings had usually been organized by Democrats hoping to lure pro-Compromise Whigs from their party. Webster predicted in the fall of 1850, "If any considerable body of the Whigs of the North shall act in the spirit of the recent convention in New York, a new arrangement of parties is unavoidable. There must be a Union party, and an opposing party under some name, I know not what—very likely the party of Liberty." Webster then tried to engineer a spontaneous non-Whig presidential nomination for himself in Massachusetts so he could seem a nonparty candidate. Failing in this effort, Webster soon gave up on the new party idea and returned to his quest for the Whig presidential nomination.[34]

More serious were the efforts of some of the Southern pro-Compromise men to create new parties. Unlike the case in most Southern

states where Whigs and Democrats continued to fight along traditional party lines, the old party lines were competely obliterated
in battles over the Compromise in Georgia, Alabama, and Mississippi.[35] Instead, ostensibly pro-Compromise Union and prosecces-
sion Southern Rights parties emerged. In actuality, the Southern
Rights parties quickly jettisoned serious plans for secession and simply
resisted the Compromise as inadequate protection for the South.
The Union parties, on the other hand, accepted the Compromise
conditionally without approving it entirely. In all three states, they
tried to establish their fealty to the South by adopting the so-called
Georgia platform, which acquiesced in the Compromise only on condition that the Fugitive Slave Law was strictly enforced in the North
and pledged "to resist even (as a last resort) to the disruption of every
tie that binds her [Georgia] to the Union" any congressional action
to abolish slavery in the District of Columbia, to bar slavery from
Utah and New Mexico, or to prevent the admission of any more slave
states.[36]

Although the gap separating the new organizations in the South
was clearly not as wide as the one that still divided North from South,
the appearance of the new parties worked a realignment in all three
states. Combining most of the Whigs and some Democrats, the Union
parties triumphed everywhere over the heavily Democratic Southern
Rights organizations. In Georgia, they elected former Democratic
Speaker Howell Cobb governor, sent former Whig Alexander H. Stephens to the House, and placed erstwhile Whig Robert Toombs in the
Senate. In Mississippi Unionists in 1851 elected pro-Compromise
Democratic Senator Foote governor over Southern Rights candidate
Jefferson Davis, who had fought the Compromise in the Senate. Ala-
bama Unionists routed the Southern Rights men in the state legisla-
tive elections of 1851.

Why traditional party lines broke down in these three states and
not elsewhere is a very important yet difficult question to answer,
because this development marked the beginning of the collapse of
the Second American Party System. The old alignment of Whigs and
Democrats would never recover fully in any of the three states. One
reason, clearly, was that the threat of secession was particularly acute
in all three—if only temporarily. Democratic governors in Georgia
and Mississippi called state conventions to consider secession after the
passage of the Compromise; in Alabama the fiery William Lowndes
Yancey led the disunionists. Friends of the Union were compelled

to organize to prevent secession. The political situation in each state also contributed to the willingness of leading politicians to discard old party names. In each a significant minority of Democrats was waging a losing battle against rival leaders who had the backing of the majority of party voters. Democratic legislators in Mississippi censured Foote for backing the Compromise. Georgia's Cobb was a long-time foe of the Calhounites in the Georgia Democracy who were known as the Chivalry and who by 1849 were taking control of the state organization. Although Cobb had a relatively safe constituency of unionist nonslaveholders in his hill-country congressional district, advancement to higher office seemed to be blocked by the state party. Certainly most of the Democratic press in Georgia denounced the Compromise that Cobb had favored. The situation in Alabama was different; there no single leader rallied Democrats to the Union party. Instead, the traditional hostility of north Alabama's nonslaveholding hill whites to south Alabama's slaveholders was the key. There the Union party was a coalition of north Alabama Democrats and south Alabama Whigs against the secessionist Democrats from south Alabama.[37]

In all three states, moreover, the Whigs were in serious trouble, and Whig politicians had to look for new ways to gain office. The Whigs had never carried Alabama and had failed to contest the governorship in 1849. In Mississippi the Whigs had garnered only 41 percent of the vote in 1849, and their poverty was shown by their willingness to give Democrats all the positions on the Union ticket in 1851, even though Whigs constituted the majority of the coalition. Whigs in Georgia were more competitive, but there, too, they had suffered incursions into their voting base, losing the elections of 1847 and 1849. In 1850 Democrats had reapportioned the state's congressional districts to the disadvantage of Whig candidates and, equally important, they had reapportioned the senatorial districts in the state legislature to guarantee a Democratic majority. Losing support among blackbelt slaveholders, their traditional base, the Whig's only hope was to attract new votes from Cobb's hill-country Democratic constituency.[38] The eagerness with which Whigs in all three states had embraced the "No Party" campaign of Taylor in 1848 had accurately forecast their response after 1850. To be elected, they needed votes from Democrats who hated the very name Whig. Political survival depended on finding a new name and a new issue. The dynamics of political competition, the need to find an attractive posture to build an electoral majority, in sum, worked in all three states by 1850 against the continued existence of the Second Party System.

Although state politics dictated the formation of Union parties in the South, men associated with them urged the formation of a national Union organization when Congress reassembled in December 1850. A bipartisan Round Robin letter was circulated pledging its signers not to support any man for any federal or state office who did not recognize all of the Compromise measures as a final settlement and who would not insist on their enforcement. Among the 44 signers were Clay, Foote, Cobb, Toombs, and Stephens. Cobb's numerous correspondents throughout the South envisioned a national Union party, and a national Union convention was called to be held in Washington in February 1851.

Regular politicians from both of the old parties resisted this effort to destroy the Second Party System. In the end, ironically, they, and not new parties, would pose the major threat to the dynamics underlying the system's continued exploitation of the slavery issue. Although Douglas had declared that the Compromise was a final settlement to all slavery matters, he refused to sign the Round Robin and denounced plans for a new party. Echoing the refrain of Democratic newspapers around the country, he asserted in a major Senate speech, "The Democratic party is as good a Union party as I want, and I wish to preserve its principles and its organization and to triumph upon its old issues."[39] National Democratic leaders, especially from the North, clearly hoped to monopolize the pro-Compromise position for their old party, and not share credit with Whigs in a new organization. Of the 44 signers of the Round Robin, only 6 were Democrats, and none came from a Northern state unless one counts William Gwin of California. Foote, Cobb, and Jeremiah Clemens of Alabama were all involved in Union parties in their home states.

The Round Robin was essentially a Whig document, but the Whig high command was no more enthusiastic about dissolving old parties than the Democrats. The genesis of the Round Robin is unclear, but Fillmore and Webster seem to have been uninvolved personally. There is no reason to doubt that the Whigs from Georgia and Alabama who signed genuinely hoped for a new party. The seven Kentucky Whigs who signed may also have shared Clay's hopes. It is more likely, however, that the majority of the 28 Southern and ten Northern Whig signees were less interested in a new party than in committing the Whig party itself to nominating only pro-Compromise men to office. Such a test would disqualify their foes within the Whig party who continued to oppose the Compromise. The identity of the 10 Northern Whigs is most suggestive. They included Senator Cooper of Pennsylvania, who was on the outs with the free-soil state administration of Johnston, Samuel Eliot of Boston, a Webster lieutenant, and eight New Yorkers who were Silver Gray supporters of Fillmore. Most Northern Whigs, who wanted to run against the Compromise, scorned the Round Robin and its authors.[40] Committing the Whig party nationally to the Compromise as a finality might help Southern Whigs in upcoming campaigns, but it would strip Northern Whigs of a potent issue and benefit their intraparty rivals at their expense.

Whatever the hazards, committing the national Whig party to the Compromise is precisely what the Fillmore administration attempted to do. In the fall of 1850 Webster proclaimed:[41]

> *The present administration will not recognize one set of Whig principles for the North and another for the South. . . .That can be regarded as no Whig Party, in New York, or Massachusetts, which espouses doctrines and utters sentiments hostile to the just and constitutional rights of the South, and therefore such as Southern Whigs cannot agree to.*

One can contrast this insistence on a national party line for both sections with the Whig response to the divisive Proviso issue in 1848. Then a Northern Whig congressman had written, "Our Southern brethren . . . threaten to draw Mason & Dixon's line between us. I tell them they may have their way south of it, & we must manage things for ourselves on the north side."[42] The Whig administration was out to destroy the flexibility of the Whig party provided by the federal system, a flexibility that had allowed Northern and Southern Whigs to take different positions on the slavery issue since the 1830s, a flexibility that had been vital to the workings of the Second American Party System since its birth.

Beginning in 1851, Fillmore, Webster, and Nathan K. Hall, the new postmaster general, employed the federal patronage and everything else at their command to impose a pro-Compromise position on the entire Whig party. A wholesale removal of anti-Compromise

Whigs in the North ensued. Webster used his influence in 1851 to prevent the election of Robert C. Winthrop, the Whig candidate for governor in Massachusetts, the reelection by the Connecticut legislature of the staunch antislavery Whig Senator Roger Sherman Baldwin, and the reelection of Pennsylvania's Governor Johnston, because all three were hostile to the Fugitive Slave Act. By purging antislavery Whigs and replacing them with pro-Compromise men, Fillmore and Webster sought to mold the Whig party into their conception of what it should be.[43]

Manuscript evidence makes it overwhelmingly clear, however, that the vast majority of Northern Whigs had a far different conception of what Whig principles were. They believed their party had opposed and should continue to oppose slavery extension and Southern aggressions. A Vermont newspaper succinctly captured their contempt for the administration strategy when it jeered that the Silver Grays "propose to walk away from the main body of the Whig party, simply exchanging the Whig principles of non-extension and non-aggression of slavery for a new cookoo [sic] song of 'Union and the Constitution' rearranged and set to music by a few restless and uneasy politicians." As a result of the administration offensive, antislavery Whigs like Seward and Johnston had no choice but to rally around a new candidate for the Whig presidential nomination in 1852, as did veterans of the Taylor administration like Clayton. Only by preventing the nomination of Fillmore or Webster, the favorities of the pro-Compromise Whigs in the North and South, could antislavery Whigs and other Taylor loyalists preserve their place in the party and their principles. When these groups boomed Winfield Scott for the presidency, therefore, he was damned in the eyes of Southern Whigs by the nature of his Northern supporters. An angry Tennessee Whig congressman described the mechanism at work precisely. Scott's candidacy was advanced, he wrote, because:

> he is not publicly identified with . . . the compromise in
> such a way as to make it impossible for that large portion
> of the Northern Whigs to support him, who are hostile
> to those measures, and who maintain their local political
> position by fomenting the prejudices of the North against
> the South. . . .In short there is a strong desire to put him
> forward as a Candidate for the Presidency upon such
> ground that hostility to the fugitive slave law and the

> *compromise generally, with strong denunciations of the*
> *same, and furious appeals to the prejudices against Slavery*
> *and the Slave States, can be indulged in by his Northern*
> *supporters.*[44]

Because of this Southern suspicion, the Whig party was seriously divided by the time its national convention met in June 1852. Sectional divisions within the Whig party over slavery had always been manageable partly because the Whigs had always been the "out" party with no national administration to impose a national party line. Things were different in 1852. Administration pressure in the North gave an advantage to the pro-Compromise forces. Even before the Whig convention met, a resolution calling the Compromise a finality passed the House of Representatives with the support of 55 percent of the Whigs and 60 percent of the Democrats. Almost a third of the Northern Whigs, including a majority from the Middle Atlantic states, had felt compelled to back it.[45] In addition, pro-administration patronage holders packed the Whig state conventions, which sent delegates to the national convention. As a result, Fillmore and Webster supporters were in the majority. They wrote a platform that explicitly committed the Whig party to the acceptance of the Compromise as a finality and to the enforcement of the Fugitive Slave Law and that denounced any further agitation of slavery. Although Scott eventually won the nomination, to the dismay of Southerners, the Whig party, unlike previous campaigns, was committed to a national party stand on the slavery issue. Many Northern Whigs denounced that platform, but they could not mitigate the force of that commitment to what was essentially a Democratic program.

While Whigs were feuding in 1851 and 1852, national Democratic leaders made concerted efforts to reunite their party on the basis of the Compromise. As the presidential election approached, pressures grew on Southern Democrats whether Unionists or Southern Rights supporters to return to the party fold and accept the Compromise. The very success of Union parties in Georgia, Alabama, and Mississippi had, in a sense, destroyed their utility. By the end of 1851, most Southern Rights Democrats were willing to admit that resistance to the Compromise was hopeless. Once they acquiesced in the Compromise and the threat of disunion dissolved, there was nothing for the new parties to fight about. Anguished Whigs who feared they could never be elected as Whigs pleaded that the Union parties be preserved, but inexorably the bipartisan Union coalitions broke down on old party lines. Democrats trooped back into the national party organization; many Whigs did not. Similarly, in the North, free-soil Democrats like the Barnburners and state organizations that had cooperated with the Free-Soilers scampered back to the party because they sensed a Democratic victory in 1852. Nominating Franklin Pierce of New Hampshire, the Democratic national convention also pledged "faithful execution" of all the Compromise measures, explicitly including the Fugitive Slave Law, and the resistance of the Democratic party to any reopening of the agitation over slavery. As in the vote in the House in the spring, little distinguished the major parties from each other on the Compromise issue during the presidential campaign.

This consensus among Whig and Democratic leaders that the Compromise had forever settled the slavery question meant that slavery as a partisan political issue was effectively dead in 1852. Although this temporary achievement may have been good for the country, it was bad for the Second American Party System. The Compromise of 1850 had become the slavery issue; yet, since the 1830s, the ability of the rival parties to offer Northern and Southern voters alternatives on the slavery issue had been one of the major props of the system itself. Clear party differences on the sectional issue had been one of the reasons voters had been loyal to the two parties. National party commitments to the Compromise in the short run meant an end to the fierce interparty conflicts over the Fugitive Slave Law that had characterized Northern state politics in 1850, 1851, and 1852, prior to the presidential campaign. In the long run, that interparty consensus meant those who wished to continue political battles over slavery would look elsewhere, not to the old Whig and Democratic parties.

With the slavery issue temporarily dead in 1852, the Whig and Democratic parties had to fall back on other issues on which they could define themselves as different from each other in order to retain support. Such a strategy was natural, since the dynamics of the two-party system had never rested on a single issue. Instead, the health of two-party competition depended on the ability of the parties to provide conflict on a broad range of issues at all levels of the federal system. When some issues had been resolved or disappeared, politicians had simply turned to other issues or provoked new ones. Since they could exploit local and state concerns as well as national matters in their appeal to the grass-roots electorate, this pattern had worked since the days of Andrew Jackson. Politicians clearly expected that it would work again in the early 1850s. When Stephen Douglas had rejected the Union party back in January 1851, for example, he had spoken of preserving the Democratic party in order "to triumph upon its old issues." Whether this optimism had any real foundation by the time of the presidential election of 1852 is the subject of the next chapter.

FIVE

The Second Party System Undermined, 1849-1853

Politicians' hopes of rallying their supporters with other issues after 1850 rested on recent experience. At the national level in the 1840s, the question of territorial expansion had supplemented the more traditional economic issues as sources of interparty combat. The actions of the Polk administration, moreover, had helped revive party lines in the states. In addition, state parties continued to battle over banking, currency, and corporate charters in state legislatures, and, in many places, over the question of revising state constitutions. Finally, Zachary Taylor's open embrace of the Native American party sharpened the distinction between the Whigs and Democrats on ethnocultural issues. The Whigs clearly seemed more hostile to immigrants and Catholics and more favorable to the passage of temperance legislation than the Democrats. If there appeared to be ground for the optimism of Whig and Democratic politicians, however, their hopes generally proved unrealistic by 1852 and 1853. Despite the impact of the Polk administration and 1848 campaign, a series of developments between 1848 and 1853 diminished and often destroyed the partisan appeal of a number of issues at the state and national levels.

Yet the developments that were so crucial to the undermining of popular faith in the Second Party System have usually been ignored in previous accounts of the politics of the 1850s. The reason for this oversight is that many historians have failed to appreciate what made the system work and have not distinguished sharply enough between the reasons for its demise on the one hand and the subsequent voter realignment of the mid-1850s and sectionalization of parties on the other. The historians who argue that sectional conflict over slavery disrupted the old bisectional parties, for example, detect a clear progression of events between 1848 and 1854. Hence they jump from divisions over the Proviso to the Compromise of 1850 to the uneasy acquiescence in the Compromise in 1851 and 1852 and finally to the Kansas-Nebraska Act of 1854, which repolarized North against South and completed the destruction of the Whigs while fragmenting the Democrats on sectional lines. The cogency of that interpretation, however, depends largely on skipping over periods *between* slavery-related events and ignoring other developments in those same years. Nor are the newer ethnocultural analyses of Northern voting behavior much more helpful, because they locate the demise of the Second Party System in the voter realignment between 1854 and 1856 and examine the years before 1854 only to look for antecedents of the ethnic and religious grievances they see as central to later voting behavior.

The Second Party System, in fact, was near death before January 1854, when the Nebraska bill was introduced, because the dynamics of interparty conflict that sustained it had already been largely eroded. The two-party system collapsed because Whig and Democratic voters lost faith in their old parties as adequate vehicles for effective political action, and they lost faith because social, economic, and political developments between 1848 and 1853 blurred the line that divided Whigs from Democrats on a host of issues. Voter loyalty had always depended on the popular perception that the parties were different from each other, that they offered real alternatives to hostile voters in elections, and that because of that choice men had a real chance to control government. Once agreement, or seeming consensus, on issues had replaced conflict between the parties at the national, state, and local levels, therefore, the ties that bound voters to their old parties frayed and often completely snapped. The result of their disillusionment in 1852 and 1853 was apathy, abstention, and alienation. Decomposition of the old parties preceded voter realignment and the rise of new parties. "Disintegration" more accurately describes what happened to the Second American Party System than "disruption" by the sudden appearance of new issues in 1854.

To explain the collapse of the party system, therefore, one must analyze when, how, and why the Whig and Democratic parties arrived at a point where they seemed more alike than different. This chapter argues that they had largely reached that point by the end of 1853 or even 1852, but demonstrating that process is difficult for a number of reasons. The complications are so troublesome that they require a brief theoretical digression to defend the approach before the substantive story itself can be told.

First, the apparently contrasting fates of the two parties that constituted the Second Party System raise doubts about the acceptability of the entire interpretation itself. The Whig party as a functioning opponent of the Democracy disappeared altogether in the 1850s, and one can date the death of the system with its demise. Yet the Democratic party seemed to thrive until 1860 and beyond. If voter loyalty to both parties depended on the sharpness of the contrast and the vigor of the conflict between them, why didn't the Democratic party collapse too? Can any interpretation that should apply to both parties possibly be correct if only one party was affected? Shouldn't one focus instead on the destructive forces that uniquely affected the Whig party? Didn't the Whig party alone disintegrate because it was more susceptible to the disruptive slavery and ethnocultural issues that emerged in the mid-1850s? In short, aren't the previous interpretations right?

In response to such arguments one can note that politicians had long recognized that the strength and cohesiveness of each individual party in the Second Party System depended on its interaction with the other party. The leaders of both had continually tried to provoke conflict between the parties at the leadership level precisely to energize the mutually hostile voters of both into action. No more perceptive explanation of this relationship can be found than that of the Indiana Free-Soiler George Julian, who jubilantly predicted the utter collapse of both the Whigs and the Democrats after the 1852 presidential election.[1]

> *One of these strongholds of slavery [the Whig party] has*
> *perished, the other [the Democratic party] has thus been*
> *deprived of its antagonist, and must follow in its foot-*
> *steps; for although intensely hostile, they have been in*
> *support of each other. Each has held the other in its orbit,*
> *whilst both have revolved around a common centre of*
> *antagonism, which was their spirit and their life.*

When the parties approached consensus in 1852 and 1853, in fact, the Democratic party did suffer erosion of its voting support and disaffection of its voters. New issues would revive the party in the mid-1850s largely because the groups exploiting those issues furiously vituperated the Democrats. That antagonism gave new meaning to Democratic identity. But one should not let this later recovery conceal the very real maladies the Democrats suffered earlier. Moreover, both the nature and constituency of the Democratic party changed considerably in the 1850s from what they had been in the 1840s. Certainly the Democratic party was altered as much in the 1850s as it would later in the 1890s and 1930s when historians also speak of new two-party systems replacing old ones. Although the label "Democratic" was retained by one of the parties that emerged from the disarray of the 1850s, therefore, one can plausibly argue that the Jacksonian Democratic party that had helped constitute the Second American Party System died just as the Whig party did.

Second, describing the process by which parties converged to a point of likeness is complicated by the federal nature of the party system. At the national level, the process is relatively easy to trace and date; most national issues were dead by the presidential campaign of 1852. Below the national level, in states and localities, however, the character of the forces producing likeness and, more important, the rate at which they operated, varied from place to place. Since state parties had always resorted to subnational issues to help establish their distinct identities and thereby reinforce voter loyalty, the longer such issues could be contested on party lines, the longer the framework of Whig-Democratic rivalry lasted. Put another way, because the parties normally approached agreement on national issues first, the less dependent state organizations were on those national questions for voter appeal the longer they evoked fealty from voters. A complete history of the undermining of the Second Party System, therefore, would systematically trace the varying politics of each state. That task is clearly beyond our limits here; illustration must substitute for systematic demonstration. Still, it is clear that because the availability and nature of partisanly contested state issues varied from state to state, the Second Party System collapsed at different times in different places. Although the years between 1848 and 1854 were most crucial for the erosion of clear party distinctions, the system limped on in some states until 1855.

A third problem is that loyalty of voters to the old party system rested not only on the reality of issue-conflict between the parties, but also on the popular perception of party difference. Subjective perception did not always reflect objective fact. The parties could have seemed different and therefore useful to voters even when they no longer disagreed or conflicted on specific policy matters. It is evident, moreover, that belief in the vibrancy of old party issues and hence in the viability and usefulness of the Whig and Democratic parties changed at different times for different people. As early as 1848, when sharp differences on a number of policy matters still separated Whigs from Democrats, for example, many politicians apparently believed the old party system was bankrupt and that voters could be lured to new organizations based on new issues. They included not only the advocates of the Southern Rights movement and Free-Soilers in the North, but also the sincere supporters of Zachary Taylor's "No Party" campaign. In the spring of 1848 the pro-Taylor New Orleans *Bee* announced, "Old party issues are worn out and have nearly disappeared," while an Alabama Calhounite reported privately that summer, "All the old issues are obsolete."[2] By the fall of 1850, still other politicians and voters thought it was time to abandon the old parties for new organizations based on new principles. In contrast, other politicians tried to preserve the Whig party as late as 1856 and 1860. Public perceptions of the usefulness of the two parties thus were diverse. Even so, it seems safe to say that from the late 1840s on, growing numbers of men became disillusioned with the Whig and Democratic parties. By the end of 1852, their numbers were significant. What follows is an attempt to indicate how events between 1848 and 1853 gave people good reason for thinking that the major parties no longer offered them clear alternative positions on any important issue at any level of the federal system.

During the administrations of Taylor and Fillmore, the clear party lines on sectional, territorial, reform, economic, and ethno-cultural issues disappeared almost entirely. Sometimes the issue that had provoked interparty conflict would be permanently resolved one way or the other and thus removed from the political arena. At other times, the issue would remain, but the parties, either because they were both internally divided by it or because one adopted the position of the other, would converge to a point where, as distinct entities, they no longer offered alternatives upon it. Thus, as shown in the last chapter, by the early summer of 1852 both the Whigs and Democrats, despite some internal resistance, were committed to the acceptance of the Compromise of 1850 and against any reopening of the slavery issue.

Territorial expansion as a salient issue of interparty combat had been shelved even before 1852. Party disagreement on the desirability of territorial acquisition did not end. The Democrats remained vigorous advocates of spread-eagle expansionism, and their national platform of 1852 even rejustified the Mexican War and gloried in its bounty. But the Whigs remained adamant foes of expansion between 1848 and 1853, and their control of the White House during those years effectively, if temporarily, killed the expansion issue. Since the President controlled foreign policy, there could be no concrete issue for the parties to fight about if he did not actively seek expansion. And the Whig presidents did not.

If Whig success in 1848 stilled partisan combat over Manifest Destiny, the triumph of constitutional reformers in a number of states also removed that issue as a source of partisan conflict. Between 1848 and 1852, New Hampshire, Maryland, Virginia, Ohio, Indiana, Michigan, Wisconsin, Kentucky, and Louisiana adopted new charters. Massachusetts wrote a new constitution in 1853, but her voters rejected it. Elsewhere, significant amendments were added to constitutions even when no conventions were called. This spate of state constitutional revision had baneful political effects on the Second Party System that have normally gone unappreciated by political historians.

First, the successful completion and ratification of those constitutions by 1853 resolved an issue that had often generated intense public interest and provoked sharp partisan conflict. Whigs generally opposed and Democrats generally favored constitutional reform. Protracted party battles occurred in state legislatures and state elections over the question of calling conventions, and the conventions themselves often witnessed interparty conflict over economic issues that had long divided the parties. While it lasted in the late 1840s, such partisan strife reinforced party identity and party loyalty. Constitutional revision, that is, was one of the most important state issues Whigs and Democrats could exploit to divert attention from national issues. The victory of reformers thus deprived the parties of a valuable resource. Here was a classic case where political parties benefited much more from the conflict over an issue than from its peaceful resolution.

Reflecting a growing popular animus toward remote and powerful public officials and responding to a demand for more direct democracy, the new constitutions also weakened party organizations by stripping them of large amounts of state patronage. Everywhere the conventions provided for the direct popular election of numerous state and local officials, like judges, auditors, justices of the peace, and sheriffs, who had previously been appointed by governors or legislators. The power to select officials had often provided glue to majority parties in state legislatures, helping to neutralize any tendencies toward factionalism on substantive issues. With patronage powers gone, such restraints on internal fragmentation disappeared. Noting the disarray of Democrats in the 1852 Ohio legislature, for example, an observer remarked that the constitutional reforms of 1851 "have broken up their principle of cohesion to any central organization." Especially in Kentucky, Maryland, and Virginia, the numerous local offices at the disposal of state leaders had provided the heart of local political machines. The new constitutions there both eroded the base of local organizations and reduced the necessity of party fealty from local politicos who could now run as independents for offices previously appointed by the governor.[3]

With organizations weakened, state parties were more dependent than ever on issues to rally voters. But the new constitutions sharply restricted the power of legislatures to act in the economic realm and thus to provide issues the parties could utilize in campaigns. For one thing, almost all constitutions replaced annual sessions of the legislature with biennial sessions, thus halving the opportunity for state parties to do battle. They also mandated a substantial amount of legislation concerning courts and governmental operations that the ensuing session of the legislature would have to pass to put the constitution into operation, and such bills, on which there was little partisan disagreement once the constitutions were ratified, replaced economic issues as the bulk of legislative business in subsequent sessions. For example, an Indianan wrote in early 1852, "Our legislature is in session and are consuming much time remodeling the laws in unison with the new constitution."[4] The new charters also settled many state economic issues that had long provoked partisan combat. They sharply restricted the amount of debt the state could incur and often banned aid to or government involvement in internal improvement projects altogether. Yet Whigs and Democrats had long clashed over such matters. They forbade legislatures to grant any privileges or immunities to corporations of any kind, thus inscribing the Democratic creed in the basic charter beyond the reach of Whig politicians. Similarly, new state constitutions specifically imposed restrictions on the kinds and operations of banks the legislature might charter, often forbidding outright the system of special individual charters that had long prevailed. In many cases, indeed, the constitutions virtually assured that legislatures would pass, as they soon did, general incorporation and free banking laws. Because those provided for the automatic chartering of businesses that met certain requirements as to capitalization, specie reserves, liability, and the like, they too worked to remove the traditional partisan squabbles over individual corporate charters that had filled state legislatures. Even before this period, the Louisiana constitution of 1845 and the Arkansas constitution of 1846 had banned the chartering of banks. Thus, the constitutions went far toward permanently resolving or depoliticizing the major Jacksonian economic issues of banking, currency, and the government's role in the economy.[5]

Historians need to do much more research on the political impact of these new constitutions, but the case of Maryland provides a suggestive example. There the question of even calling a convention was the major legislative and state campaign issue dividing the Whigs from the Democrats between 1845 and 1850. Closely related to it and also a source of interparty conflict was the matter of state aid for transportation projects to connect the western part of the state with Baltimore and the Chesapeake Bay. Whig planters from the Eastern Shore and southern portion of the state feared a new constitution would grant Democratic Baltimore and western Maryland greater representation in the state legislature. Those Whigs feared that the Democrats would then pursue a vigorous program of state aid to economic projects to benefit Baltimore and the west that would in turn increase the state's debt for which the planters were already taxed. When the Democrats finally pushed a convention call through the legislature in 1850, the apprehensive Whigs managed to write into the new constitution prohibitions on the state promotion and indebtedness they feared. Thus the ratification of the constitution of 1851 removed not only the revision issue itself but the most important economic issue in the state from the partisan political arena. The completion by 1853 of both the Chesapeake and Ohio Canal and the Baltimore and Ohio Railroad helped render the internal improvements issue obsolete. Furthermore, the constitution fixed liability and other requirements for banks that had long been fought over. The effects of those articles in defusing the banking issue became apparent in the 1853 session of the legislature when Whigs and Democrats unanimously passed an act extending the charters of 20 banks until 1880 and incorporating the constitutional restrictions in the renewed charters. That law virtually settled the banking issue in Maryland for the rest of the decade.

By 1851, indeed, the parties had little to fight over. The Baltimore *Sun,* one of the few truly nonpartisan newspapers in the country, rejoiced, "Amongst the people by whatever party name they may happen to be known, it is now almost impossible to find a division of sentiment upon any measure of government. There never was a time perhaps in which the sentiments of the people were more happily blended." Because the new constitution deprived the governor of the power to make literally hundreds of local appointments, moreover, it severely weakened party discipline in local organizations. The *Sun* again perceptively summarized the impact: "With . . . executive patronage destroyed, and no nucleus for undue exercise of political power within the economy of government . . . systematic organizations are dismembered." As soon as the new constitution was ratified, party lines in Maryland began to disintegrate both in the legislature and at the polls, where a plethora of independent candidates began to vie for local and legislative offices. In effect, one can date the demise of the Second Party System in Maryland from the passage of its new constitution in 1851.[6]

Where new state constitutions were adopted, they contributed to what was undoubtedly the most important development between 1848 and 1853 that undermined the Second Party System—the muddying of the clear and different positions the parties had taken on the proper role of the government in the economy. Since the 1830s, those stances had served as guideposts for distinguishing Democrats from Whigs. Because shaping or responding to economic growth was a basic responsibility of government at all levels, economic questions were the most fundamental supports of the two-party system. The

Whig argument that the inadequacy of individual resources required government to supply capital and to facilitate its accumulation by private entrepreneurs through corporate charters, tariffs, and subsidies in order to spur growth was one of the few positive positions shared by almost all Whig politicians. Although the Democrats opposed such a positive role for government, they also defended their policies as ones that would produce the soundest economy of all. Because the economic role of government was so basic, the sharp alternatives the parties had provided on that role did much to enhance popular belief that through the party political process, men could change government policy, that through the Whig and Democratic parties, they could achieve the republican ideal of self-government. Hence the blurring of traditional party distinctions on economic issues between 1849 and 1853 dealt the parties a particularly severe blow.

More important than even state constitutions in erasing sharp party lines on economic issues was the sudden transformation of the nation's economy after 1848. Beginning suddenly in 1849, the country enjoyed a sharp boom that lasted until a recession in late 1854. Because of the California gold rush and a dramatic increase in British investment—after the English withdrew funds from the European continent in the wake of the revolutions of 1848—the country's money supply mushroomed. Antebellum foreign investment peaked in 1853, as did the specie reserves of banks in 1854.[7] The economic and political consequences of this unprecedented surge were enormous. The new availability of private capital helped undermine the entire rationale of the Whig economic program, which had been based on the dearth of private capital and the consequent necessity of governmental promotion to achieve economic growth. The enlarged money supply as well vastly complicated many of the staple issues of party conflict such as banking, business incorporations, the tariff, internal improvements, and land policy. More abundant specie reserves, for example, defused the ancient controversy over paper bank notes, because now almost all notes could be sufficiently backed. Whigs now agreed to Democratic demands for more stringent reserve requirements, while formerly antibank Democrats bombarded Democratic governors like Pennsylvania's William Bigler with pleas to expand both the number of banks and the supply of paper currency. Not only did rank-and-file Democrats become much more receptive to banks, but they also urged the creation of other business corporations in order to capitalize on the new prosperity.[8] Divisions between pro- and anti-business Democrats, which had largely been submerged in the mid-1840s behind the party's antimonopoly orthodoxy, now reappeared. Although this trend posed problems for the Democrats, it also meant that the Whigs would have no corner on the advocacy of legislation to promote private business now that direct state subsidization seemed superfluous in many places.

Clear evidence of this neutralization of the banking issue came in the movement for free banking laws in the five states of the Old Northwest in 1851 and 1852. Michigan failed by a single vote to pass such a law in 1851, but Wisconsin, Illinois, Indiana, and Ohio all succeeded. Even though the Democratic governors and much of the Democratic press in those states continued to denounce all forms of banking, large minorities, and in some cases majorities of Democratic legislators joined the probanking Whigs in each case to vote for the bills. A significant discrepancy between Democratic rhetoric and Democratic behavior had developed. As it did so, the line separating the parties on banking policy faded. Once the laws were passed, there continued to be partisan division in Ohio over the question of taxing banks, but by and large banking as a political issue remained quiescent until the Panic of 1857.[9]

Similarly, the Whigs' demand for a high protective tariff lost saliency as both wages and profits rose. Assaults on the low rates of the Walker Tariff seemed useless with both workers and manufacturers flourishing. By 1850 large textile manufacturers like Abbott Lawrence opposed a higher tariff because it would benefit their inefficient competitors more than them and help lure new firms into the textile business during the boom. By 1851 Whigs admitted they could not hold the worker vote with the tariff issue any longer in textile towns like Lowell, Massachusetts. Whig discouragement was also apparent in Pennsylvania where, by 1852, the tariff issue occupied much less of the legislature's time and Whig state platforms than it had earlier. When the national Whig platform of 1852 abandoned the all-important term "protective" in favor of a "revenue" tariff and weakly called for duties that would provide encouragement "equally to all classes and to all parts of the country," the Whig surrender was complete. As astute Democrats were quick to charge, little now distinguished the Whigs' tariff stance from that of the Democrats in 1844. The two parties were in substantial agreement.[10] In sum, although both parties were affected by economic developments after 1848, the Whigs were the biggest losers. Their programs now often seemed unnecessary, while the wisdom of Democratic measures seemed confirmed.

The chief product of the economic boom between 1849 and 1854, the extraordinary surge in railroad construction, also helped dissolve old party lines. Railroads attracted most of the foreign investment, and the completion of the trunkline railroads between the Atlantic coast and Western waters—the Erie in 1851, the Pennsylvania in 1852, the Baltimore and Ohio in 1853, and the New York Central in 1854—altered methods of manufacturing, shifted trade routes, and encouraged an agricultural boom. But, as men rushed to build these and hundreds of other roads, politicians eagerly promoted lines regardless of party affiliation. To cite one example of this bipartisan boosterism, the federal land grant to the Mobile and Ohio Railroad passed the House of Representatives with the support of 51 percent of the Democrats and 64 percent of the Whigs. Railroad building also erased party lines at the other—or local—end of the political spectrum. As one Wisconsin politician wrote in 1853, "Politically we are at this moment very much 'mixed.' Party lines are pretty much extinguished by a deluge of railroad excitement at both ends of the county." As contemporaries noted, moreover, the demands of railroad construction made the tariff issue a two-edged sword, because so many of its former advocates became railroad promoters who wanted cheap British rails. As a result, both Whigs and Democrats pushed for lower rates on railroad iron that the American iron industry could not yet supply in sufficient amount.[11]

The scramble for state railroad charters itself often took the form of one region or locality versus another, not party lines, at least as long as the issue was granting the original charter instead of regulating the corporate rights of previously chartered companies. As numerous railroad projects swamped state legislatures in the late 1840s and early 1850s, therefore, geographical conflict often replaced party conflict. A perfect example of this trend occurred in the Pennsylvania legislature in 1846 when a battle developed between the proponents of chartering the Pennsylvania Railroad from Philadelphia to Pittsburgh and the advocates of granting the rival Baltimore and Ohio a right of way to Pittsburgh. This contest in effect pitted Philadelphia and eastern Pennsylvania against Pittsburgh and western Pennsylvania. The numerous roll-call votes on the measure reduced party lines to a shambles that year, as other contests for charters would in later years.[12]

All in all, the new prosperity after 1848 as epitomized in the railroad boom went far toward obliterating the coherent party lines on economic issues that had existed since the late 1830s. A Baltimore businessman summarized what had happened precisely in a letter to his brother, who was then the Whig minister to Spain. First he reported that banks had so much money that they were desperate for investment opportunities and that merchants, anticipating investments in railroads, "say that never before has the world been so largely and so regularly supplied with gold." Then he assessed the political impact of this burgeoning money supply. "The great dividing lines between the two old parties are fast melting away—and such changes are taking place in the world, that, issues formerly momentous are now of comparatively trifling importance."[13]

That impact was readily apparent in Congress. In January 1851, at almost the same time that Stephen Douglas bravely spoke of triumphing on old Democratic issues, other observers stressed their absence. William A. Graham, the Whig Secretary of the Navy in the Fillmore administration, reported that "there is but little party feeling manifested between the old parties" in Congress, while the Democratic Washington *Union* pronounced an epitaph for the old economic issues, which, it asserted, the Polk administration had permanently settled. Similarly a Whig wrote in 1852, "I think members here are becoming more independent of party. There has not been a division in the Senate yet on party grounds. Nor is anything heard yet of party debate in our body." In fact, the traditional party lines that had characterized voting on economic issues in the 1840s disappeared in 1850-1851 and especially in the 32nd Congress, which met during 1852. By the presidential campaign of 1852, neither the record of voting in Congress nor even the kinds of issues debated gave either party a distinctive economic program to take to the voters.[14]

The disappearance of interparty conflict is not quite so clear-cut at the state level because of variations from state to state, but the trend toward bipartisan agreement is plainly evident. The internal cohesion of the Whig party generally remained high on most economic issues, except railroad charters, but the degree of disagreement or conflict between the parties shrank because the Democrats were much less cohesive than they had been earlier. For example, studies of roll-call voting in Ohio, Kentucky, Pennsylvania, Maryland, Connecticut, Vermont, and New Hampshire indicate that many traditionally partisan economic issues ceased to attract as much legislative attention as earlier, and that on those that did produce votes, the level of interparty conflict had generally declined by 1852 from what it had been in the 1840s. Indeed, interparty conflict on almost all legislative business, whether measured by individual category or the sum of all business in each session, seems to have subsided from earlier levels.[15] (See Table 3 and compare it with Table 1.) Even the indexes presented in Table 3 understate or camouflage the trend toward party likeness on economic matters. In Maryland, for example, while there continued to be slight party disagreement on the seven individual bank bills that came up in 1854, much more significant was the single unanimous vote in 1853 for the omnibus act extending 20 bank charters until 1880.

Those studies also reveal the variations over time and from state to state in the availability of state issues as sources of interparty conflict. Banking provoked more partisan combat in Ohio and Pennsylvania than in Vermont or Kentucky, even though the level of disagreement was declining in the former states. By the early 1850s, moreover, non-economic issues were usually most important in sustaining party identity. The Connecticut and Vermont legislatures remained relatively polarized in 1852 and 1853, respectively, for example, because of the high proportion of votes on temperance and patronage elections of state officials by the legislature in the total legislative business. Connecticut's overall level rose in 1854 because half the roll calls then concerned the Kansas-Nebraska Act, which sharply reinforced party lines in the Nutmeg state.

Similarly, Pennsylvania's relatively high average indexes for all votes in 1851 and 1852 rested on a unique combination of issues. As noted in Chapter Four, there was intense partisan conflict over repeal of the state's personal liberty law, which was finally passed in 1852 and which, in any case, was neutralized as a campaign issue later that year by the national party consensus on the Compromise. In both years, as in 1850, there was a high proportion of purely partisan votes concerning the redrawing of legislative and congressional districts to favor one party or the other. Politicians everywhere could fight bitterly about matters such as patronage dispensation and reapportionment, but they could hardly appeal to voters on those matters, since they only created the image of the parties as spoils-oriented machines instead of vehicles to represent the people. Finally, Pennsylvania's Whig and Democratic legislators in the early 1850s fought about the competitive relationship between the state-owned Pennsylvania Canal System and the parallel but privately owned Penn-

TABLE 3

Average Indexes of Party Disagreement on State Legislative Roll-Call Votes on Various Issues 1847-1854[a]

State	1847	1848	1849	1850	1851	1852	1853	1854
Banking and Currency								
Vermont		9.1	33.9	30.6	17.6	2	33.5	
Connecticut		72	67	48	59	68.6	–	51
Pennsylvania	85.7	62.6	67.1	48.5	63.5	54.3	70	50.2
Ohio	89	95.5	98	87	100	52		61
Kentucky				27.2	31	35.7		31.1
Maryland		–		50	–	–	0	26
Incorporations and Corporate Privilege								
Vermont		25.4	3	21	–	5	–	8.5
Connecticut		77	–	–	–	–	48	
Pennsylvania	84.4	45	65	34.4	44.3	53.1	46.9	28.2
Ohio	48.1	78.1	62	81.6	73	33.5		30
Railroads and Internal Improvements								
Vermont		34	31.5	3	13.6	8	12.5	–
Connecticut		31	12.7	–	–	–	9.2	
Pennsylvania railroads[b]	34	28.7	39.6	42.9	38.3	52.3	38	20.3
Pennsylvania state works[b]	92.9	24.9	54.6	41	58.1	53.8	55.2	44.1
Ohio	62	73.3	58	49	69	–	38	79
Maryland	–	18		7		6	4	3
Constitutional Revision								
Ohio	91	65	89	6.5	53	–	–	–
Maryland		88		81		–	–	–

			Temperance				
Vermont		—	—	17.3	39	17.5	43.6	67
Connecticut		—	—	76.5	32	81.2	68.2	
Pennsylvania	15.2	40.5	25.1	49	44	16.3	26	36.4
Ohio	23	21	31.5	—	—	30.3	—	41.3
Maryland		11		26		6	22	21.2
Slavery								
Vermont	60.3	—	—					
Connecticut	55.5	12.7	71.5	—	—		11	
Pennsylvania	0	59	85.9	77.8	62.4	—		85
Ohio	91.7	85.5	8	20.7	33.7	—		
All Roll Calls								
Vermont		42.6 (N = 41)	24.9 (N = 44)	22.4 (N = 44)	16.6 (N = 64)	16.4 (N = 38)	36.1 (N = 83)	
Connecticut		73.9 (N = 24)	76 (N = 25)	76.2 (N = 24)	59.6 (N = 27)	67.7 (N = 16)	47.7 (N = 16)	69.9 (N = 22)
Pennsylvania	57.7 (N = 201)	36.2 (N = 376)	44.5 (N = 471)	43 (N = 495)	48.5 (N = 277)	46.6 (N = 433)	45.1 (N = 363)	31.3 (N = 411)

aThis table is based on the sources listed in footnote 15. I have calculated the figures for all sessions of the Pennsylvania house myself, except for 1850, 1853, and 1854. Those were computed by Eric Leininger of the University of Virginia. The figures for Vermont, Connecticut, and Pennsylvania are based on all votes, while those for the other states are based on samples chosen by my former students. It must be admitted here that I have no idea how representative those samples are, but the figures are certainly comparable to those in Table 1, which were also based on samples. A dash (—) indicates that no votes were taken in that year on that issue or at least not included in my students' samples. "A complete blank ( ) indicates either that the legislature of the state did not meet that year or that the year was not included in my students' samples." My student, Harry Volz, III of the University of Virginia, has thus far generated figures for only the banking issue in Kentucky, although he will eventually analyze all legislative votes in that state from 1850 to 1860. Remember that the higher the disagreement index, the more cohesively parties were aligned against each other.

bIn Pennsylvania it was possible to distinguish votes on private railroad corporations from those on the state-owned canal system, and I have done so. The two kinds of bills provoked very different levels of party conflict, except in 1850 and 1852, when they became entangled.

sylvania Railroad. That controversy was much too complex to detail here, but in general the Whigs opposed while the Democrats defended the canal—and the patronage it supplied their party—while the Democrats attacked and the Whigs defended the Pennsylvania Railroad on votes explicitly involving its competitive position vis-à-vis the canal.[16] In a reversal of traditional roles, the Democrats championed public enterprise and an active role for the state, while Whigs championed private enterprise and demanded an end to the state's involvement in the economy.

The availability of such unique state issues was vital in prolonging the life of the Second Party System in certain states, because there state parties could shift attention to such matters when they approached consensus on national issues concerning economics, slavery, and territorial expansion. Conversely, the states in which such partisan issues disappeared first were the states in which the two-party system first collapsed. Several additional examples should clarify the vital importance of state issues in either lengthening or shortening the life of the system.

Probably no Northern state witnessed such serious internal divisions over the slavery issue in both parties as New York. The Democrats had suffered massive defections to the Free Soil party in 1848, and even though the Barnburners returned in 1849 and accepted the Compromise, tensions on the sectional issue remained acute. In 1850 the Silver Gray supporters of President Millard Fillmore bolted the Whig state convention because the antislavery supporters of Senator William H. Seward refused to endorse the Compromise as a finality. Although the feuding factions supported the same ticket that year, the Compromise issue remained potentially divisive unless attention could be diverted from it. In this situation, Whig boss Thurlow Weed, an ally of Seward, seized on a traditional state issue to unite his fragmenting party and redraw party lines. Unlike Pennsylvania, Whigs in New York had traditionally supported expenditures for expansion of the canal system, while Democrats opposed them. In the spring of 1851, therefore, Weed pushed a $9 million bond issue through the legislature to enlarge the Erie Canal network.

Observers testified to the efficacy of this scheme in revitalizing the party system, and it became a major issue in the state campaigns of 1851 and 1852. Democrat William L. Marcy, who had been hopeful of exploiting Whig divisions over the Compromise, lamented, "Its political bearing is to rerun old political lines—to fuse into a homogeneous mass the fragments into which both parties were previously broken." Similarly, Free-Soilers saw their hopes for a reorganization of parties over the slavery issue go aglimmering.

> *Seward, by forcing upon us the question of the nine million loan for enlarging the canal, has created a new issue of local nature, which, for the present, predominates over every other. It will have the effect of uniting the Whigs, which was probably intended; it will in considerable degree, bring together the democrats also.*

Seward congratulated Weed for his "splendid victory," which would ensure Whig success in New York "for a period which will carry us through the efforts at disorganization which are so ferociously carried on by our old masters."[17] There is evidence, indeed, that the canal enlargement issue cemented the loyalty of many Whigs, especially in western New York, even in the election of 1853, when the Whigs were dissolving elsewhere. Largely because of the canal issue, the New York Whig party, and with it the Second Party System, survived in New York until 1855 while it collapsed earlier in states like Ohio and Michigan.

In contrast, the absence of interparty conflict on state issues helps account for the early demise of the Whig party and of the old system in Alabama, Georgia, and Mississippi where Union and Southern Rights organizations replaced the old parties in 1850 and 1851. The apparent threat of secession, long-term voting trends, and personal political vulnerability prompted leaders in those states to form new parties, but other politicians and voters were willing to follow them in jettisoning old party names because the traditional economic issues that had long provided a rationale for Whig-Democratic rivalry disappeared more quickly there than elsewhere in the South, or at least they were not replaced by other state issues. Banking and internal improvements issues lost their saliency in Mississippi by 1847 and in Georgia by 1848. Alabama's Democrats had long defined themselves as the antiprivilege party by opposing charters for banks and railroads, but in 1849 Democratic leaders dramatically embraced the normal Whig position in favor of such corporations and state-aided economic development. Then all the parties had left to fight over was the national slavery issue in the form of the Compromise of 1850. By the end of 1851, the new organizations in all three states had reached consensus even on that issue. By then, the Alabama Whig party was for all intents and purposes dead. It failed to attend the national Whig convention in 1852 and to offer a gubernatorial candidate in 1853.[18] In all three states, moreover, turnout dropped precipitously in 1852 because there seemed to be no party issues in the race, and it recovered partially at best in 1853. There was simply little left in the way of issue-conflict to sustain the Second Party System.

Conversely, the Second Party System lasted longer in other Southern states because the Whigs and Democrats were simultaneously fighting over other issues besides the Compromise. Men saw a reason to preserve the old vehicles of political action. The parties battled over the question of constitutional revision in Virginia, Maryland, Kentucky, and Louisiana between 1849 and 1852. In North Carolina Democratic endorsement of and Whig opposition to a change in the state's suffrage requirement for voting in state senate elections produced enormous interest in the gubernatorial elections of 1848, 1850, and 1852. Consequently, those summer elections brought out much larger votes than the presidential contests in 1848 and 1852. Although the diversionary issues were not always explicitly economic, they still were available to give the Whig and Democratic state parties continuing appeal to the electorate.

Such disparate state issues, however, had their limits in helping the national parties as they faced the presidential campaign in the summer of 1852. New York's Whigs might control the state legislature with the Erie Canal issue, but the national Whig party could hardly use it to bring out the vote for Winfield Scott. And it was the Whigs who were especially desperate as the campaign began. The Democrats had achieved much greater unity behind their pro-Compromise platform and their candidate, Franklin Pierce, than the Whigs had. Rightly or wrongly, Southerners regarded Scott as a lackey of Seward and the antislavery Whigs, who could not be trusted to enforce the Compromise. Correspondents accordingly were quick to predict massive Whig defections in the Deep South.

The Whigs, therefore, would be more dependent than ever on carrying the North and border states, but there, too, they had problems. Fillmore and Webster supporters were disgruntled with the candidate, and other Northern Whigs were unhappy with the platform, which prevented them from campaigning as an anti-Southern party. Their traditional economic issues like the tariff and government subsidization, moreover, had lost their relevance. The new prosperity seemed only to show that the Democrats had been right all along about national economic policy. Advocacy of an active economic role for government was one of the few positive programs uniting Whigs, and the apparent unimportance of government and political parties to the self-sustaining economic growth then prevailing dealt the Whigs a body blow. As a Cincinnati Whig and future president, Rutherford B. Hayes reflected perceptively in the fall of 1852:[19]

> The real grounds of difference upon important political questions no longer correspond with party lines. . . .Politics is no longer the topic of this country. Its important questions are settled. . . .Government no longer has its ancient importance. Its duties and powers no longer reach to the happiness of the people. The people's progress, progress of every sort, no longer depends on government.

Aggravating Whig difficulties in carrying the North in 1852 was the huge growth in the immigrant population since 1848. Although that surge began in 1846 because of the Irish famine, it swelled markedly after 1848 as refugees from the German revolutions joined the Irish streaming across the Atlantic. Altogether, almost 3 million foreigners flooded American shores between 1846 and 1854. That infusion amounted to a startling 14.5 percent of the 1845 population, the largest proportionate addition of immigrants in American history. Mostly Catholic, the aliens transformed the old-stock communities of the border states and the North where they clustered, and those were exactly the regions the Whigs had to carry to counterbalance their anticipated losses in the cotton South.

The wave of immigrants presented the Whigs with a terrible political dilemma. On the one hand, because immigrants had traditionally gravitated to the Democratic party, the Democrats seemed assured of a much larger vote in the North in 1852 unless the Whigs could reverse that trend. Not only were there hundreds of thousands of additional aliens, but more of them could vote. Those who had arrived in 1846 and 1847 could, by 1852, meet the five-year naturalization requirement for U.S. citizenship and the right of suffrage that went with it. Many states, moreover, allowed aliens to vote before they became citizens, and the spate of new state constitutions had extended that privilege and shortened residency requirements. Many Whigs believed, in any case, that Democrats fraudulently naturalized immigrants on a massive scale. Without limiting or neutralizing the Democratic gains in some way, the Whigs had no chance of electing Scott.

On the other hand, the party could not move to capture part of the new immigrant vote without alienating nativist and anti-Catholic voters who traditionally had sided with the Whigs and whose hostility grew in direct proportion to the immigrant population. To apprehensive and often bigoted Protestant Americans, the tide of Catholic aliens inundating their communities seemed to spawn slums, violations of the Sabbath, public drunkenness, pauperism, and crime. The cheap competition supposedly offered by immigrant workers was already being blamed for holding wages down just when prices were rising because of the swelling money supply. Long warned by shrill propagandists of a papal plot to take control of America through the agency of European minions, horrified Protestants bemoaned the growing number of Catholic churches, bishops, priests, and parishioners. Finally, the immigrants seemed to pervert the democratic political process because they voted in blocs that were easily manipulated by party bosses who illegally naturalized them, bought their votes, and marched them to the polls or who, even more alarmingly, seemed all too willing to give positions of political power to Catholic immigrants.

By 1852, such unvarnished anti-Catholic nativism was only in the incipient stages of a growth that would crest later in the decade. At that time, the reaction to immigration most often found an outlet in the burgeoning crusade for state legislation to ban the manufacture, distribution, and sale of alcoholic beverages. Early temperance advocates had relied on moral suasion or local option laws for licensing tavern owners and banning Sunday drinking. As public drinking and the other social evils that went with it seemed to accompany the arriving Irish and Germans, however, anxious citizens demanded statewide prohibition. Joining temperance associations by the thousands, they questioned candidates of all parties as to how they would vote on such legislation and threw their support to those who replied most favorably. The passage of the famous Maine Law in 1851 not only symbolized the success of the new strategy, but catalyzed the drive for prohibition in other states. At the same time, prohibition was a concrete political issue that angered the newly arrived Irish and

Germans. Long accustomed to gathering at beer gardens and neighbor-
hood taverns, they began voting in much larger numbers in the early
1850s to defeat the prohibitionists and protect their traditional mores.
Openly endorsing either side of the issue would have a price.

The essence of the Whig dilemma was simple. Should they woo
the immigrants to reduce Democratic gains or should they woo their
nativist and prohibitionist foes to offset those gains? In 1848 Zachary
Taylor had attempted the latter by an allegiance with the Native
Americans and by his "No Party" campaign to lure native-born Democrats. By 1852, however, the Taylor Republican movement had aborted, and the risk in offending immigrants seemed much higher. So did
the risk of alienating the nativists, however. From Boston, where the
soaring Irish population threatened Whig hegemony unless the Whigs
could win their votes, the patrician Robert C. Winthrop explained
the choice before Whigs everywhere. "One has to steer these days
between Scylla and Charybdis. The Native Americans are wide awake,
& my wall is scribbled with 'No Popery' every night. Meantime, the
Irish have reasons enough to support me, if they understood them."[20]

The alternatives available to the Whigs, in fact, were not equal.
The advantages of seeking the nativist and temperance vote were not
as evident as the danger in offending the immigrants. The Whigs were
undoubtedly aware of the escalating anti-Catholic and nativist back-
lash, but its potency in terms of total votes was difficult to calculate.
If only traditional nativists were affected, their votes were scarcely
numerous enough to offset the expected immigrant turnout. Temperance advocates were easier to count, but the benefits of siding with
them seemed just as dubious. The prohibition question did not just
polarize immigrants against natives. Native-born workers who wanted
to drink on Sundays as well as Americans who resented the infringe-
ment on personal freedom inherent in prohibition, people involved
in the manufacture and sale of liquor, and especially the numerous
native-born farmers who converted their crops into hard cider, corn
whiskey, or beer opposed the legislation.

At the same time, the temperance forces had a poor record of
concentrating their votes. Because so many votes were at stake on
both sides of the issue, in most states neither major party had dared
to take a clear stand on the issue. Instead, they tried to straddle it
by ignoring the queries of temperance associations, letting individuals
vote their consciences in legislatures without adopting a party line,
or pushing public referenda on the question so their parties could

avoid responsibility for what politicians everywhere deemed unpopular laws. As a result, temperance advocates were found in both parties, and prohibitionist support was divided between them. When the Whigs openly bid for that support as in the Connecticut gubernatorial campaign of 1852, moreover, they lost. Whig "wets" defected to the opposition, while Democratic "dries" refused to aid them.[21] With both parties internally divided, temperance seemed too hot a political potato to touch.

On the other hand, a tremendous surge in the immigrant vote was a virtual certainty, and it would be overwhelmingly Democratic unless something was done to attract it. Faced with this hard fact, internally divided over their platform and candidate, bereft of traditional issues with national or even regional appeal, and plagued in many states by disintegrating local organizations, the Whigs made a conscious choice in 1852 to reverse their traditional stand and actively seek the Catholic immigrant vote.

There were a number of specific reasons for this decision. Foremost was the influence of Seward and his followers in the movement for Scott's nomination. Always scornful of the prohibitionists, Seward since 1840 had urged the Whigs to go after the Catholics and immigrants instead of aligning with nativists. As governor in 1841, he had even urged public support for parochial schools. In 1848 many Sewardites had preferred Scott to Taylor because of Scott's potential appeal to the Irish. During the Mexican War, Scott had been especially solicitous not to damage Catholic church property, and he had educated two daughters in Catholic convents. Whigs hoped this record could be exploited. By early 1852, Whigs and Democrats were reporting Seward's hopes of using Scott's candidacy to woo Catholic voters, and Pierce was warned after he received the Democratic nomination that "the Catholic question is to be one of the principle [sic] elements in the coming contest, provided Gen. Scott should get the Whig nomination. . . .Scott having two daughters Catholics, it is expected by the Seward wing to make great capital out of it."[22]

With Pierce's nomination, the Whigs thought that the Democrats were especially vulnerable to the "Catholic question." When New Hampshire revised her constitution in 1850, a clause to repeal the state's ban disqualifying Catholics from holding public office was defeated in the popular referendum. Because Democrats were the majority party in the state and because Pierce was the head of that party, the Whigs falsely charged that the Democrats had voted against the repeal en masse, that Pierce had favored retention of the religious test, and that he was therefore a bigot whom no good Catholic could support. "To your Tents, Catholics," warned Whig campaign slogans when publicizing the accusation.

Special circumstances in certain states with large Catholic populations, moreover, encouraged Whigs to think they could wean Catholics from their Democratic allegiance even before Pierce was nominated. In Illinois, the Democratic gubernatorial candidate was supposedly unpopular among Catholics. In Pennsylvania, as scores of Democrats reported, Irish Catholics seemed particularly ripe for Whig plucking. They were furious that the lone Democrat on the 1851 state ticket to lose was James Campbell, an Irish Catholic leader from Philadelphia. Because the Irish blamed anti-Catholic Democrats for cutting their hero, "the blandishments of the Scott and Seward school of politicians, fall now upon open ears and ready minds." In Massachusetts, Boston's Irish denounced the Free Soil-Democratic coalition's support for the state's prohibition law and for constitutional revisions that would strengthen the nativist western regions of the state at the expense of Boston and her Irish. Both the Whigs and the Democrats were divided on regional lines by those issues, and Boston's Whigs had struck out on their own to woo the Catholics by opposing both.[23]

If unique opportunities spurred Eastern Whigs to adopt the pro-Catholic strategy, fear of being deluged by a huge new immigrant vote converted Midwestern Whigs. In September 1852, after speaking with Schuyler Colfax of Indiana, Truman Smith wrote Thurlow Weed, Seward's long-time ally in the pro-Catholic strategy, a remarkable letter revealing both the Whigs' problem in the Northwest and their solution to it.

> He [Colfax] says Indiana would be sure for Scott were it not for some 10 or 15,000 new German voters brought in by a recent amendment of their constitution and he fears the accession of locofoco strength may turn the scale there against us. The same cause may defeat us in Ohio & in the other states of the Northwest. We both agree on this—that you must devote your whole time to bringing the Catholic element into full play. No one can do this as well as you can & in short you can do it & must. . . . Colfax says Bishop Purcell [of Cincinnati]

> *can put this matter right in the NW if he can be induced*
> *to act. I think you should see him at the earliest day*
> *practicable.*

Smith then urged Weed to visit other bishops around the country to line up their support to influence Catholics to vote Whig and thus cut into the Democratic hold on the immigrant vote.[24]

Whether Weed made a grand tour of bishops as Smith begged is unclear, but the Whigs sought the Catholic and immigrant vote with a vengeance. Pierce's purported anti-Catholicism was propagandized, pro-Irish tracts were circulated, congressional Whig voting records favoring famine relief for Ireland were dredged up, and Scott himself made foolish speeches praising the Irish brogue. The Whigs, moreover, took care to softpedal the temperance issue so as not to alienate the immigrants on that score. In September the most renowned prohibitionist in the nation, Neal Dow of Maine, wrote Seward that because Pierce "is an intemperate man," all the Whigs had to do to win the entire temperance vote and thus elect Scott was to publicize that fact. Aware that the temperance vote had never yet united and that such a tactic would neutralize the appeal to Catholics, Seward jotted at the bottom of the letter when he forwarded it to Weed, "Of course I don't think so. But I send the letter." Whig newspapers like the Pittsburgh *Gazette* denied that a moral issue like temperance had any place in the campaign, and the Massachusetts Whigs openly adopted an antiprohibition position to secure the Irish vote. Their gubernatorial candidate in 1852 was a notorious "wet," and Boston's Whigs went even further by printing tickets for a slate explicitly pledged to repeal the state's prohibition law that consisted of the Whig gubernatorial candidate and the Democratic candidate for lieutenant governor, because the regular Whig was considered too favorable to prohibition.[25]

The reasoning behind the desperate Whig stratagem in 1852 is understandable, but it proved to be a colossal mistake that failed to salvage the election in the short run and had particularly calamitous consequences for the Whigs in the long run. Quite consciously, the Whigs had destroyed the last thing distinguishing them from the Democratic party. In 1852 the Democrats easily defused Scott's appeal to immigrants by trotting out letters he had written earlier demanding a longer naturalization period for immigrants and by pointing to their own long record of tolerance toward immigrants. After the election, an Ohio Whig despaired, "We are overwhelmed by the Foreign vote," and others agreed that the Irish and Germans had voted solidly for Pierce.[26]

All the Whigs managed to do was to alienate nativist and anti-Catholic voters in and outside their coalition, just at a time when anti-Catholic sentiment was rising. As early as March 1852, a Philadelphia Whig had warned that "the Scott men count here on the Roman Catholic vote, which is exceedingly unsafe reckoning, whilst the bare suspicion of it, drives from his support the ultra protestant feeling which is strong here, and very strong in the interior of this state." Similarly, an Ohio Whig who anticipated Scott's nomination demonstrated the intensity of anti-Catholic bigotry even when he misjudged how the Catholics themselves would act.

> It is very presumable that our military, sop-headed, Roman Catholic Scott comes next. He compelled the American Armies to prostrate themselves in mud whenever a crucifix or an Idolatrous Doll Baby passed along. His children are all ultra roman catholics, and therefore he will get every roman catholic vote in the United States.

Later, other nativists reacted with equal vehemence to the Whig campaign for Scott. Nativist organizations such as the Order of United Americans in New York bitterly opposed him, and Lewis C. Levin, chief of Pennsylvania's Native American party, assured the Democrat William L. Marcy that "the feeling among my friends is intense —intense hostility to the Whigs." Other observers from Pennsylvania wrote Pierce before the election: "Many honest Protestants among the Whigs [especially Methodists and Presbyterians] are disgusted at the course Scott has taken to secure the Catholic vote and will vote against him." Finally, a Whig reported from western Pennsylvania after the election: "A Presbyterian doctor, a consistent and old fashioned Whig in politics, who practices in some four or five townships in this county, says that a number of Old Presbyterians refused to vote with the Whigs, because Scott was an Episcopalian and had a daughter in a nunnery."[27]

Although anti-Catholics were especially infuriated by Whig tactics in 1852, the more general response to the disappearance of clear party lines on matters relating to expansion, slavery, constitutional revision, economics, and immigration was boredom. Nothing seemed to separate the parties. Little seemed at stake other than the spoils of office. "There were no issues," the Tennessee Democrat Andrew Johnson complained after the election. This perception was widespread. As a result, the campaign provoked little more than a yawn in many places. "Genl. Apathy is the strongest candidate out here," reported a Cincinnati Whig; the Baltimore *Sun* remarked that "there is no issue that much interests the people." "Unexampled prosperity renders it difficult to create excitement about party politics," it explained later. "Let either [party] win that may," summed up the *Baltimore County Advocate,* "we have nothing at stake."[28]

At first glance, the numerous observations of widespread voter apathy seem controverted by the results of the 1852 election. The total vote was larger than in 1848, and Pierce won a smashing victory in the electoral vote, 254 to 42. The Whigs managed to carry only four traditional strongholds, Vermont, Massachusetts, Kentucky, and Tennessee, and in each of those their popular vote dropped from 1848. Historians have traditionally attributed this rout to the fact that Pierce seemed a truer friend of the Compromise than Scott. Unionist Whigs in both sections supposedly stayed home or supported Pierce. There is undoubtedly some truth to this assertion. Scott was unpopular among Southern Whigs, and the party lost 67,500 votes in the slave states from its 1848 total. The Whigs lost votes everywhere except Virginia, which had extended the suffrage in the 1851 constitution, but defections were especially severe in the Deep South states where Union parties had been formed in 1850 and 1851. The Whig vote plummeted by 66 percent in Georgia, 50 percent in Alabama, and 30 percent in Mississippi.

A closer look at the popular results, however, raises doubts that there were widespread Whig conversions to the Democracy. For one thing, the Democrats gained only 35,000 votes in the South, and 27,000 of those came from the enlarged electorate in Virginia. The Democrats, in fact, also lost votes in Georgia and Alabama and only retained their 1848 total in Mississippi. Pro-Compromise Southern Whigs may have refused to support Scott, but they did not join the Democracy on a large scale. In the Northeast, the Whig popular vote remained about even with the 1848 total; they gained votes in New York, but lost them elsewhere. In the Midwest, moreover, the Whigs actually gained 61,000 votes since 1848. The Democrats won, not because of Whig conversions, but because their vote grew so much faster. They gained 84,000 new votes in the Midwest and 208,000 in the Northeast. Returning Van Burenites and immigrants voting for the first time undoubtedly accounted for the bulk of this increment, although anti-Catholic Whigs and Unionist Whigs may have contributed to it.

The Whigs' ability to retain and even increase their vote in the North is puzzling in light of their loss of issues. If voter loyalty and voter interest depended on an issue conflict that people perceived was gone, why did so many people bother to vote? In part, the answer is that in certain states like New York and Pennsylvania there still was conflict over state issues such as the Erie Canal and the Pennsylvania Mainline Canal System. Also, the sheer mechanism of the presidential campaign with all its organizational work to stir up voters activated the mutual animosity between Whigs and Democrats. If the parties had lost their issues, they still retained their names, and many voters would still do all they could to defeat the other. As a Democrat wrote Pierce in the summer of 1852, the Whigs "are so bitter against the Democrats, that, unless they are stirred up with a very long pole, they will be very likely to disregard the consequences & results, re their present wishes, not to elect Scott so much as to defeat you."[29] Put another way, because the presidential election could provoke mutual hatreds, it provided an artificial stimulus to the dying party system. It was an electric shock to a patient whose heart was stopping. Even when voters longed for new parties to express their grievances, a presidential election was the most difficult time to start one because of the organizational problems of distributing ballots around the country. In 1852, the issues that concerned voters were local in orientation. There was no new issue of sufficient intensity and breadth around which to organize a new national party. In this situation, even disillusioned voters responded to the call to defeat the traditional enemy.

Not all disillusioned voters did so, however. In fact, the apathy of many was translated into abstention on election day. Although higher than 1848, the turnout in 1852 was abnormally low when measured against the number of potential voters. The absolute vote in presidential elections had always increased every four years simply because of population growth and the admission of new states. Almost 75,000 of the votes in 1852, for example, came from the new state of California. In many old states the total vote dropped absolutely from 1848, and elsewhere the rate of increase in participation between presidential elections caused by population growth was lower than usual. In Maryland, for example, turnout rose less between 1848 and 1852 than in any other four-year interval between 1836 and 1860. In Tennessee, the estimated proportion of the potential electorate voting fell from 90 to 93 percent in 1844 and 83 to 86 percent in 1848 to only 72 to 75 percent in 1852.

Even though disgusted Whigs were most likely to abstain, thousands of Democrats also stayed home instead of voting in an election that seemed to mean little because the parties no longer stood for anything distinct. In Georgia, Alabama, and Mississippi, where the Compromise was the only issue and both parties agreed on it, this trend was certainly apparent. The Democratic vote was down from 1848 by 22 percent in Georgia and 14.2 percent in Alabama. The Democrats gained a few votes over their 1848 presidential total in Mississippi, but their 1852 presidential vote was 13.2 percent below their gubernatorial total in 1849. Similarly, total turnout in North Carolina in 1852 dropped from the gubernatorial election in August, where there was a hotly contested state issue, to the presidential election in November by 13.8 percent, and the Democratic vote fell by 18 percent. In Florida, Tennessee, Vermont, and even Pierce's New Hampshire, the same trend prevailed. Both the total vote and the Democratic vote declined from the preceding gubernatorial contest.

Recently, historians, using a highly sophisticated quantitative technique known as ecological regression, have estimated that the proportion of nonvoters, men who could vote but did not, climbed between 1848 and 1852 from 33 to 64 percent in Alabama, from 11 to 37 percent in Mississippi, and from 51 to 54 percent in Louisiana. Similar studies of 302 counties in Indiana, Illinois, Michigan, Ohio, and Wisconsin found that those not voting increased from 22 percent in 1848 to 26 percent in 1852. Put another way, one-sixth of the Democrats who voted in 1848 did not vote in 1852, one-eleventh of the Whigs abstained, and almost half of the Free-Soilers of 1848 stayed home. In Massachusetts, 30 percent of the Whigs who voted for Taylor in 1848 remained home in 1852, as did one-tenth of the 1848 Democratic voters and one-fourth of the Free-Soilers. Nationally, the Free Soil vote fell from 291,000 in 1848 to 156,000 in 1852. In New York, many of the Barnburners undoubtedly returned to the Democratic column, but elsewhere they simply did not vote.

With the Compromise seemingly settling the territorial issue, they had no reason to participate.[30]

Despite the additional stimulus to the voters provided by the presidential sweepstakes in 1852, therefore, considerable erosion in the voting support of both major parties did occur. That decomposition would advance considerably in the state and local elections of 1853 when it was both more difficult for the major parties to arouse apathetic voters and more feasible for dissident groups to organize third parties to meet their needs. From Massachusetts in the spring of 1853, Whig editor Samuel Bowles of the Springfield *Republican* urged the Whigs to take up constitutional reform as a new issue. "Now is the time to start new; the old issues are gone, we can't live under them. We are beaten out." By the fall, a Boston Democrat reported, "Never was the Whig party so apathetic here as at present." Although the Whigs eventually did rally to oppose the state constitution, which was written in 1853, the defeat of the document in the fall referendum stripped them of even that issue. In Connecticut, Whigs described their party as "disheartened & divided by temperance, Maine Law & abolition," while a Democrat exulted, "The Whigs here seem disposed to let the election go pretty much by default." In Pennsylvania, where the Whigs could offer only a vague one-sentence platform pledging that they adhered "steadfastly to the cherished and often avowed principles of their party," a Whig editor wailed that "party ties are measurably weakened, and partially broken. Indifference and apathy have taken possession of the public mind." Voting returns confirmed this response to the lack of concrete issue-conflict. Participation in statewide elections in Pennsylvania, Massachusetts, New Hampshire, Connecticut, New York, Tennessee, Alabama, and Florida fell from previous levels in similar off-year elections. The Whig vote usually declined most dramatically, but Democrats also abstained in larger numbers than normal.[31]

Little separated the palpable loss of interest in party battles from a loss of faith in the old parties and the politicians who led them. The evident bankruptcy of the two-party system combined with the sudden change produced by massive immigration, rapid urban growth, and dislocating economic transformation fostered a widespread sense of malaise. Everywhere people began to suspect that something had gone wrong with American society and that reform was needed. Voters who had a specific idea of what was wrong and what the remedy should be formed new parties to meet their needs.

Impatient with the refusal of the major parties to take an open stand on temperance, prohibitionists had been ready to bolt even in 1852. During the midst of the presidential campaign that year, an upstate New Yorker reported:

> *The Temperance question however will govern not only a large share of the Whig votes but many of the Democrats have pledged themselves to vote for temperance men only let the consequences be what they will to the two Political Parties. They think the temperance questions is of far more importance to the people of this State than any other that agitates the public mind.*

In Michigan, Pennsylvania, Maryland, and elsewhere in 1853, prohibitionists entered separate slates in the state legislative elections in various localities, and everywhere they fragmented former party lines. The temperance ticket carried normally Democratic Baltimore, and a Philadelphian summarized the Democracy's experience all over his state: "So many Democrats are voting for the prohibitory ticket and so many combinations are against it that I am afraid of the results."[32]

In certain gubernatorial races, the prohibition issue revived the fortunes of the failing Free Soil party when it was the only party to take a clear stand in favor of a Maine Law. Connecticut provides a perfect example. In 1852 both the Whig and Free Soil candidates were regarded as temperance men. Then the Whigs received about 45 percent of the popular vote, and the Free-Soilers garnered 4.6 percent. In 1853, the Whigs spurned the advances of the temperance men who threw their support to the Free-Soilers. The Whigs lost 8000 votes, while the Free-Soilers gained 6000. The Whig proportion of the vote fell to 34.2 percent; the Free Soil share increased to 14.8 percent. Similarly, the Free Soil share of the vote soared in Wisconsin and Ohio because the party endorsed prohibition, while in Maine itself the Free-Soilers and a "dry" faction of Democratic dissidents cut heavily into the two-party share of the vote.[33]

The growing numbers of anti-Catholic voters who could no longer trust either of the major parties also thought they had a remedy for society's ills. And they, too, turned to splinter parties to effect that remedy. Furious at the Whig betrayal, rabid Protestants also detested the pro-Catholic Democrats. By 1853, they were especially distrustful because Democratic legislators in Michigan, Ohio, Pennsylvania, Maryland, and elsewhere endorsed Catholic demands to provide public tax support for Catholic parochial schools. Because division of the school funds would reduce the monies available for the Protestant-dominated public schools, the Catholic demands articulated in 1852 and 1853 seemed like an assault on the cherished public school system. To blunt that attack, frantic Protestants started new parties of their own in the local elections of 1853. Even before the school issue arose, an anti-Catholic demagogue named Joe Barker was elected mayor of Pittsburgh in 1850 as an "Anti-Catholic and People's Candidate," and he ran strongly in local elections the next two years. The school issue spread the resort to third parties to other cities. Anti-Catholic Democrats in Detroit nominated an Independent ticket in the municipal election of 1853 whose main platform was the protection of public schools from Catholic designs, and with Whig support the Independents swept the election. In Cincinnati's municipal election in the spring of 1853 four parties ran: Democrats, mildly anti-Catholic Independents, a vehemently anti-Catholic Free School party, and dissident anti-Catholic German Democrats known as Anti-Miamis. The Democrats won over the divided opposition, but the three splinter parties polled three-fifths of the vote, with the Free School party winning 35 percent by itself. By the time of the county elections in the fall of 1853, the temperance issue had further dissolved party lines in Cincinnati. An incredible seven tickets contested the race for state legislators.[34] Although the anti-Catholic and temperance issues aroused intense popular interest in some states and localities, in sum, they only increased the fragmentation of Whig and Democratic voting coalitions instead of reinforcing two-party lines.

In many places, however, the reform impulse was not so focused on specific issues. Instead, it took the form of simple rebellion against the old parties and the politicians who led them. The purpose of many independent parties was to oust party hacks from public office and recruit new, honest, and more responsive men to replace them. The result was the same, in any case: the severing of the ties that bound voters to the old two-party system. In Boston's municipal election of 1853, for example, two independent, clean government parties, the Citizen's Union Party and the Young Men's League, outpolled the Whigs and Democrats combined. From Maryland, where independent candidates were contesting congressional and state legislative seats throughout the state, a Democrat worried, "I was mortified to find so much disorganization." Some Pennsylvanians articulated the spirit behind the revolt precisely. A rural Democrat explained to Governor Bigler that an independent was elected judge in his district instead of the regular Democratic nominee "simply because the people in the district were tired of the spirit of [party] dictation." From Philadelphia an independent accounted for the victory of his state legislative ticket in similar terms.[35]

> Politics—so called—have assumed a strange shape. Without any present questions of political importance to preserve the old lines of parties, parties yet preserve the old names which prove convenient vehicles to convey certain individuals to places of trust and distinction and emolument. . . . I had the satisfaction of being one of an organization which proved sufficient to break down for once the power of party organization in this city in the late election, and succeed in electing an independent ticket composed of highly meritorious men to our state legislature. . . . It seems to me the public are tired of what you may justly call the day of small things, and that they are ready, throughout the country, for abandoning a system which brings up none but obscure men for the most distinguished stations. Our System of party nomination . . . ought to be abandoned.

What united the men who passively abstained in 1853 with those who actively bolted to new parties was a mounting antagonism to politicians and the mechanisms of the old parties, like conventions, which enhanced their control over the rank and file. There was a growing demand that power be removed from such politicos and returned directly to the people. Because politicians no longer offered distinctive programs to the people, they were increasingly viewed as corrupt and tyrannous spoilsmen interested only in their own self-advancement. Party "controversy is continued not for measures, but for men—not for the public good, but for public offices," complained a Baltimore newspaper. Politicians and the parties they commanded no longer seemed agents of the people; instead, they now seemed to stand between the people and true self-government. Such suspicion of entrenched politicians had, in fact, been growing since the late 1840s. Surely part of Zachary Taylor's appeal as a "No Party" or "People's" candidate had been his promise to break the control of regular party politicians over the White House, and his calculated use of the name "Republican" was meant to reassure people that self-government would be restored. Similarly, much of the impulse behind the wave of state constitutional revisions with their specific prohibitions on legislative initiatives and substitution of direct popular election for patronage appointments was an effort to return power to the people. Explaining why so many Ohio Whig voters supported the state's new constitution, which Whig leaders had labored so long to prevent, an observer reported that "so unpopular had the administration of the appointing power of the general and state governments become, that many . . . voted and lent their influence for its adoption, to give to the people directly, as far as they will, the appointing power."[36]

The disappearance of perceived party alternatives on almost all issues by 1852 enormously increased popular resentment of politicians by exacerbating a fear that republican government itself was endangered. It is not too great an oversimplification to say that since 1776 the essence of American politics had been the battle to secure republicanism—government by and for the people, a government of laws whose purpose was to protect the liberty and equality of the people from aristocratic privilege and concentrations of tyrannous power. Since the Revolution, Americans from both sections had been obsessed with the fragility of republics, with the danger power in any form posed to liberty, and with the susceptibility of republican self-government to usurping conspiracies and plots. A number of code words had pervaded political rhetoric that signified their apprehensions. "Corruption" was viewed as an omen that republicanism was being undermined because rulers put their own self-interest ahead of the public interest. Once they did that, it was feared, the people no longer controlled their governors. Corruption then led to "tyranny," "oppression," or "slavery," the quashing of the individual freedom and independence it was the purpose of government to protect.

It is of the utmost importance in understanding the events of the 1850s, therefore, to recognize that the word "slavery" had a political meaning to antebellum Americans quite apart from the institution of black slavery in the South. It implied the subjugation of white Americans to another's domination. It meant the absence of independence. It was the antithesis of republicanism. When men denounced slavery before the Civil War, in other words, they were not always referring to Negro slavery; instead, they were often concerned with the rights and liberties of white Americans. Slavery was the status Americans had rebelled to escape in 1776, and to preserve the fruits of the Revolution they were convinced that they had to be ever vigilant to prevent it.

The legitimacy of the Second Party System with the electorate had always rested fundamentally on the belief that through the Whig and Democratic parties, men could protect and perfect republican society. Since the days of Jackson, men had kept faith in the political process because parties had offered alternative ways to secure self-government, promote liberty and equality, and answer more specific needs. The presence of sharp party alternatives not only satisfied this last requirement, but also persuaded men that they had a way to change government policy and thereby achieve self-government, government by and for the people. Equally important, the parties had debated almost every issue that entered the political arena since 1820 in terms of its implications for republican government in order to reinforce faith that the parties were truly defenders of republicanism. Much more than Andrew Jackson, banking, Masonry, reform, Manifest Destiny, or black slavery, the tensions between power and freedom had been the crux of political conflict between Jacksonians and Whigs. Continually the parties did battle against supposedly tyrannous concentrations of power— be they usurping executives, corrupt legislatures, the lawless Masonic conspiracy, or monopolistic corporations.

The politicization of economic issues had been the most basic to the parties' ability to convince people that they could protect liberty and equality from power and privilege through the party political process. When attacking the probusiness measures of the Whigs, for example, Democrats constantly portrayed themselves as foes of antirepublican monsters. Thus the *Cleveland Plaindealer* asserted in 1850:

> *It must not be left to the corrupt cupidity and caprice of future Legislatures to say whether this State shall be dotted over with Bank Corporations or cut up with Plank and Railroad Corporations, with such tyrannical and exclusive privileges as shall make them masters, we their slaves.*

Similarly, a Democratic sheet in Illinois denounced all forms of banking as "a curse—a legacy that the aristocratic tendencies of a bygone age has left, as a means to fill the place of baronial usurpation and feudal exactions. They are the engine of the new form of oppression."[37] Whigs, on the other hand, had argued cogently that by promoting economic growth, by increasing the capital available for investment and speeding the pace of economic diversification, they were increasing the freedom of all Americans by enlarging the range of economic choices open to each individual. Because the wealthy were so few, the Whigs had maintained, they would widen and democratize access to the resources necessary for growth and thus reduce the power of the monied aristocracy over less wealthy individuals. Whereas the Democrats promised to protect individuals from heinous concentrations of power and privilege, the Whigs promised to liberate men from the dependent status of wage earner and the dead-end of subsistency by increasing the opportunity for economic mobility to the independent status of entrepreneur, whether as farmer, merchant, or manufacturer.

Much more was at stake in the waning of perceived party alternatives on issues by 1852, therefore, than the mere loss of specific issues to fight about and thereby galvanize voter loyalty. The lack of choice between the parties was equated with an end of republicanism, a loss of popular control over government, government removed from and even threatening to the people. And even though the convergence of the parties on ethnic and religious matters had the most immediate overt results, the bipartisan scramble to promote the economic boom of the early 1850s probably had even more serious consequences. As Democrats and Whigs alike chartered railroads and banks, the parties lost their main chance to pose as paladins of republicanism, and as the people lost faith in their traditional champions, their anxiety about the vulnerability of republican values became all the more grave. The sudden economic and social changes of the period seemed to threaten those values, but the Democratic and Whig parties no longer seemed willing to slay dragons in order to protect them.

Once people lost faith in the efficacy of the political process, their most common response was to denounce politicians and the old parties themselves as the subverters of republicanism that stood between the people and true self-rule. The felt need for reform was first expressed as a desire to change the old party machinery, restore power to the people, and thus save the Republic. In late 1852 an Ohioan succinctly expressed the widespread perception of what had gone wrong. "We are Republicans, so-called," he lamented, "and yet men placed in power are often too far removed from the people —are not easily approached, seldom comply with the expressed wishes of the people, but on the contrary repulse them." In 1852 and 1853, complaints about politicians and parties that readily identified them as antirepublican reached a crescendo. From Maryland Francis P. Blair wrote that the people were furious at "the prevailing corruptions in the conduct of public affairs," and a Whig denounced the control of his party by "a Court House clique composed of a set of unprincipled men, selfish, immoral & tyrannical." A St. Louis newspaper declared that "the convention system must be abolished if we would preserve the supremacy of the popular will." Philadelphia Whigs protested the "high handed attempt" by Whig officeholders to "frown down an expression of public opinion," while Connecticut Democrats complained that "selfish office-seekers," "managers[,] time-servers[,] and place men" dominated the party and frustrated the popular will. Mississippi's Whigs tried to salvage the election of 1853 by vilifying the corruption of party caucuses and conventions, condemning the tyrannical *"spirit of party"* that ruled the state, and endorsing dissident Democratic candidates already in the field as the "choice of the people." In Ohio, Wisconsin, and elsewhere, independent parties consciously called themselves "People's Parties" to indicate their defiance of domineering wirepullers and reassure voters they would restore republican self-government. As Tennessee's ambitious Andrew Johnson, who was angling for the Democratic gubernatorial nomination in 1853, shrewdly noted, if "there were to be no convention and by general consent . . . the candidate whoever he may be have the track as the *'people's candidate'*, it would be worth many votes to the party."[38]

Usually ignored by historians in their rush to get to the more exciting events of 1854, 1853 was the year that the consensus that had developed between the parties during the previous five years took its most serious toll. In the absence of new issues with widespread salience and in the presence of pervasive antiparty sentiment, that impact took the form of fragmentation and a disintegration of loyalty to the old parties instead of a major voter realignment and the formation of coherent new parties. In the long view, however, even that development was ominous. Although the collapse of popular confidence in the Second American Party System had had very little to do with the sectional conflict between North and South—indeed, it had occurred during a temporary lull in that conflict—that collapse had serious implications for the course the sectional conflict might take. Between the late 1820s and early 1850s, the sectional conflict had been contained and prevented from disrupting the nation. As long as men had placed loyalty to their own party and defeat of the opposing party within their own section ahead of sectional loyalty, neither the North nor the South could be united into a phalanx against the other. More important, as long as men believed that the party political process could protect the values they cherished most—self-government, freedom, and equality—they had continued to look to the normal party political process to defend even sectional interests. By the end of 1853, the danger was that, with faith in the old parties eroded, men might reverse their priorities between party and section and change the methods they used to secure republican government.

Politicians in 1853, however, were not aware of the long-range consequences of what had happened. Their immediate concern was to revive loyalty to the old parties or to build new parties that could attract jaded and distrustful voters. To enlist the alienated and apathetic in such parties and relieve the sense of crisis and helplessness caused by the bankruptcy of the Second Party System, those politicians would not only have to convince the voters that they were agents of the people and not their masters. They would also have to identify some new and powerful conspiracy that seemed capable of usurping government, subverting republican institutions, and enslaving white men. In their quite conscious efforts to find new ways to appeal to the republican beliefs of Americans in the North and South to replace the old ones that events had obviated, ambitious politicians would shape the developments and enlist the passions that led to Civil War.

SIX

Realignment, Reorganization, and Reform, 1854-1856

When the 33rd Congress assembled in December 1853, the returning Whig and Democratic senators and representatives, most of whom had been elected in 1852 or earlier, were aware of the erosion of their parties' voting support at the grassroots level. But they still had hopes of reinvigorating and reinforcing traditional party loyalties as politicians had done for the past 20 years. Loss of popular faith in the Second Party System, after all, had been manifested primarily by abstention, alienation from self-interested and unresponsive politicos, and alarm that republicanism could no longer be protected through the party political process. The Whig and Democratic organizations still existed. No new major party had yet emerged to challenge them for the electorate nor had any issue of sufficient intensity and widespread salience arisen to provoke a massive shifting of voters' allegiances. Hence, reviving the old parties seemed possible if popular confidence that they stood for something distinctive and were therefore useful to voters could be restored. Ironically, the very effort to define distinctive identities and represent certain constituent groups would have the effect of completing the destruction of old party lines, encouraging the creation of powerful new parties, and producing a dramatic voter realignment.

At the end of 1853, many politicians still believed that adroit action could save the old system. Although some Whigs had been so discouraged by their defeat in 1852 that they spoke of abandoning the Whig party altogether to create some new combination, others recommended finding new issues around which to rally the old Whig party. And while Samuel Bowles of Massachusetts and other like-minded Whigs turned to state issues in 1853, it was natural for Whig congressmen at Washington to hope that the new Democratic administration would provide them ammunition for future campaigns, just as actions of the Polk administration had enabled the Whigs to come back in the late 1840s.

The Whigs were also encouraged by Democratic difficulties, The scope of the Democratic triumph in 1852 and in the congressional elections of 1853 presented the Democracy with a special problem. They had a two-thirds majority in the House and one almost as large in the Senate. As the Whig opposition appeared to evaporate, they faced the age-old problem of holding their own party together when there was no strong external force to give it cohesion. Nor did the Democrats have a program to unite them. Tennessee's Andrew Johnson had accurately predicted in December 1852 that "the Whig party is now in fact disbanded leaving the [Democratic] party without external pressure to keep it together." Since the 1852 election had been issue-less, the administration "comes into power to carry out no Set of measures, nothing in fact to bind the party together with except the *'cohesive ties of public plunder'* which will soon give out." Hence, many Whigs thought they could rebound simply by exploiting the inevitable divisions in the Democracy.[1]

Since his inauguration in March 1853, President Franklin Pierce had exacerbated those divisions. Pierce had tried to unify the victorious Democrats by rallying the party behind its platform pledge to enforce the Compromise of 1850, by allocating patronage to all elements who had supported him, and by reviving the expansionist foreign policy of Polk now that domestic issues seemed to be dead. Thus he proclaimed in his Inaugural Address, "The policy of my Administration will not be controlled by any timid forebodings of evil from expansion." The location of the United States rendered "the acquisition of certain possessions not within our jurisdiction eminently important for our protection."[2] To that end, Pierce dispatched James Gadsden to negotiate the purchase of more of northern Mexico, and he envisioned capturing a larger prize, Cuba, although at first he made no overt moves in that direction.

With negotiations going on in secret and Congress out of session during most of 1853, however, public attention was attracted to Pierce's patronage distribution. Pierce faced severe difficulties here, because the Democratic party was divided in almost every state. Sometimes factionalism reflected the conflicting personal ambitions of leaders alone, as in Pennsylvania, but often it was based as well on disagreements over principle or strategy. In many Northern states, for example, Democrats still disagreed over the advisability of forming state-level coalitions with Free-Soilers, while in the South tensions still existed between the Democrats who had fought on opposing sides when Union and Southern Rights parties had been created. Pierce might have attempted to lead the party in the direction he wished by appointing only men who had been firm friends of the Compromise from the beginning, but he chose instead to reward all groups. His conglomerate cabinet revealed his approach. For Attorney General he appointed Caleb Cushing of Massachusetts, a former Whig and staunch foe of those Democrats who favored coalition with the Free-Soilers. On the other hand, the new Secretary of State William L. Marcy had opposed the Fugitive Slave Law and, much to the consternation of the most conservative pro-Compromise Democrats in New York, had co-operated with the returning Barnburners. To offset Marcy, Pierce named Jefferson Davis, erstwhile gubernatorial candidate of the Mississippi Southern Rights party, as Secretary of War. He further antagonized pro-Compromise Democrats in the South by appointing other extremists like Louisiana's Pierre Soulé to foreign posts. To retain the foreign and Catholic vote he had won in 1852, he made James Campbell, the Irish Catholic leader from Philadelphia, Postmaster General, even though many Protestant Democrats resented the choice. Pierce's appointments, in short, were catastrophic; by trying to please everybody, he alienated all factions.

The Democratic party was divided everywhere, but factionalism in New York was especially severe and relevant to impending events. Since the early 1840s, the friends of Van Buren, the Barnburners, and their conservative opponents, known as Hunkers, had divided over economic issues. When they took opposing sides on the Wilmot Proviso, the tensions had intensified. The two factions held separate state conventions in 1847 and 1848, and the Barnburners had stormed out of the national

convention to start the Free Soil party in 1848. When the Van Burenites began to return to the party fold in 1849, the Hunkers divided
between Softshells, who welcomed them back, and Hardshells, who
would deny them any party spoils as punishment for their apostasy. By
1853, three factions could be identified: the Barnburners, now led by
John A. Dix; the Softs, led by Marcy; and the Hards, led by ex-Senator
Daniel S. Dickinson.

Pierce tried to distribute patronage evenly among all three factions
in New York, especially in the New York City Customs House, which
was headed by a Hard. Dickinson and the other Hards, however, were
furious at the appointment of Marcy to the cabinet, of Dix himself to
the subtreasury in New York City, and of scores of other Softs and
Barnburners to lesser posts. They complained so bitterly during 1853
that the administration publicly assailed them. When the Hards and
Softs, who were now buttressed by the Barnburners, nominated separate state tickets in 1853 and allowed the Whigs to win the state election, Pierce openly sided with the Softs by removing the Hard as
Collector of Customs, the most lucrative plum that faction had received, and appointing a Soft in his place.

Relying on Dickinson's influence among his former colleagues in
the Senate, the Hards sought revenge when Pierce's appointees came up
before that body for confirmation. As newspapers openly reported in
1853, the Hards hoped to define a new test of party orthodoxy, inter-
preting the party's pledge to the principles of the Compromise in such
a way as to embarrass anti-Southern Democrats. If Pierce's Barnburner
and Soft appointees did not toe this new line, they would be rejected.
What made this threat ominous is that many Southern Democrats
were just as angry as the Hunkers about Pierce's Northern appointees,
because the only ammunition some Southern Whigs had had during
the 1853 campaigns were taunts that Pierce's appointment of antislavery men showed that the Democrats were unsafe on the slavery
issue. Led by the four most powerful men in the Senate, who were
known as the "F Street Mess" because they boarded together on F
Street—David R. Atchison of Missouri, president pro-tempore of the
Senate and the man who would succeed Pierce if he died because the
Vice-President had died in April 1853; James M. Mason of Virginia,
chairman of the Foreign Relations Committee; Robert M. T. Hunter
of Virginia, chairman of the Finance Committee; and Andrew Pickens
Butler of South Carolina, chairman of the Judiciary Committee—

Southern Democrats were determined to demonstrate their influence in the party and reject Pierce's free-soil appointees if necessary.

By the end of 1853, therefore, many Democrats were just as anxious as the Whigs to find a new issue. The Hunkers and Southerners needed a vehicle they could use to redefine party orthodoxy. Others were simply concerned with provoking interparty conflict so they could regain the loyalty of their disintegrating legions. The publicity given Democratic patronage quarrels only increased the public antagonism toward parties as spoils-oriented machines that seemed to stand for nothing distinctive. From Pittsburgh a Democrat wrote Cushing that the Pennsylvania Democrats were in great disarray. The best way to unite the party, he argued, was for Pierce to initiate a policy "that will raise invective from the other side and compel us to quit our domestic squabbles." Similarly, Stephen A. Douglas was warned in December that unless Pierce "promptly marks out a line of sound national and Democratic policy, and boldly makes it known to the country by unmistakable *action,* it will be utterly impossible for him to save his Administration from total Failure." Nothing but the "boldest and most decided action can turn the current" and prevent the Democratic party from being "shivered to atoms."[3] Instinctively, that is, Democrats recognized that only by provoking interparty conflict with the Whigs, only by dramatically defining themselves as different from their opponents, could they save themselves from fragmentation, indeed, from utter dissolution.

The Congress that met in December 1853 was thus remarkably similar to the one that greeted Zachary Taylor four years earlier. It was the first chance that angry members of the President's party had to respond as a group to his patronage allocation. Democratic and Whig politicians from both sections, moreover, were looking for ways to improve their competitive position in relation to the other party and in relation to rival factions within their own party at home. Southern Whigs were again particularly desperate; their contingent in the House numbered a mere two dozen as compared to 64 Democrats. What was different in 1853, however, was that the new President seemed unwilling to provide any leadership. Unlike Taylor, he offered no concrete program, either foreign or domestic, to the assembled solons in December. It would be up to the divided men of Congress themselves to generate the issues for which they searched, and their efforts would have fateful consequences not only for their parties but for the nation.

Douglas of Illinois, chairman of the Senate Committee on Territories, became the pivotal figure. At this juncture, pressure was growing for Congress to organize the remaining portion of the Louisiana Purchase west of Iowa and Missouri. Settlers were anxious to move in, but they could not legally buy the land until Congress organized a territory, the land was surveyed, and the government put it up for sale. In addition, railroad promoters were anxious to build a line to the Pacific coast, and any central route from St. Louis or Chicago or even a northern route from Minnesota would have to pass through the area and would necessitate its organization. A devout Unionist, Douglas had long championed the development of the West to form a balance wheel between North and South, and he had pushed unsuccessfully for the organization of the Nebraska Territory since 1844. In the previous session of Congress a Nebraska bill had failed to pass the Senate because of Southern opposition. The catch was that, according to the terms of the Compromise of 1820, slavery was "forever prohibited" from the area to be organized, and Southern senators made it clear they would not accept the organization of any more territory on those insulting terms. As early as November 1852, Douglas had written that the Missouri Compromise ban would have to be bypassed in order to get a Nebraska bill through Congress. During 1853, Democratic newspapers in both the North and South called for the organization of the area on the popular sovereignty basis of the Compromise of 1850, and in December 1853 Douglas promised that he would write a Nebraska bill incorporating that principle.[4]

Douglas saw a marvelous opportunity at the end of 1853 to pursue his program and at the same time provide an issue that could unify the Democratic party. Like other Democratic politicians, he had been flooded with letters indicating that the party's voting strength was dissolving and that only active promotion of a distinctively Democratic program could save it. He himself had written shortly before the session began that "the party is in a distracted condition & it requires all our wisdom, prudence, & energy to consolidate its power and perpetuate its principles."[5] Western development through three bills that were linked together in Douglas's mind—organization of Nebraska, a Pacific railroad bill with government land grants, and a homestead bill to encourage settlement—could serve as the necessary program. It would be distinctive because the Whigs had traditionally been reluctant to develop the West.

Douglas realized that he would have to make a concession to the

South by substituting popular sovereignty for the Missouri Compromise prohibition against slavery, but he saw even in that an opportunity to put the Democratic stamp on the territorial bill. The Democrats had long pushed popular sovereignty as the proper solution for slavery in the territories, and the party was pledged to the principles of the 1850 Compromise in their 1852 platform. Why not assert that the solution of 1850 was meant to apply to all territories, not just Utah and New Mexico? A decision by settlers in the territory would prevent sectional strife in Congress, but, even more important from Douglas's point of view, the principle of self-government, freedom from congressional dictation, was a way to reaffirm the Democratic party's commitment to the republican tenet of popular rule just when people were worrying that political parties and government were beyond popular control. As he wrote Howell Cobb in April 1854, "The great principle of self government is at stake, and surely the people of this country are never going to decide that the principle upon which our whole republican system rests is vicious and wrong." Because Whigs opposed it, Western development on the principle of local self-determination would provide the Democrats with a unifying and winning issue, just as Manifest Destiny had done in the 1840s. "The only way to avoid a division of the party is to sustain our principles," Douglas wrote an Illinois Democrat in February. "The principle of this Bill will form the test of Parties, & the only alternative is either to stand with the Democracy or to rally under [the Whig, William H.] Seward."[6]

So convinced, Douglas reported a bill from his committee on January 4, 1854 organizing the entire area north of 36°30' to the Canadian border into a single Nebraska Territory. States eventually formed from it were allowed to prohibit or establish slavery in their new constitutions. In an accompanying report, Douglas compared the Missouri Compromise ban with the prohibition of slavery in the Mexican Cession by Mexican law. Just as Congress had replaced Mexican law with popular sovereignty in 1850, he explained, he was replacing the 1820 ban with the same principle.

Douglas fervently hoped to bypass the Missouri Compromise without direct repeal by simply substituting popular sovereignty for it. Once the slavery question was again on the floor of Congress, however, other groups of politicians who were also searching for issues saw an opportunity to exploit it for partisan advantage. One of these was the New York Hunkers and their Southern allies in the F Street Mess. At the same time, but for different reasons, they also saw advantages in arguing that the Democratic platform meant that popular sovereignty should apply to all territories. Southern Democrats had long been galled by the insult of the Missouri prohibition, and they welcomed a chance to discard it. Here was the pro-Southern standard of Democratic orthodoxy they could use to test Pierce's free-soil appointees when they came up for confirmation. But the Southerners feared that Douglas's original bill was not explicit enough. The 1820 prohibition might still apply to a territory until it was ready for statehood, in which case no slaveholders would enter it. Hence they put pressure on Douglas to clarify the bill, and, on January 10, he reported a version with a new section making it explicit that all questions concerning "slavery in the territories were to be left to the people residing therein." The Hunkers were jubilant. "I am . . . glad," one wrote Douglas, "that there is now a measure before Congress which will test the sincerity of the late Free Soil Democrats whom Gen. Pierce has taken to his bosom." "The Hards or Dickinsonites . . . are exulting," a New York Soft later lamented to Marcy. "They say that they have at last cornered the President with the Nebraska bill, that he will be obliged to dismiss part or all of his Cabinet or be set aside himself."[7]

Even then, however, the Nebraska bill remained a political football, because the Whigs too saw opportunities in it to revive their expiring party. Douglas's revision still allowed the possibility that slaveholders would be prohibited from the territory until there were enough settlers to elect a territorial legislature. If so, the decision of that body against slavery would be foreordained. A number of Whigs spotted that loophole, and, on January 16, Whig Senator Archibald Dixon of Kentucky, after conferring with another Whig senator from Tennessee, offered an amendment repealing the Missouri Compromise ban outright. Later the free-soil Whig William H. Seward of New York would assert that he had put Dixon up to this move.[8] Whether or not Northern and Southern Whigs acted in concert, they clearly saw possibilities of exploiting the slavery-extension issue as they had done in the 1840s. The next presidential election was almost three years away; Whigs who still hoped to save their party were more concerned with the state and congressional elections of 1854 and 1855 when they would not be restrained by the need of national party unity and could run different ways in different sections. By being first to demand explicit repeal of the prohibition of slavery north of 36°30′, Southern Whigs could present themselves as better advocates of Southern Rights than Southern Democrats. Seward and the Northern Whigs, on the other hand, anticipated that by making this Democratic measure as obnoxious as possible to Northern voters, they could generate a Whig comeback in the North in 1854.

Douglas, who had hoped to avoid overt repeal, was dismayed by Dixon's move, but Southern Democratic senators refused to be outflanked by Southern Whigs and put pressure on him to adopt it. An Alabama Democrat introduced a similar amendment in the House about the same time. Douglas gave in, wrote a section that said the Missouri Compromise had been "superceded" by the principles of 1850 and was declared "inoperative," and together with the F Street Mess extorted administration backing for the measure. Pierce, who dreamed of making his mark with an expansionist foreign policy, dared not offend the powerful Southerners who could wreck his program by refusing to ratify his treaties. As the Hunkers had hoped, the bill was made a test of Democratic orthodoxy, and the administration threw all its weight behind it. Despite a growing protest in the North, it was pushed through the Senate in March and the House in May and signed into law by Pierce on May 30, 1854. The Kansas-Nebraska Act in its final form created two territories instead of one, avoided direct repeal of the Missouri Compromise but declared it "inoperative and void," and dropped the section that explicitly gave territorial settlers all power over slavery for the vaguer wording of the measures of 1850, which left territorial power over "domestic institutions" subject to the Constitution. This last change was crucial. Southerners doubted the constitutional power of territorial legislatures to prohibit slavery. The clause thus perpetuated the artful ambiguity by which Northern Democrats would argue that the decision could be made in the territorial stage and Southern Democrats would argue that it could not be made until the territory was ready to apply for statehood.

The Kansas-Nebraska Act had been shaped largely by the divergent intentions of politicians who had specifically partisan and not sectional goals in mind. Most important were Douglas and Seward, who saw the bill as a chance to revive the flagging Second Party System by creating a new issue that Whigs and Democrats could once again fight about on party lines. The bill was meant to reinforce the lines dividing the old parties, not create new ones. Over a year after Douglas introduced his bill, a perceptive Kentucky editor analyzed its origins precisely.[9]

He must be blind indeed to the logic of events during the last few years, who has not observed the decadence of party

> spirit, and a gradual approximation to a coincidence of measures, destined in all probability to render a reconstruction of issues essential to the separate existence of the two parties. It was the pressure of this necessity for agitating and dividing topics, that induced Mr. Douglas to spring upon the country the Nebraska bill, involving the repeal of the Missouri Compromise. The politician constructed a new arena for party gladiators at the expense of the repose and temper of the nation.

In their hopes of resurrecting old party lines and regalvanizing voter support with the Kansas-Nebraska Act, however, Whig and Democratic politicians had made a serious miscalculation. The Act permanently severed the Northern and Southern wings of the Whig party and eventually obliterated what remained of it in the South. Except for those politicians who had specific and narrow partisan goals in early 1854, most Southerners were at first apathetic about the bill. Few saw any real chance of actually taking slavery to Kansas, and many deplored the reignition of sectional agitation, which had been dampened for several years. But the growth and ferocity of Northern assaults on the bill and on Southerners during the spring of 1854 changed the Southern perspective. Whatever they expected to gain, passage of the act became a symbol of Southern honor, just as resistance to the Proviso had been. Northern attacks defined a new Southern orthodoxy that left no room for dissent, and few Southern Whigs dared openly oppose it. Thus, in the Senate, only John Bell of Tennessee voted against the bill, while seven other Southern Whigs voted for it. In the House the Georgia Whig Alexander H. Stephens played a major role in expediting its passage, and only 7 of 24 Southern Whigs, all but one from the upper South, voted against it. Indeed, because most of the opposition to the bill came from Northern Whigs, the very name "Whig" became a grave political liability in the South. It stood as a challenge to the new Southern orthodoxy, and, in 1855, when the next major elections were held in most Southern states, foes of the Democrats would be forced to organize under a new banner.

In contrast, passage of the Kansas-Nebraska Act ignited an explosion of rage in the North, an outpouring of wrath that was almost universal. Because the law seemed to provide an opportunity for slavery to spread to Kansas, which was directly adjacent to slaveholding regions in Missouri, it reinforced all of the existing reasons for Northern hostility to slavery expansion—moral antipathy to black slavery, fear that the Northern free labor economy would be prevented from growing, racism, and jealousy of the Slave Power. But Northern animosities were much more intense in 1854 because the areas involved were not distant like New Mexico but contiguous to populated states. Many Northerners, especially Midwestern farmers, had a real interest in moving to Kansas and Nebraska, and the territorial issue thus had more immediacy than in the 1840s. More important, the area involved had been promised to free soil for thirty-five years. The overthrow of the Missouri Compromise seemed like concrete evidence of a genuine Slave Power conspiracy to use its domination of the national government to spread slavery against the will of the majority of Americans.

For a while it appeared that this new excitement could be channeled into old party lines and that the expectations of Douglas and certainly of Seward would prove accurate. Not a single Northern Whig had voted for the bill in Congress, while half of the Northern Democrats had supported it, and the Pierce administration had given the bill a Democratic imprimatur. Northern Whigs like Seward and Abraham Lincoln of Illinois jubilantly viewed the law as the issue they needed to revive the Whig party in the congressional and state elections of 1854 and 1855 when they could run unfettered by their Southern wing. All Northern Whigs, even the conservatives who insisted on enforcement of the Compromise of 1850, had always opposed slavery expansion; during the spring of 1854, Whig and Democratic politicians throughout the North reported, in the words of a Pennsylvanian, "The Whig party of the North is, this day, stronger than at any former period." "I think a mistake had been made in this Nebraska business," wailed a New York Democrat. "The effect will be to consolidate the Whig party in the North & divide the Democrats." Whigs and Democrats alike predicted that the Whigs would elect the next president, probably Seward, because of the law, and an anti-Seward Silver Gray in New York gloomily recognized the new prestige the revival of the slavery issue had given the Sewardites: "The Nebraska Swindle had driven National & Sectional Whigs into the same camp where they must mess together. . . . The Whigs will be united . . . and will swallow anything, on account of Nebraska."[10]

In 1854 Whig parties in Maine, Connecticut, Massachusetts, Pennsylvania, New York, Illinois, and elsewhere confidently campaigned as an anti-Nebraska party through which angry Northern voters could repudiate the Democracy. Those Whig assaults often rallied Democratic

149

voters to their former standard, even when they disliked the Nebraska Act itself. Referring to the fortunes of Pennsylvania's Democratic Governor William Bigler, who was running for reelection, a Democrat reported in September, "The Whigs are boasting, and that is driving many Democrats to his support who had made up their minds not to vote at all, and others who had intended to vote against him, that will now vote for him when the day of election arrives." Similarly, a Free-Soiler fearful that the revival of old party animosities would divide the North predicted from New York that when the Whigs tried to exploit the Nebraska issue against the Democrats, the "hunker democrats will use the hatred to Whigs to reunite their party & then claim a popular verdict in favor of their fraudulent measures."[11]

The state and congressional elections of 1854, however, did not bear out predictions, whether optimistic or pessimistic, that the Nebraska issue would rekindle the old loyalties of Whig and Democratic voters. Although the apathy of 1853 was abruptly disspelled, the fragmentation of two-party lines evident that year continued at an accelerated rate. The Democrats suffered crushing defeats, losing 66 congressional seats in the North alone, control of most state legislatures, and most gubernatorial chairs that were contested. Many former Democratic voters had clearly joined the opposition, if only temporarily. But they had not realigned behind the Whigs; while the Democrats lost, the Whigs failed to resurrect their party as so many had expected. In most Midwestern states Whigs abandoned their old organization for new fusion anti-Nebraska coalitions, called "People's," "Independent," or "Republican" parties, that were bewilderingly heterogeneous in their makeup. As an Indiana Democrat reported in words that could be extended to other states, "The Whig party, *as a party,* are entirely disbanded. They have not *as a party,* brought out a single candidate."[12] In Maine, where the Whig party continued to run as an anti-Nebraska vehicle, its voters if not its leaders joined the fusion movement. But even in old Eastern Whig strongholds like Massachusetts, Connecticut, New York, and Pennsylvania, where the Whigs did not face significant rival anti-Nebraska parties, their showing was pathetic. Even when they won, it was in multiparty races where they received only a fraction of their former vote.[13] Whig support declined further in 1855 when many Eastern organizations joined the Republicans, and by 1856 Whig organizations in Northern states were virtually extinct.

A combination of reasons account for the dismal Whig performance and the final disruption of the Second Party System in the North. In the Midwest and upper New England, new anti-Southern organizations immediately challenged the Whigs for the anti-Democratic vote. Varying in name, those anti-Nebraska coalitions were much more attractive to Free-Soilers and angry Democrats seeking a new party than the old Whig party, because the Whigs still bore the stigma of their Southern allies who had helped pass the Nebraska Act and because long-time opponents of the Whigs simply could not stomach joining that party. Anger at Democratic actions did not make them pro-Whig. On the other hand, the Whigs had usually been in such a minority in the areas in which fusion parties were formed that they readily discarded their old standard in hopes of finally sharing in a victory over the Democrats. Exclusively Northern in their support and often started by Free-Soilers, the new organizations were much more vigorously anti-Southern than the Whigs, who still hoped to win the presidency as a national party in 1856, dared to be. They developed a powerful appeal by exploiting preexisting fears that the Republic was endangered, identifying the Slave Power conspiracy that had been revealed by the Kansas-Nebraska Act as the major threat to it, and calling on Northerners to join a crusade to crush the Slave Power and save the Republic.

Here is the key to understanding why Northern antagonism toward the South was so much more powerful in the 1850s than in the 1840s and why, as a result, the sectional conflict had more potential both as a partisan weapon in different sections and for disrupting the Union than it had ever had before. By 1854, many more people were prepared to accept the existence of a Slave Power plot that abolitionists and Free-Soilers had long warned of. Equally important, they were much more fearful of its consequences than they had ever been. Developments antedating the introduction of the Nebraska bill had created a sense of crisis about the viability of republicanism, and, as had been the case since the Revolution, anxiety about the preservation of liberty, equality, and self-government was easily translated into fear of powerful conspiracies that threatened the fragile republic. This is not to say that Northern anger at the South was in any sense an invention of politicians and not authentic. It is to say, instead, that for over thirty years the fundamental purpose of political action had been to protect and perfect republicanism and that, by 1852 and 1853, people were alarmed that they could no longer do so. Thus, opposition to the Nebraska Act and the Slave Power conspiracy provided a cathartic opportunity to restore to political activity its basic purpose, to regain a sense that vigilant citizens could save republican government. Precisely because Northerners had *already* lost faith in their political parties as champions that could adequately protect republicanism from threats to it, precisely because they were *already* so concerned about dangers to republican values for reasons that had almost nothing to do with the sectional conflict itself, they were extraordinarily receptive to rhetorical exposures of tyrannical conspiracies that subverted the liberty and self-government they sensed was lost and eager to enlist in crusades against them.

It was the weakness of faith in the responsiveness of the old two-party system, in short, that gave sectional propaganda such resonance and not the strength of sectional animosity that weakened faith in the two-party system. Parties that promised to resist the supposed aggressions of the South against Northern rights, parties that insisted on humiliating the Slave Power itself, could restore faith in the efficacy of the party political process by convincing Northerners that they could once again save the republic through political action. Because politicians who wished to exploit the revived sectional conflict to build a new Northern party recognized this fact, the major way they would politicize that conflict from 1854 until the election of Abraham Lincoln in 1860 was by constantly warning Northerners of the continued threat of a Slave Power plot to subjugate the North to its tyranny and oppression. What was at stake, those politicians iterated, was not just the wrong of black slavery or even the possibility of its spread, bad as that might be. What was ultimately at stake in the sectional conflict was the enslavement of white Americans in the North by despotic slaveholders bent on crushing their liberties, destroying their equality in the nation, and overthrowing the republican principle of majority rule. Only by supporting Northern parties that resisted the aggressive slavocracy instead of parties like the Whigs and Democrats that abetted it by meekly cooperating with the South could freedom be saved.

The first to articulate this powerful theme and to exploit its potential for partisan purposes were a small group of Free-Soilers in Congress who, in January 1854, issued an "Appeal of the Independent Democrats in Congress to the People of the United States." The signers included Senator Salmon P. Chase of Ohio and Senator Charles Sumner of Massachusetts, who had earlier been elected by Free Soil-Democratic coalitions that had since collapsed during the quiescence over slavery in 1852 and 1853, and four representatives who had narrowly won their seats in three-way contests in 1852. All were looking for a new issue to revive anti-Southern agitation, to provoke the reorganization of parties along sectional lines that they had been seeking since the 1840s, and, incidentally, thereby to perpetuate their careers. Citing their "duty to warn [their] constituents, whenever imminent danger menaces the freedom of our institutions," they vilified the Nebraska bill as "a gross violation of a sacred pledge; as a criminal betrayal of precious rights; as part and parcel of an atrocious plot to exclude from a vast unoccupied region immigrants from the Old World and free laborers from our own States, and convert it into a dreary region of despotism inhabited by masters and slaves." It was a "bold scheme against American liberty" whose success would subjugate the whole country "to the yoke of a slaveholding despotism." "Shall a plot against humanity and democracy so monstrous, and so dangerous to the interests of liberty throughout the world, be permitted to succeed?" "Not without the deepest dishonor and crime can the free States acquiesce in the demand. . . .We warn you that the dearest interests of freedom and the Union are in imminent peril." Even if the bill should pass, "we shall go home to our constituents, erect anew the standard of freedom, and call on the people to come to the rescue of the country from the domination of slavery."[14]

By May the Free-Soil newspaper in Washington urged all Northern congressmen who had voted against the bill—Whigs, Democrats, and Free-Soilers alike—to call "upon the people to disregard obsolete issues, old prejudices, mere party names, and rally as one man for the re-establishment of liberty and the overthrow of the Slave Power." In Michigan, where the disparate foes of slavery extension did abandon old party names and unite in a new coalition that called itself Republican, the first state platform adopted in July 1854 made explicit the rationale of the new party. After denouncing Negro slavery as "a relic of barbarism," calling for defiance of the Fugitive Slave Act, and insisting that Congress prohibit slavery expansion to check the "unequal representation" of the South, it declared that the purpose of the Kansas-Nebraska Act was to "give to the Slave States such a decided and practical preponderance in all measures of government as shall reduce the North . . . to the mere province of a few slaveholding Oligarchs of the South—to a condition too shameful to be contemplated." It included, finally, a ringing justification for the name "Republican."[15]

> That in view of the necessity of battling for the first prin-
> ciples of republican government, and against the schemes
> of aristocracy the most revolting and oppressive with which
> the earth was ever cursed, or man debased, we will co-oper-
> ate and be known as Republicans until the contest be ter-
> minated.

Using this potent appeal, the Republican party spread quickly in the Midwest where the Whigs had always been weak, but it did not emerge immediately in the old Whig strongholds of the East where the Whigs themselves tried to run as the anti-Nebraska party. Yet, as noted, the Whigs failed to retain their former strength in the East. There, more than the vitality of anti-Southernism accounted for their demise. The very unanimity of anti-Nebraska sentiment helped to frustrate Whig hopes for a comeback. Unlike the Midwest where state Democratic parties openly endorsed the Nebraska Act, hoping to capitalize on the genuine appeal of popular sovereignty as Douglas had envisioned, Democrats in old Whig strongholds, especially New York and Penn-sylvania, assiduously tried to defuse the issue by ignoring it entirely, by refusing to endorse the Act, by denying its relevance to state and local elections, and often by attacking the measure outright in local Democratic newspapers. Because almost everyone was against the Nebraska Act, the Whigs often found it difficult to draw clear party lines on the issue.

No matter how much excitement an issue provokes, it cannot cause a voter realignment—as Republicans hoped—or even reinforce former loyalty—as Whigs hoped—unless it polarizes large blocs of the electorate against each other and unless competing parties adopt stances at op-posite poles of opinion so that it makes sense for voters to support one party instead of another to express opinion on that issue. The Nebraska Act had repolarized North against South, but within certain Northern states, it was often difficult to translate sectional antagonism into party terms. Half of the Northern Democratic congressmen, after all, had voted against the act, and in many congressional and gubernatorial elections, it was difficult to see any difference between the parties on that issue. It must be remembered that for many Americans state governments, especially state legislatures, were more important than Congress, and the slavery issue did not seem germane to the battles to control them. As even an anti-Democratic newspaper in Buffalo as-serted:

> *Every person of common understanding knows that the*
> *election tomorrow in this State, turns about as much upon*
> *the Nebraska issue as upon the question of the opium trade*
> *in China, and that one will be about as much affected as the*
> *other by the result. Ninety-nine out of every hundred*
> *voters will think as much of Nebraska when they go to the*
> *polls as of Timbuctoo.*[16]

At the same time, Northern voters in those states found it much easier to make a choice between the Democrats and their foes in 1854 and 1855 on other issues that mattered as much and often more to them than slavery expansion because state governments could address them—temperance and nativism. "The Nebraska-Kansas bill is obsolete, or in the language of its famous Author 'is superceded & inoperative' in comparison with these immediate and practical questions," reported an upstate New Yorker by August 1854.[17] Although those ethno-cultural matters clearly hurt the Democrats, who were identified with liquor interests, foreigners, and Catholics, however, they did not help the Whigs, who were no longer trusted on those issues because of their evasions and open courtship of wets and immigrants in 1852 and 1853. Sewardite antislavery Whigs were especially anathema to anti-Catholics because of Seward's long pro-Catholic record.

As a result, the salience of temperance and nativism increased the tendency toward fragmentation of the old two-party system instead of allowing its resurrection or the formation of new party lines on the basis of the slavery or sectional issue alone. Thus, in Maine, dries as well as dedicated free-soilers bolted the Whigs and Democrats for the new Republican party, which took a forthright stand on both issues. Thus a separate temperance candidate siphoned off a fifth of the popular vote in the Connecticut gubernatorial election of 1854, frustrating the comeback of Whigs who ran on the Nebraska issue. In New York, too, the temperance issue foiled the hopes of Seward and Weed that they could revive their party on the slavery issue alone. In the spring of 1854 Democratic Governor Horatio Seymour vetoed a prohibition law, thereby polarizing dries who abhorred his action against wets who applauded it. Because Seymour was running for reelection, he seemed assured of getting the antiprohibition vote if the Whigs made an issue of the veto. And because the Soft wing of the Democracy to which Seymour belonged was also denouncing the Nebraska Act, temperance seemed a much clearer issue on which the Whigs could campaign. Yet the temperance issue posed a twofold problem for Seward and Weed. First, the duo was personally disliked by temperance Whigs because of Seward's reputed fondness for potables and their well-known contempt for temperance advocates, but prohibitionist sentiment was widespread among the most dedicated antislavery Whigs in upstate New York, precisely the constituency on which Seward and Weed had always depended. Second, the temperance men threatened to bolt unless the Whigs openly endorsed prohibition, but such a platform would undoubtedly drive anti-Nebraska Whigs who opposed prohibition into the camp of Seymour. Recognizing that the anti-Nebraska Whig vote was bound to be divided, Weed gambled that the dries outnumbered the wets and secured the Whig gubernatorial nomination for an antislavery Whig who was also the state's leading prohibitionist politician. Even that concession, however, could not rally the Whig legions that opposed Nebraska and favored prohibition.[18]

The real problem for the Whigs in New York and elsewhere was not so much the temperance issue, embarrassing as that might be, but the emergence of a new political party, the Know Nothings or Americans, which exploited the growing animosity toward Catholics and foreigners and which rivaled both the Whigs and the Republicans for the anti-Democratic vote. In New York and other states the Know Nothings attracted sincere antislavery men and sincere prohibitionists, but they placed priority on the purported menace to republican institutions posed by immigrants and especially by Catholics. Like the Republicans who appeared simultaneously, the Know Nothings benefited from preexisting apprehensions that republicanism was ailing, but they offered a different diagnosis of the debilitating disease and prescribed a different remedy to cure it.

The party evolved from a superpatriotic secret fraternal society known as the Order of the Star Spangled Banner, which had been founded in 1849 and resembled Masonry in its hierarchical degrees of membership, initiation rites, and secret oaths of allegiance. Membership was usually restricted to native-born Protestants, and members were sworn to obey the will of the local lodges and keep their affiliation secret. When asked by outsiders if they belonged, they were to reply "I know nothing" about it, and hence the popular sobriquet for the organization. From the start the order hoped to proscribe Catholics and foreigners from the political process by pressuring existing parties to nominate only native American Protestants for public office, but it did not really grow until 1853 and 1854 when, under the dynamic leadership of a New Yorker named James Barker, lodges were established throughout New York State, the rest of the North, and even the South. As membership grew, an elaborate structure was created in pyramid fashion from local councils or lodges to citywide and county councils to state councils, and finally to a grand national council composed of seven delegates from each state council. By June 1854, the national council had adopted a national charter that defined membership requirements and postulated oaths for various degrees of membership. Although the secrecy and fluctuating membership of the order makes exact calculation of its total strength impossible, contemporary estimates ranged from 800,000 to 1,500,000 nationally.

Beginning in late 1853 and early 1854, the order entered politics secretly by backing its own members or other candidates from the tickets of existing parties who shared its desire to restrict officeholding to native-born Protestants and to prevent immigrants from voting by lengthening the naturalization period for aliens and allowing only citizens to vote. In those early elections, Know Nothings frequently astounded political observers by keeping their choices secret and electing men for local offices whom the regular parties did not even know were in the race. "Nearly everybody appears to have gone altogether deranged on Nativism here," shrieked a worried Democrat from central Pennsylvania early in 1854. "There are too many of our young men in it, sons of Democrats, that dont care, have no idea of the rong [sic] that they are doing to the country," complained another from Philadelphia, while a Connecticut Democrat moaned that the Know Nothings "are making havoc with the Democratic party here." But Whigs, too, flocked to the order, which was as hostile to the old Whig leadership as it was to the Democrats. The Whig stronghold in the "Burned Over District" of upstate New York was described as "very badly infected with Knownothingism," while another Whig called the "American feeling . . . the lever to move mountains" throughout the state. The stunning spread of the movement was constantly described as a "tornado," a "hurricane," "a freak of political insanity." The presence of the Know Nothings and the palpable interest of voters in issues besides Nebraska caused the initial confident predictions of a clear referendum on the Nebraska Act to give way to widespread lamentations about the utter confusion into which party lines had been thrown. "The 'Know Nothing' fever is epidemic here," wrote a Pennsylvanian. "We are without chart or compass and must for the present give up our vocation of political 'seer.'" Similarly, a New Yorker reported, "There are so many elements that are to be mixed up in the coming contest that no one can predict the result," while a loyal Sewardite despaired to Weed that "there never was a time when party ties seemed of so little account. The new questions have destroyed everything like party discipline, and many staunch old Whigs are floating off they don't know where."[19]

Such forecasts of disarray proved accurate; there was no clear realignment of voters or reorganization of parties on the basis of the slavery issue in 1854 and 1855. In many parts of the country, the Know Nothings were the fastest growing party. Shifting anti-Democratic voters realigned behind them, not behind the Whigs or the Republicans. In 1854, Know Nothings captured the governorship, almost all the seats in the legislature, and all of the congressional seats in Massachusetts, even though both the Whigs and the Free-Soilers were trying to exploit anti-Nebraska sentiment. They made impressive showings in congressional elections in New York, New Jersey, Pennsylvania, and elsewhere, and they also ran strongly in statewide races. By 1855, when they often operated openly as the American party, they controlled all the New England states except Vermont and Maine, and the Know Nothings, not the rival Republicans, were the major anti-Democratic party in the Middle Atlantic states and California. In direct contests that year with the Republicans, who tried to run on the anti-slavery issue alone, they defeated them in Massachusetts and New York and overwhelmed them in Pennsylvania. Elsewhere in the Northeast the Know Nothings were so strong that the Republican party had not yet organized, and even in the Midwest where the Republicans did become the major anti-Democratic party, they did so partly because they merged openly with the Know Nothings against the administration. Equally important, Know Nothingism spread to the slave states. In 1855 they carried Texas, Kentucky, and Maryland, where a dramatic realignment occurred as former Democratic areas went Know Nothing while former Whig strongholds became Democratic. Inheriting much of the Whig vote and attracting converts, the nativists also provided strong competition to the Democrats in Virginia, Tennessee, Georgia, Alabama, Mississippi, and Louisiana. Because the Americans had strength everywhere, many predicted that they, and not the Republicans, would become the next major party and would elect their presidential candidate in 1856.

Two aspects about the Know Nothing performance require emphasis. First, in many parts of the North, no matter how outraged voters were at the Nebraska bill, they were even more worried about Catholics and foreigners. "This election has demonstrated that, by a majority, Roman Catholicism is feared more than American slavery," wrote a New Yorker in 1854; a dejected Massachusetts Republican bitterly reported after the 1855 election, "The Election is most disastrous. . . . The people will not confront the issues at present. They want a Paddy hunt & on a Paddy hunt they will go." "At the bottom of all this is a deep seated religious question—prejudice if you please, which nothing can withstand," wailed a Philadelphia Democrat in the spring of 1854. "Our party is made to bear the sin of *Catholicism* and every other evil sentiment promulgated in the country." "How people do hate Catholics," exclaimed a Cincinnati Whig after the state and congressional elections there in 1854, "and what happiness it was to thousands to have a chance to show it in what seemed like a lawful and patriotic manner." Second, it is clear that the emergence of the Know Nothings and not the slavery issue destroyed state Whig parties in their old Northern strongholds, even when they ran as an anti-Nebraska party. "The old northern Whig party has ceased to exist—it is swallowed up routed, and merged into the great 'American Union party,'" exulted a Philadelphia Know Nothing. "If we are in a fix," wrote a Bay State Democrat, "how is it with the Whigs? Look here in Massachusetts; who has the ascendancy here—why not the *Whigs*—nor the free soilers—but literally the Know Nothings. . . : If there be anything in the idea that misery loves company, we surely have company enough in our overthrow."[20] Only after Know Nothing incursions into Whig ranks had clearly aborted a Whig comeback did antislavery Whigs like Seward, Weed, and Lincoln join the new Republican party.

Because the Know Nothings were so palpably important in contributing to the final disruption of both old parties, the voter realignment, and the party reorganization of the mid-1850s, one must account for their phenomenal rise in 1854 and 1855 and their equally sudden demise, which allowed the Republicans to become the major anti-Democratic party by the end of 1856. Clearly, the Know Nothings benefited from the fears engendered by increasing numbers of foreigners. Immigration surged to its highest annual levels between 1851 and 1854, and nativists constantly charged that the disproportionate numbers of foreigners filling hospitals, poorhouses, and prisons proved that Europe was dumping its paupers and criminals on American shores. Moreover, severe economic dislocation simultaneously lent credibility to assertions that cheap immigrant competition was endangering the welfare of American workers. The national economy had boomed since 1849 because of the California gold strikes and foreign investment in railroads, but there was a sharp recession during the last half of 1854 and first third of 1855, precisely the time when Know Nothing membership soared. Unemployment suddenly accompanied the inflation of prices caused by new money supplies. Compounding this general problem was a drought in the summer of 1854 that brought trade on the Ohio River and its tributaries to a standstill. Workers connected with the river trade in Pittsburgh, Cincinnati, Louisville, and St. Louis may have lost their jobs or had their wages lowered. Know Nothings were strong in the river-front wards of those cities, and it seems reasonable that unemployed or poorly paid workingmen who faced higher prices vented their wrath on immigrants whom they blamed for their economic woes.[21]

Furthermore, the massive railroad construction between 1849 and 1854, especially the completion of the four trunklines between the Atlantic coast and the Midwest, abruptly transformed patterns of commerce, methods of manufacturing, and what a New York official called "the social conditions of our people." Relatively isolated and homogeneous communities were now brought into contact with men of different backgrounds as railroads and the telegraph increased communication among towns and as armies of railroad workers arrived with the tracks in area after area. From Pennsylvania, Virginia, Illinois, New York, Tennessee, and elsewhere, nativists complained that the immigrant construction crews provided the Democrats with a powerful and illegal floating vote. As railroads began to take trade away from water routes and to alter manufacturing and commercial relationships, many workers confronted with high prices probably lost their jobs. Some towns along rivers and canals were bypassed entirely, but railroads proved mixed blessings to the communities they came to as well. Through lines destroyed the jobs of men in former transshipment centers. Midwestern merchants and manufacturers faced increasing competition from the East and had to cut wages or lay off workers to keep up. Eastern manufacturers, on the other hand, now that railroads opened up fast, all-weather transportation to Midwestern markets, began to mechanize their factories and use interchangeable parts on a large scale in the 1850s—developments that changed the regimen of new factory hands, caused technological unemployment among skilled workmen, and threatened to reduce others to wage-earner status.

In sum, the railroad building between 1849 and 1854 produced wrenching structural changes in the economies of many communities, either by displacing men employed in the old businesses—whether they be river and canal men or artisans not employed in the new factories—or by eliminating the geographical advantages certain groups had enjoyed by ending isolation and subjecting smaller communities to the economic domination of larger cities, which now reached them by railroad. Such disorientation increased prejudice and frustration and caused men to lash out at Catholic immigrants.

Adjustment to new economic conditions has often caused an intensification of ethnic identities and intergroup animosities, and it is likely that the economic and social tribulations of native Protestant workingmen and farmers were translated into hatred of immigrants. What quantitative and qualitative evidence we have about Know Nothing membership indicates that Know Nothingism was overwhelmingly a movement of the poor and middle classes. Know Nothing sympathizers described the membership as honest but poor workingmen, artisans, and mechanics, while their foes characterized them as a rabble or thugs. In cities, workers and many from the huge floating population that drifted from one town to the next in search of employment, men who suffered most from the traumatic economic changes of the decade, flocked to Know Nothing lodges. After blaming "the vast influx of immigrants" for lowering wages, raising the price of food and rent, and inflicting "a thousand evils . . . [on] the working classes," a New York nativist despaired, "It is true that much of the evil exists in Cities, but are cities not part of the U.S.? and are American *mechanics* to be borne down, crushed, or driven to western wilds?"[22] No better statement can be found to show that to many in the North, the major threat in 1854 was not that the presence of black slaves might keep them out of Kansas and Nebraska, but that the presence of immigrant Catholics in the East might force them to go there. Along with farmers who feared the cultural menace of alien groups and the residents of small towns suddenly swamped by outside forces, these disoriented groups struck out at Catholic immigrants on whom much of the disorder and dislocation in society could be blamed.

It was indeed the Catholicism of most immigrants and the palpably growing political power of the Catholic Church, once immigrants voted in large numbers, that stimulated the initial spread of Know Nothingism. Know Nothings made the apparent perversion of American political processes by the growing foreign and Catholic participation the chief justification for their secret political action. Specific "aggressions" by the Catholic hierarchy in 1853 and 1854 provided nativists with concrete evidence of a papal plot to control America. Led by Archbishop John Hughes of New York, Catholic bishops around the country began to demand ecclesiastical ownership of church property —that is, a transfer of the physical properties of Catholic churches from lay trustees to the clergy. Protestants viewed this as an attempt to increase the economic power of the Church, and when the Pope sent a special nuncio named Gaetano Bedini to persuade certain individual congregations who refused to sell to the Church, propagandists labeled Bedini the vanguard of a papal invasion. Even more menacing were the continuing efforts by the Catholic clergy to agitate for, and by Democratic legislators who represented them to introduce, laws that would stop Bible reading in public schools and obtain public funding for parochial schools. Additional evidence of the political clout of Catholics came with the increased immigrant vote for Pierce in 1852 and his appointment of the Irish Catholic Campbell to his cabinet. Not only Nativists and Whigs, but Protestant Democrats were appalled by such blatant subserviency. Even in 1853 a Philadelphia Democrat warned Governor William Bigler that "the better part of the Democratic party . . . will not be led by the Irish vote, or contented with it either. If persisted in, the Party will, as large as it is, . . . *cave in.* This Irish influence must & will be put down."[2 3]

Exploiting such resentment, Know Nothings skillfully employed the idiom of republicanism, as had the Republicans, to portray *their* party as a necessary reform crusade to save the Republic just at the time when so many people were increasingly anxious about its survival. The Catholic Church instead of the Slave Power was identified as the chief subverter of the Republic. It was assailed as a "despotic faith" whose hierarchical government "is diametrically opposed to the genius of American Republicanism." "Yet this Church, relying on the 'profligacy of our politicians,' has freely declared its intention (being an alien), to substitute the mitre for our liberty cap, and blend the crozier with the stars and stripes!" In its schools a "crafty priesthood" taught "anti-republican . . . sentiments," while its attempt to divide the public school fund would subvert "the very Citadel of Republican strength in the free education of youth and the consequent independence of mind." Know Nothings demanded a lengthening of the naturalization period for immigrants in order to "guarantee the three vital principles of Republican Government—*Spiritual Freedom, Free Bible,* and *Free*

162

Schools—thereby promoting the great work of Americanizing America." Because the papal plot was so dangerous, one group summarized:

> *it therefore becomes the duty of every American and naturalized protestant citizen throughout the Union, to use his utmost exertions to aid the cause by organizing and freeing the country from that monster which has long since made his appearance in our midst and is only waiting for the hour to approach to plant its flag of tyranny, persecution, and oppression among us.*[24]

Most important, the Know Nothings specifically linked the foreign and Catholic menace to the growing disgust with politicians and political parties as corrupt, tyrannical, unresponsive, and useless that had been the first manifestation of the loss of faith in the efficacy of the political process to secure republicanism. The Know Nothing movement was the culmination of the revolt against politics as usual that had appeared in 1852 and 1853, and in their attempt to exploit antiparty sentiment the Know Nothings initially had a great advantage over those politicians who stressed the Nebraska issue instead. Although Republicans could identify the Slave Power plot as the reason why the national government was no longer responsive to the Northern majority, Know Nothings provided a persuasive diagnosis of what had gone wrong with local and state government everywhere. And, until the presidential election of 1856, when sectional control of the national government seemed directly at stake, reform of government at those lower and more immediate levels seemed more important to many voters.

The political process had been perverted, Know Nothings argued, because Catholics and foreigners had infiltrated it and usurped political power from Americans and because toadying Whig and Democratic politicians had prostituted themselves to those foreign elements instead of truly representing Americans. As early as 1852, a Democrat complained from Pittsburgh that Catholics had seized control of the local Democratic machinery and that "the movement was made in so open and unblushing a manner . . . that I have heard some of our best men say they would never again attend a primary meeting unless some different plan can be fixed upon, in choosing delegates." By 1854 another credulous Democrat reported that Catholics were boasting "that they are, through the instrumentality of their Bishops and Priests entirely united, and that the visit of Nuncio Bendini . . . is intended to form among them an organization so perfect that they will act as a unit . . . in all our future elections." From Tennessee the Know Nothing Parson Brownlow explained that the Catholics had accumulated such political power because "associated with them for the purpose . . . of securing the Catholic vote, are the worst class of American politicians, designing demagogues, selfish office-seekers, and bad men, calling themselves *Democrats* and 'Old-Line Whigs.'" A comprehensive statement of the combination of grievances producing Know Nothingism appeared in a letter from a Detroit judge to Supreme Court Justice John McLean in 1855.

> You know that for the last quarter of a century political traders and gamesters have so manufactured public opinion, & so directed party organization, that our Union has been endangered, & bad men elevated to place & power, contrary to the true sentiment of the People. And there seemed to be no hope for us. Both parties courted what was called the foreign vote; & the highest aspirants of the Senate, to ensure success, strove which could pay more homage to a foreign Prince, whose ecclesiastical subjects, constituted so large a portion of this imperium in imperio. The Papal Power at Rome, apprised fully of this state of things, gave direction to her vassal priesthood, to use their supposed power for the propaganda files, and hence the attack on our school systems in Cincinnati, New York, Baltimore, and Detroit. I give thanks to God, that they commenced the warfare at the time they did, and that their plan was discerned and defeated.

After condemning the Whigs and Democrats for fearing to offend the Pope during this crisis, he rejoiced that good men had united secretly so "that *secret jesuitism* in America might be triumphantly met by a *secret American movement*—the leading object of which—is good and competent men for public stations, and the preservation of the freedom of conscience and the right of private interpretation of the scriptures."[2 5]

Everywhere, indeed, politicians in and outside the order attributed both the failure of the old parties, especially the Whigs, to reinforce former party lines with the new issues of 1854 and the phenomenal rise of the Know Nothings to the pervasive disgust with wirepulling politicians who stood for nothing and the widespread desire for reform that would replace them with men who represented the people. From Connecticut, Gideon Welles, an arch-foe of the Know Nothings, perceptively analyzed the Whig failure.

> It has been one of the mistakes of Seward and his friends [in New York] —of the Whig leaders in Massachusetts—and in this state also—that the Whig party would gain what the administration lost. The truth is there is a general feeling to throw off both the old organizations and their intrigues and machinery.

"Thousands flocked into the order, not that they approved its principles, but for the purpose of relieving themselves from the obligations and abuses of the old organizations. To rebuke these, to defeat these, to rid the country of what men no longer believed useful appears to have been the mission and purpose of the order." From Massachusetts the Republican Charles Sumner was more trenchant in explaining Know Nothing success in 1854. "The explanation is simply this. The people were tired of the old parties & they have made a new channel." A New York Know Nothing newspaper interpreted the party's attraction in similar terms. The people "saw parties without any apparent difference contending for power, for the *sake of power*. They saw politics made a profession, and public plunder an employment." From Pittsburgh a Know Nothing editor attributed success to "the profound disgust every right-thinking man entertained for the corrupt manner in which the machinery of party had been perverted to suit the base purpose of party wireworkers—an evil they honestly believed the orders would remedy." A Cincinnatian predicted that thousands who did not like the order's proscriptive principles would vote for the Know Nothings in 1856 because they saw it as "the only chance for restoring the government, from a state of utter corruption, to comparative health and soundness."[26]

Even in the South where, unlike the North, Know Nothingism was largely a vehicle for former Whigs to continue opposition to the Democrats once the Whig party had collapsed, some viewed Know Nothingism as a reform movement necessitated by the declension of republican government. "Whatever many have divided us in other times this *crisis* brings us together," vowed a Mississippian to his party's gubernatorial candidate. "This new and mysterious party called 'Know Nothings,'" wrote one Virginian, "may, and I think will, do good in ridding the country of the trading and trafficking politicians who have had controul [sic] of its affairs for years past." Similarly, an American candidate for a judgeship in the Old Dominion wrote that he had "been sick of politics" and had abstained from them for years, but that he had joined the Know Nothings in order "to rebuke the insolent spirit of party tyranny," to overthrow "the present corrupt . . . dynasty," and to save the American republic from "that state of degeneracy and corruption" which "it took five hundred years for the roman republic to arrive at." The Kentucky editor who had divined the motives behind Douglas's Nebraska bill, finally, astutely recognized that Know Nothingism arose because of the same circumstances—the loss of faith in old parties.

> The people could not fail to perceive the change that time was working in the state of political affairs. Many old measures that once divided the two parties were settled by incorporation into the policy of the country, others had totally failed or lost their significance, and a large portion of the people had come to regard parties as only the machinery used for securing or retaining the emoluments of office. Under the influence of this impression . . . it was perceived, that, while Americans were about equally divided on all important topics, there existed a third element [foreign Catholics], which, by union and concert of action, had obtained a power that enabled it to control all elections. The danger of this element was perceived only when its power had been developed by ascertained results, and then it led to the formation of a new party [the Know Nothings], made up of seceders from both of the old ones.[27]

South and North, hundreds of thousands embraced Know Nothingism as a vehicle of reform because of its clearly expressed purpose to destroy both old parties, drive hack politicians from office, and return political power directly to the people. Thus an apprehensive Mississippi Democrat warned that Know Nothings enlisted voters "in a crusade against parties, as part of the people, determined in spite of parties to rectify abuses, and they are led naturally and easily to refer to their own feelings that, it is a spontaneous movement of the people, in opposition to parties." At the other end of the country, a New York Know Nothing vowed, *"We are* determined to give old party lines and old party hacks a glorious drubbing this fall," and others in the Empire State made it clear that their special targets were Seward and Weed, precisely those Whig politicians trying to resurrect their party in the North with the Nebraska and temperance issues. "We shall sweep Sewardism & Political Catholicism off the face of the Earth," exulted one, while Horace Greeley legitimately complained that "in this state Know-Nothingism is notoriously a conspiracy to overthrow Seward, Weed, and Greeley, and particularly to defeat Mr. Seward's re-election to the Senate." Those disgruntled New York Whigs objected to the tyrannical power of Weed's machine and to Seward's pro-Catholic proclivities, but the effort to reform politics and break up machines prevailed everywhere. Even the American national platform of 1855 pledged "hostility to the corrupt means by which the leaders of party have hitherto forced on us our rulers and our political creeds [and] Implacable enmity against the prevalent demoralizing system of rewards for political subserviency, and of punishment for political independence."[28]

One way the Know Nothings promised to return power to the people was to provide a kind of direct primary system by choosing the party's nominees by majority vote in the local lodges or councils. Complaints about the domination of party conventions by wirepullers and patronage holders were rampant, and the Know Nothings answered the desire for a new nominating procedure by allowing much more influence from the bottom up. In states like Massachusetts the Know Nothings also embraced reform measures to reapportion state legislatures, equalize representation, and make government more responsive to the people.

Most important, the Know Nothings represented themselves as the people's party, and they endeavored to make sure that their candidates represented the people and not the political machines. In the Midwest, the fusion parties that Know Nothings joined and dominated in some states, such as Indiana, referred to themselves as "People's Parties," and individual congressional candidates elsewhere were run as

"People's Candidates." A Bostonian wrote that one of the Know Nothings' "cardinal principles is to send Representatives 'fresh from the people'—no professional, no politician or any office seeker can have part or lot with them." Pittsburgh's Know Nothings demanded that Pennsylvania's U. S. senator, to be elected in 1855, "should be a new man, fresh from the ranks of the people—clad in American raiment, and not in the cast off garments of Whiggery or Democracy." A Know Nothing from western New York summarized the party's appeal to frustrated and rebellious voters in December 1854:

> There is a prestige surrounding new measures and parti-
> cularly new men which it is worth our while to concentrate
> and secure. Under this we have shook off the yoke of politi-
> cal bondage. Under it more than all else we are indebted
> for our success. Our acts must tally with our throng. Let it
> be generally understood during the coming presidential
> campaign that new men are to be the leaders and all the
> offices filled from the ranks, and I care little by what name
> we are known, success is sure—but once by our own acts
> disipate [sic] this impression and half our prospects are
> gone.

Perhaps there is no better proof that rank and file Know Nothings demanded a genuine people's party than the fawning letter of that perpetual presidential aspirant Justice John McLean to a member of the order who had suggested him as the party's presidential nominee. "You are the party of the people; make your own candidates from the highest to the lowest, and give no countenance to those who endeavor to make themselves candidates. This should be the work of the people, and they can do it better than the politicians can do it for them."[29]

In its early campaigns the Know Nothing party did select most of its local leaders from new men, men who were younger and poorer than former political leaders and thus more representative of the people. Out of a sample of Know Nothing leaders in Pittsburgh, over half were younger than 35 years, 60 percent owned property worth less than $5000, a proportion much larger than in the contemporary Whig and Republican parties, and almost half were artisans and clerks. Know Nothings in the Massachusetts legislature elected in 1854 were predominantly artisans from the building trades and shop industries, clerks and rural clergymen, not the farmers and lawyers who had been prominent in former legislatures. Know Nothing leaders in Maryland apparently came from wealthier families than elsewhere, but they were also strikingly young and political amateurs. A New Haven, Connecticut resident noted that Know Nothings there would "put an entire set of new men in office who are very little known in any way." "Some of them [are] young men only four years from College and others are quite uneducated and as it now appears unfitted for their places." One of the major complaints about Know Nothings who took office concerned their inexperience and incompetence, and those suggest that most of the initial Know Nothing officeholders were, indeed, political novices.[30]

By pledging to defeat the papal plot that menaced the Republic, restore politics to their early republican purity, and return political power to the people, the Know Nothings generated a powerful reform appeal that attracted hundreds of thousands of voters who were disillusioned with the old Whig and Democratic parties, thereby contributing to the final destruction of the Second Party System. Where the old parties seemed hopelessly subservient to Catholic and foreign interests, the Know Nothings promised action to proscribe those groups from the political process. Where they had seemed dominated by unresponsive political manipulators beyond the reach of the people, the Know Nothings vowed to choose new leaders fresh from the ranks. Where they had seemed useless because they no longer stood for anything distinctive, Know Nothings portrayed themselves as the only party that could save republicanism because they alone openly challenged the foreign and Catholic menace and they alone of all political parties were dedicated to having Americans rule America. The essence of the Know Nothings' appeal to a distraught electorate in the mid-1850s, in short, was that, just like but even better than the Republicans, they restored faith in the efficacy of political action to save the republic. "What happiness it was to thousands," Rutherford B. Hayes had written from Cincinnati, "to have a chance to show [their hatred of Catholics] in what seemed like a lawful and patriotic manner" by voting Know Nothing.[31]

Equally important, however, although the appeal of the Know Nothings was similar to that of the Republicans, it prevented Know Nothing supporters in the North from joining the rival Republican party, which stressed the sectional issue just when anti-Southern sentiment should have been the strongest because of the passage of the Kansas-Nebraska Act. Between 1854 and 1856, therefore, Northerners who feared for the safety of the Republic and who disliked the Democrats because of their responsibility for the Nebraska Act *and* for their open favoritism of Catholics and foreigners were offered a choice between a party that stressed the need for Northerners to unite to resist the Slave Power and a party that stressed the need for native-born Protestants to unite to resist a Catholic conspiracy. By the end of 1855, the Republicans had emerged as the major opposition party west of Pennsylvania; the Know Nothings had assumed that role in most states east of Ohio.

It is tempting to explain this pattern by arguing that because many Midwesterners actually intended to move to Kansas and Nebraska, they were more interested in the slavery extension issue than Easterners, and that the Easterners were more attracted to Know Nothingism because there were larger concentrations of Irish and Germans there than in the Midwest. Such a dichotomy of regional motivation is far too simplified, however. Know Nothing lodges also proliferated in the Midwest, and the Republicans succeeded there only by combining openly with the nativists, dividing tickets with them as in Ohio, or incorporating nativist planks in state Republican platforms as in Indiana. On the other hand, there is massive evidence that most Know Nothing voters in the Northeast were also hostile to slavery expansion. Know Nothing leaders like Henry Gardner of Massachusetts went to great lengths to defend their antislavery pedigree, and a Connecticut Republican complained in May 1856 that even though the Republicans would take advanced antislavery ground in order to build up the party, they could not distinguish themselves sufficiently from the Know Nothings to lure away voters by that strategy, because "the Americans express themselves with so much decision upon the subject, and come so fully up to our standard that it will be difficult to keep our party friends separated from their organization."[32] Northern voters, then, were motivated by a combination of grievances against the Democrats, and even though they may have given issues different priorities, that differential does not explain the regional pattern of party strength.

What seems to have been crucial, instead, was the attitude of Republican leaders toward the Know Nothings. In the Midwest Republicans like Chase of Ohio and Lincoln of Illinois, who detested the proscription and bigotry they associated with Know Nothings, pragmatically refused to attack them publicly and embraced coalition so as to build the broadest anti-Democratic party possible. In the Northeast Republican leaders like Seward and Weed in New York were often personally anathema to Know Nothings, or else they explicitly presented the Republicans as an anti-Know Nothing party. In many places, the Republican party was started in 1855 and 1856 specifically as a refuge for those who could not tolerate either the Democrats or the Know Nothings, a Hobson's choice as one put it, between the party of "Rum and Slavery" and "a system of Northern Slavery to be created by disfranchising the Irish & Germans." Often former Antimasons who despised the secrecy of the Know Nothings were influential in founding the Republican party, which pledged opposition to secret proscriptive societies because they were antirepublican. The structure of the Know Nothing order itself, critics argued, was similar to that of the Roman Catholic Church and just as alien to republican principles.[33]

As the presidential election of 1856 approached, however, even Eastern Republicans realized that they would have to combine with the majority of Northern Know Nothing voters in order to defeat the Democrats. They managed to win over most of them by the fall of 1856 and almost all of them by 1860, but historians disagree over how the Republicans accomplished that feat. Pointing to Republican platforms and rhetoric, which emphasized the slavery and sectional issue, some argue that Republicans won Know Nothing support without making any concessions to the Know Nothings, that nativism and anti-Catholicism lost their political relevance during the late 1850s, and that the Republicans achieved dominance in the North above all else because antislavery and anti-Southern attitudes shaped voting behavior.[34] To buttress their case, they point out that the Know Nothings, too, split into sectional wings over the slavery extension issue. In June 1855 and again in February 1856 Northern Know Nothings bolted from national conventions of the American party when the platform did not take staunch enough ground against the Nebraska Act and slavery expansion. And when the latter convention gave its presidential nomination to Millard Fillmore, who was supported primarily by Southerners and who was still detested by many in the North for signing the Fugitive Slave Act, the bolters called a North American convention to meet in New York City in June, a week before the Republicans convened in Philadelphia. Although that body hoped to nominate their own candidate whom the Republicans would be forced to adopt, they eventually supported the Republican nominee John C. Frémont in the 1856 campaign. Thus there is no denying that the

171

slavery issue could rupture the Know Nothings, just as it was dividing the nation, or that Northern nativists were also against slavery expansion. Still, antislavery or anti-Southern sentiment alone cannot explain why the Republicans eventually absorbed most of the Northern anti-Democratic vote.

The relationship between the decline of the Know Nothings and the rise of the Republicans as the major anti-Democratic party was symbiotic. The two rivals had more in common than opposition to the Democracy. Both reacted to preexisting fears about the survival of republicanism by identifying despotic conspiracies and calling on Americans to enlist in crusades to save freedom and liberty. And no matter how bigoted some Know Nothings were, their commitment to freedom and obsessive fear that it was menaced by a form of despotism seems to have been just as authentic as that of the Republicans. Just as a disillusionment or loss of confidence in the Whigs and Democrats preceded and was exploited by the Know Nothings, so the Republicans capitalized on the bitter disappointment of men who had eagerly joined the Know Nothings but quickly left them. Put another way, the Republicans played on what the rivals had in common to beat the Know Nothings at their own game. Through shrewd political maneuvering, they won the support of anti-Catholics without adopting the secret machinery and all of the proscriptive principles of the Know Nothings. Equally important, they adroitly adopted an antiparty, reform image of their own, which made them seem an even better champion than the Know Nothings to save republican liberty and equality from corruption and tyranny, to purify the political process, and to restore self-government.

The Know Nothings, in fact, were not a static or solid bloc that emerged in 1854 only to fragment over the slavery issue in 1856. The order seemed to lose its charm rapidly for many who had rushed to join. It could attract initiates much more easily than it could retain members. As a result, its support was remarkably fluid from one election to the next. A rare membership list of an individual lodge in the city of Worcester, Massachusetts,' for example, reveals that only 200 of the 1120 men who had belonged in 1854 were still members in 1855, while 214 new men had joined. Similarly, careful statistical studies of voting returns in Massachusetts and New York, show that the party drew its support from different areas in 1854 and 1855. As one New Yorker astutely reported after the latter election, "There is one thing about this contest quite discernible—that where they were strong last year they have now lost & where they were weak now they are strong." In part this shifting was attributable to the defection of some antislavery nativists to the Republicans in 1855, while conservatives, as one Democrat put it, "rushed blindly in, to defeat 'republicanism.'" But many became disillusioned with the secret order for reasons that had little to do with the slavery issue even before the Republican party became a viable alternative for their vote.[35]

First, enthusiasm waned when the Know Nothings failed to take concrete action against immigrants and Catholics. In contrast to Whigs and Democrats, the Know Nothings had promised to *do* something to redress the grievances of nativists, but their performance in office could not match their rhetoric. In certain states they banned ownership of church property by the clergy, passed temperance laws, and began witch-huntlike investigations of Catholic schools, but generally they were inept as legislators. Foremost, they failed to restrict the vote to legally naturalized citizens and to extend the naturalization period itself as they had promised. Their incompetence destroyed their appeal as being the only effective anti-Catholic party.

Second, many nativists grew disenchanted with the secret machinations of the order. From Delaware, New York, Pennsylvania, and elsewhere, complaints reached Know Nothing leaders that many who agreed with the anti-Catholicism of the party, especially old Antimasons, could not tolerate its secrecy, which they deemed a threat to the republic. "Can there be a different organization that will accomplish our object and obviate the great objection now made to us as a party?" asked a New Yorker. A Pennsylvanian writing to Simon Cameron, who had joined the order at the end of 1854, provided an answer. The way to succeed in the Keystone State, he argued, was to drop secrecy and "step on two planks of a new platform and carry the state with a rush—viz Americanism and antislavery."[36] In essence, that is precisely what the Republican party in Pennsylvania and elsewhere would do in 1856 and for the remainder of the decade.

Equally damning in the eyes of those who sought genuine reform of the political process was the violence and lawlessness associated with Know Nothingism. In many cities, gangs of armed thugs sided with the nativists, and in cities like Baltimore, Cincinnati, and Louisville they resorted to mayhem and murder to stop immigrants from voting. If all else failed, Know Nothings were wont to seize the ballot boxes in immigrant precincts and destroy the ballots before they could be counted. Such tactics seemed just as subversive of honest politics and the republican rule of law as illegal immigrant voting.

Finally, the very success of the Know Nothings helped to tarnish their image as an authentic people's party. The early triumphs and growing membership of the order attracted to it, in the words of an indignant member, "a set of selfish politicians who cared not a straw about its principles [but] were trying to *use* the order for the promotion of their heartless and sordid aims." The inexperience of the first Know Nothing leaders allowed those shrewd politicos to achieve dominance in statewide offices. In Massachusetts, for example, Henry Wilson and a small band of Free-Soilers rose to leadership by supporting Henry Gardner for governor in return for Wilson's subsequent election to the U.S. Senate. Wilson's adeptness at manipulating Bay State Know Nothings has caused some historians to view the movement there simply as an extension of the Free Soil and antislavery reform drive, but there is no denying the intensity of anti-Catholic sentiment in the state, especially in view of Know Nothing victories over a separate Republican party in state elections in 1855 and 1856. Similarly, the rapid rise of the erstwhile Democrat Simon Cameron in the Pennsylvania party or of Daniel Ullmann, Millard Fillmore, and other officeseeking Silver Gray Whigs in the leadership of the New York Know Nothings does not mean that the anti-Catholicism and antiparty sentiment which motivated the vast majority of Know Nothing voters was any less real. Rank and file Know Nothings in Pennsylvania denounced those legislators who had voted for the crafty Cameron for senator, and Ullmann's voluminous correspondence contains many letters warning against an open alliance with the Silver Grays because it would offend so many of the members. Indeed, the eminence of seasoned politicians in the party by 1855 disillusioned thousands who had joined the order to escape the rule of politicos and return power to the people. Hence a North Carolinian complained in 1855 about the developments in Pennsylvania and New Hampshire, where the order helped to reelect John P. Hale to the Senate:

> This struggling and scrambling for office and promotion was one of the very great evils it was the object of our organization to remedy—and yet our success is likely to be jeoparded by the very same evil. The masses are sound but

the old party leaders and political hacks who have come into the order, from selfish purposes, will ruin us, if we are not strictly on our guard.[37]

With enormous skill the Republican leadership played on the various sources of discontent with the Know Nothings and exploited the republican idiom common to both parties to unite most of the Northern anti-Democratic voters in 1856 into a powerful opposition party. Just when the American party was losing its image of newness and true concern for the people, the Republicans evinced it. From the inception of the Republican party, its leaders had recognized and profited from the popular mood of protest against established parties. Early anti-Nebraska coalitions in Ohio and Indiana were called People's Parties, and Republicans also employed that name in Connecticut in 1856 and later in Pennsylvania and New Jersey. Elsewhere they used the name Independent as frequently as the name Republican. Anti-slavery politicians clearly needed an inoffensive title that could attract mutually suspicious Whigs, Democrats, and Free-Soilers, but they also hoped to appeal to the public demand for popularly controlled parties. That the Republicans did attract men who hated politicians and the mechanisms of party politics became evident during the initial meeting to organize a national party at Pittsburgh in February 1856. There a German delegate from Cincinnati, Charles Reemelin, opposed holding a national nominating convention, because "the people would find their *men,* if it was taken out of the hands of *bargaining politicians.*" He protested that he had hoped the Republican conclave "was the inauguration, of a new and purer political party that would avoid the corruptions incident to political conventions & especially not . . . name, the *time* & place, which was an advertisement to the political jesuits to commence their work."[38]

Although the Republicans held a nominating convention in June, they took advantage of the old-fashioned, machine-controlled aura around the American and Democratic parties. Fillmore's nomination in February fell "like a wet blanket" among Northern lodge members, who warned Nathaniel P. Banks that the North American and Republican nomination should emanate directly from the people and not merely be the choice of a convention. Nor did the Democratic nomination in May of the old Pennsylvania wheel-horse James Buchanan satisfy the craving for new leadership. "There is no enthusiasm for

Buchanan which has its origins in the hearts of the people." They wanted "a man fresh from the loins of the people—a mechanic—able and jealous of the hierarchy of Rome—a Democrat—prudent in times of trouble amid the usurpations of petty tyrants," another Northern Know Nothing informed Banks. While this supporter thought that Banks himself, whom Know Nothings and Republicans had elected Speaker of the House, should be the North American and Republican nominee, Fremont at age 43 seemed a much fresher face than the shopworn Fillmore, who was 56, or Buchanan, who was 65. Republican editorialists shrewdly presented the Pathfinder as "a new man, fresh from the people and one of themselves . . . [who] has been singled out by the people themselves to retrieve the government from maladministration and restore it again to the cause of liberty, justice, and humanity."[39]

As they would again in 1860 the Republicans also organized Wide Awake clubs, marching societies whose members paraded the streets in uniform with lanterns burning. Many of the original Know Nothing lodges had been called Wide Awakes, and these militaristic societies attracted the young and the poor, workingmen and mechanics, precisely the kind of men who had rushed to the Know Nothing lodges in 1854 and 1855. Through their candidate, appeals, and imitative campaign paraphernalia, the Republicans bid for those Know Nothings who opposed slavery expansion, found nothing new in Millard Fillmore, and yearned for a genuine people's party to restore self-government.

The Republicans had to do more to lure North Americans than adopt a reform image, however. The Northern Know Nothings who bolted their party in February 1856 expected to be treated as equals in any coalition with the Republicans, and, as Banks's correspondence indicates, they insisted on some deference to their anti-Catholicism. But Republicans could not adopt Know Nothing principles wholesale, because it would offend original Republicans in the East who hated their secrecy and because it would antagonize Protestant Germans and Protestant Irish, whom Republicans also hoped to include in their party. Such immigrant Protestants despised their Catholic countrymen even more than native-born Protestants, and many had formed secret anti-Catholic societies of their own in 1854 and 1855. Yet they were put off by the antiforeign aspects of the Know Nothings and by the prohibitionism of other groups who opposed the Democrats. Nativism, anti-Catholicism, prohibitionism, and anti-Southernism were crosscutting issues among foes of the Democrats that pushed voters, especially Protestant immigrants, in opposite directions. The difficulty of combining all the anti-Democratic groups in a single party was made clear in a letter from a Cincinnati German named Stephen Molitor to the Ohio Republican leader Salmon P. Chase. He denounced "the Jesuitical influence" in the local Democratic convention where a Catholic who "a few years ago denounced our public schools as institutions of Satan, played one of the principal parts." He then deplored the fact that the Catholic-dominated Democratic ticket would be elected, because Germans of all religions were appalled by the Know Nothing and prohibitionist influence in the Ohio Republican party. No matter how much those Germans hated slavery, he explained, they would never vote for the Republicans as long as those influences prevailed. Everywhere, indeed, observers reported that the Know Nothing surge had rejuvenated the Democracy by 1855 by causing more immigrants to vote and by driving them to the Democrats in self-defense.[40] Men moved in both ways during the realignment of the 1850s, and because the Democrats were first and most vociferous in denouncing the Know Nothings, the order's bigotry gave its targets a new appreciation of the Democracy.

The Republican leadership was well aware that open identification with the Know Nothings would doom them with immigrants, but that they would also have to make some concessions to Know Nothing principles. Selecting a common presidential candidate exemplified the dilemma. The North Americans hoped to nominate their own candidate first in New York and then impose him on the Republicans, who were meeting five days later in Philadelphia. The Republicans, in turn, wanted Know Nothing support for their own nominee without the stigma of a nativist nomination. They accomplished this considerable feat through the pivotal role of Speaker of the House Banks, who was trusted by both North Americans and Republicans. Concealing his ultimate plans from many delegates, Banks won the North American nomination but delayed acceptance until the Republicans met. When they selected Frémont, he declined the Know Nothings' nomination, as had been prearranged, and urged the North Americans to support Frémont, which most eventually did.

They did so, however, only because there was far more to the merger than common support for a presidential ticket. Beneath the national level, Republicans bargained blatantly with the Know Nothings, and the nativists proved to be tough negotiators. They skillfully divided the state ticket with the Know Nothings in Pennsylvania, where the local party was called the Union party because of the anti-Know Nothing connotations of the name Republican. In Massachusetts most Republican backed the Know Nothing gubernatorial candidate in 1856 in return for Know Nothing support for Frémont. Even more important, the Republicans did make concessions to Know Nothing biases, despite the insistence of some historians to the contrary. Because of the need to win the immigrant vote, however, they tried to soft-pedal antiforeignism and temperance whenever possible, but they openly exploited the one thing besides anti-Southernism that united Protestant immigrants and Northern Know Nothings—their intense hatred of Catholics. The Union state platform in Pennsylvania, for example, was evenly divided between anti-Southern and Know Nothing planks. The latter resolutions censured the interference of "foreign influence of every kind" in American government, castigated "the pandering of any party to foreign influence as fraught with manifold evils to the country," and pledged to defend the common school system from any attempts "from whatever quarter" to pervert it to sectarian purposes. Indiana's Republican platform in 1856 contained a clause condemning alien suffrage before the five-year naturalization period required by Congress—a demand that was not that offensive to the *previously naturalized* Protestant immigrant voters to whom Republicans appealed. Michigan's Republicans endorsed a book because it demonstrated the "antagonism of Romanism to Freedom and true Progress."[41]

Nor was the national Republican leadership unaware of the potency of anti-Catholic prejudice or hesitant to appeal to it. Edwin D. Morgan, chairman of the Republican National Committee, carefully won the public endorsement of James Barker, the ex-president of the Know Nothings' grand national council and the man who had done so much to build up the lodges in 1853 and 1854; he informed one correspondent that "the anti-Catholic tract is to be out soon. . . . It has been too long delayed"; and he sent an ex-Know Nothing workingman as a speaker to New Jersey because he "will do good among mechanics or among religous people." Even the Republican national platform written in June before the final merger was effected contained indirect appeals to the Know Nothings. The last plank stated that "believing that the spirit of our institutions as well as the Constitution of our country, guarantees liberty of conscience and equality of rights among citizens, we oppose all legislation impairing their security." This clause is normally interpreted as a victory of the German element in the Republican party over the proscriptiveness of Know Nothingism, and to a degree it was. But one should note that it spoke of "citizens," not aliens, and that "liberty of conscience" was a standard Know Nothing and anti-Catholic idiom when arguing for Bible reading in public schools. To them it meant protection from the priesthood and the right of individual interpretation of the scriptures, and the Republican pledge could be interpreted to mean opposition to the laws demanded by Catholics banning the Bible from public schools.[42]

Ethnocultural and religious animosities, in sum, did not cease influencing the electorate once Northern Know Nothings were absorbed into the Republican party. Those historians who differentiate between nativism as a political force when men voted Know Nothing and nativism as a cultural force without political importance when they voted Republican make a spurious distinction. It is true that Republican campaign rhetoric and platforms focused on sectional matters, not ethnocultural issues, but that rhetoric reflected a campaign strategy, not necessarily the value priorities of the Northern electorate. The refusal of antislavery Germans in Cincinnati and elsewhere to support the Republicans because of their nativist and prohibitionist taint alone shows that. The issues that mattered most to them were precisely the issues that the Republicans consciously *omitted* from their platforms when possible so as not to offend them, not the issues they included. Certainly many Republicans complained that their gravest single handicap in 1856 was the false charge that Frémont was a Catholic, a charge they believed prevented tens of thousands, if not hundreds of thousands, of sincere antislavery men from joining the Republicans because they could not abide a Catholic no matter what his position on slavery. As one informed Chase after Frémont lost that election, largely because Fillmore drew off anti-Democratic voters in crucial states,

> *The element most to be dreaded is the American vote. . . .*
> *If we make judicious nominations and emphatically show*
> *no disposition to court the Catholic vote, and if practicable,*
> *open our batteries against the political tendencies of that*
> *institution, we can command the largest portion of this*
> *vote.*

Republicans did precisely that; in many localities of the North the worst thing a Republican could call a Democrat for the remainder of the decade, indeed for the remainder of the century, was that he was a Catholic or a Catholic sympathizer. It must never be forgotten that the Republicans did not just contest for national offices such as congressman or president. In terms of raw numbers, they ran far more campaigns for state legislator, county commissioner, and other local and state offices, and in those races a candidate's religion was often more important to voters than his attitude toward slavery.[43]

There is a difference between the Republicans' strategy as encapsulated in their platforms and the reasons why hundreds of thousands of voters coalesced behind Republican candidates after 1855. Voters often support parties for very different reasons than leaders form those parties. And voters often align with one party more because they are *against* its opponent than because they are *for* it. That was especially true in the 1850s when the Republican party was so new and inchoate that men had not yet formed strong positive identifications with it. Nativism and anti-Catholicism had turned many voters against the Democrats in 1854 and 1855, when realignment occurred behind the Know Nothings. When it became clear in 1856 that the Republicans would have the best chance of defeating the Democrats whom they regarded as agents of the papal plot and when Republicans at the local level took frequent opportunities to denounce Romanism, such voters readily joined them.

Yet anti-Catholicism alone did not cause men to vote Republican. Northern Know Nothings and Protestant immigrants were also anti-Southern. Hundreds of thousands of other Republican voters, moreover, had never been Know Nothings. Although anti-Catholicism did not wane, the most important fact to remember is that it was not the Know Nothings but the Republican party—which stressed the sectional issue—that became the major anti-Democratic party in the North. Clearly, more was involved in the rise of the Republican party than simply the skill of Republican leadership in exploiting the disillusionment with Know Nothings and coopting their appeal. The Republican leaders had consciously chosen to try to convince Northern voters that it was necessary to have an exclusively Northern party. The mere fact that 1856 was a presidential election year when, unlike 1854 and 1855, the North and South were actually pitted against each other for control of the national government made that appeal more credible. But, ultimately, what was most important in explaining the triumph of the Republicans over the Know Nothings in 1856 and over the Democrats in 1860 was the plausibility of the Republican case against the South, their success in convincing men that a Northern party was truly needed to resist Slave Power aggression. The cogency of that appeal, in turn, had always rested on concrete events that seemed to prove that a Slave Power conspiracy truly intended to subjugate the North. The Kansas-Nebraska Act by itself had persuaded many Northerners of that menace, but not enough to build a winning party. What was needed for the Republican party to rise to power in the North and in the nation was a series of events that increased Northern resentment of the South.

The story of those events, the Republican exploitation of them, and the Southern response to the Republican party is the story of how American politics were sectionalized, of how the North and South became so fundamentally polarized against each other that they no longer participated in the same party system. The sectional conflict had not destroyed the Second Party System between 1848 and 1854. Nor had it alone produced the realignment of voters following its collapse, by which the Democrats were reduced to a minority of the national electorate between 1854 and 1856. But exacerbation of the sectional conflict between 1856 and 1861 was the most important reason why the Republicans combined anti-Democratic elements in the North and why the South seceded.

SEVEN

Slavery, Republicanism, and the Triumph of the Republican Party

Between 1856 and 1861 sectional wrangling over slavery dominated political debate and snapped the ties of mutual allegiance to national parties that had linked Northerners and Southerners since the 1830s. The ostensibly bisectional Democracy became more pro-Southern in orientation, and Northern and Southern Democrats increasingly eyed each other with suspicion instead of trust. Opponents of the Democrats from the rival sections could no longer even combine in the same party. Within each section, moreover, the most militantly sectional party, the Republicans in the North and the Democrats in the South, rose to power. Consequently, national elections came to be viewed by many as less a question of which party than of which section would control the government in Washington, and, when the anti-Southern Republicans won in 1860, seven slave states seceded instead of accepting the result. By focusing first on the North and then the South, this and the following chapter will investigate why and how this sectionalization took place, what the relationship between the dynamics of the political system and the escalation of sectional conflict was, and what role black slavery played in the ultimate breakup of the Union.

The sectionalization of American politics was emphatically *not* simply a reflection or product of basic popular disagreements over black slavery. Those had long existed without such a complete polarization developing. Even though a series of events beginning with the Kansas-Nebraska Act greatly increased sectional consciousness, it is a mistake to think of sectional antagonism as a spontaneous and self-perpetuating force that imposed itself on the political arena against the will of politicians and coerced parties to conform to the lines of sectional conflict. Popular grievances, no matter how intense, do not dictate party strategies. Political leaders do. Some one has to politicize events, to define their political relevance in terms of a choice between or among parties, before popular grievances can have political impact. It was not events alone that caused Northerners and Southerners to view each other as enemies of the basic rights they both cherished. Politicians who pursued very traditional partisan strategies were largely responsible for the ultimate breakdown of the political process. Much of the story of the coming of the Civil War is the story of the successful efforts of Democratic politicians in the South and Republican politicians in the North to keep the sectional conflict at the center of political debate and to defeat political rivals who hoped to exploit other issues to achieve election.

For at least thirty years political leaders had recognized that the way to build political parties, to create voter loyalty and mobilize support, and to win elections was to find issues or positions on issues that distinguished them from their opponents and that therefore could appeal to various groups who disliked their opponents by offering them an alternative for political action—in sociological terms, to make their party a vehicle for negative reference group behavior. Because of the American ethos, the most successful tactic had been to pose as a champion of republican values and to portray the opponent as antirepublican, as unlawful, tyrannical, or aristocratic. Jackson, Van Buren, and Polk, Antimasons and Whigs, had all followed this dynamic of the political system. Stephen A. Douglas and William H. Seward had pursued the same strategy in their unsuccessful attempt to rebuild the disintegrating Second Party System with the Kansas-Nebraska Act in 1854. After faith in the old parties had collapsed irreparably, when the shape of future political alignments was uncertain, Republican politicians quite consciously seized on the slavery and sectional issue in order to build a new party. Claiming to be the exclusive Northern Party that was necessary to halt slavery extension and defeat the Slave Power conspiracy was the way they chose to distinguish themselves from Democrats, whom they denounced as pro-Southern, and from the Know Nothings, who had chosen a different organizing principle—anti-Catholicism and nativism—to construct their new party.

To say that Republican politicians agitated and exploited sectional grievances in order to build a winning party is a simple description of fact. It is not meant to imply that winning was their only objective or to be a value judgment about the sincerity or insincerity of their personal hatred of black slavery. Some undoubtedly found slavery morally intolerable and hoped to use the national government to weaken it by preventing its expansion, abolishing it in federal enclaves like the District of Columbia, and undermining it within Southern states by whatever means were constitutionally possible, such as opening the mails to abolitionist literature and prohibiting the interstate slave trade.[1] The antislavery pedigree of Republican leaders, however, was in a sense irrelevant to the triumph of the Republican party. The leaders were divided over the policies they might pursue if they won control of the national government, and leadership views were often far in advance of those held by their electorate. Much more important was the campaign they ran to obtain power, their skill in politicizing the issues at hand in such a way as to convince Northern voters that control of the national government by an exclusive Northern party was necessary to resist Slave Power aggressions. The Republicans won more because of what they were against than because of what they were for, because of what they wanted to stop, not what they hoped to do.

As the presidential campaign of 1856 approached, Republican success remained uncertain. Although the bolt of the North Americans in February had reduced American or Know Nothing support primarily to the slave states, the Americans campaigned vigorously for Millard Fillmore in those areas of the North that were most in doubt and that the Republicans had to carry in order to win—Illinois, Indiana, and especially the Middle Atlantic states. There is ample evidence that the Democrats secretly funded the Know Nothing campaign to keep their opponents divided. The Americans officially renounced secrecy in 1856 and softened their most proscriptive positions, but they still called for an increase in the naturalization period, denounced foreign and Catholic interference in politics, and proclaimed that only Americans ruling America could purify politics and restore the nation to early republican ideals. Vilifying the Democrats as tools of the papal plot, they also denounced corruption and fraud in the Pierce administration and cried that true reform could be achieved only by expelling Democrats from power. But the Americans also condemned the Republicans as pro-foreign and raised the fatal charge that Frémont was Catholic. Always superpatriotic in their rhetoric, the Americans added the potent issue of Unionism to their arsenal. The Republicans were abolitionist fanatics whose victory would provoke secession, they charged, while the Demo-crats were dominated by secessionist fire-eaters from the South. Only an American victory could assure the permanency of the Union and with it of the republican experiment.

The major challenge to the Republicans, however, came from the Democrats, whose strength in the South they could not rival. The Democrats could win merely by preserving their majorities in a few of the Northern states they had swept in 1852, and in the 1855 state elec-tions they had begun to make a comeback from the disaster of 1854 in New Jersey, Pennsylvania, Indiana, Illinois, and Wisconsin. Opposition to Know Nothingism and prohibitionism had bolstered the Democrats in 1855, and in 1856 they stressed their long-time defense of religious and ethnic minorities and of personal freedom from the attacks of in-tolerant bigots and self-righteous moral reformers who, they argued, were prominent in both the American and Republican parties. The secret machinations of Know Nothingism constituted a conspiracy against republican government, they complained, and for the remainder of the decade they charged that Know Nothings controlled the Re-publican party. To improve their chances in all-important Pennsylvania, the Democrats selected James Buchanan as their presidential candidate. The national Democratic platform endorsed the Kansas-Nebraska Act, lauded the principle of congressional noninterference as the proper solution to the problem of slavery in the territories, and insisted that new states be admitted with or without slavery, as their constitutions prescribed. Thus it drew a sharp line between the Democrats and the Republicans who denounced the Act, demanded congressional prohi-bition of slavery from all territories, and often vowed to prevent the entry of any more slave states no matter what their constitutions said. The Republican advantage was not as great as it seemed, however; after the initial shock of 1854, many long-time Democratic voters in the North seemed disposed to see how the doctrine of self-government actually worked in Kansas. To reinforce their loyalty, Democrats de-fended popular sovereignty as a perfect manifestation of government by the people and a logical extension of traditional Democratic states rights principles that would preserve a heterogeneous society. Equally important, Northern Democrats continued to promise that popular sovereignty would bar slavery expansion just as surely as congressional prohibition.

To offset the Republican appeal on the slavery issue even more, the Democrats launched a two-pronged attack. Like the Americans, they labeled the Republicans as dangerous sectionalists whose victory would disrupt the Union. All Union-loving Democrats and former Whigs, they contended, must vote for Buchanan to prevent that catastrophe, because Fillmore could not possibly win. More insidious, but equally effective, the Democrats viciously race-baited the Republicans. Castigating them as "Black Republican Abolitionists" and "nigger lovers" who cared much more about blacks than Northern whites, they charged that the Republicans would abolish slavery in the South and thus inundate the North with a horde of freed blacks who would rob white workers of their jobs, ruin their neighborhoods, and even marry their daughters. "To elevate the African race in this country to complete equality of political and economic condition with the white man, is the one aim of the party that supports Fremont," wrote one Democratic paper in a mild version of this appeal, and later it pronounced the single issue in the contest to be "the white race or the Negro race."[2]

The Republicans thus faced two foes who not only offered compelling versions of their own as how best to save republican principles and the Union, but who also exploited palpably powerful prejudices. To counteract them, the Republicans had to develop a persuasion that could win the widest possible support from a Northern constituency that was racist and overwhelmingly believed federal abolition in the states unconstitutional and dangerous to the Union. The most delicate problem was black slavery, and historians have disagreed about what the Republican position on it was and how central that stand was to their appeal. Evidence exists in Republican platforms, pamphlets, speeches, and editorials to support widely varying interpretations of what the party stood for and, by inference from that rhetoric, why Northerners supported it. Some historians, for example, argue that the Republicans were abolitionists dedicated to eradicating slavery as soon as it was constitutionally feasible, while others insist that humanitarian or moral antipathy to the institution, if not outright abolitionism, was the moving force behind the party.[3] They point out that the 1856 Republican national platform condemned slavery as a "relic of barbarism" and a patent violation of the Declaration of Independence's proclamation that "all men are created equal and have inalienable rights

187

to life, liberty, and the pursuit of happiness." Together with other assaults on slavery's inhumanity, demands that it be extinguished, and paeans to freedom and liberty, these can provide evidence that Republicans sincerely wanted to remedy the plight of the black slave.

Yet juxtaposed to demands that slavery be ended and freedom extended were constant Republican denials that the federal government had any right to interfere with slavery within Southern states or that Republicans had any intention of doing so. Similarly, along with enlightened talk of the equality of all men appeared blatant racism or at least strained arguments that concern for the black, free or slave, had nothing to do with the Republican party, evidence that seems to refute assertions that moral antipathy to black slavery or humanitarianism was the basic force behind Republicanism. "NO NEGRO EQUALITY IN THE NORTH," pledged a Republican banner at an Illinois rally in 1860. A Pittsburgh orator and future Radical Republican congressman proclaimed in 1856 that "he cared nothing for the 'nigger'; it was not the mission of the Republican party to preach rebellion—he had a higher mission to preach—deliverance to the white man." The Hartford *Courant* ringingly defended the party's free-soil principles that same year: "The Republicans mean to preserve all of this country that they can from the pestilential presence of the black man." Less insultingly, a Pennsylvania Republican editor declared in 1855 that "the real question at issue between the North and South in the present contest, is not a sentimental difference growing out of the oppression of the negro," while Seward echoed in 1860, "The motive of those who have protested against the extension of slavery [has] always been concern for the welfare of the white man, not an unnatural sympathy with the negro."[4]

Historians have tried to reconcile these contradictory appeals in various ways. Some simply admit that the party was a heterogeneous coalition ranging from radicals to conservatives on the slavery issue whose rhetoric reflected the diverse views of its different elements. Others have excused the Republicans' racist remarks as an attempt to defend the party from Democratic charges that it cared more about blacks than whites. In reality, they argue, the Republicans were more favorable to black rights than Democrats, as their voting records against discriminatory laws in Northern state legislatures demonstrate. Still others have accepted the racism of some Republicans and the reluctance of the vast majority to interfere with slavery in the South by arguing that the Republicans were essentially a free-soil party, not an abolitionist or antislavery party. Opposition to slavery extension, which sprang from a number of sources, constituted the party's central thrust. Many sincerely believed that slavery had to expand to survive and that restricting it would bring about its ultimate destruction. Others wanted to protect the free labor system of the North by preserving areas for its expansion, while some wanted to keep blacks out of the territories for racist reasons. Many Republicans, finally, desired to stop the growth of Southern political power.[5] *why?*

Prohibition of slavery expansion was the specific policy most frequently voiced by the Republicans and one with which everyone in the party agreed, if for different reasons. Northern hostility to slavery extension was authentic and deep-seated. Yet to assert that free-soilism constituted the core of Republicanism is to miss the essence of the Republican appeal. Prevention of slavery extension was the issue the Republicans seized on to politicize their message, but it was not the heart of that message. It was a goal of the party, but not the party's fundamental purpose. As Charles Sumner admitted when congratulating Henry J. Raymond, who wrote the address from the Republicans' national organizational meeting in February 1856, an address that focused on the need to keep Kansas free:

> For a long time my desire has been to make an issue with the slave oligarchy; & provided this can be had I am indifferent to the special point selected. Of course, at this moment Kansas is the inevitable point. In protecting this territory against tyranny we are driven to battle with the tyrants, who are the oligarchs of slavery.[6]

The words of Sumner, who was much more sympathetic to blacks than most Republicans, suggest that the majority of the party disliked white slaveholders more than black slavery or even slavery extension. The Republicans, in fact, presented themselves basically as an anti-Southern or antislaveholder party. What was at stake, they cried, was not the future shape of Western society but the present condition of the American republic. Skillfully they portrayed the sectional conflict in terms of the republican ideology that had suffused American politics since the time of the Revolution. This was not a case of a new sectional ideology overwhelming a political system that had previously been nonideological or of new antagonisms toward black slavery displacing old concerns about banks, monopolies, and executive tyranny. This was a case of the Republicans consciously applying the traditional republican idiom to the issue they had selected to define their party and using that idiom to explain what the sectional conflict meant to Northern whites who were generally apathetic about the plight of blacks or were hostile to them. "Convince the laboring class that [slavery] is at war with our republican institutions and opposed to their interests," advised an Indiana Republican in 1856. In one form, the Republicans' case did focus on black slavery. Arguing that the Founding Fathers had envisioned the eventual extinction of the institution, they maintained that Southern attempts to extend and perpetuate it perverted the original purposes of the republic from freedom to slavery. Yet their most effective argument was much more general and traditional and had little to do with the institution of slavery itself. Identifying the Slave Power conspiracy as the major threat to republican liberty, equality, and self-government, the Republicans promised, as parties had since the 1820s, that voting for them was the best way to preserve the republican institutions of whites from despotism, unrestrained power, and privilege. Thus a Republican Congressman demanded in June 1856: "Are we to have a government of the people, a real representative Republican Government? or are the owners of slave property, small in number but with the power in their hands, and strongly entrenched in every power, to rule us with arbitrary and undisputed sway?"[7]

The key to unraveling the paradoxes in Republican rhetoric, the juxtaposition of egalitarianism and racism, of pledges not to interfere with slavery in the South alongside calls to end slavery and join a great crusade for freedom, is to remember that the word "slavery" had long had a definite meaning aside from the institution of black slavery in the South. It was in this sense that many Republicans used the word. Slavery implied subordination to tyranny, the loss of liberty and equality, the absence of republicanism. Slavery resulted when republican government was overthrown or usurped, and that, charged Republicans, was exactly what the Slave Power was trying to do. Hence the slavery that many Republicans objected to most was not the bondage of blacks in the South but the subjugation of Northern whites to the despotism of a tiny oligarchy of slaveholders bent on destroying their rights, a minority who controlled the Democratic party and through it the machinery of the federal government. Thus one Republican complained privately in 1857, "The Slave power will not submit. The tyrants of the lash will not withhold until they have put padlocks on the lives of freemen. The Union which our fathers formed seventy years ago is not the Union today. . .the sons of the Revolutionary fathers are becoming *slaves* or *masters.*" Thus a Chicago Republican congressman, after reciting a litany of supposed Slave Power aggressions against the North, later recalled, "All these things followed the taking possession of the Government and lands by the slave power, until we [in the North] were the slaves of slaves, being chained to the car of this Slave Juggernaut." Thus the black abolitionist Frederick Douglass perceptively observed, "The cry of Free Men was raised, not for the extension of liberty to the black man, but for the protection of the liberty of the white."[8]

The basic objective of Republican campaigns from 1856 to 1860, therefore, was to persuade Northerners that slaveholders meant to enslave them through their control of the national government and to enlist Northern voters behind the Republican party in a defensive phalanx to ward off *that* slavery, and not in an offensive crusade to end black slavery, by driving the Slave Power from its control of the national government. For such a tactic to succeed, the Republicans required two things. First, to make an asset and not a liability of their existence as an exclusive Northern party, they needed events to increase Northern antagonism toward the South so that men believed the South, and not foreigners and Catholics or the Republicans themselves, posed the chief threat to the republic. More important, they had successfully to identify the Democratic party as an agent or lackey of the South. Because the Republicans campaigned only in the North, because Northern voters chose among Northern candidates instead of between Northerners and Southerners, only by making Northern Democrats surrogates for the Slave Power could they make their case that Republicans alone, and not simply any Northern politicians, were needed to resist and overthrow the slavocracy. Because they dared not promise overt action against slaveholders except for stopping slavery expansion, in other words, Republicans could not exploit Northern anger, no matter how intense it was, unless they could convince Northern voters that supporting the Republicans and defeating Northern Democrats was an efficacious and constitutional way to defeat the Slave Power itself.

By the summer of 1856 it was much easier to identify the Democracy with the South than it had been earlier. For one thing, the results of the congressional elections of 1854 and 1855 had dramatically shifted the balance of sectional power within the Democratic party, a result that was plainly evident when the 34th Congress met during 1856. From 1834 to 1854 the Democratic congressional delegation had usually been reasonably balanced between North and South. In the 33rd Congress, Northern Democrats had even outnumbered Southern Democrats in the House by a margin of 91 to 67. But in 1856 there were only 25 Northerners as compared to 63 Southerners, and even though Northern Democratic representation would increase after the 1856 elections, the sectional balance would never be restored before the Civil War.[9] The South seemed to dominate the Democracy, and that fact was especially difficult to hide during a presidential election year. Because the Democrats, unlike the Republicans, met in a common national convention with Southerners and campaigned in both sections, Democrats could not deny their Southern connection. The Democratic platform endorsing the Kansas-Nebraska Act strengthened that identification, thereby flushing out regular Northern Democrats who had tried to evade the Nebraska issue in 1854 and 1855 and infuriating anti-Nebraska Democrats who had clung to the party in hopes of reversing its policy but who now bolted to the Republicans.[10]

What made the Democratic platform commitment especially damaging in the North were events in Kansas itself. Many Northern voters sincerely revered the principle of self-determination by local majority rule, and because they had been assured by Northern Democrats that nonslaveholders would move to Kansas in greater numbers than slaveholders, they anticipated that popular sovereignty would produce free soil in the West. If their expectations had been fulfilled, if popular sovereignty had worked as Stephen Douglas envisioned it, the course of American history might have been different. But things did not go according to plan in Kansas, and it became a whip that Republicans used to flay the Democracy. To understand why, one must differentiate between what actually happened on the plains of Kansas and what political propagandists said was happening.

Although there was much publicity about groups in the Northeast and Deep South, like the New England Emigrant Aid Company, which organized to send settlers to Kansas to control it for free or slave states, most people who went there came from the Midwest and border slave states. Their main interest was acquiring land and making money. Insofar as they cared at all about the slavery issue, the vast majority, including nonslaveholding Missourians, wanted to keep both black slaves and free blacks out of the territory. There was much turmoil and some violence typical of a frontier situation, but most of this concerned disputed land claims, competition for lucrative government contracts, and rivalry for the location of county seats, not slavery. A minority of the settlers from free states, however, had been sent from New England by antislavery societies, and some of them were authentic abolitionists. Unlike most settlers, the New Englanders opposed slavery on moral grounds, denounced the exclusion of free blacks, and insisted that blacks be granted equal rights. Their presence frightened nonslaveholding Southerners, who wished Kansas to be free, into following the small group of slaveholders in the territory because they feared that the New Englanders would make Kansas an abolitionist sanctuary for fugitive slaves.[11]

The New Englanders also scared slaveholders in neighboring Missouri, who wildly exaggerated the number and influence of the abolitionists. When popular sovereignty received its first real test in the election of a territorial legislature on March 30, 1855, Missourians, led by U.S. Senator David R. Atchison, poured across the border to vote and secure a proslavery government for Kansas. At that early date, when few Northern settlers had arrived, the proslavery men would probably have won the election without the Missourians' interference, but the invasion of the "Border Ruffians" made a mockery of local self-government. The territorial governor threw out some of the fraudulent returns and put a few antislavery men in the legislature, but the proslavery men were in firm control. They then passed a series of incredible laws that stripped antislavery men of basic constitutional rights. Officeholding in Kansas was limited to men who would take an oath that they favored slavery. Asserting that slavery was illegal in the territory was declared a felony. Harboring a fugitive slave was punishable by ten years' imprisonment; inciting a slave to escape or circulating abolitionist literature became a capital offense. As if to practice what they preached, the proslavery men then expelled antislavery representatives from the legislature. Vowing that "we owe no allegiance to the tyrannical enactments of this spurious legislature,"[12] Northern settlers responded by organizing their own government at Topeka in opposition to the "bogus legislature" at Lecompton. That government brazenly declared Kansas a free state and elected its own governor and legislature. Kansans were polarized not so much by attitudes toward slavery or blacks as by allegiance to rival governments; for many who supported the Lecompton legislature wanted to keep slavery out of Kansas. Its laws were so unjust, however, that by the end of 1855 a majority of the people in the territory aligned with the Topeka regime.

The ostensible division of Kansas between Northerners and Southerners over the question of slavery extension, when the real division was over the legitimacy of the territorial legislature, gave Republicans in the East a marvelous opportunity. Friction between the two camps, both of which were heavily armed, was inevitable, because neither recognized the laws of the other government as binding or its officials as legal. Efforts by the agents of one government to enforce laws against settlers who paid fealty to the other, even for the many crimes that had nothing to do with slavery, took on the aura of a war between antislavery and proslavery factions, a conflict that Republican propagandists distorted far beyond reality. When the Lecompton government sent a posse to arrest several free state leaders in the town of Lawrence and when that posse, which included Missourians, burned some buildings and destroyed two printing presses but killed no one in the town on May 21, 1856, Republicans labeled it "The Sack of Lawrence." "The War Actually Begun—Triumph of the Border Ruffians—Lawrence in Ruins—Several Persons Slaughtered—Freedom Bloodily Subdued," hyperbolized the Eastern Republican press. Ignoring more serious atrocities like the fanatical John Brown's brutal massacre at Pottawatomie Creek of five nonslaveholding Southerners affiliated with the territorial government, Republicans shrieked that Kansas was bleeding because lawless slaveholders were butchering defenseless Northern settlers in their effort to force slavery on the territory. What gave Kansas such partisan value to Republicans was that President Pierce denounced the Topeka government as revolutionary, officially recognized the proslavery legislature as the only legal authority in the territory, and pledged to use federal force to uphold its laws. The national Democratic administration was seemingly helping the South and the Missouri Border Ruffians to impose slavery on the unwilling settlers of Kansas. The Democracy had apparently aligned itself with the antirepublican forces, which violated the law, trampled majority rule, and deprived citizens of basic liberties. The Republican Seward made the case explicit in a Senate speech when he likened Pierce to King George III, a despotic tyrant who oppressed Kansans just as the British monarch had subjugated American colonists.[13]

If the prolonged imbroglio in Kansas helped the Republicans by arousing the North against the South and the Democratic party, so did a much briefer but related incident in Washington. On May 19 and 20, 1856, Charles Sumner, the Republican Senator from Massachusetts, delivered a carefully rehearsed speech called "The Crime against Kansas" in which he insultingly excoriated slavery, the South, and several individual senators, among them South Carolina's Andrew Pickens Butler. On May 22, the day after the so-called "Sack of Lawrence" a cousin of Butler who was determined to avenge the family name, Representative Preston S. Brooks of South Carolina, strode into the Senate chamber, accosted Sumner who was seated at his desk, and in less than a minute beat him senseless with a gutta percha cane. Sumner's bloody head wounds were so severe that he could not attend the Senate regularly for over three years, but the immediate sectional reaction to Brooks's dramatic act was more important than Sumner's lingering personal agony. Throughout the South, Democratic newspapers praised Brooks for chastising an insolent Yankee abolitionist, and he was sent scores of new canes from admiring Southerners to replace the one he had splintered on Sumner's head. For Republicans Sumner became a martyr, an actual victim of naked Southern aggression who personified the plight of the entire North. Nothing else could have given so much credibility to the Republican charge that the arrogant slavocracy meant to subjugate and enslave Northern whites just as they had their black slaves. The assault, proclaimed Republicans, clearly demonstrated the need of Northerners to unite behind a party with backbone, which could resist the impudent Southerners. "The remedy for ruffianism resides in a united North," asserted one Massachusetts Republican paper. "Old party names must be forgotten, old party ties surrendered."[14]

"Bleeding Kansas" and "Bleeding Sumner" electrified the North. More than anything else in 1856 they accounted for the Republicans' success in enlisting diverse and often mutually hostile Northern voters behind their standard. Together they had created an issue "that properly directed, might carry the election by storm," wrote one observer at the end of May, while a New Yorker testified, "The feeling all over our State, in relation to Kansas affairs and the assault on Sumner, is more intense and determined than I thought it would be." By June Republicans were exulting that "the outrage upon Sumner & the occurences in Kansas have helped us vastly." At the same time, Southern Know Nothings recognized that Northern anger doomed all hopes of maintaining the national American party at full strength. Thus a Virginian despaired to a Northern Fillmore man, "Recent events in Kansas and Washington seem to be driving the masses of your people into the arms of the Republican party and forcing a coalition between them and the Americans who disapprove of Mr. F[illmore]'s nomination."[15]

Kansas and Sumner provided Republican propagandists with an

invincible combination. Both were direct clashes between Northern whites and Southern whites in which the Northerners could be cast as the victims of aggression. Neither directly involved black slavery or black rights. The race question was acutely embarrassing for Republicans, and the more they could ignore blacks—free and slave—the more they could keep their appeal lily white, the more they liked it. In addition, the incidents could be politicized in the broadest terms employing the idiom of republicanism, for they presaged the actual enslavement of Northern whites. "Did you ever see such infernal, outrageous, liberty-crushing, persecuting, tyrannical, I can't find any word to express it but damnable, proceedings as those engineered by Pierce & Douglas in Kansas? It makes my blood boil," wrote an Indiana Republican. Similarly, a Massachusetts Yankee fumed that the fate of Northerners in Kansas showed that "the *Missouri Savages* seem determined to prevent their settlement in the Territory except as servants or slaves of the South. . .what has taken place in Kansas and at Washington within the last few months is a disgrace to the country and a reproach to our republican form of government." The incidents, in sum, had much wider resonance in the North than any attacks on the institution of black slavery or even slavery extension could have had. "The anti-slavery sentiment in New Jersey is not a moving power among the people," wrote one Republican. "The Sumner outrage is however severely condemned and has had its effect." The Republican national platform in 1856 illustrated perfectly the balance of campaign themes. It denounced slavery as immoral, demanded that Congress prevent its expansion and admit Kansas immediately as a free state, and devoted the bulk of its space to cataloging and protesting the violation of the rights of Northern white settlers in Kansas by the despotic proslavery legislature, which was aided by the Democratic administration.[16]

Kansas and Sumner provided the main ammunition in 1856, but in that campaign and for the remainder of the decade the Republicans utilized the republican idiom in other ways against Southerners and Democrats. To complement their argument that slavery expansion must be stopped to preserve the opportunities of free labor, for example, Republicans portrayed planters as supercilious aristocrats contemptuous of the common man while the Republicans were an egalitarian party that protected the poor from the privileged. "The contest ought not to be considered a *sectional* one but the war of a *class*—the slaveholders—against the laboring people of *all classes*," wrote the border state Republican and former Jacksonian Francis

P. Blair to his son in 1856. Seward iterated in 1860 that "it is an eternal question between classes—between the few privileged and the many underprivileged—the eternal question between aristocracy and democracy." Over and over, as well, Republicans denounced the apparent usurpation of the national government from the people by a tiny minority of planters. Pledging "to resist the spread of Slavery and the aggressions of the Slave Power, and to secure a free government for a free people," a Republican association in Buffalo announced:

> We require for our country a government of the people, instead of a government by an oligarchy; a government maintaining before the world the rights of men rather than the privilege of masters. . . .We insist that there shall be no Slavery outside the Slave States, and no domination over the action of the National Government by the Slave Power.

Similarly, a Republican meeting in Hartford castigated "the maladministration and abuse of powers" by the Democratic administration, which was controlled by "the nullification dynasty."[17]

The way to restore the government to the people, the Republicans argued, was to revive the republican doctrine of majority rule. Whereas the Know Nothings had promised to return power to the people by ousting hack politicians from office and the Democrats did so by calling for local self-determination, the Republicans argued that if people were free and equal in a republic, then only majority rule fairly represented the equal rights of all. Because the North was a majority section in the nation, the North and not the South ought to control the government. Protesting as undemocratic and un-American the idea that 20 million free whites in the North should be ruled by slaves and their 350,000 masters, a Pennsylvania Republican meeting demanded "the reestablishment of the rule of the majority." When confronted with threats of Southern secession if the Republicans won in 1860, a Pittsburgh editor scornfully replied, "This is the merest rant. It is an insulting demand to the majority to disband and give up their cherished views and purposes." The Republicans' success in translating the sectional conflict politically into a fundamental principle of republican government is attested to by the postwar memoirs of General Ulysses S. Grant, who had been largely apolitical before the war. Referring to the major Southern and Northern candidates in the 1860 election, he tersely summarized, "The contest was really between Mr. Breckinridge and Mr. Lincoln; between minority rule and rule by the majority."[18]

Even though the Republican organization was still embryonic in 1856, the party's appeal was so compelling and its tactics for combining with the North Americans so skillful that Frémont almost won the presidential election. The Republicans carried every free state except California, Illinois, Indiana, Pennsylvania, and New Jersey. Buchanan and his running mate John C. Breckinridge of Kentucky carried those states as well as all the slave states except Maryland, thereby securing election, even though they garnered only 45 percent of the popular vote in the three-way race. Frémont won 33 percent of the popular vote (45 percent in the North) and Fillmore 21 percent. Fillmore carried only Maryland, but he ran very strongly in other slave states, expecially Kentucky, Tennessee, Louisiana, and Florida.[19] More important to the result, Fillmore won about 165,000 votes in the free states that Frémont failed to carry and almost 400,000 in the entire North. Together the Frémont and Fillmore votes totaled more than Buchanan's in California, New Jersey, and Illinois and almost equaled it in Pennsylvania and Indiana. As important, although the Democratic vote declined in the Northeast from 1852, except in Buchanan's home state of Pennsylvania, the Democrats gained over 100,000 votes in the Midwest. Immigrant revulsion from the Know Nothing stigma of Republicanism, continued faith among farmers in popular sovereignty, racial fears stirred up by the Democratic campaign, and genuine fears for the Union probably accounted for that accession.

The basic lesson of the election for the Republicans was that they would have to improve their fortunes in the lower North. If they had carried Pennsylvania and either Illinois or Indiana, they could have won. Specifically, the Republicans would have to offset the continuing appeal of the Democrats in that region and especially to capture those anti-Democratic voters who had supported Fillmore instead of Frémont. Die-hard nativists and anti-Catholics had backed Fillmore, but both Fillmore and Buchanan had benefited from the cry that Republican victory would disrupt the Union. The voters the Republicans had to add to their coalition in order to win the presidency were more conservative than those they had already drawn to the fold. They had not yet been persuaded that the national Democratic party was a mere tool of the Slave Power, that the Slave Power's aggressions posed the greatest danger to the Union by undermining its republican basis, and that the preservation of the Union of the Founding Fathers therefore required the replacement of the Democratic regime by the Republican party. To triumph, in sum, the Republicans had both to broaden their appeal to include Fillmore Americans and to strengthen their basic case against the South and the Democratic party.

On the other hand, despite the Republicans' impressive performance in 1856, their status as the second party in a new two-party system was by no means secure. It was still uncertain what shape political strife would permanently assume, and many former Whigs in the North still hoped to recreate a bisectional opposition party that combined Northerners and Southerners, something the Republicans could never do by running as an anti-Southern party. With a fifth of the popular vote, the American party remained a potential base for a new nonsectional opposition party that might replace the Republicans if the need for an exclusive Northern party disappeared. Many Know Nothings and former Whigs had backed Frémont in 1856 only because blatant Slave Power aggressions against Northern rights and the threat of slavery expansion into Kansas had seemed to dictate its necessity. If those supposed aggressions stopped, if the menace of a Slave Power plot appeared to recede, and if different nonsectional issues arose that could be used against the Democracy, then the rationale of the Republican party would dissolve and the way might be opened for a very different anti-Democratic party. Because that threat soon materialized, more was involved in the history of the Republican party between Frémont's defeat and Abraham Lincoln's victory than merely expanding its 1856 base. Republicans had to fight a vigorous holding action to prevent erosion of that base.

In the fall of 1857 a sudden financial panic prompted bank suspensions and a sharp if brief recession in agricultural, commercial, and industrial activities. In the past such slumps had helped the Democratic party by fomenting animosity against bankers and paper money. Democratic leaders around the country, therefore, saw a golden opportunity to divert attention from sectional issues and resurrect traditional Jacksonian rhetoric against monopolies and aristocratic bankers in the elections of 1857 and 1858. Because those elections primarily involved state and local offices, Democrats could argue with justice that immediate economic needs should be more important than the national sectional issue in determining their outcome. As Martin Van Buren had done twenty years earlier, Democratic President Buchanan attempted to orchestrate this campaign in his annual message to Congress in December 1857 by blaming the Panic on the excesses of banks and calling on state governments to restrict banknote issues, require larger specie deposits, and revoke charters of banks that suspended specie payments.

Following that lead, Democrats throughout the North attempted to exploit the economic grievances aroused by the Panic, but their hopes of substituting economic for sectional matters as the axis of party conflict were frustrated for a number of reasons. For one thing, the financial panic itself was of brief duration. Most banks resumed specie payments by the spring of 1858. Although pockets of unemployment persisted in certain sectors of the economy, especially in iron manufacturing and coal mining, the banking and currency issue itself was partially defused by the banks' steady performance. Even in 1857 and 1858, however, when economic issues were still salient, they did not help the Democrats.

The general reason was that economic grievances growing out of the Panic were so complex and localized that they were not susceptible to manipulation by statewide parties. Three concerns had political relevance at the state level: banking and currency reform; rabid antagonism toward railroads, whose high rates, low taxes, and monopolistic powers offended men who could not afford to ship goods; and demands to reform state-owned and money-losing canal systems either by enlarging them, as in New York, or by selling them to private investors in order to relieve the public of a tax burden, as in Pennsylvania and Ohio. Attitudes toward both railroads and canals tended to follow regional patterns that were not amenable to exploitation by state parties. Whether men favored or opposed railroads and canals depended on their location, not their party, and the Democrats could develop no coherent and distinctive party program concerning them. The Democratic party, moreover, remained internally divided in legislatures on banking questions, especially on bills concerning note issues and specie reserve requirements. Those divisions, too, often reflected regional or at least rural-urban disagreements. In addition, Republican politicians and editors were often just as vocal as Democrats in calling for bank reform, while others denied that the Republicans had an official stand on banking. As a result, the Democrats usually could not draw a party line on the banking issue. The sole exception came in Ohio, where special circumstances allowed the Democrats to carry the legislature in 1857 and, by party line votes, pass new laws taxing private banks and removing state government deposits from them. Even in Ohio, however, the Democrats could not generate coherent policy recommendations concerning currency reform at the state level, and like others they called more and more for national legislation to limit note issue.[20]

Once economic issues were shifted from a state to a national perspective, the Democrats lost whatever advantage they might have had. They had lowered tariff rates in the spring of 1857; when imports fell during the recession, government revenue, which was largely dependent on tariff receipts, plummeted. Instead of retrenching federal expenditures on public works like post office and ship construction—which provided jobs for good Democrats—or raise the tariff—which Southern Democrats adamantly opposed—the Buchanan administration, led by Secretary of the Treasury Howell Cobb, resorted to deficit financing by selling interest-bearing Treasury notes to see the government through its crisis. Whatever the economic wisdom of this decision, it allowed the Republicans to charge the administration with gross extravagance and financial mismanagement and to demand a higher tariff that would balance the federal budget and restore jobs to the unemployed by protecting American industry from foreign competition. By the fall of 1858 Republicans throughout the North, but especially in Pennsylvania, New Jersey, New York, and Massachusetts, had taken up the cry for tariff revision. When the Southern-dominated Democracy also frustrated increased demands for railroad land grants, rivers and harbors improvements, and a homestead act to promote recovery, the Republicans simply added those issues to their stockpile of weapons. In terms of national policy, the Panic worked against the Democrats instead of for them.

If economic fluctuations briefly challenged the priorities of the Republicans, developments affecting the slavery issue seemed to threaten their very purpose as a party. Two days after Buchanan's inauguration in March 1857, the Supreme Court handed down its notorious Dred Scott decision. Scott was a Missouri slave who in the 1830s had lived for several years in Wisconsin Territory, from which slavery had been banned by the Missouri Compromise. In the late 1840s, while once again in Missouri, Scott sued for his freedom in that state's courts on the basis that once having lived in free territory, he was free. Losing in that domain, Scott sued his new owner, a New York citizen named John A. Sanford, in federal courts under the Constitution's diverse citizenship clause, and the case eventually came to the Supreme Court on appeal from a lower federal court that upheld the state decision.

The Court might have followed precedent and ruled narrowly that state law prevailed in the matter and that Scott was therefore still a slave. Instead, it chose to rule broadly. In an intricate decision supported by six justices who argued differently in individual opinions, the Court held that Scott remained a slave, that as a black and a slave he was not a citizen and therefore not entitled to sue in federal courts, and, most important, that the Missouri Compromise ban on slavery north of 36°30', on which Scott rested his claim to freedom, was unconstitutional because congressional prohibition of slavery deprived slaveholders of their property without due process of law in violation of the Fifth Amendment.

Although the 1820 ban itself had been overturned by Congress three years earlier, the Court's majority, six Democratic justices, five of whom where Southerners, were declaring that the major concrete policy that united Republicans—congressional prohibition of slavery from the territories—was unconstitutional. In a single stroke they threatened to destroy the party's principal reason for being. If Congress could not bar slavery expansion as Republicans demanded, Democrats asked, what purpose did the party serve? The decision implied that the Northern majority was powerless to keep slavery out of the territories if Southerners chose to take it there.

Republicans greeted the Court's decision with outrage. They could not simply urge defiance, however, since their posture as champions of republicanism would be destroyed by flouting the rule of law. Instead, they attacked the decision in two ways. Incorrectly, they argued that the Court had no need or right to decide on congressional authority over slavery in the territories and therefore that that part of the decision was a mere *obiter dictum* and not the law of the land. With slightly more justice they charged that the decision itself was part of the Slave Power conspiracy between the executive and judicial branches to usurp the government from the people and nullify the wishes of the majority. In February, before his inauguration, Buchanan had been informed of the impending decision. Because he regarded agitation over the territorial question as dangerous to both his party and the nation, he had urged the justices to make a broad decision settling once and for all whether Congress had power over slavery in the territories. Then, at his inauguration, Buchanan had whispered to Chief Justice Roger B. Taney for several minutes before announcing in his address that the Court should settle the disputed question and that he would "cheerfully submit" to the Court's impending decree. When Taney issued the Court's decision two days later, a plot did indeed seem to exist that fit perfectly the Republicans' strategy of ignoring black slavery and portraying Democratic and Southern actions in classical terms of despots crushing out republican liberties. "The question of African Slavery sinks into insignificance compared with the enslavement of the people of Kansas, and the subjugation of all the free states to the principles of Dred Scott vs. Sanford," protested one Illinois voter in 1857. To mobilize such resentment Seward charged in the Senate in 1858 that Buchanan's inauguration had been "desecrated by a coalition between the executive and judicial departments to undermine the national legislature and liberties of the people." Comparing Buchanan at one point to "the worst of all the Roman emperors," he said that Buchanan had received the justices when they made their traditional formal call on a new president "as graciously as Charles the First did the judges who had, at his instance, subverted the statutes of English liberty."[21]

The Dred Scott case showed the Republicans' ability to convert a crippling disadvantage into a powerful weapon of their own. Continued jousting over Kansas followed the reverse pattern. Developments that initially seemed to make the Republicans unbeatable evolved to a point where they endangered the very existence of the Republican party. Realizing that squabbles over slavery in Kansas Territory had, since 1854, provided the Republicans with their most compelling evidence of Slave Power aggressions, Buchanan quickly determined to admit Kansas as a state as rapidly as possible and thereby spike the Republicans' biggest gun. He persuaded Robert J. Walker, who had been so important in Democratic politics in the 1840s, to serve as territorial governor, and he urged Walker to see that Kansas applied to Congress with a new constitution settling the vexed slavery question once and for all. Pledged to popular sovereignty, he assured Walker in writing that he would back Walker's insistence that the entire constitution be submitted to a popular referendum so that the will of the majority of actual settlers in Kansas would be determined.

Kansans remained divided in their loyalties to the Topeka and Lecompton governments, however, and even before Walker was appointed the Lecompton legislature had called for an election of delegates in June 1857 to a convention that was to meet at Lecompton in September to write a constitution for statehood. Despite Walker's pleas the free-state men refused to participate in an election called by the "bogus legislature," and in June only about 2000 from an estimated electorate of 24,000 chose extreme proslavery men to attend the

Lecompton convention. Before that assemblage acted, however, another election was held for the territorial legislature in October. This time Walker persuaded the free-staters to vote, and when Walker threw out some obviously fraudulent proslavery returns, antislavery men won control of the official territorial legislature for the first time. Furious at Walker's action, the proslavery delegates to the Lecompton convention wrote a constitution that guaranteed slaveholders their property rights to the slightly more than 200 slaves already in Kansas and to their descendants. Instead of submitting the entire constitution for popular approval as Walker, Buchanan, and the Democratic party had promised, the convention ordered that the voters could only choose between two versions of it: one with a clause allowing the entry of more slaves into the state, and the other with a clause prohibiting future entry. Either way, Kansans had to accept the constitution itself, which contained several other objectionable features aside from that regarding slaves already in Kansas. Free-state settlers again refused to take part in the referendum on December 21, 1857, and the provision for the admission of additional slaves passed 6143 to 569. On January 4, 1858, however, the free-state men voted in another referendum called by the new territorial legislature that they controlled, and over 10,000 votes were cast against the entire constitution. In this election, the proslavery men abstained. Despite the evidence that the majority of Kansans opposed the Lecompton constitution, Buchanan, who feared the ire of Southern Democrats should he reject it, accepted the constitution and December referendum as legitimate. In early 1858 he urged Congress to admit Kansas under it. The President used every threat and inducement at his command, including outright cash bribes, to persuade Northern Democratic congressmen to pass the statehood bill.

Buchanan's actions presented the Republicans with a splendid issue. Here was a Democratic president ignoring the party's commitment to popular sovereignty and apparently bowing to Southern pressure by attempting to ram slavery down the throats of Kansans despite the wishes of the local majority. Thousands of Democratic voters who in 1856 had kept faith in the party's guarantees to obtain free soil with popular sovereignty now lost confidence in that solution and appeared ready to convert to the Republican cause. Republicans also took glee in the obvious discord Buchanan's decision had provoked among Democratic leaders. Even before the December referendum in Kansas, Stephen A. Douglas, author of the Kansas-Nebraska bill, denounced the constitution as a fraud.

Long a sincere champion of self-determination by local majorities, Douglas realized that his entire political career depended on the viability of that doctrine. He had been embarrassed by the Dred Scott decision; the Court had not ruled directly on the power of territorial legislatures over slavery, but many had asked how Congress could delegate to them the power to prohibit slavery if it did not constitutionally possess that power itself. By June 1857, Douglas had deflected such criticism by arguing that legislatures could block slavery simply by refusing to pass the positive slave codes necessary to establish the institution. No argument, however, could justify the denial of majority rule in Kansas. Facing reelection by the Illinois legislature to be chosen in 1858, he knew that the Republicans could carry that legislature on the Kansas issue unless he broke with Buchanan and opposed Lecompton.

Openly joining the Republicans in excoriating Lecompton as a travesty, Douglas led an unsuccessful fight against it in the Senate. In the House, however, Douglas and his lieutenants rallied enough Democrats to combine with the Republicans and prevent its passage. The Northern Democratic party was split between Douglas and Buchanan supporters and would remain so until the Democratic national convention in 1860. Eventually a compromise was worked out in Congress that resubmitted the question of statehood under the Lecompton Constitution to another popular referendum of all Kansans. On August 2, 1858, it was overwhelmingly defeated. Kansas would remain a territory instead of becoming a slave state. By 1860, only two slaves remained within its borders.

The Lecompton fight marked a turning point for the Democratic party. Buchanan and Douglas would never patch up their differences. The President worked to defeat the Little Giant's bid for reelection in Illinois in 1858 and for the presidential nomination in 1860. In the congressional campaigns of 1858, anti-Lecompton Democrats ran separate candidates or aided the Republicans against proadministration Democrats, and by 1860 the majority of Northern Democrats insisted that only Douglas's nomination would give them any chance against the Republicans.

Yet the Lecompton fight had permanently soured Southern Democrats on popular sovereignty and on Douglas. At the critical moment, they complained, Douglas had rejected the legal workings of self-determination in Kansas and had joined the hated Republicans in preventing the entry of another slave state. When Douglas, during his famous debates with Lincoln in 1858, reiterated his "Freeport Doctrine" that territorial legislatures could prohibit slavery simply by not passing positive proslavery laws, it was the last straw. In 1859 Southern Democrats in the Senate stripped Douglas of his committee chairmanship. Some, like Albert G. Brown and Jefferson Davis of Mississippi, demanded that Congress pass a federal slave code to protect slave property in the territories.

By the time of the Democratic national convention at Charleston, South Carolina in April 1860, several slave state delegations were pledged to bolt the convention unless the platform committed the party to a federal slave code, and almost all Southerners were intent on blocking Douglas's nomination. The Northern majority at the convention, however, refused to concede to the demands of the Southern minority on either the platform or the candidate. When threats failed, enough Southerners left the convention to prevent any nomination at Charleston. Eventually the Democrats nominated two presidential candidates; Douglas, who was supported by the vast majority of Northern Democrats and a minority of Southerners, and Vice-President John C. Breckinridge, who ran on the Southern platform of a federal slave code and who had the support of most Southerners and of Buchanan loyalists in the North.

At first glance, the disruption of the Democracy over the slavery extension issue and personal feuds seemed to guarantee the triumph of the Republican party, and in 1860 those divisions may have aided the Republicans by discouraging Democratic voters who saw no hope of victory with a divided electoral vote. In 1858, however, the benefits of the Lecompton struggle for Republicans were not so clear. By joining the Republicans in the fight against Lecompton and Southern Democrats, Douglas and his Northern Democratic followers seemed just as opposed to Slave Power aggressions and slavery extension as the Republican party, especially since its own policy of congressional prohibition had been jeopardized by the Dred Scott decision. The rift in the Democracy had broken the link between the South and the Northern Democratic party that the Republicans were trying to forge. By erasing the clear line of difference between the parties, Douglas's action vitiated the Republicans' argument that only they could resist the South. The seriousness of that development became clear when many Eastern Republicans urged the Illinois party not to oppose Douglas's reelection to the Senate.

Equally important, the final referendum in Kansas had for all intents and purposes permanently settled the slavery extension issue, which had provided the primary justification for the existence of the Republican party. No one expected slavery to spread to the larger Nebraska Territory, and the fate of slavery in the Southwest had been determined by the Compromise of 1850 and by climate. There were a few slaves in New Mexico who were primarily house servants but not enough to arouse much interest in the North. Although some Southerners pushed for a federal slave code, others argued that there was no area available in which slavery could flourish and that the South had no excess slaves to send to one if it existed. Besides, the adamant opposition of Douglas Democrats and Republicans effectively doomed such a proposal. Finally, some Southern Democrats did demand annexation of new territories for slavery expansion in Mexico and the Caribbean, but the possibility of congressional approval of and appropriations for such acquisitions was remote. Only Kansas had given immediacy to the slavery extension issue, and on August 2, 1858 the fate of slavery in Kansas was settled by the antislavery majority. By that date, the Republicans had lost their major issue and their major distinction from their Northern Democratic opponents.

The resolution of the slavery issue in Kansas also created the possibility that a new, nonsectional opposition party could challenge the Republicans' credentials as the best anti-Democratic party. Buchanan's Lecompton policy was so egregiously unfair and his economic policies so open to criticism that Southerners who had supported Fillmore in 1856 joined the assault on the administration. Inheriting former Whig strength, the Americans had run strongly in the upper South, and by 1858 old Whigs like John Bell of Tennessee and especially John J. Crittenden of Kentucky saw that Buchanan's policies had created a chance to revive a national conservative opposition party that could replace the Republicans in a new two-party system. Their experience with the Second Party System naturally disposed them toward a national alignment of party competition instead of the sectional alignment that Republicans were fomenting. In the spring of 1858 Crittenden gave two major speeches in the Senate to define a basis for the new party the former Whigs envisioned. The first vilified Buchanan's Lecompton policy, demanded resubmission of the Lecompton Constitution to a vote of all Kansans, and called for true majority rule in the territories even if it produced free soil, a stand that mirrored that of the anti-Lecompton Democrats but sharply distinguished Southern Americans from Southern Democrats, who pressed for Kansas's admission as a slave state. The second speech flayed Buchanan's fiscal extravagance and demanded a higher tariff to protect workers from a depression prolonged by Democratic policies. Coupled with nativism and assaults on official corruption, these themes would provide the platform for a new party that all opponents of the administration, and not just Yankees, could support.

From all over the country congratulations flowed to Crittenden along with predictions that he would be elected president in 1860. Northern Whigs and Americans rejoiced that his position on Lecompton had given them new life. Southern opposition to Lecompton had destroyed the stigma of cooperating with the South that had plagued Americans in the North in 1856. "You can have no conception of the importance of your position," wrote Washington Hunt from New York. "It gives assurance to the whole country that patriotism and love of justice do not belong to North or South, but that both sections have men true to the Union, and to the principles of constitutional liberty." From Buffalo a correspondent predicted that Americans and Republicans would unite in a *"new party"* behind Crittenden's position and elect him president, while a resident of Erie, Pennsylvania echoed, "I look for a reorganization of parties within the next year on a basis similar to the principle embodied in your great speech." A Kentuckian was more detailed.

> Will not this Lecompton Business present . . . a field for a
> new organization of parties, or rather the organization of
> a new party with a new name having the principles of truth
> and justice of the old Whigs, the national principles of the
> Americans, without their fanaticism and proscription, and
> some of the best features of the National democracy, in
> which all the Americans, all the national [anti-Lecompton]
> Democrats North, all the old line Whigs, and the soundest
> portion of the Republicans could unite.[22]

Here was the rub for the Republicans. With the slavery extension issue shifted by the Dred Scott decision and the Lecompton fight to the question of whether the free-state majority was really ruling in Kansas and with that question settled by August 1858, the need for an exclusive Northern party, such as the Republican party, seemed over. Not only might a new conservative party based on mere opposition to

Buchanan and not to the South prevent the Republicans from absorbing the Northern Fillmore voters they needed to win in 1860, but it could also draw off Frémont voters who no longer saw any need for the Republican party and its Wilmot Proviso principles. In 1858 and 1859 Republican leaders like national committee chairman Edwin D. Morgan of New York and Governor Salmon P. Chase of Ohio were inundated with letters worrying that antislavery sentiment was receding, that voters were becoming more conservative toward the South, and that the new polyglot opposition party might consign the Republicans to an early grave. "The object is to break down or override the Republican party & elevate John Bell or some other Old Line Tariff Whig to the Presidency or in other words the object is to reestablish the old Whig party under a new name & crush out all 'Slavery agitation,'" wrote a Philadelphian to Morgan. Similarly, Ohioans complained to Chase that the political comeback of the former Whig Thomas Corwin as a Republican congressional candidate was meant to "bring down our doctrines and position to the Fillmore level in order to make Corwin our leader and *Senator* and Crittenden our President in 1860."[23] From August 1858 until the 1860 presidential campaign finally began, the Republican party faced its sternest challenge.

The response of Republicans to this conservative challenge varied. Most insisted that, despite developments in Kansas, the Slave Power plot against Northern rights still existed and that the need for Republican victory was therefore just as compelling as ever. A circular published by the Republican national committee at Morgan's urging in the spring of 1859 illustrates this tack perfectly. "The republican party had its origin in the obvious necessity for resistance to the aggressions of the slave power," it began. Although some of the problems forcing its organization in 1856 had been resolved, "the attitude of the slave power is persistently insolent and aggressive. . . .It is not content with the absolute control of the national government. . .not content with its well known influence, always pernicious, over the legislature at the national capital, but it demands fresh concessions from a free people" in its new cries for a slave code and the reopening of the African slave trade. "Upon no organization, except the republican party, can the country rely for successful resistance to these monstrous propositions, and for the correction of the gross abuses which have characterized the present national administration."[24]

At the state level, Republicans employed even more extreme rhetoric to perpetuate fear of a Slave Power conspiracy, distinguish themselves from Northern Democrats, and rejustify the need of a principled Northern party to prevent defections to the conservative opposition. Thus Republicans resurrected charges first made by the Liberty party and revived briefly after the passage of the Kansas-Nebraska Act that the Slave Power, in conjunction with the Democratic party, was plotting to spread black slavery not only to the territories but to the free states themselves. Abraham Lincoln's famous campaign against Douglas for the Illinois Senate seat in 1858 provides a perfect example. Because of Douglas's new popularity as a foe of Lecompton, Lincoln desperately needed an issue to draw a line between himself and Douglas and to show that his credentials as an anti-Southern candidate were superior. To establish that distinction, he argued that he believed black slavery was immoral and should be placed on the road to "ultimate extinction"; Douglas, Lincoln charged, did not care whether it spread or not so long as the local majority got its way.

Lincoln raised the moral issue, however, less to draw distinctions on the ground of humanitarian sympathy for black slaves than to supplement his primary theme first developed in his keynote address in which he asserted that a house divided against itself could not stand and that the nation could not remain half slave and half free. Either slavery would be stopped from spreading and eventually die, "or its *advocates* will push it forward, till it shall become alike lawful in *all* the States, *old* as well as *new—North* as well as *South*." All that was needed was another Supreme Court ruling declaring state laws prohibiting slavery unconstitutional. As evidence that this might happen, he constantly reiterated the steps that had been taken since 1853 to spread slavery that had been unimaginable until then—the Kansas-Nebraska Act, proslavery tyranny in Kansas, the Dred Scott decision, and the effort to make Kansas a slave state under the Lecompton Constitution. Equally important, he iterated the complicity of prominent Democrats like Douglas, Pierce, Taney, and Buchanan in the proslavery plot. "In *such* a case, we find it impossible to not *believe* that Stephen and Franklin and Roger and James all understood one another from the beginning, and all worked under a common *plan* or *draft* drawn up before the first lick was struck." Nationalization of slavery by a new Supreme Court decision was the next act in the scenario, and Douglas was still following the script. His "don't care" attitude about slavery's immorality and expansion was meant to undermine Northern resistance to the idea of its spread and thereby to prepare the North to submit to the

Court's next decision. Lincoln's theme, in short, was not just slavery's immorality or the danger of it spread, but also the continuing danger of a malignant conspiracy against the North.[25]

In New York Seward made a very similar case in October before the fall elections of 1858. Explicitly condemning slavery as antagonistic to republicanism and vilifying the attempt of Southerners to pervert "a republican Constitution [into] an aristocratic one," he proclaimed that an "irrepressible conflict" existed between slavery and free labor and that the United States would become "either entirely a slaveholding nation, or entirely a free-labor nation." Rehearsing the past aggressions of the Slave Power, he, too, charged that slaveholders meant to spread slavery to Northern states. "The designs of the slaveholders can and must be defeated," and there was only one way to do that. "The Democratic party must be permanently dislodged from the Government," because the Democratic party "is identical with the Slave Power." "To expect the Democratic party to resist Slavery and favor Freedom, is as unreasonable as to look for Protestant missionaries to the Catholic Propaganda of Rome." When informed that the radical tone of the speech would offend conservative Americans and might prevent them from joining the Republicans in New York, Seward explained privately why he had given the speech. It "was needful to stay and brace up the Republican party" in the face of the conservative renaissance and to "justify its purpose to lead, not to follow, to exact concessions not to make them under any circumstances."[26]

Elsewhere Republicans also moved in a radical direction, but they turned to a different issue to draw a line between themselves and the Democrats. With the Kansas issue dead, Republicans in Wisconsin, Ohio, New York, Massachusetts, and Pennsylvania demanded renewed resistance to the Fugitive Slave Act of 1850 by passing personal liberty laws that provided jury trials, defense attorneys, and other procedural safeguards for accused fugitives. Because Democrats universally condemned such laws as an unconstitutional form of nullification and called for obedience to the 1850 law, agitation of the issue allowed the Republicans to stake out a distinct and advanced anti-Southern position. In 1858, for example, the new Democratic legislature in Ohio repealed a personal liberty law that Republicans had passed in 1857. In 1859 the Republican state platform was devoted solely to the fugitive slave issue and called for repeal of the federal law, while in 1860

Republican legislators pushed for a new state personal liberty law. Republicans in the New York legislature introduced a bill in the spring of 1859 that would automatically free any slave brought into the state by a Southerner on a visit and pushed it through the house. During the debates, one speaker boldly and baldly defended its purpose.

> The tendency of laws like that now under consideration is to check the Slave Power in its aggressive march, to roll back the black and threatening wave of Southern oppression, to teach the Slave Power that it will have absolute need of its utmost efforts to preserve its existence within its present boundaries, without grasping by robbery and bribery the territories of other governments in order to aggrandize and perpetuate slavery.[27]

Some Republicans moved to the left to combat the appeal of anti-Lecompton Democrats and a new conservative party, but others moved to the right to attract nativist and conservative voters who might be lured to the new party, especially in the Northern states Frémont had failed to carry in 1856. In New Jersey and Pennsylvania Republicans and Fillmore Americans in 1858 openly merged in People's Parties that not only incorporated the principles of both and gave prominence to the new tariff issue, but were far milder on the sectional issue than Republicans elsewhere. In effect, they virtually adopted the position of Crittenden and the anti-Lecompton Democrats by denouncing the denial of local majority rule in Kansas as "subversive of the principles of our government" instead of insisting that no more slave states be admitted to the Union. Indiana's Republicans also endorsed popular sovereignty as their new policy on slavery extension in 1858. In Massachusetts the American-Republican Governor Nathaniel P. Banks tried to combine the elements by running in 1857 and 1858 primarily on economic issues, denouncing Democratic extravagance and calling for a higher tariff, bank reform at the state level, and retrenchment of state expenditures. To woo die-hard Know Nothings, Banks also endorsed, and Republicans and Know Nothings in the legislature passed, an amendment to the state constitution barring naturalized citizens from voting until after two full years from the date of their naturalization. Although many Republicans in Massachusetts and elsewhere denounced this amendment and most Republican voters boycotted the referendum on it in May 1859, Banks's endorsement, like his stress on economic issues, should still be seen as a Republican attempt to broaden the Republican coalition, reduce Know Nothing recalcitrance, and prevent any slippage to a separate conservative party running on those same issues. Elsewhere, too, in Ohio and New York, for example, while Republicans were speaking boldly on the sectional issue, they were privately dividing tickets with Know Nothings to win their support.[28]

The diverse Republican tactics brought success in the state and congressional elections of 1858. The Democrats suffered a net loss of 18 congressional seats in the North, with particularly severe reversals in New York and Pennsylvania. Internal bickering among the Democrats over patronage and Lecompton weakened them, but the Republicans were clearly strengthened by their more effective mergers with Americans and continued exploitation of sectional grievances. Especially encouraging was their performance in the crucial swing states. The Democrats lost votes in New Jersey, Pennsylvania, and Indiana while the Republicans increased their absolute totals to carry those states. In Pennsylvania the Democratic vote dropped dramatically from 1856, while the new People's Party combined most of the Frémont and Fillmore voters. As a result the People's Party share of the vote was 53.6 percent, as compared to Frémont's 32 percent. In Illinois the Republicans actually won more votes in the important legislative elections, but malapportionment and Democratic holdovers kept the legislature in Democratic hands and allowed Douglas's reelection to the Senate. The prospect for 1860, however, seemed bright. Despite the challenges, the Republicans had managed both to add Fillmore voters and to reduce the Democrats' appeal, as they had to do, and by the beginning of 1859 one Republican confidently rejoiced to Chase, "The disposition and efforts of those who desire to form a party upon opposition merely have not produced much impression upon the great body of Republicans who have united for the sake of giving success to their principles."[29]

Such optimism was premature, but the Republican gains in 1858 did blunt the most efficacious appeal of those who wanted a more conservative bisectional party: the argument that only a party with support in the South could defeat the Democrats in 1860. The results of the Southern elections in 1859 further damaged that case. Although the Know Nothings carried Maryland again and the conservative Opposition parties ran well elsewhere, their failure in Virginia, Kentucky,

Tennessee, and North Carolina, let alone in the Deep South, weakened Northern faith that sufficient backing was available in the South to risk a bisectional campaign that might alienate part of their Northern support. "If the rotten democracy shall be beaten in 1860, it has to be done by the North; no human invention can deprive them of the South," Lincoln warned a conservative advocate in 1859. Then, on October 16, 1859, the abolitionist John Brown invaded Harper's Ferry, Virginia in an abortive attempt to foment a slave uprising. By increasing Southern fears of Northern intentions, Brown's raid gave such a potent issue to Southern Democrats that it doomed the chances of any conservative party in the South that would cooperate with Republicans.[30]

To offset whatever residual appeal a conservative party retained for Fillmore voters in the North, the Republicans seized the initiative on another issue dear to the hearts of Know Nothings, but one that also fit their own republican rhetoric perfectly—corruption in government. Since the era of the Revolution, corruption and conspiracy had been inseparably linked as twin dangers to republican government, and Democratic malfeasance could be made another compelling reason why the salvation of the Republic required the ouster of the Democratic regime. Fortunately, from the Republicans' point of view, the administration of James Buchanan was undoubtedly the most corrupt before the Civil War and one of the most corrupt in American history. Equally fortunate, many of its peculations and improprieties involved not just the President's men, but the entire Democratic party. Public printing funds were illegally subcontracted to support Democratic newspapers and used to buy votes at elections, campaign contributors were granted government contracts without competitive bidding, federal officials embezzled public money, and cash was offered to congressmen for their votes on Lecompton. Much that went on under Buchanan was not new, but the graft and gross overexpenditures of government money to favor Democratic contractors were illuminated for the first time during his term. Aggressively and partisanly, Republican congressional committees investigated virtually every department and activity of the executive branch. The most notable and biased was the Covode Committee, which looked into the President's relations with Congress and election frauds. The Republicans joyfully exposed every sleazy activity they could find, and they ordered that thousands of copies of committee reports be printed to be distributed as campaign material. To an electorate seeking reform, the Democrats seemed impossible.[31]

Sectional division, corruption, and complicity in both the Slave

Power conspiracy and the papal plot doomed Democrats to defeat in the presidential election of 1860. But the Republicans took no chances of squandering their many advantages. They had fought too long and skillfully to establish a distinct identity that could appeal to a broad spectrum of Northern support. Thus the party did not give its presidential nomination to its foremost leader, Seward of New York. Seward's apparent radicalism was regarded as a liability in the swing states of the lower North, but more important his long pro-Catholic and anti-Know Nothing record was considered fatal. Scores of Republicans warned that Seward was anathema to the nativists and that his nomination would drive off the Fillmore Americans and other Know Nothings that the Republicans had worked so hard to attract. Instead, they nomianted Lincoln of Illinois, whose House Divided speech had seemed almost as radical as Seward's Irrepressible Conflict effort. Lincoln, however, had not alienated the all-important Know Nothings as Seward had, and his popularity in Illinois might guarantee that key state. Despite the prominence he had gained from the debates with Douglas, his relative obscurity on the national scene and railsplitter background allowed him to be presented as a new man, "fresh from the ranks of the people." Expanding their use of the Know Nothing-like Wide Awake marching clubs to attract the young, exploiting anti-Catholic appeals where valuable, circulating conservative speakers like Corwin and New York's Daniel Ullmann to woo Fillmorites, and carefully emphasizing different economic issues like the homestead law in the West and the tariff in the East, where they had most impact, the Republicans maintained the gains they had made in 1858 and even extended their support.

Four candidates contested the 1860 election: Lincoln, Douglas, Breckinridge, and John Bell of Tennessee, nominee of the Constitutional Union party, which was the successor of the American party and a refuge for Union loving Whigs who still thought the Republicans too extreme. The race in the North, however, was essentially between Douglas and Lincoln, and Lincoln swept every Northern state except New Jersey by garnering almost 500,000 votes more than Frémont had won in 1856. The Republicans' success in courting Fillmore voters is attested to by the small Bell vote. Whereas Fillmore had attracted 395,000 votes in the North, Bell lured only 78,000. Lincoln also seems to have been inordinately successful with young voters participating in a presidential election for the first time. The accretion from those two sources was crucial to Republican triumph; surprisingly, the Democratic

215

party, if one combines the votes won by Douglas and Breckinridge, also increased their Northern vote by over 200,000 since 1856. Douglas was popular with immigrants and Catholics for his vociferous opposition to Know Nothingism. But his break with the South was probably the key to the continued popularity of the Democratic party among nonimmigrants in the North. As even a Republican admitted in 1860, "The North is anti-slavery to the core. The democratic party, today, if the leaders were removed so as to permit its real sentiments to be shown, is as anti-slavery as the republicans."[32] Southern antagonism to Douglas made him a credible candidate for those Democratic voters to support.

By 1860, then, antislavery sentiment did not distinguish Republican voters from Democratic voters in the North, and attributing Republican victory to antislavery sentiment is too simplistic. Instead, the Republicans' skill in broadening their case against and defining a line of difference between Northern Democrats and themselves so as to attract all the diverse groups who opposed the Democracy must be given credit. So, too, must their ability to shift the focus of the sectional conflict from black slavery to republicanism. In the end, however, the Republicans' greatest achievement and the thing most responsible for their victory was that they restored Northern faith in the efficacy of political action. By making the Democratic party a surrogate for the South and the Catholic Church, they argued that slavery could be ended and freedom secured, republicanism saved, and politics reformed simply by driving the Democracy and with it the slavocracy from power. And nothing more! By labeling the Democracy a receptacle of aristocracy, slavery, tyranny, and corruption—antirepublicanism incarnate—they redirected the sectional antagonism that was intensified by events and the Republicans' politicization of those events into traditional political channels. As one Republican had reported in 1856 about Northern anger over the outrages against free-state settlers in Kansas, "The people in many sections are perfectly furious; and nothing but the vent which our elections afford, prevents them from resorting to arms." Although some Republicans actually hoped to use their control of the executive branch to undermine slavery in the South, for most Republican voters Lincoln's victory and Democratic defeat was the only triumph over the South, the Slave Power, and slavery they required. Seward again incapsulated the view of the vast majority of the party when he pithily remarked a few days after Lincoln's inauguration "that the battle for Freedom had been fought and won."[33]

To Republican voters, in short, the political result had settled the sectional conflict. Their goal had been to save the Republic from a Southern conspiracy and to protect themselves from enslavement, not to attack or end black slavery. Later, they and other Northerners would take up arms against the South and during the ensuing war move against black slavery itself. They would do so, however, only because of further Southern assaults on the republic, only because certain Southerners refused to accept the political result that Northerners regarded as the legitimate conclusion of the sectional conflict, an end to strife not a beginning. It was only that last defiant Southern action that transformed a cold war, which had been carried on for seventy-five years within peaceful political channels, into a shooting war between the North and the South.

EIGHT

Politics, Slavery, and Southern Secession

Lincoln's election initiated a headlong rush to secede in seven slave states. Radicals who had advocated disunion for over a decade were intent on acting before Lincoln assumed office in March 1861. South Carolina led the way on December 20, 1860, and, by February 1, 1861, Mississippi, Florida, Alabama, Georgia, Louisiana, and Texas had followed her lead. On February 7, 1861, almost a full month before Lincoln's inauguration, the Confederate States of America was formed.

Nor was disunion the work of a tiny cabal in defiance of the popular will. As soon as the results of the presidential election were in, the drive for secession developed tremendous momentum. Local Democratic politicians committed to Breckinridge had argued throughout 1860 that the election of a Republican president was sufficient cause for secession; after the election, Democratic governors and legislatures quickly called for the election of delegates to state conventions to consider it. To make sure that prosecession delegates won, radicals orchestrated a powerful campaign of propaganda and pressure. Organizations like South Carolina's "Association of 1860" distributed secessionist tracts, and paramilitary Minute Man marching clubs and vigil-

ance associations insisted that a crisis existed that could only be resolved by separation. They seem to have been extraordinarily successful. Reports from widely diverse sources concurred that popular enthusiasm for secession was zealous and widespread.[1] Participation in
a crusade for Southern independence seemed cathartic.

In contrast, conservatives who opposed secession were woefully
disorganized and often intimidated into silence and inaction. Few outright Unionists ran in the delegate elections. Instead, what opposition
there was to immediate state secession came from candidates known as
Cooperationists, who argued that Lincoln's election alone was not
sufficient cause and who urged delay until he acted against the South
or until all the slave states acted together. Some Cooperationists opposed secession altogether, but many desired eventual secession and
most believed Republican aggressions against the South would justify
it. The question was whether Lincoln's election alone constituted that
aggression. The difference was more over means and timing than over
ends. The elections themselves were often very confused, since some
delegates refused to announce their position and others ran unopposed.
As a result, participation dropped sharply from the presidential poll in
November. Even though the election results and the balance between
Cooperationists and Immediatists at conventions were close in several
states, they probably did not accurately gauge the true strength of
secessionists and unconditional Unionists. What is clear is that Immediatists prevailed everywhere, that Cooperationists, after losing
early convention votes concerning the method of secession, usually
joined in backing the final secession ordinances, and that the public
responded with hosannas of joy.[2]

The drastic nature of secession becomes evident when it is placed
in a political context. Whatever else secession represented, it was a
rejection of the normal political process. It was a refusal not only to
tolerate Republican possession of the executive branch but to trust the
Democrats in Congress and the Supreme Court to protect Southern
Rights. The Republicans had not won control of either house of Congress in 1860. Democrats had a majority in the Senate, and Democrats,
along with members of the Southern Opposition, could dominate the
House. Presumably the Republicans would be powerless to effect any
anti-Southern action if Southerners did not withdraw from Congress.[3]
Southerners of all parties might oppose Republican policies for sectional reasons, as all had opposed the Wilmot Proviso earlier; Democrats from both sections might be expected to do so for the traditional

partisan purpose of generating interparty conflict. The Republicans, moreover, were a new and heterogeneous coalition united primarily by hostility to past Democratic actions, and they might not be able to coalesce behind any concrete or positive program for the future. Certainly the fate of the two previous Whig administrations suggested that opposition parties were more disrupted by control of the executive branch than strengthened by it. Why not wait it out until the next presidential election in 1864 or the congressional elections of 1862, as conservatives suggested? Why not rely on the normal ebb and flow of electoral results and the natural dynamics of competition between Republicans and Democrats to meet the South's needs?

One immediate response to these questions is that developments in the late 1850s had destroyed Southern faith in the reliability of the Democratic party. Douglas's fight against Lecompton and rejection of a federal slave code had infuriated many Southern Democrats. When the Northern majority had refused to knuckle under to the Southern minority at the Democratic national convention at Charleston, Southerners may have given up on the national party because they thought they had lost control of it and because they considered Douglas Democrats as untrustworthy as Republicans. Southerners, however, still controlled the congressional Democratic party, both numerically and in terms of key committee assignments, yet secessionists seemed to have no faith in Southern Democratic congressmen either.[4]

What is most striking about secession is that state leaders promoted it in defiance of, almost as a revolt against, prominent national politicians from the South. In many ways secession was an antiparty, antipolitician movement akin to the early stages of Know Nothingism and Republicanism in the North. Advocates of secession had long disliked political parties and argued that they had to be bypassed in order to achieve their goal. Thus Alabama's William Lowndes Yancey wrote in 1858:

> No national party can save us, no sectional party can do it.
> But if we could do as our fathers did, organize Committees
> of Safety all over the cotton states (and it is only in them
> that we can hope for any effective movement), we shall fire
> the Southern heart—instruct the Southern mind— give
> courage to each other, and at the proper moment, . . . we
> can precipitate the cotton states into a Revolution.

221

Radicalism could not flourish, secessionists realized, if men remained loyal to political parties and normal political processes. "So long as the Democratic party, as a National organization, exists in power at the South, and so long as our public men trim their sails with an eye either to its favor or enmity," fumed Robert Barnwell Rhett in early 1860, "just so long need we hope for no southern action for our disenthrallment and security." Another South Carolina fire-eater, Congressman Lawrence M. Keitt, was more epigrammatic when he wrote in 1857, "Loyalty to party is treason to the South." That secessionist message seems to have taken hold. During the weeks following Lincoln's election, state conventions repudiated the advice of national politicians who urged their states to delay until Lincoln did something or at least to cooperate with other states instead of seceding alone—men as prestigious as former Whig Alexander H. Stephens of Georgia and Democratic Senators James Hammond of South Carolina, Benjamin Fitzpatrick of Alabama, and Jefferson Davis of Mississippi.[5] Southerners who rejected the political process by exultantly embracing secession seemed, if only briefly, to abandon Southern Democratic leaders. If local Democratic politicos went along with secession, they often did so to save their skins. They were just as likely to be followers as leaders.

The problem to be explained is why secessionists, who had languished for years on the fringe of Southern politics and who had long but vainly made the same arguments against political parties and political remedies and in favor of Southern independence, suddenly gained such frenzied popular support in the winter of 1860-1861. What about the mere victory of a Republican president was so dreadful or so intolerable that Southerners were persuaded to or felt compelled to secede even before Lincoln was inaugurated? Men may have accepted secession for different reasons. Long-time advocates of secession probably had different motives from others, especially the nonslaveholding majority of whites, whom they induced to go along. Still, one must ask why so many Southerners who had been as fanatical in their loyalty to the Union, republicanism, and the political system as any other Americans rejected that system in favor of Southern independence.

The normal answer to these questions is that Southerners regarded the Republicans as a threat to black slavery and seceded to protect it. There is absolutely no doubt that many did. Yet historians have disagreed about precisely how it was menaced and who was most alarmed. Some, for example, see the Republicans' free-soilism as a sufficient cause for secession. Southerners were correctly convinced, they contend, that slavery could not survive economically unless it could expand to new areas. Restriction would destroy the basis of the planter class's hegemony in the South and shut off economic opportunities for small slaveholders hoping to join that class. Racist nonslaveholders who supported the institution primarily as a system of racial subordination also demanded expansion, they argue. Convinced that slavery would wither and die without expansion, the majority of Southern whites whose sense of worth depended on the continued debasement of blacks through slavery and whose sense of security depended on their continued dispersal to new areas feared they would be inundated by a growing black population if new areas for slavery were not acquired. The Republican program of confining slavery thus threatened "the profits of the plantation, the hubris of the planter, and the racial phobias of all Southern whites." When Republican victory seemed to foreclose the possibility of expansion within the Union, Southerners seceded to achieve it on their own.[6]

Some secessionists did stress the need for continued slavery expansion. Envisioning the enlarged boundaries of an independent South, Rhett's Charleston *Mercury* boasted that "we shall colonize Texas throughout, and Chihauhaua [in Mexico] and a few more good Southern States. We shall have all the Gulf country when we have once shaken ourselves free of the puritans." Similarly, the Augusta *Constitutionalist* announced, "Expansion is the peculiar necessity of the southern people." Yet one wonders if the thirst for territorial expansion was really the force behind secession. As pointed out earlier, many planters evidently felt no economic pressures for more territory in the 1850s. To the argument that nonslaveholders demanded the dispersal of blacks, one can point out that other secessionists wanted to increase the number of black slaves to reduce their price, not diffuse them to new areas and thereby raise slave prices. Finally, many Southerners, including the large planters who supported John Bell in 1860, considered the whole expansion question a phony issue, and very prominent fire-eaters like Yancey were against it.[7]

Other historians cite evidence that Southerners seceded because they sincerely feared that the Republicans were genuine abolitionists whose purpose was to destroy black slavery as soon as possible. For example, Mississippi's commissioner to the secession convention in Virginia justified his state's action by arguing that the purpose of the Republican party was "the ultimate extinction of slavery," while Henry

L. Benning gave as the reason for Georgia's secession "a conviction, a deep conviction on the part of Georgia, that a separation from the North was the only thing that could prevent the abolition of her slavery. This conviction, sir, was the main cause." All slaveholders, and not just the tiny oligarchy of planters who owned more than 20 slaves, faced a severe economic loss if uncompensated abolition occurred. The proportion of white families who owned slaves, especially in the Deep South states, was surprisingly large. All Southerners, slaveholders and nonslaveholders alike, moreover, feared the racial consequences of abolition or even antislavery agitation. The sheer number of blacks in their midst—almost 4 million slaves among 8 million whites—worried many. In 1860 the proportion of slaves in the seven states that seceded averaged 47.5 percent and, in many regions within those states, whites were heavily outnumbered by blacks. To petrified whites, abolition meant the end of a necessary system of control over a despised race. It meant devastating social and economic competition for poor whites. Even worse, it meant insurrection, rape, massacres of white families, and eventually a bloody race war until one race or the other in the South was exterminated.[8]

During 1860, a wave of terror about the probability of slave uprisings and their bloody consequences swept the South. John Brown's raid at Harper's Ferry traumatized many Southerners, because Brown had brought along a number of cast-iron pikes to arm the slaves he expected to flock to him. With little effort, frightened Southerners could imagine on whom those pikes were to be used. Brown's raid was not regarded as an isolated incident, but as part of a gigantic conspiracy, fomented by abolitionists and Republicans, to infiltrate the South and instigate slave insurrections. In 1860 hysterical Southerners tended to see an abolitionist behind every bush. Rumors of slave plots to poison wells in Texas and murder whites elsewhere circulated widely. Vigilance committees were formed to ferret out agitators, helpless poor whites and Northerners living in the South were beaten and driven from their homes, and others were unceremoniously lynched. For many in 1860, anxiety about slave rebellions was especially acute.

Still, one might ask why Southerners believed the Republicans could achieve abolition when the party did not control Congress and when its platforms constantly denied the right or intention of interfering with slavery in Southern states. Secessionists provided some plausible answers. Republicans would disregard the Constitution, they argued, as the personal liberty laws of the North demonstrated. Republican control of the executive branch was dangerous enough. Some simply said that the Republicans' long-range goal of ultimate extinction and their belief that slavery was wrong were so pernicious that Southerners must secede. The election had marked a turning point that doomed the South. But others presented what seemed like more immediate dangers that required immediate responses. The mere news that an antislavery man had taken office as President, argued some, would provoke spontaneous slave insurrections, and the South must escape before Lincoln's inauguration took place. Georgia's Senator Robert Toombs listed for that state's legislators the patronage, revenue, and military might that would fall into "the hands of your enemy" on March 4, 1861, and frantically urged them to "strike, strike while it is yet time." A Republican administration, it was charged, would encourage fanatics like John Brown and aid other abolitionists by opening up the U.S. mails to abolitionist literature, thus exposing the South to incendiary material that it had barricaded itself against since the 1830s. Such auguries were not entirely paranoic; a minority of Republican leaders had, indeed, publicly called for opening the mails as well as for the immediate abolition of the interstate slave trade.[9]

More likely but equally dangerous, secessionists prophesized, a Republican administration could shatter the unity of the Southern defense of slavery by building up an antislavery Republican party *within* the South on the basis of federal patronage. Slaveholders had always worried about the reliability of the nonslaveholding majority, which could easily end slavery by state law if it chose, and many feared that such men would provide recruits for a Southern wing of the Republican party. A writer in *DeBow's Review* warned in 1860 that "among the no-property men of the South," there was *"a feeling of deep-rooted jealously and prejudice, of painful antagonism, if not hostility, to the institution of negro slavery, that threatens the most serious consequences, the moment Black-republicanism becomes triumphant in the Union."* Similarly, Toombs predicted in 1860 that Republican control of the federal government "would abolitionize Maryland in a year, raise a powerful abolition party in Va., Kentucky, and Missouri in two years, and foster and rear up a free labour party in [the] whole South in four years." Given the racial fears of nonslaveholding whites, such predictions that they would join a true abolition or antislavery party seem exaggerated. The Republicans, however, were not and did not present themselves as an abolitionist party. Instead, they

225

posed as an egalitarian, antiprivilege, antiplanter party, a party that would restore the principles of republican government, a party of democracy versus aristocracy. Such a party based on class tensions among whites, as distinct from attitudes toward black slavery, may have had much greater potential in the South. As a South Carolinian warned in 1860, "For you know that even in our lower Country, there are many who could be marshalled against the Planters, upon the idea that they were fighting against the aristocracy."[10]

The overwhelming majority of Southerners feared and hated the Republican party, even if they did so for different reasons. Although that revulsion was often based on a misconception of what the Republican party stood for, confusing the wishes of a radical minority with the purpose of the party as a whole, fear and irrationality had to play a role in causing secession. The question is not the authenticity of Southern fears and grievances, however. It is why they took the form they did—immediate secession before Lincoln could take office—*where* they did—in the seven slave states of the lower South but *not* in the eight slave states of the upper South. As helpful and as well-documented as previous interpretations are, they leave two nagging problems unanswered.

First, they are based on the motives of entire groups who supposedly effected secession, be those groups planters, all slaveholders, or all whites with a racial stake in the preservation of slavery. In every Deep South state that seceded, however, with the possible exception of South Carolina, none of those groups acted as a unit. Enthusiasm for secession, once it was accomplished, may have been widespread, but on the question of whether or not to secede before Lincoln was inaugurated, merely because he had been elected, there were genuine differences. Yet planters, smaller slaveholders, and nonslaveholding whites all divided between the opposing camps of Cooperationists and immediate secessionists. The largest slaveholders in the South, indeed, the cotton planters from the Delta region of Mississippi and the sugar planters of Louisiana, were staunchly opposed to immediate secession. If class demands that slavery be extended or fears of racial inundation prompted secession, why did they oppose it? Because members of all the groups identified as the proponents of secession behaved in opposite ways, motives that applied to the groups as a whole cannot explain their members' divergent behavior.

The latest and most sophisticated research finds little significant relationship between any socioeconomic variable (wealth, slaveholding, the concentration of slaves, crop production, etc.), and the way voters divided on the question of immediate secession. There was a slight tendency for slaveholding counties to support secessionists more strongly than nonslaveholding counties, but there was no distinct polarization of slaveholders against nonslaveholders on the question of secession. The best predictor of behavior was by all odds present and former political affiliation. At both the leadership and voter levels, Breckinridge Democrats supported secession, while the former Whigs who backed John Bell in 1860 and the Douglas Democrats in the South generally opposed it. By no means did all former Whigs oppose secession; in certain states almost half the Bell voters who participated in the secession elections favored it. Bell supporters, however, were much more likely that Breckinridge voters to abstain from the elections altogether; in most states almost all who voted for Cooperationists were Bell supporters or Douglas Democrats.[11]

The key to explaining the secession of the Deep South, therefore, is to explain why the Democrats who were the majority party in every state were persuaded to embrace it. When one realizes that the bulk of Democratic strength had traditionally come from nonslaveholders, the need to account for their behavior becomes more pressing. Democratic slaveholders led the drive for secession, but Democratic nonslaveholders allowed its success either by voting directly for it or by abstaining and refusing to vote against it.

Second, and much more serious, all theories based on the fear of the Republican menace to black slavery would seem to apply equally well to the states that refused to secede merely because Lincoln was elected as to those that did secede. Democratic slaveholders demanded secession in the upper South too, but they were woefully unsuccessful. During February 1861, the voters of Virginia, Tennessee, Arkansas, Missouri, and North Carolina either rejected proposals to call secession conventions at referenda or elected overwhelming majorities of genuine Unionist delegates to conventions or both. In Kentucky, Maryland, and Delaware secessionists could not even get proposals to call conventions before the public. Yet most men in the upper South, regardless of party, despised what the Republican party seemed to stand for just as those in the lower South did. The question is why the latter felt it necessary to bolt the Union before Lincoln took office and the former did not. Why did extremism prevail in one region and not the other?

Historians have long been aware of this anomaly in the behavior of slave states. They have correctly pointed out that special circumstances played a role in each individual state, but they have generally attributed the hesitancy of the upper South to the greater strength of Unionism there as shown by the continued prominence of former Whig politicians like John Bell of Tennessee and John J. Crittenden of Kentucky, and by the results of the presidential election of 1860. Bell, the Constitutional Union candidate, carried Virginia, Kentucky, and Tennessee and came close to carrying Maryland and Missouri, the latter being won by Stephen A. Douglas, the other conservative candidate. Assuming that those results were based on attitudes toward national affairs instead of local political patterns, historians attribute Unionist sentiment to the closer economic ties of the upper South to the North and to the smaller stake it had in black slavery. One wonders, however, whether Tennessee or Arkansas really had closer economic ties to the North than Louisiana with its great trading center of New Orleans, or whether North Carolina had closer ties than South Carolina.

On the other hand, it is clear that by certain measures the Deep South had a greater stake in black slavery than the upper South (see Table 4). In every state that seceded before Lincoln's inauguration except Texas, the proportion of slaves and slaveholders in the population was greater than it was in any of the upper South states. Because of this differential, the argument runs, fears of the Republican party were more intense and more widespread in the Deep South. The significance of that differential is questionable, however; neither slaveholders nor nonslaveholders united on one side or the other of the secession question. In terms of absolute numbers, moreover, the differential was not so stark. Virginia had more slaves and slaveholders than any state in the nation. Kentucky, Tennessee, and North Carolina contained more slaveholders than any of the states that seceded immediately except Georgia, although individual holdings were clearly not so large. Still, one wonders whether Mississippians or Floridians really felt the need of slavery expansion more than Kentuckians, Tennesseans, and North Carolinians. Are we to believe that Virginians feared abolition or slave rebellion any less than Georgians or Alabamians? Yet if it was John Brown's raid that exacerbated fears of abolition and insurrection, why did the latter respond so differently to Lincoln's election than the people of Virginia, where Brown's raid had taken place, or the neighboring Marylanders? It is not clear that those who refused to secede were any less committed to slavery than those who did secede. As a North Carolina paper that opposed secession vowed, "North Carolina will never permit Mr. Lincoln or his party to touch the institution of domestic slavery. Her people are at least a unit on this point."[12]

TABLE 4

Slaves and Slaveholders in the South in 1860[a]

	Number of slaves	Proportion of slaves in the population	Number of slaveholders	Proportion[b] of slaveholding families
Upper South				
Delaware	1,798	1.6%	587	3.8%
Maryland	87,189	12.7	13,783	14.5
Virginia	490,865	30.9	52,128	27.3
North Carolina	331,059	33.3	34,658	29.1
Kentucky	225,483	19.5	38,645	23.5
Tennessee	275,719	24.8	36,844	24.9
Missouri	114,931	9.7	24,320	12.7
Arkansas	111,115	28.	11,481	20.1
Lower South				
South Carolina	402,406	57.1	26,701	47.1
Georgia	462,198	48.2	41,084	37.6
Florida	61,745	43.9	5,152	34.5
Alabama	435,080	45.1	33,730	35.1
Mississippi	436,631	55.1	30,943	49.2
Louisiana	331,726	46.8	22,033	31.
Texas	182,566	30.2	21,878	28.5

[a]This table is based on Appendix A in James M. McPherson, *The Negro's Civil War* (New York: Vintage Books, 1965), pp. 317–318 and the table on "Slaveholders in 1860" in James G. Randall and David Donald, *The Civil War and Reconstruction* (2nd ed. rev.; Boston: D. C. Heath & Company, 1969), p. 68.

[b]These proportions were calculated by dividing the number of individual slaveholders by the number of white families in each state.

It seems more logical, therefore, to assume that what differentiated the lower South from the upper South was not the degree of either's fear of Republican action against slavery, but the degree of their confidence in preventing that action. The difference was less in attitudes toward the supposed Republican program than in the perception of what the election of a Republican president, by itself, meant for the South. Instead of focusing on the common Southern anxiety about black slavery, a different approach may be more fruitful in suggesting why groups and regions behaved differently during the secession crisis.

Throughout Dixie, Democratic leaders and voters provided the bulk of support for secession, although it is clear that larger proportions of nonslaveholding Democrats followed the lead of slaveholders in the Deep South than in the upper South. Otherwise the majorities against immediate secession in the upper South would not have been so lopsided. At the same time, secessionist leaders called on Southerners to repudiate the national Democratic party, Democratic leaders in Congress, and the normal party political process in favor of more drastic action. The question is why more voters and politicians, especially Democratic voters and politicians, in the upper South than in the lower South seemed willing, at least temporarily, to keep faith in the Democratic Congress and the normal give and take of party politics to check Republican designs. Evidence suggests that the answer to this question lay in the different political experiences of the Southern states during the 1850s which, in turn, engendered different perceptions of the efficacy of party politics to achieve desired ends.

In October 1860 the South Carolinian Keitt astutely explained why the Palmetto State would inevitably be the first state to secede. "This State I think will have to lead. The absence of party spirit enables us to do so." South Carolina, indeed, had never developed a two-party system, and men there had never regarded politics in party terms. As a result, South Carolina had always been the most radical of the Southern states. Conversely, extremism had been weakest, and faith in the political process to protect Southern Rights had been strongest where two-party systems flourished and loyalty to political parties consequently was strong. Back in 1849, for example, the Charleston *Mercury* had complained that Southerners had not rallied behind Calhoun's Southern Address, moderate as that was in comparison with secession, because "the antipathies of Whig and Democrat are too strong in Washington and their exercise forms too much the habit of men's lives there."[13] Those antipathies had, in fact, permeated the Southern electorate as well until the early 1850s, thus stymying the efforts of more radical agitators than Calhoun when they demanded secession after the passage of the Compromise of 1850.

When the Second Party System collapsed in the South, however, new frameworks of two-party competition for national, and more important for *state* offices did not emerge with equal strength everywhere. Interparty competition remained fairly close in most of the upper South states, so that both contending parties seemed to be legitimate alternatives to control the government. Within the states of the lower South, however, the Democratic party achieved such dominance after the Whigs collapsed and Know Nothingism faded that they became virtual one-party polities. In terms of confidence in the political process, which rested on the presence of perceived and viable party alternatives, the Deep South states had approached the status of South Carolina by 1860. This fact may have been why Yancey thought that secession as an antiparty movement could succeed in the cotton states alone.

Only gross measures of the degree of interparty competition in Southern states during the 1850s can be presented here. The most important gauge would be an analysis of the intensity of interparty conflict in Southern state legislatures after 1852, but only a very few states have been so studied. In addition, Democrats in several Deep South states enjoyed such overwhelming preponderance in state legislatures that even high levels of party conflict would lose significance. The closeness of party strength in popular elections, however, provides an approximate index of the health of interparty competition and allows one to contrast the upper South states with the lower South states. By simply measuring the difference between the proportion of votes won by the Democrats and that won by the opposition, whatever its name, one gets a sense of the degree of party rivalry. The smaller the margin, the stronger the two-party system was; the larger the margin, the weaker it was.

Table 5 presents the margins between the Democrats and their opponents in presidential elections from 1848 to 1860. A minus (−) sign indicates that the anti-Democratic party had more votes. Two figures were calculated for the average margins in the upper and lower South. The first is simply the absolute average of party difference, regardless of who won. The second figure, given in parentheses, was the measure of the Democratic margin in each region and was calculated by subtracting anti-Democratic margins from Democratic margins and dividing the result by the number of states in each region. Hence the (−.8) average for the upper South in 1848 means that overall the Whigs had a margin of .8 in that region. In most cases where more than two candidates received votes, I have combined all the opponents of the Democrats in the Opposition and all Democrats together, since my interest was measuring party strength and not candidate strength.[14] This procedure was especially important for 1860, because I combined the

TABLE 5

Indexes of Interparty Competition Between the Democrats and Their Opponents in Presidential Elections, 1848-1860[a]

	1848	1852	1856	1860
Upper South				
Delaware	−3.6[b]	.2[b]	9.6	4.2
Maryland	−4.4[b]	6.4[b]	−10	4.2
Virginia	1.6	11.4	19.8	8.4
Kentucky	−5.4[b]	−2.8	4.6	7.8
Missouri	9.8	12.4	8.8	8.8
Arkansas	10	24.2	34.2	25. 8
Tennessee	−4.8	−1.4	5.4	4.8
North Carolina	−10	.8	13.2	6.6
Average	6.2 (−.8)	7.4 (6.5)	13.2 (10.7)	8.8
Lower South				
Georgia	−3	29.4	14.2	19.4
Florida	−15	20	13.2	27.8
Alabama	1.2	31.8	24	38.2
Mississippi	1.4	21	19.4	27
Lousiana	−9.2	3.8	3.4	20
Texas	37	46.8	33.2	51
Average	11.1 (2.1)	25.5	17.9	30.5

[a]This table is based on the election statistics listed in Walter Dean Burnham, *Presidential Ballots 1836-1892* (Baltimore: The Johns Hopkins University Press, 1955). It was constructed by subtracting the proportion of the vote received by the anti-Democratic party from that received by the Democrats. In 1856 and 1860 votes for Democratic candidates were combined as were votes for various anti-Democratic candidates.

[b]I have not included the small Free Soil vote in these calculations.

Douglas vote with the Breckinridge vote and the few votes Lincoln received in the upper South with the Bell vote. Hence the table understates the anti-Breckinridge vote, particularly in the upper South. Still, the table gives a rough index of the health of interparty competition in the two regions. Texas and Arkansas were so disproportionately Democratic that they skew the averages for both regions, but the trend is evident. Even in 1848 parties were more evenly balanced in the upper South than in the lower South, and by 1860 the levels of competitiveness had grown far apart.

It is possible, however, that figures from presidential elections are artificial indicators of the health of the party system within individual states. The candidates were nominated by national organizations outside the states. Their votes may suggest the potential support for opposing parties, but they do not measure the strength of state parties themselves. The vote for John Bell in the Deep South, in fact, greatly exaggerates the vigor of anti-Democratic *parties* there. The presidential election of 1860 was like an electric shock that momentarily revived a corpse, an external stimulus that disguised the moribundity of opposition parties at the state level. Because state governments remained closest to the people and did most of the things that affected their everyday lives, what really determined the public's sense of efficacy in the political system was the degree of interparty conflict at the state level and the substantive or insubstantive nature of state-level politics. What was crucial was whether parties existed to provide alternatives to control state government and its policy.

Table 6 presents the margins between the parties in races for state offices, primarily for governor, wherever it was possible to do so, and Table 7 aggregates the results from Table 6 in order to clarify the trends and regional differences. An uncontested election in Alabama in 1857 and a one-sided race in Missouri in 1858 inflate the Democratic margins in both regions, but the pattern of elections for state-level offices confirms that for presidential elections. Although the meteoric appearance of the Know Nothings intensified interparty conflict in both regions in 1855, 1856, and 1857, by the end of the decade, there was markedly greater two-party competition in the upper South than in the lower South. These figures, moreover, *under*state the bankruptcy of opposition parties in the lower South once the American party dissolved. Although the incumbent Democratic governor in Georgia was challenged in 1859, for example, his opponents were so poorly organized that they could not even find a name for their party. The elections in Texas, Mississippi, and Alabama that same year were contests between rival Democratic factions, not between two organized parties.[15] In all four states, finally, the only issue was which candidate was the more determined defender of slavery and Southern Rights; the elections did not provide alternatives on state policy.

Even before examining the substance of Southern politics in the

TABLE 6

Margins Between the Parties in State Elections 1850–1860[a]

	1850	1851	1852	1853	1854	1855	1856	1857	1858	1859	1860
Upper South											
Delaware	.3						12b(c)				3.2b(c)
Maryland	2	2.6		5.8		-3.6		-10	1.4	-12c	
Virginia		5.6			-5.2	6.4		21(c)		3.8	
North Carolina	3.2		6	5.6b(c)	2.2		12.2		16.8		5.6
Kentucky		.8		1.8		-3.2		10.2c		6.2	
Tennessee		-1.4				1.6		8.8		5.6	
Missouri		15.4c	19		-3b		28.6d	.2			8.2e
Arkansas		14.8b(c)	9				29.2		35c		-3.4
Average	1.8	6.7(6.5)	11.3	4.4	3.5(-2)	3.7(.4)	20.5	10(6)	17.7	6.9(.9)	5.1(3.4)
Lower South											
Georgia	-5.6b(c)			.6		3.8		10.2		20.4	
Florida		-19.2f			10.4		3.6		22.8b(c)		14.2
Alabama				23.8b(c)		15.4		100		46	
Mississippi		-1.8f		8		8.2		32.8		54	
Louisiana		-.8c		9b(c)		7		13.4c		22	
Texas						-3.8c		1.7		-13.6	
Average	-5.6	-7.3		10.3	10.4	7.6(6.8)	3.6	34.7	22.8	31.2(28.5)	14.2

[a]This table is based primarily on election returns in the Tribune Almanac and is based on the votes from gubernatorial elections except where noted. The return for the gubernatorial election of 1860 in North Carolina is taken from Andrew R. L. Cayton, "Political Rhetoric and the Secession Crisis in North Carolina, 1856-1861" (seminar paper, University of Virginia, 1975), p. 22, and the vote for the 1859 gubernatorial election in Alabama was found in J. Mills Thornton III, "Politics and Power in a Slave Society: Alabama 1806–1860" (unpublished Ph.D. dissertation, Yale University, 1974), p. 457.

bThese were based on the total votes for congressmen in the States instead of on a single statewide race.

cThese were races for state offices other than governor. They were respectively: judge in Missouri in 1851; auditor in Louisiana in 1851; land commissioner in Texas in 1855; secretary of state in Kentucky in 1857; auditor in Louisiana in 1857; school superintendant in Missouri in 1858; and comptroller in Maryland in 1859.

dIn this election I combined the Benton and anti-Benton totals in the Democratic column, although the Democracy was sharply divided. In actuality, the margin of the victorious anti-Benton Democrats over the Know Nothings was much smaller.

eHere I have combined the votes for two Democratic candidates in the Democratic column and the votes of the Opposition and the Republicans in the anti-Democratic column.

fThese two votes were between Southern Rights and Union candidates. There was no similar gubernatorial race between those parties in Alabama.

TABLE 7

Aggregate Indexes of Interparty Competition in State Elections in the Upper and Lower South[a]

	1850–1853	1854–1856	1857–1860
Upper South	6.9 (6.8)	9.7 (7)	9.4 (6.3)
Lower South	6.7 (1.3)	6.5 (5.5)	29.3 (27)

[a]This table is based on the same election returns as Table 6. The figures in parentheses are again Democratic margins and are calculated by subtracting anti-Democratic margins from Democratic margins and dividing by the number of cases for each set of years.

1850s, one can suggest ways in which this disparity in the vigor of two-party politics influenced responses to the drive for secession. At the simplest level, because political affiliation affected the decision of voters on immediate secession, there obviously was a greater organizational base for the foes of secession in the upper South than in the lower South. The disarray of conservatives in the Deep South, even though Bell and Douglas together did quite well, indicates the critical difference between the presence of an organized state opposition party and the existence of potential voters for such an organization. At the same time, Democratic politicians, if they chose, could take a more extreme proslavery position in the Deep South, even to the point of advocating secession if the Republicans won, because they need not fear that the feeble local opposition party could win by asserting that Democrats were disunionists. Put differently, there was no institutionalized check on extremism in the lower South. As we will see, Democrats in the Deep South took advantage of this situation by constantly escalating their demands for the protection of slavery and Southern Rights. Another result of the opposition's weakness was that Democratic state parties in the lower South were much less dependent on the patronage, the aid, and the good graces of the national Democratic party to win elections than Democrats in the upper South. They could be and were much more critical of the Democratic administration in Washington and congressional Democrats who aided it than were state Democratic parties in the upper South, thus helping to weaken faith in national political solutions for Southern grievances.

Finally, it is probable that the fears of local Democratic politicians and of planters in the Deep South that the Republicans could establish an antiplanter opposition party were more intense and more justified than they were in the upper South. It is a significant irony that the creation of a Southern wing of the Republican party was much less feared in states like Maryland, Virginia, Kentucky, and Missouri, where Frémont and Lincoln actually won some votes, than it was in the Deep South, where there were no Republican tickets. Leaders from the upper South scorned the possibility that a strong Republican party could be created there, and with good reason.[16] In their states opposition parties already flourished. They had no room or need for a new anti-Democratic party. It was clear in any event that the Republican party would be thrashed. The Deep South states, on the other hand, were tending toward a one-party situation. There was a political vacuum in which a new opposition party that had outside backing to build an organization might blossom. In the lower South, in short, there was a need for a new opposition party, and the potential of the Republicans was unknown.

That potential, of course, rested on the availability of disaffected voters who would be willing to join an egalitarian, antiplanter party pledged to restore the principles of republican government. It is doubtful that anyone expected the large planters from black belt areas who had voted for Bell to be attracted to the Republican party, but the nonslaveholding artisans, laborers, and farmers who had voted for Bell and Stephen Douglas might be. Douglas ran very poorly in Florida, Mississippi, and Texas, but he won 10 to 15 percent of the vote in Alabama, Georgia, and Louisiana, and almost all of his votes came from nonslaveholders. As South Carolinians and others feared, even nonslaveholders who had voted for Breckinridge bore grudges against planters, and they might be attracted to the Republican party. Their loyalty to the Democracy had always depended partly on a sense of competition with other intrastate parties, which was clearly waning. In the end, however, their willingness to join such a party rested primarily on the degree of their satisfaction with present political arrangements, on how well they thought the dominant Democracy was representing the needs of nonslaveholders.

The nonslaveholders, who constituted over two-thirds of the Southern white population, held the key to Southern actions during the secession crisis. They not only represented potential Republican voters, but would provide the critical support for secessionists who exploited their weakened party loyalty. Strange as it seems, there were striking similarities between the appeals of the secessionists in the South and those of the Republicans in the North. Secessionists not only went out of their way to discredit the Republican party to prevent non-slaveholders from ever considering it, but they presented secession itself as an alternative—and more effective—way to secure the principles of republicanism.

It must be reemphasized that white Southerners had always shared the same devotion to republican values as other white Americans. Identifying an antirepublican dragon, associating it with the opposition party, and crusading to slay it had been the basic tactic of Southern politics since the 1820s. As in the North, contests between the Whigs and Democrats had been explicitly portrayed as battles to save self-government, liberty, and equality from power, privilege, and despotism. Southern Democratic voters, most of whom were nonslaveholders, had ardently embraced the Jacksonian fight against banks, paper money, corporations, and positive state action of any kind. Party conflicts, moreover, had often reflected regional antagonism within states between wealthy planters from the black belt and poor nonslaveholding whites from the hill country or piney woods areas. The Second Party System had provided an outlet for class and regional hostilities in Georgia, Alabama, Mississippi, and Louisiana as well as in the upper South states by identifying *within* those states parties whose programs fostered some powerful or privileged menace to the freedom, equality, and interest of voters and by allowing people to defeat those supposed antirepublican forces by voting against the opposition party in local, state, and national elections. Because parties presented alternative ways to secure republicanism and alternative vehicles through which contending groups could seek to control government, Southerners, just like other Americans, had believed that republican government could be preserved and perfected through the political process. And for Southerners, like other Americans, that achievement, and not the protection or extension of black slavery, was the preeminent political goal.

Just like other Americans, Southerners had reacted to the emerging congruence between the Whig and Democratic parties and to the eventual collapse of the Second Party System by becoming more and more suspicious of politicians, impatient with the unresponsiveness and unrepresentativeness of political parties, and alarmed about the very survival of republicanism. They, too, grew hypersensitive about hints of corruption and conspiracy that seemed to be subverting the

POLITICS, SLAVERY, AND SOUTHERN SECESSION

Republic and its rulers. They, too, demanded reform to restore political power to the people and early republican purity to the society and its politics. Hence, Know Nothingism also mushroomed briefly in the South in 1855 and 1856, and, although it was largely a refuge for homeless Whigs, it employed everywhere the same reform rhetoric that Know Nothings used in the North. Even those Southerners who doubted the viability of Know Nothingism in the South thought there was a need for a reform party like it. Thus William C. Rives of Virginia urged the Know Nothing party there "to install itself as the American *Republican* party, faithful to the tradition of a *Republican* ancestry & consulting the genius, usages, & habits of a *Republican* people." Such a transformation would "enable the new party in Va. . . . to secure its permanence & a lasting & salutary power to check the extravagances & corruptions of *modern Democracy.*" Similarly, when the opposition in Georgia, which had rallied to the American party in 1855 and 1856, searched for a new image in 1857, they considered renaming themselves the "People's Party," the "Independents," or the "Reform Party."[17]

Even Democratic reactions to Know Nothingism indicate the pervasiveness of republican values among Southerners, although Democrats obviously located the threat to them in a different place. For a short time in 1854 and 1855, the Know Nothing crusade seemed capable of winning numerous converts from Democratic voters and sweeping the South, and Democratic politicians throughout Dixie waged a desperate campaign to crush it. In states like Mississippi and Alabama, where the Democracy was not dependent on foreign voters for its majority, Democratic politicians tried to neutralize the Know Nothings' appeal by admitting that illegal immigrant voting had corrupted the political process and calling for reform of the naturalization laws. As in the North, however, their major tactic was to denounce the secrecy and structure of the Know Nothing order as "antirepublican." Their private correspondence makes clear, moreover, that such vituperation reflected sincere love for republican government and fears about its survival, not simple opportunism. Expressing "abhorrence for the recent antirepublican development of opinion, as exhibited in the 'Know-Nothing' organization," one alarmed Alabamian warned that "this stupendous and farspreading leprosy . . . this terrible system of *espionage*—this imitation of the most odious practice of foreign despotism, will, as certainly, if it continue unchecked, bring about the ruin of our Govt. and the failure of our Republic, as night follows day." Similarly, a Mississippi congressman protested, "The *secret* notion of Know Nothingism is enough to keep Democrats out of it. . . . Let Kings and Despots plot in secret, but let us who glory in being free govern openly."[18]

Finally, the secessionist rhetoric, the paranoic belief that an all-powerful abolitionist conspiracy had infiltrated the South, and the frenzy that characterized the Deep South after Lincoln's election as young men thronged to militia units, Minute Men clubs, and vigilance associations indicate the same kind of crisis atmosphere that spawned Antimasonry in the 1820s, Know Nothingism in the mid-1850s, and the early Republican party with its Wide Awake clubs. There is an especially striking similarity between the rumors of slave plots to murder masters and earlier rumors in the North that Irish servants were plotting to murder their employers. Secessionism rose in the Deep South in the late 1850s in response to this sense of crisis, just as Republicanism rose to meet it in the North. Southern secessionism was the mirror image of Northern Republicanism in a number of ways. Secessionists denounced politicians and political parties as corrupt, dishonest, and unreliable, and revelations of Democratic election frauds in the North in 1856, the maddening evasiveness and ambiguity of popular sovereignty, and exposures of corruption in the Buchanan administration only increased their disgust with and strengthened their case against politicos in Washington. Just as the Republicans portrayed the North as the victim of aggression, moreover, so secessionists pictured the South as under assault.

Most important, however, the core of the secessionist persuasion was aimed at the same republican values of Southerners that Republicans appealed to among Northerners. Although the secessionists and their allies did, indeed, warn of the dangers of abolition and escalate demands concerning slavery in the territories, the essence of their appeal had less to do with black slavery than with protecting the rights of Southern whites from despotism. The central issue was neither race nor restriction, but republicanism. Where the Republicans had located the antirepublican monster in the Slave Power conspiracy, secessionists identified it with the Republican party, which they labeled a threat to self-government, the rule of law, Southern liberty, and Southern equality. Thus a Georgia newspaper condemned the Republican party in rhetoric akin to denunciations of earlier antirepublican dragons.

[It] stands forth today, hideous, revolting, loathsome, a menace not only to the Union of these states, but to Society, to Liberty, and to Law. It has drawn to it the corrupt, the vile, the licentious, the profligate, the lawless. . . . It is a fiend, the type of lawless Democracy, a law unto itself, its only Lord King Numbers, its decrees but the will of a wild mob.[19]

Southerners had long boasted that theirs was the most egalitarian and free society on earth because it was based on black slavery. "The presence of the black race in America [has] enabled the white man to treat as his equal all of his own race," wrote one. "A base was thus formed for liberty, as broad as the population; and hence popular sovereignty was a reality, not a fiction." Not only would the success of Republican abolition schemes undermine the basis of this egalitarian society, argued secessionists, but a Republican victory even without abolition would destroy the glories of that society. Since the 1840s, Southerners had insisted that slavery restriction was a denial of Southern equality in the nation; in the 1850s Democrats echoed that theme when vilifying the Republicans' free-soil principles. Thus Southern Rights, and not positive desires for expansion, remained central in the territorial issue of the 1850s. Just as with the Republicans, however, the slavery extension issue was often but a pretext for secessionists. The essence of their message was that Republicanism was antirepublican. The election of a "Black Republican President will be a virtual subversion of the Constitution of the United States," warned the South Carolina Minute Men in October 1860. Because the Republicans organized exclusively as a Northern party, government by the Republicans could not possibly be government of, by, or for the Southern people. By insisting that the Northern majority rule, moreover, the Republicans persistently identified the South as a minority that was inherently unequal and inferior. Southerners, insisted the secessionists, could not and would not tolerate that degradation. "Can you be really a friend to the South," the South Carolina novelist and secession enthusiast William Gilmore Simms wrote a Northern acquaintance in December 1860, "when you desire *us,* the *minority* states to submit to the uncontrolled legislation of a majority . . . which has declared its determined purpose

241

to subdue, rule and destroy the minority, and abrogate all its rights and securities?"[20]

Repeatedly, Southern extremists denounced the very idea of majority rule as subversive of republicanism. During the debates on the Nebraska bill in 1854, for example, one Senator had vowed "never to trust the simple despotism of a majority," while Simms later wrote that the founders of the Republic "strove to guard their people, with all their vigilance, against the danger equally of a majority and Federal usurpation." The Southern states were a helpless minority, declared one secession convention, "in imminent peril, being in the power of a majority, reckless of Constitutional obligations and pledged to principles leading to [their] destruction." Northern majority rule meant the end of equality, the absence of law, and subjugation to tyranny.[21]

Without question the most persistent theme in secessionist rhetoric was not the danger of the abolition or restriction of black slavery, but the infamy and degradation of submitting to the rule of a Republican majority. To acquiesce in Lincoln's election, to allow his inauguration, was to legitimize and accept the Republican doctrine that Southerners were inferior to Northerners and should not have an equal voice in the government. And, by definition, inferiors were slaves in the Southern lexicon. As Jefferson Davis put it in his inaugural address as Confederate president, Southerners "believed that to remain longer in the Union would subject them to . . . a disparaging discrimination [by a sectional majority], submission to which would be inconsistent with their welfare, and intolerable to a proud people." Others were blunter. "I should rather my state should be the graveyard of martyred patriots than the slave of northern abolitionists," shrieked Keitt in 1856. The South could not remain in the Union "stigmatized, dishonored, reviled, plundered, and degraded" by the Republican majority. The Republicans were "mongrel tyrants who mean . . . to reduce you and your wives and your daughters on a level with the very slaves you buy and sell," charged a South Carolina "Minute Man in 1860." "Talk of Negro slavery," proclaimed George Fitzhugh, "it is not half so humiliating and disgraceful as the slavery of the South to the North." Here, then, is the key to why the mere election of Lincoln could provoke secession. The Republican party did not have to do anything against black slavery to humble the South. Its victory alone meant the end of republican government and the enslavement of white Southerners. As Edmund Ruffin of Virginia wrote in 1860:

> *A Northern sectional party, and majority, directing the*
> *action of the federal government, need not exercise any*
> *unconstitutional power, or commit any "overt" act of*
> *usurpation, to produce the most complete subjection and*
> *political bondage, degradation, and ruin of the South.*[22]

But if Republican rule meant the end of republicanism and slavery, argued secessionists, republicanism could be restored simply by preventing Republican rule. The heart of the secession appeal, like that of the Republicans, was that reform was necessary to save republican government. Just as the Republicans promised that defeating Democrats would protect Northern white men from enslavement to the Slave Power, moreover, secessionists promised to protect Southerners from enslavement to the Northern majority. Since remaining in the Union and accepting Republican rule was for Southerners to assume the status of slaves to Northern masters, republicanism could be saved simply by withdrawing from the government in which Republican tyranny could be exercised. In sum, Southerners did not secede simply to protect black slavery. Although many did view the Republican party as a legitimate threat to the existence of that institution, the vast majority of Southerners saw the protection of slavery as a means, not as an end in itself—a means to preserve the most free and egalitarian white society on earth. The central impulse behind secession was thus less to save black slavery than to escape white slavery by avoiding Republican tyranny and by allowing Southerners to pursue republican principles on their own. As Jefferson Davis proclaimed in his inaugural, the South had seceded to escape "the tyranny of an unbridled majority, the most odious and least responsible form of despotism" and "to renew such sacrifices as our fathers made to the holy cause of constitutional liberty."[23]

Once it is recognized that secessionist rhetoric was aimed primarily at ideological values shared by all white Southerners, not at the economic interests of slaveholders alone, that Democratic nonslaveholders were the decisive group throughout the South, and that secession was portrayed for them as a way to achieve the goals Southerners had sought through the normal political process for the preceding forty years, then the question concerning the different behavior of the upper and lower South can be rephrased. Why did men, and especially Democratic nonslaveholders, in the lower South feel it was more necessary to withdraw from the Union to save republicanism than did nonslaveholders in the upper South? Here is where the different political experiences of the two regions had their greatest impact. Voters in the upper South had much greater confidence that republicanism could be secured through the normal political process than voters in the lower South, who accepted instead the secessionists' message that drastic action alone could achieve the same goal. Their perceptions differed because of the nature of Southern politics in the late 1850s.

Briefly, politicians and voters in the upper South continued to channel the desire to preserve and perfect republicanism internally by locating the chief menace to republicanism in the programs and practices of opposing parties *within* their states, thus assuring nonslaveholders that they could protect their values by voting against that opposing party. In the Deep South states, however, as the Democratic party increasingly assumed unassailable control, the opposition party could not be made a credible threat to crusade against, even if the Democratic politicians wanted to. As a result, Democratic politicians, who were goaded by secessionists and the remnants of the opposition, crusaded almost exclusively against a foe external to the South and Southern state politics—the Northern Republican party. Crudely put, by 1860, the Republican party had become the chief symbol of anti-republicanism in the Deep South, while politicians in the Upper South still found dragons to slay at home.

The nature and strength of the opposition was not the only thing determining whether a state's politics were internally or externally oriented. The strategies pursued by ambitious Democratic politicians helped to shape this result, and those strategies, in turn, reflected the different social structures of the upper and lower South. As Table 4 suggests, slaveholders formed a considerably larger share of the electorate in the latter region than in the former. This imbalance did not necessarily impart different degrees of commitment to the preservation of black slavery or of dislike for the Republican party, but it did mean that politicians in the two regions had to follow different strategies to build winning majorities. In the upper South, the composition of the population as well as the nature of the Democrats' opponents forced Democratic politicians to concentrate on winning nonslaveholder votes. And nonslaveholders were simply less interested in an external threat to slavery than slaveholders. Other issues were more important to them. In the Deep South, demography and political exigencies dictated the opposite strategy—a competition for the votes of slave-

244

holders. Thus, by the end of 1860, Democratic state parties in the two regions were often led by men who had come to power by very different routes. The following brief synopsis of Southern politics in the 1850s attempts to show how those contrasting patterns developed.

After 1854, political conflict in the Deep South, such as it was, was dominated by the sectional issue. In part this development resulted from the lack of other issues to form an axis for interparty competition. The American party temporarily provided a rallying point for anti-Democratic voters in 1855 and 1856, and consequently it was a viable opponent for Democratic politicians to campaign against, especially since its secret organization and proscriptive principles could be labeled antirepublican. In most places, however, the Democrats neutralized its nativistic appeal by agreeing that naturalization laws should be reformed. As soon as Millard Fillmore was defeated in 1856, Know Nothing strength rapidly dissolved except for isolated pockets such as New Orleans, where lines between the parties on the immigrant issue were sharply drawn. Thus the Democrats lost a worthy foe. Nor could the opposition rally support against the Democrats on economic issues, which had been so basic to the republican images of both parties in the 1830s and 1840s. As in the rest of the nation, Democratic state parties in the South were adopting Whiggish stances in favor of railroad promotion, business incorporations, and banking expansion in order to facilitate a boom in cotton production in the 1850s. The probusiness wing of the Democracy was so strong that even the revival of antibanking sentiment by the Panic of 1857 did not allow competing parties to draw distinct lines on economic issues. So many Democrats continued to vote with the remnants of the opposition in favor of banks that antibanking elements found no coherent partisan vehicle to channel their anger.[24]

The Democratic party within the Deep South had, in fact, changed in significant ways. During the 1830s and 1840s, it had normally been controlled by and represented the interests of nonslaveholders from the hill country and piney woods regions. Even at that time slaveholders and their lawyer allies from the normally Whig black belt areas had contested for leadership of the Democracy. Sharing the same economic concerns as their Whig neighbors in those plantation regions, concerns that nonslaveholding Democrats generally opposed, Democrats from the black belt had bid for control of the party by trying to shift attention to national issues and asserting that the threat to Southern equality posed the greatest menace to the liberties of all

Southern voters. During the 1850s, for a variety of reasons, those slaveholding elements took over the Democracy, and in state after state it became much less receptive at the state level to the wishes of the nonslaveholding majority who nonetheless remained Democrats because of traditional Jacksonian loyalties. For one thing, Franklin Pierce favored Southern Rights Democrats in the distribution of federal patronage. Second, as the Whig party dissolved, Democratic politicians from the slaveholding regions won over some of its former adherents by stressing the menace to slaveholders' interests, thereby increasing their own power within the Democratic party. Finally, during the 1850s, the cotton culture spread away from the old black belt to staunchly Democratic regions, thus enlarging the constituency that would respond to politicians riding the slavery issue.

As a result of this transformation, the economic priorities of the Democratic party changed. Democratic newspapers openly advised Democratic legislators not to offend their new Whig allies, and the new Democratic leaders wanted positive economic programs in any case. Occasionally the nonslaveholders found individual champions of the old Jacksonian orthodoxy like Governor John Winston of Alabama and Governor Joe Brown of Georgia who vetoed probusiness legislation, but Democratic legislatures invariably overrode those vetoes. To nonslaveholders, the Democratic party, as a party, and the political process as a whole no longer seemed as responsive as they once had been.[25]

The shift of power within the dominant Democracy hastened the almost exclusive concentration of political rhetoric on the slavery and sectional issues. For one thing, slaveholders were more genuinely concerned about potential threats to black slavery than nonslaveholders. For another, the Democrats attributed their rise to dominance by 1852 to their ability to appear more pro-Southern than the Whigs, and they saw no reason to change a winning strategy. Third, the new leaders of the party continued to feel the need of holding the loyalty of the nonslaveholding backbone of the Democratic electorate. That support had always been won by identifying and crusading against antirepublican monsters. Because the new leaders did not want to attack the economic programs they were themselves promoting and because internal opposition was so weak from former Whigs who approved of those programs, they more and more portrayed the external Republican party as the chief danger to the liberty, equality, and self-esteem of all Southerners, slaveholders and nonslaveholders alike. Like the Republicans in the North, they translated the sectional conflict into the republican idiom in order to win the votes of men who were not primarily concerned with black slavery.

There were two additional pressures, however, that pushed the Democracy to more extreme pro-Southern positions. Because the foes of the Democrats could find no state issues on which to campaign and because they also despaired of winning over the traditionally Democratic hill whites who despised them as aristocrats, they saw their only hope as winning back former Whig slaveholders who had joined the Democracy in the early 1850s. To do this, they tried to beat the Democrats at their own game by taking a more extreme pro-Southern position than the Democrats. Here they focused on the untrustworthiness of the national Democratic party and tried to tar Southern Democrats with guilt by association. Hence, in 1857, opposition parties blasted Buchanan's Kansas policy and especially Governor Robert J. Walker's actions in Kansas as a betrayal of the South because they would prevent Kansas from being admitted as a slave state. Similarly, in 1859, some of them would call for a federal slave code in the territories as an alternative to the Democracy's professed commitment to popular sovereignty. Simultaneously, outright secessionists and an extreme Southern Rights faction within the Democracy applied pressure in the same direction by calling for a complete repudiation of the national Democratic party as corrupt and pusillanimous and for severing the nation to secure Southern freedom. These were the men who were contesting gubernatorial elections against the Democrats in some states by 1859.

Squeezed between these two forces and committed to agitation of the sectional issue in any case, state-level Democratic politicians responded by attacking the national Democratic administration themselves and moving to more and more advanced or extreme ground in order to prove the trustworthiness of the Democratic party on the sectional issue and to keep one step in front of their various challengers. After 1856, therefore, there was a continual escalation in the proslavery demands that Deep South Democrats made on the Democratic party and the nation: first that Walker be cashiered and replaced by a "fairer" governor in Kansas; then that Kansas be admitted as a slave state under the Lecompton constitution; then that a federal slave code for the territories be enacted and that the African slave trade be reopened; then that state delegations bolt the Democratic national convention in 1860 if a proper platform were not adopted; and, finally, that the South secede if a Republican were elected president in 1860.

Although the proponents of Bell briefly provided a genuine conservative alternative to these demands in the presidential campaign of 1860, Deep South politics were dominated at all levels by the national or sectional issue, and the tendency was overwhelmingly in a more radical direction. Southern Democrats had narrowed the focus of politics and destroyed confidence in Democrats at Washington to such a degree that they left themselves and their voters few options if Lincoln should win the election.

The political experience of the upper South states after the collapse of the Second Party System was strikingly different. The conservative renaissance of Bell and Crittenden, which was based on the national Lecompton and tariff issues, clearly was more successful in the upper South in 1858 and 1859 than in the lower South, but the vibrancy of two-party competition there did not rest on national issues alone. It was not simply a product of greater conservatism or Unionism. State-level politics had a life of their own there and, more important, the substance of that competition continued to be over alternative methods to perfect republicanism. It is suggestive indeed that except for Louisiana, the wave of constitutional reform in the early 1850s to make state governments more responsive to the people by restricting legislative prerogatives and making patronage offices elective was confined to the upper South. But the impulse for internal reform did not stop there.

In Maryland, for example, state political battles from 1850 to 1860 revolved around the issue of reform. First Whigs and Democrats had conflicted over revision of the state constitution. Then, in 1853 and 1854, temperance advocates and Know Nothings had launched a crusade against the Democratic state administration to clean up political corruption, restore the glories of the old Republic, and protect the purity of American institutions from the alien Catholic menace. In Maryland, at least, that menace seemed genuine; tens of thousands of immigrants were crowding into Baltimore and other parts of the state. The emergence of the Know Nothings worked a realignment of Maryland's voters very similar to that in the North and forged lasting and intense allegiances to new parties that shaped voting behavior for the remainder of the decade. The Know Nothings controlled the state government from 1854 until 1859, but their power was based on extensive fraud and violence in Baltimore. Immigrants were literally maimed or murdered to prevent them from voting. As a result, the state Democratic party campaigned from 1856 on as a reform party that would restore honesty, purity, and virtue to the state by over-throwing the lawless and corrupt Know Nothings and by protecting the political process from the violence people associated with Know Nothingism. Although Breckinridge carried the state in 1860, he did so primarily because of the stigma of Know Nothingism that men attached to the supporters of John Bell. Throughout the decade, in sum, state-level politics in Maryland had real substance—reform to protect liberty and equality from intolerable concentrations of power and corruption and to restore government to the people. In Mary-land, the fundamental goal of American voters could be and was achieved within the normal political process.[26]

The very strength of Know Nothingism also gave vitality to party competition in Kentucky. There, too, Know Nothings captured control of the state government in 1855, and there, too, unrepublican violence and intimidation characterized their electoral tactics in the city of Louisville. As in Maryland, therefore, Democratic voters had the sense that they could achieve reform simply by overthrowing the Know Nothings within the state. Although the Democrats regained control of the lower house of the legislature in 1857, the Know Nothings continued to hold the governor's office and state senate until 1859, when the opposition party, based on Crittenden's principles, waged a strong but losing campaign. The Americans and Democrats, more-over, seemed to be able to provide party alternatives on other issues just as the Whigs and Democrats had done earlier. Thus, when the banking issue rekindled in Kentucky after the Panic of 1857, there was significantly sharper interparty conflict on it than there had been in the first part of the decade and than there was in legislatures of the Deep South at the same time.[27] Parties within Kentucky once again seemed to stand for something distinctive, and people once again perceived legitimate alternatives through which they could fight to influence government. Hence faith in the political process was re-stored.

Perhaps the best example of how intrastate party competition could divert attention from the sectional conflict and diminish the perception that only secession could save republicanism, however, comes from North Carolina. Like the states of the Deep South, North Carolina politics had long reflected antagonisms between nonslave-holding hill whites and wealthy planters from the black belt. Unlike the lower South, however, the interests of nonslaveholders from the western part of the state had never been exclusively championed by the Democratic party. From 1835 to the late 1840s, the Whigs had represented the nonslaveholders against the planter-controlled Democracy. In the early 1850s, however, the Democrats had won enough nonslaveholder support to rule the state by favoring suffrage reform for the poor and internal improvements for the west. During the remainder of that decade, both parties bid for nonslaveholder support in battles over issues like railroad building, the corruption and extravagance of state and national administrations, and state taxation in language that was astoundingly similar to that employed by the secessionists.

The crux of North Carolina politics in the 1850s was the preservation of liberty from tyranny, equality from privilege, and self-government from subversion through the corruption of Democratic officials at the state and national level. The crux of politics was the battle to save republican government. Although Democrats there, as elsewhere, tried to focus attention on the external Republican threat to republicanism, moreover, their opponents explicitly argued that other menaces were more dangerous. The threat of abolition "is a *decoy* cry which they [the Democrats] hope will distract your attention from the *true issue*," charged one opposition newspaper in 1859. "What is the true issue? The true issue is the *corruptions of the Democratic party—the profligacy* of the Administration, the wasteful extravagance of the party!" Similarly, the opposition's Raleigh *Register* protested in January 1860, "While Federal issues are of the highest importance, we have State concerns which should attract our earnest attention." Anti-Democratic politicians made it clear that the real antirepublican monster was not the Republican party, but the North Carolina Democratic party. "Corruption now stalks abroad under the name and sanction of the Democracy of the present day," proclaimed the *Register* in 1856. "Tell this wicked, corrupt, and impudent administration in trumpet tones," it repeated in 1859, "that the freemen of the Old North State indignantly refuse to surrender to its bidding, their glorious heritage of freedom." State legislation sponsored by the Democrats, cried the Asheville *News,* had produced "the curse of an oppressed, down-trodden, betrayed, and plundered people." Actions "not more tyrannical" had caused the Revolution, and these would produce "a peaceful revolution" at the next election.[28]

Foes of the Democrats found their most potent issue in the question of taxation. Nonslaveholders regarded the low taxes on slaves compared to other kinds of property as an unfair privilege for the slaveholders, especially when the Democratic state administration had raised other taxes to pay for the railroads it was building to appease the western part of the state. In 1860 the opposition reclaimed the Whig name and wrote a platform calling for "a sound and thorough reformation of public affairs." Democratic policies were so unjust and tyrannical that "a free people, jealous of liberty" ought to offer them "determined resistance" to preserve "the cherished institution of liberty." Democrats might try to divert attention to the Republican menace, they warned, but the greatest danger to the liberty and equality of North Carolinians came from the "great inequality . . . in the present mode of taxation."[29]

Democrats did, indeed, try to divert attention away from state issues, but, when that tack failed, they countered Whig proposals by arguing that new taxes on slaves would put a tax collector in every household. The Whigs, charged the Democrats, would infringe on freedom by creating a leviathan state. Although it ingeniously employed the same republican idiom, the Democratic counterattack could not stem Whig incursions into the nonslaveholder vote. The Democrats won the gubernatorial election of 1860 by their narrowest margin since the original Whig party had collapsed.

By the gubernatorial election in August 1860, the Whigs had improved their fortunes to such a degree that they were sure they would win the next contest in 1862. "We have lost . . . by a small vote—but yet all the prestige of success is ours," wrote one. "One more such a day & they [the Democrats] are ruined. So may it be."[30] Parties were now so closely matched and the ability to build new majorities so evident that the faith of the nonslaveholding majority in the political process continued to flourish. Until 1857, the Democracy had offered them suffrage reform and internal improvements for the regions where they lived. After that date, when the Democracy appeared once again to champion the hated slaveholders by opposing the equalization of taxes on slave property and to undermine republicanism by corruption and extravagance in office, the Whig party had reorganized to save nonslaveholders from such injustices. State parties continued to provide realistic political alternatives through which nonslaveholders and slaveholders alike could seek their desired goals, and both promised to advance republican principles as parties had during the life of the Second Party System.

Although the specific issues differed in other states of the upper South, the dynamics of interparty competition worked throughout the region to quell radicalism and perpetuate the faith of nonslaveholders in the utility of the political process. The two parties in Virginia and Tennessee, for example, offered alternative versions of state-oriented reform, and the success of populistic Democratic governors such as Andrew Johnson of Tennessee and Henry Wise and John P. Letcher of Virginia prolonged confidence that the Democracy remained the party of the people. To a great extent, indeed, the central theme of Virginia politics in the 1850s was a competition for the allegiance of nonslaveholders in the western part or the state. At the same time, the Americans and then the Opposition achieved sufficient strength in those states to be both a credible internal opponent for the Democrats to campaign against and a check on any Democratic proclivities toward extremism. In Virginia, at least, intraparty rivalry between the state's two major Democratic leaders, Wise and Senator R. M. T. Hunter, worked to the same end. Both hoped for a place on the Democratic national ticket in 1860, and therefore both quashed any talk of secession by Virginia Democrats lest it hurt them with Northern Democrats. Unlike state-oriented Democratic politicians to the south, in other words, Virginia's Democratic leaders had not been campaigning against the national Democratic party for half a decade.

The differing political experiences of the upper and lower South thus engendered quite different responses to the secessionist persuasion. Secession was presented as a necessary means to save the republican principles of individual autonomy, equality, and self-government by escaping enslavement to Northern tyranny. It was necessary, disunionists argued, because the old political parties had proved themselves hopelessly corrupt and unreliable. Lincoln's election meant Northern despotism, and there was no way to stop it other than separation, so that Southern whites would once again be their own governors in a society where all were considered equal.

This argument made sense to men from the lower South, especially to the nonslaveholders who provided the critical support for secession. For almost a decade the political process had seemed unresponsive to them, and they were prepared to believe that republican self-government was indeed in jeopardy. For half a decade, moreover, the Republican party had been presented as the only menace to republicanism, yet within their state polities they were powerless to defeat it by voting. Thus Lincoln's election seemed a fundamental and irreversible turning point. It meant that a majority of Northerners were dedicated to the subjugation of the South. Lincoln's support was not just an ephemeral aggregation of voters attracted to the same party on election day, but instead represented the "huge mountainous waves . . . beating down on the South with resistless force." For men from one-party states who had not experienced any shift in majorities for over a decade, such a perception was understandable. As a result, the lower South had no faith in dissipating that majority, and without confidence in the possibilities of future elections it had no way to pursue reform and resist Republican tyranny other than to withdraw from the Union. "With such a prospect before them," argued one Louisiana newspaper,

> the Southern States may well pause ere they consent to go on as they have hitherto done, trusting either to the conservatism of the North, or to the strength of party to neutralize Black Republican hatred. It is manifest that the South cannot possibly consent to dwell in the Union upon suffrance; the mere vassal and thrall of a party which aims at her ruin and degradation. . . . Such a state of practical servitude and submission where all sense of equality would be lost, and where we should be placed at the mercy of a relentless master, would necessarily become perfectly intolerable.[31]

Most of the slaveholders and nonslaveholders who had traditionally supported the Democratic party therefore responded enthusiastically to the message of the secessionists, since they at least had identified a devil subverting the Republic and had a way to deal with it. Secession—independence from Northern aggression—would provide a fresh start in achieving a government where liberty, equality, and self-government were secure. The promise of secession, indeed, accounts for the apparently atypical behavior of Democratic nonslaveholders in Alabama. There, north Alabama hill whites who had feverently supported Breckinridge in the presidential election selected Cooperationists instead of Immediatists to the state's secession convention. Their action, however, did not represent opposition to secession as a crusade to save republicanism, but was, instead, a maneuver to achieve even greater reform. Throughout the 1850s those fervent Jacksonian farmers had chafed with resentment at the takeover of the state's Democracy by south Alabama slaveholders and their lawyer allies, who were associated with

253

William Lowndes Yancey. They had been appalled by the Democracy's endorsement of probusiness measures because they saw banks, corporations, and railroads as concentrations of power and privilege that were themselves inimical to their equality and freedom. But they had been powerless to stop those measures because they were without a potent political voice. No longer able to control the Democratic party, they could not stomach aligning with an opposition they associated with hated aristocratic Whig planters. They voted for the Cooperationists, therefore, not to stop secession, which they ardently favored, but to elect men to the secession convention who would oppose the Yanceyites from south Alabama. To them secession represented not only an escape from the external tyranny of the North, but an opportunity to restore government by nonslaveholders within Alabama. The secession convention would, in effect, be a constitutional convention, since a new government was to be established, and Alabama's constitution had not been revised since 1819. North Alabama's hill whites were determined to write into the new charter prohibitions against the type of state legislation they had futilely resisted in the 1850s, and they did precisely that at the convention.[32] Such men viewed secession as a suprapolitical or nonparty way to advance republican principles, not only vis-à-vis the federal government, but within the state itself.

The same secessionist rhetoric had much less resonance among the residents of the upper South, and they rejected the demands to join their sister states to the south. They did not perceive Lincoln's victory as the end of republicanism, but as the product of its normal workings. To men accustomed as they were to the ebb and flow of party competition, it was simply a single triumph in a continuous series of elections. Someone, after all, had to win elections. To them a majority did not mean tyranny. It was defined politically as simply more than half of the electorate at any particular election—a temporary aggregation that every party tried to attract and that one's own party could construct by working harder at the next election. Surely the experience of the upper South indicated that political fortunes changed and that different parties could achieve majority status. In Maryland, Kentucky, Tennessee, and North Carolina one majority party had been replaced by another during the previous decade, and the new majority party had itself often been replaced. In Virginia, although the Democrats won all the statewide elections during the decade, their opponents had steadily narrowed the gap from 1851 to 1859, so that they, too, could envision being in the majority some day.

The confidence inspired by their own political experience had two specific results. Voters in the upper South did not regard Lincoln's majorities in Northern states as evidence of permanent sectional hostility to them. Instead, they regarded Lincoln's election as a fluke caused by the temporary Democratic divisions in 1860 and universal revulsion at the Buchanan administration, which many Southerners shared because the corruption and extravagance of that administration had been highlighted in their own campaigns. "Its unparalleled corruption, apart from the Slavery question, had arrayed against it the undoubted majority of the American people," argued a Virginia newspaper. "The Republican vote was made up in very large proportion, not of the sympathizers with MR. SEWARD, but of enemies of MR. BUCHANAN." A North Carolina paper stressed the other cause of the Democrats' defeat. "It would be a nice piece of folly to dissolve the great and glorious Union simply because" the intraparty quarrels of the Democrats had "permitted a minority to gain *temporary* ascendancy." All that was needed to check the Republicans, men from the upper South therefore believed, was to wait for the elections of 1862 and 1864, when the Democrats would not have to bear such an impossible burden.[33]

Thus, while residents of the upper South were as emphatically opposed to Republican programs as other Southerners, they had much more confidence that the new administration could be checked by Congress and vanquished at future elections when their majorities would fade away. Government tyranny could be stopped, argued a Nashville newspaper, "because the government belongs to the people and the laws are theirs. They have the power to alter, amend, or repeal the laws at their will, in a constitutional and peaceful manner" by voting out of office the politicians who passed them. Similarly, Tennessee Senator Andrew Johnson promised in a major speech against secession that "in four years from this day [December 19, 1860], Lincoln and his administration will be turned out, the worst-defeated and broken-down party that ever came into power. It is an inevitable result from the combination of elements that now exists."[34]

Residents from the upper South, then, did not view secession as the only way to salvage republicanism and avoid slavery. They not only continued to believe that they could achieve those goals at the national level through the normal political process, but they also thought that they were being attained already within their states so that there was no need to create new governments. Where people from the lower South thought that they required secession to attain self-government and the liberty and equality that went with it, residents from the upper South firmly believed they already enjoyed it.

For many nonslaveholders in the upper South, indeed, the real threat against republicanism came not from the Republican party, but from the slaveholders who demanded secession in response to the Republican victory. Thus a Tennessean charged that the "oligarchs and aristocrats" pushing secession "despise the people and hate the political constitution which recognizes the equality of man to man. I love this constitution, because it does maintain this very equality. . . ." North Carolina's Whigs, who vilified slaveholders in their own state, turned on South Carolina's planters with equal fury when they urged North Carolina to secede. "Will you suffer yourself to be spit on in this way?" asked the Wilmington *Herald*. "Are you submissionists to the dictates of South Carolina?" For North Carolinians to "submit" to the "insufferable arrogance, and conceited self-importance" of South Carolina would be to sacrifice "their independence and their manhood." "It is deeply humiliating (or ought to be) to any citizen of a Border State if they will allow these arrogant Cotton Oligarchys South of them to dragoon them into their service," wrote another Tarheel.[35] Nonslaveholders, in short, believed not only that it was unnecessary to secede in order to save republicanism and escape slavery, but that secession itself would entail slavery to the haughty planters.

The divergent paths followed by the upper and lower South during the secession crisis provide the ultimate evidence that the relationship between state and national politics was crucial. Democratic advocates of secession justified that drastic action not only as a way to protect black slavery, but also as the only means of saving republicanism—the self-government, liberty, and equality that Americans everywhere cherished. To Democratic nonslaveholders in the South, the latter part of that message was more important than the former. The credibility of that message, in turn, depended less on perceptions of the Northern Republican party than on conditions at home. Only a widespread fear among the nonslaveholding majority that republicanism was indeed in danger created a receptive constituency for the secessionist appeal. Because political conditions differed markedly in the upper and lower South, that constituency existed in the latter region but not in the former. Hence the immediate secessionists prevailed in the Deep South, where nonslaveholding Democratic voters continued to believe that a dire crisis faced republican government, whereas they failed in the states of the upper South because state-level political developments had dissipated the necessary sense of crisis among nonslaveholding Democrats.

Many in the upper South, however, agreed that even though

Lincoln's election did not justify secession any overt action to coerce Southern states would do so. Coercion would actually represent the enslavement of the South that Lincoln's election alone did not. Thus, when Republicans refused to compromise with Southerners early in 1861, when Fort Sumter was fired on, and when Lincoln called up troops to quell the insurrection, men obsessed with protecting Southern freedom had all the evidence of tyranny they needed. In response to Lincoln's action, therefore, Virginia, North Carolina, Tennessee, and Arkansas joined the Confederacy. When obstreperous governors, federal military intervention, and the sheer numbers of unconditional Unionists prevented like action in the remaining slave states, some of their citizens seceded on their own by marching off to fight for the Confederacy. Although they had needed "a smoking gun" to persuade them, these Southerners seceded in April and in the following months for basically the same reason that others had done so before Lincoln's inauguration, to escape what one North Carolinian called "absolute subjection and abject slavery."[36]

Yet from the Republicans' point of view, coercion was absolutely necessary. To tolerate secession was for them to allow the destruction of republican government. If the South could reject the results of an election merely because they did not like the victor, then the principle of majority rule that was the only guarantee of the freedom and equality of Northerners in the Union would be destroyed. "If a minority will not acquiesce, the majority must, or the Government must cease," Lincoln stated in his Inaugural Address.

> There is no other alternative, for continuing the Government is acquiescence on one side or the other. . . . Plainly the central idea of secession is the essence of anarchy. A majority held in restraint by constitutional checks and limitations, and always changing easily, with deliberate changes of popular opinion and sentiments is the only true sovereign of a free people. . . . The rule of a minority, as a permanent arrangement, is wholly inadmissible. . . .

To the Republicans, therefore, secession was not the salvation of republican principles but the ultimate proof that the Slave Power conspiracy was intent on obliterating them. As an Ohio farmer explained in early 1862, "This civil war was commenced by the Southern

Rebels to continue the inordinate power of a class of men, the representatives of the Slave Oligarchy, who were crushing Republicanism out in this country."[37]

The sectional conflict over slavery had been crucial in causing the Civil War, but the basic issue had less to do with the institution of black slavery than has been thought. If the institution had not existed, there probably would never have been a war. Black slavery's primary role in intensifying the sectional conflict, however, was that, in one form or another, it provided concrete issues over which Northern and Southern politicians clashed in the national political arena. Its extension into Western territory was an especially volatile issue. Those clashes, in turn, increasingly caused the constituents of those politicians to view people in the other section as enemies of their rights, and as they worried about their own rights they shifted their focus away from the institution of black slavery itself. The vast majority of white Northerners abhorred black slavery and wished it could be done away with. Similarly, the vast majority of white Southerners were appalled at the prospect of its abolition. Most white Americans, however, were not obsessed with black slavery, and they refused to make its destruction or perpetuation a political priority. Hence neither the Republican voters who elected Lincoln nor the Southern non-slaveholders who allowed secession were primarily concerned with it. The slavery that was important to them was an abstract status men hoped to escape, a status they equated with the end of republican government.

Most Americans' perception of the imminence of that status was a function of the responsiveness, output, and efficacy of the political system that they had come to believe depended on the presence of two parties in conflict that provided them with alternative ways to achieve self-government and protect liberty and equality. Because the Whig and Democratic parties had done that, partly by offering differing party stands on sectional issues themselves, the sectional conflict between North and South was contained during the life of the Second Party System. Once faith in those parties collapsed, however, a sense of crisis developed that government was beyond control of the people, that it had become a threatening power dominated by some gigantic conspiracy, and hence that republican institutions were under attack. Politicians in the North and South responded to this sense of crisis by making an enemy in the other section the chief menace to republicanism who would enslave the residents of their own section. As a result, sectional antagonism became much more inflamed in the 1850s than it had ever been. Along with Know Nothingism, this strategy restored a sense of political efficacy in most of the nation, because antirepublican devils were associated with rival parties that could be stopped simply by voting against them. In the Deep South, however, no internal enemy was identified who could be defeated through the normal political process. Men there thought that more drastic action was necessary to escape slavery. The consequence was secession and a tragic Civil War.

SELECTED BIBLIOGRAPHY

The following does not pretend to be a complete bibliography for the forty-year period covered in this book. For one thing, as my notes indicate, I have relied quite heavily on primary sources, but I have chosen to confine suggestions here to the secondary accounts that were most helpful in the preparation of this study—both as sources of information and as stimulants to my thinking because I disagreed with them. The literature on Jacksonian and antebellum politics, moreover, is too vast to be listed here. Those interested in fuller guides should see the excellent bibliographies in Edward Pessen, *Jacksonian America: Society, Personality, and Politics* (Homewood, Ill.: The Dorsey Press, 1969) and in James G. Randall and David Donald, *The Civil War and Reconstruction* (2nd. ed. rev.; Boston: D.C. Heath & Company, 1969). The intent here is to provide a brief guide that will be useful to undergraduates.

Much of the historiographical debate on the causes of the Civil War is assessed in Thomas J. Pressly, *Americans Interpret Their Civil War* (Princeton: Princeton University Press, 1954). This should be supplemented with the reviews of the literature in David M. Potter,

The South and the Sectional Conflict (Baton Rouge: Louisiana State University Press, 1968); David Donald, "American Historians and the Causes of the Civil War," *South Atlantic Quarterly, 54* (1960), 351–355; and Eric Foner, "The Causes of the American Civil War: Recent Interpretations and New Directions," *Civil War History, 20* (1974), 197–214.

For general treatments of the prewar period, students should first consult David M. Potter, *The Impending Crisis, 1848-1861* (New York: Harper & Row, 1976), completed and edited by Don E. Fehrenbacher. Although I disagree with its emphasis on the morality of black slavery as the root of the sectional conflict, it is the wisest and fairest synthesis of the period yet to appear in print and is literally crammed with shrewd insights on virtually every event in those years. Its footnotes alone are treasures. For a still broader account, where the emphasis is not so exclusively on politics, students should see Allan Nevins's massive four-volume history, *The Ordeal of the Union* (2 vols.; New York: Charles Scribner's Sons, 1947) and *The Emergence of Lincoln* (2 vols.; New York: Charles Scribner's Sons, 1950), which is written in the grand tradition of narrative history but still advances the author's vigorous, if disputable, interpretations. Avery Craven, *The Coming of the Civil War* (2nd ed. rev.; Chicago: University of Chicago Press, 1957) is a classic revisionist study of the period 1800 to 1861.

My understanding of the republican values and ideology that shaped Americans' political perceptions in the years 1820 to 1860 rests on a number of sources. Excellent analyses of that ideology in an earlier period are Bernard Bailyn, *The Ideological Origins of the American Revolution* (Cambridge: Harvard University Press, 1967) and Gordon S. Wood, *The Creation of the American Republic, 1776-1787* (Chapel Hill: University of North Carolina Press, 1969). Richard B. Latner, "The Nullification Crisis and Republican Subversion," *Journal of Southern History, 43* (1977), 19–38, argues that the same republican ideology continued to influence politicians in the Jacksonian period. One can easily draw the same inference from Alexis de Tocqueville, *Democracy in America,* edited by Phillips Bradley (2 vols.; New York: Vintage Books, 1945). Rush Welter, *The Mind of America, 1820-1860* (New York: Columbia University Press, 1975), which I read after completing the manuscript, makes much the same point as I do. Although his terminology differs from mine and although he relied on different sources, he demonstrates that what I have called republican values permeated American consciousness in the Middle Period and that the dialog between parties was primarily about alternative ways to secure those values.

Special mention should be made in this regard of J. Mills Thornton's brilliant dissertation, "Politics and Power in a Slave Society: Alabama 1806 to 1860" (Ph.D. dissertation, Yale University, 1974). It has influenced virtually everything I have written about Southern ideology and Southern politics. By proving that the battle to preserve self-government, freedom, and equality was the crux of Alabama's politics from territorial days until secession, Thornton has written the finest study of antebellum politics in a Southern state that I know of. Happily, it will soon be published by the Louisiana State University Press.

My theory that party systems require conflict to survive and that they are endangered by consensus stems mostly from my own reading of the primary sources. But I have benefited from Michael Wallace, "Changing Concepts of Party in the United States, 1815-1828," *American Historical Review, 74* (1968), 453–491, and the essays in William N. Chambers and Walter Dean Burnham, eds., *The American Party Systems: Stages of Political Development* (New York: Oxford University Press, 1967), especially Paul Goodman's essay on "The First Party System." I have also learned much from Walter Dean Burnham, *Critical Elections and the Mainsprings of American Politics* (New York: W. W. Norton, 1970) and James L. Sundquist, *Dynamics of the Party System: Alignment and Realignment of Political Parties in the United States* (Washington: The Brookings Institution, 1973), although both tend to equate voter realignments alone with the death of old party systems and the formation of new ones. For an example of the contrary view—that party systems can only exist in the absence of serious issue conflict—see Rudolph M. Bell, *Party and Faction in American Politics: The House of Representatives, 1789-1801* (Westport: Greenwood Press, 1973).

Because of its sweeping scope, the best general introduction to Jacksonian politics is still Arthur M. Schlesinger, Jr., *The Age of Jackson* (Boston: Little, Brown & Company, 1945). Although many of Schlesinger's contentions have been disproved by further research, although he often accepts uncritically the truth of Democratic rhetoric, and although his portrait of the Whig party is unduly negative, his contention that there was sharp ideological and programmatic conflict between the Whig and Democratic parties is more persuasive than those that posit little difference between the parties. In part, Schlesinger achieves this insight because he recognizes that the Democratic party possessed both an antibusiness and a probusiness wing and that it was only gradually over time that the antibusiness wing emerged as the dominant faction in the party. The various critiques of Schlesinger's book are reviewed in the Pessen book mentioned above, which itself denies, incorrectly, that the parties differed over anything of note. Perhaps the most pugnacious critic of Schlesinger, however, is Lee Benson, *The Concept of Jacksonian Democracy: New York as a Test Case* (Princeton: Princeton University Press, 1961), which argues that in New York, Whigs were more reformist than Democrats, and that ethnocultural and religious differences more sharply defined Whig from Democratic voters than the class differences posited by Schlesinger. Benson's contention that the Texas issue had little impact in the 1844 election in New York is more persuasive.

The origins of the Second Party System are specifically studied in Richard P. McCormick, *The Second American Party System: Party Formation in the Jacksonian Era* (Chapel Hill: University of North Carolina Press, 1966), which contends that presidential elections and the regional identification of presidential candidates formed the occasion for and determined the timing of party formation in various states. McCormick, however, both understates the importance of issues in the formation of parties at the state level in the 1820s and exaggerates the inability of the major parties to handle the slavery issue. The most useful studies of the influence of economic issues growing out of the Panic of 1819 on party formation in the 1820s are Charles G. Sellers, *James K. Polk: Jacksonian, 1795-1843* (Princeton: Princeton University Press, 1957) and the following analyses of individual states: Donald B. Cole, *Jacksonian Democracy in New Hampshire, 1800-1851* (Cambridge: Harvard University Press, 1970); Kim T. Phillips, "Democrats of the Old School in the Era of Good Feelings," *Pennsylvania Magazine of History and Biography, 95* (1971), 363-382, and "The Pennsylvania Origins of the Jackson Movement," *Political Science Quarterly, 91* (1976), 489-508; Donald J. Ratcliffe, "The Role of Voters and Issues in Party Formation: Ohio, 1824," *Journal of American History, 49* (1973), 847-870; Lynn L. Marshall, "The Genesis of Grass-Roots Democracy in Kentucky," *Mid-America, 47* (1965), 269-287; Charles G. Sellers, "Banking and Politics in Jackson's Tennessee, 1817-1827," *Mississippi Valley Historical Review, 41* (1954), 61-84; and Thornton's dissertation on Alabama.

The impact of the Missouri Compromise debates on politics can be traced in Glover B. Moore, *The Missouri Controversy, 1819-1821* (Lexington: University of Kentucky Press, 1953) and especially Richard H. Brown, "The Missouri Crisis, Slavery, and the Politics of Jacksonianism," *South Atlantic Quarterly, 65* (1966), 52–72.

For the origins of Antimasonry in the 1820s and its contributions to the Whig party, I have relied on Benson, *The Concept of Jacksonian Democracy;* Charles McCarthy, *The Antimasonic Party: A Study of Political Antimasonry 1827-1840* in the Annual Report of the American Historical Association for 1902, Vol. I (Washington, 1903); Bertram Wyatt-Brown, "Prelude to Abolitionism: Sabbatarian Politics and the Rise of the Second Party System," *Journal of American History, 58* (1971), 316–341; and Michael F. Holt, "The Antimasonic and Know Nothing Parties" in Arthur M. Schlesinger, Jr., ed., *History of U.S. Political Parties* (4 vols.; New York: Chelsea House and R. W. Bowker, 1973) Vol. I, pp. 575–737.

The reasons for and consequences of the failure of a two-party system to develop in South Carolina are explored in William W. Freehling, *Prelude to Civil War: The Nullification Controversy in South Carolina, 1816-1836* (New York: Harper & Row, 1965) and James M. Banner, "The Problem of South Carolina," in Stanley Elkins and Eric McKitrick, eds., *The Hofstadter Aegis: A Memorial* (New York: Alfred A. Knopf, 1974), pp. 60–93.

For the clarification of party lines during the Jackson and Van Buren administrations see, in addition to Schlesinger, Robert Remini, *Andrew Jackson and the Bank War* (New York: W. W. Norton, 1967); David J. Russo, "The Major Political Issues of the Jacksonian Period and the Development of Party Loyalty in Congress, 1830-1840," *Transactions of the American Philosophical Society, 62* (1972); and Michael F. Holt, "The Democratic Party, 1828-1860," in Schlesinger, *History of U.S. Political Parties,* Vol. I, pp. 497-571. I have also learned much about national politics from Sydney Nathans's perceptive and beautifully written *Daniel Webster and Jacksonian Democracy* (Baltimore: The Johns Hopkins University Press, 1973). The best study of Van Buren's presidency is James C. Curtis, *The Fox at Bay: Martin Van Buren and the Presidency, 1837-1841* (Lexington: University Press of Kentucky, 1970), and the best account of the divisions over the banking issue within the Democracy is James Roger Sharp, *The Jacksonians versus the Banks: Politics in the States after the Panic of 1837* (New York: Columbia University Press, 1970).

The origins of the Whig party are discussed in some of the books mentioned above as well as Lynn L. Marshall, "The Strange Still-Birth of the Whig Party," *American Historical Review, 72* (1967), 445–468, and Glyndon G. Van Deusen, "The Whig Party," in Schlesinger, *History of U.S. Political Parties,* Vol. I, pp. 333–493. There has been considerable controversy about why the Whig party formed in the South. The old but still valuable standard account, Arthur C. Cole, *The Whig Party in the South* (Washington: American Historical Association, 1913) argues that states rights men who were miffed at Jackson's actions during the nullification controversy began the party. Charles G. Sellers, in "Who Were the Southern Whigs?" *American Historical Review, 49* (1954), 335–346, contends that Whigs were led by urban merchants and bankers who objected to Jackson's Bank War. William J. Cooper, Jr., "The Politics of Sectionalism: Some Thoughts on the Second Party System in the South," (seminar paper, The Institute of Southern History of the Johns Hopkins University, 1972), maintains that it was the Whig campaign against Van Buren and his supposed abolitionist proclivities in 1835 and 1836. Professor Cooper will develop this and other points about Southern politics in the Middle Period in his forthcoming study, *The Politics of Slavery,* which is to be published by the Louisiana State University Press and which he very generously let me read in manuscript form. Whatever the motivation of Whig leaders in the South, Joel H. Silbey's authoritative "The Election of 1836," in Arthur M. Schlesinger, Jr. and Fred Israel, eds., *History of American Presidential Elections* (4 vols.; New York: Chelsea House, 1971), Vol. I, pp. 577–600, makes clear that it was the election of 1836 that established a voting base for the Whig party in the South, a point suggested earlier by McCormick.

Characterizations of the ideological differences between the parties once the system had crystallized by 1840 can be found in the Schlesinger, Benson, Welter, and Pessen books mentioned above. That the parties hewed to these different ideological positions when voting against each other in national and state legislatures is demonstrated by: Joel H. Silbey, *The Shrine of Party: Congressional Voting Behavior, 1841-1852* (Pittsburgh: University of Pittsburgh Press, 1967); Thomas B. Alexander, *Sectional Stress and Party Strength: A Computer Analysis of Roll-Call Voting Patterns in the United States House of Representatives, 1836-1860* (Nashville: Vanderbilt University Press, 1967); Herbert Ershkowitz and William Shade, "Consensus or Conflict? Political Behavior in the State Legislatures during the Jacksonian Era," *Journal of American History, 58* (1971), 591–622; Rodney O. Davis, "Partisanship in Jacksonian State Politics: Party Divisions in the Illinois Legislature, 1834-1841," in Robert P. Swierenga, ed., *Quantification in American History: Theory and Research* (New York: Atheneum, 1970); the Sharp book mentioned above; William G. Shade, *Banks or No Banks: The Money Issue in Western Politics, 1832-1865* (Detroit: Wayne State University Press, 1972); Peter Levine, "State Legislative Parties in the Jacksonian Era: New Jersey, 1829-1844," *Journal of American History, 62* (1975), 591-608; and M. Phillip Lucas, "The Second American Party System in Mississippi" (unpublished seminar paper, University of Virginia, 1975).

For the Whig break with Tyler, the emergence of the Texas issue, and the impact of that issue on the 1844 presidential election, see George Rawlings Poage, *Henry Clay and the Whig Party* (Chapel Hill: University of North Carolina Press, 1936); Frederick Merk, *Slavery and the Annexation of Texas* (New York: Alfred A. Knopf, 1972); James C. N. Paul, *Rift in the Democracy* (New York: A. S. Barnes & Company, 1961); and especially Charles G. Sellers, *James K. Polk: Continentalist, 1843-1846* (Princeton: Princeton University Press, 1966). Sellers presents a different interpretation of the motivations of Robert J. Walker than does James P. Shenton, *Robert John Walker: A Politician from Jackson to Lincoln* (New York: Columbia University Press, 1961), who argues that Walker was using Texas annexation simply as a pretext to stop Van Buren. Shenton makes clear, however, that Walker had no direct economic investments in Texas when he began to push for annexation.

Frederick Merk, *Manifest Destiny and Mission in American History* (New York: Vintage Books, 1963), argues that territorial expansion in the 1840s was a product of party initiative, not popular pressure, and that Americans divided on the question by party instead of sectional lines. Norman E. Tutorow, "Whigs in the Old Northwest and the Mexican War" (Ph.D. dissertation, Stanford University, 1967) provides both literary and quantitative evidence to show that parties polarized against each other on Texas annexation and the Mexican War. There is a great deal of information on the Whigs' reaction to territorial expansion in the 1840s in Robert F. Dalzell's excellent *Daniel Webster and the Trial of American Nationalism, 1843-1852* (Boston: Houghton-Mifflin, 1972), which also provides a superb account of Webster's role in national and Massachusetts politics. Whig opposition to the Mexican War is outlined in John H. Schroeder, *Mr. Polk's War: American Opposition and Dissent, 1846-1848* (Madison: University of Wisconsin Press, 1973). Both the Silbey and Alexander studies of congressional voting, finally, show that party lines held on the expansion question in the 1840s, and Silbey takes explicit and forceful exception to the traditional portrait of party disruption during the Polk administration there and in "John C. Calhoun and the Limits of Southern Congressional Unity, 1841-1850," *The Historian, 30* (1967), 58–71. On the other hand, the disruptive impact of the slavery extension issue in a Northern state is argued in Kinley J. Brauer, *Cotton versus Conscience: Massachusetts Whig Politics and Southwestern Expansion, 1843-1848* (Lexington: University Press of Kentucky, 1967).

Historians have now concluded that Democratic factionalism played a major role in causing the introduction of the Wilmot Proviso, and their arguments can be found in Sellers, *James K. Polk: Continentalist* and Chaplain W. Morrison, *Democratic Politics and Sectionalism: The Wilmot Proviso Controversy* (Chapel Hill: University of North Carolina Press, 1967). Eric Foner, "The Wilmot Proviso Revisited," *Journal of American History, 56* (1969), 262–279, adds the important point that Van Buren Democrats from New York also feared repudiation by their antislavery constituencies if acquisition from Mexico was made to seem a proslavery measure.

The Janus-faced strategies adopted by the major parties on the slavery extension issue during the presidential election of 1848 are alluded to in Morrison; Norman Graebner, "1848: Southern Politics at the Crossroads," *The Historian, 25* (1962), 14–35; and Joseph G. Rayback, *Free Soil: The Election fo 1848* (Lexington: The University Press of Kentucky, 1970). Rayback, however, underestimates the role of traditional economic issues in that campaign and exaggerates moral antipathy to slavery as a component of Northern free-soil sentiment.

My own understanding of the reasons for Northern opposition to slavery expansion rests on Morrison, who stresses both racism and hostility to Southern political power; Larry Gara, "Slavery and the Slave Power: A Crucial Distinction," *Civil War History, 15* (1969), 5–18, the emphasis of which is connoted by its title; Eugene Berwanger, *The Frontier against Slavery: Western Anti-Negro Prejudice and the Slavery Extension Controversy* (Urbana: University of Illinois Press, 1967), which stresses the racist element in free-soilism; and Eric Foner, *Free Soil, Free Labor, Free Men: The Ideology of the Republican Party before the Civil War* (New York: Oxford University Press, 1970), a deservedly influential book that argues that Northerners opposed slavery expansion primarily because they feared their own free labor economy could not coexist with the slave-based plantation economy of the South.

My view of the Southern stake in the slavery expansion question rests heavily on my own reading of the sources, Thornton's superb study of Alabama, and inferences drawn from Morrison and from George Fredrickson, *The Black Image in the White Mind: The Debate on Afro-American Character and Destiny, 1817-1914* (New York: Harper & Row, 1971). It is at odds with the prevailing view that economic pressures for slavery expansion caused Southerners to demand more territory for slavery. The major proponents of that interpretation are Eugene Genovese, *The Political Economy of Slavery: Studies in the Economy and Society of the Slave South* (New York: Vintage Books, 1967); William L. Barney, *The Road to Secession: A New Perspective on the Old South* (New York: Praeger Publishers, 1972); and Barney, *The Secessionist Impulse: Alabama and Mississippi in 1860* (Princeton: Princeton University Press, 1974). The critics of that interpretation maintain that Southern planters neither objectively had nor perceived any economic pressures to expand slavery in the 1840s and 1850s. They are: William J. Cooper, Jr., "The Cotton Crisis in the Antebellum South: Another Look," *Agricultural History, 49* (1975), 381–391; and Robert Fogel and Stanley Engerman, *Time on the Cross, Volume I* (Boston: Little, Brown, & Company, 1974).

My analysis of Zachary Taylor's genuine desire to change or even replace the Whig party is based on my own reading of the primary sources. Allusions to the "No Party" strategy of 1848 can be found in Poage and Holman Hamilton, *Zachary Taylor: Soldier in the White House* (Indianapolis: The Bobbs-Merrill Company, 1951), the second volume of the best existing biography of Taylor. Neither fully understands the origins or purpose of that strategy, however.

Holman Hamilton has also written the best existing study of the Compromise of 1850, *Prologue to Conflict: The Crisis and Compromise of 1850* (New York: W. W. Norton, 1966), which offers a slightly different interpretation of the reasons why the Compromise passed than the one presented here. Hamilton has persuasively revised the story of the Compromise as told by Allan Nevins in *Ordeal of the Union,* Vol. I, but he, in turn, should be supplemented with David Potter's account of the Compromise in *The Impending Crisis* and with Robert W. Johannsen's detailed analysis of Stephen A. Douglas's role in his exhaustive biography, *Stephen A. Douglas* (New York: Oxford University Press, 1973). Robert Dalzell's study of Webster also has much that is fresh to say about the Compromise. I have also used Jonathan F. Fanton, "The Politics of Compromise" (seminar paper, Yale University, 1973).

The standard account of the Fillmore administration is Robert J. Rayback, *Millard Fillmore: Biography of a President* (Buffalo: Buffalo Historical Society, 1959). The most important political ramifications of the Compromise of 1850, however, were felt at the state level. I have found especially useful for Southern states: Cole, *The Whig Party in the South;* Potter and Nevins; Thornton's dissertation on Alabama; Paul Murray, *The Whig Party in Georgia, 1825-1853* (Chapel Hill: University of North Carolina Press, 1950); Horace Montgomery, *Cracker Parties* (Baton Rouge: Louisiana State University Press, 1950); and Daniel J. Hoisington, "From Whig to Union: The Whig Party in Georgia, 1849-1853" (unpublished seminar paper, University of Virginia, 1975). A number of other studies of Southern states during the crisis of 1850 are listed in the bibliography in Randall and Donald.

My interpretation of the forces that undermined the Second Party System is based on a number of disparate sources. The nature of the constitutional revisions of the early 1850s is discussed in Ralph A. Wooster, *Politicians, Planters, and Plain Folk: Courthouse and Statehouse in the Upper South, 1850-1860* (Knoxville: University of Tennessee Press, 1975) and Fletcher M. Green, *Constitutional Development in the South Atlantic States: A Study in the Evolution of Democracy* (New York: W. W. Norton, 1966). For evidence of the dramatic economic changes that occurred between 1848 and 1854 I have relied on: Thomas D. Willett, "International Specie Flows and American Monetary Stability, 1834-1860," *Journal of Economic History, 28* (1968), 28–50; Jeffrey G. Williamson, *American Growth and the Balance of Payments, 1820-1913* (Chapel Hill: University of North Carolina Press, 1964); Alfred D. Chandler, Jr., *The Railroads: The Nation's First Big Business* (New York: Harcourt, Brace, and World, 1965), and "The Organization of Manufacturing and Transportation," in David T. Gilchrist and W. David Lewis, eds., *Economic Change in the Civil War Era* (Greenville, Del: Eleutherian Mills-Hagley Foundation, 1965); Peter Temin, *Iron and Steel in Nineteenth Century America: An Economic Inquiry* (Cambridge: Harvard University Press, 1964); Albert Fishlow, *American Railroads and the Transformation of the Antebellum Economy* (Cambridge: Harvard University Press, 1965); Harry N. Scheiber, *The Ohio Canal Era: A Case Study of Government and the Economy, 1820-1861* (Athens: Ohio University Press, 1969);

and Paul W. Gates, *The Farmer's Age: Agriculture, 1815-1860* (New York: Harper & Row, 1960).

The political impact of the economic changes at the national level can be seen in the Silbey and Alexander studies of congressional voting, but, for the influence of constitutional revision and the new prosperity in eroding party lines at the state level, one must consult individual state studies. Among the published accounts, I have used: Shade, *Banks or No Banks* on the Midwest; on Maryland, Douglas Bowers, "Ideology and Political Parties in Maryland, 1851-1856," *Maryland Historical Magazine, 64* (1969), 197–217, and William J. Evitts, *A Matter of Allegiances: Maryland, 1850-1861* (Baltimore: The Johns Hopkins University Press, 1974); on Louisiana, Perry H. Howard, *Political Tendencies in Louisiana* (2nd ed. rev.; Baton Rouge: Louisiana State University Press, 1971) and George D. Green, *Finance and Economic Development in the Old South: Louisiana Banking, 1804-1861* (Stanford: Stanford University Press, 1972).

I have relied very heavily, however, on the unpublished papers of my former undergraduate and graduate students at Yale University for the story of party disintegration in the early 1850s. To distinguish the former from the latter, I will cite their papers as being done in Yale College. These are respectively: Mark W. Summers, "The Rise of the Republican Party in Democratic Maine, 1850-1858" (seminar paper, Yale College, 1972); Thomas Bright, "The Anti-Nebraska Coalition and the Emergence of the Republican Party in New Hampshire: 1853-1857" (seminar paper, Yale College, 1972); Peter Olberg, "Coalition Politics: Party Formation in Vermont, 1845-1855" (seminar paper, Yale College, 1972); Kevin Sweeney, "Rum, Romanism, Railroads, and Reform: The Twilight of the Second Party System in Massachusetts, 1849-1854" (seminar paper, Yale University, 1973); Alexander Deland, "Rum, Romanism, Regionalism, and Slavery: Requiem for a Whig Party in Connecticut, 1848-1855" (senior thesis, Yale College, 1972); William Sharp, "The Collapse of the Whig Party in New Jersey" (seminar paper, Yale College, 1973); Robert Hampel, "The Ohio Whig Party, 1848-1854" (senior thesis, Yale College, 1972); and Stephen Green, "The Election of 1852 in Maryland" (seminar paper, Yale College, 1972) and "The Collapse of the Whig Party in Maryland" (seminar paper, Yale College, 1973). Hampel, now a graduate student in Cornell University, allowed me to use his "Constitution-Making at Mid-Century: Indiana, 1850-1852" (unpublished seminar paper, Cornell University, 1973). Both the Bright and Sweeney essays listed above have been published in slightly different form. See Thomas Bright, "The Anti-Nebraska Coalition and the Emergence of the Republican Party in New Hampshire, 1853-1857," *Historical New Hampshire, 27* (1972), 57–88, and Kevin Sweeney, "Rum, Romanism, Representation, and Reform: Coalitional Politics in Massachusetts, 1847-1853," *Civil War History, 22* (1976), 116–137.

We still need works on the emerging importance of ethnocultural and religious issues in the early 1850s, especially in the presidential election of 1852. There is no full-scale modern study of the temperance issue in politics in the 1840s and 1850s, for example, but Joseph R. Gusfield, *Symbolic Crusade: Status Politics and the American Temperance Movement* (Urbana: University of Illinois Press, 1963), which covers a much broader period, is useful. So, too, are the studies that stress cultural issues but that are primarily concerned with the voter realignment of middecade instead of party dissolution in the early 1850s. See, for example, Joel H. Silbey, *The Transformation of American Politics, 1840-1860* (Englewood Cliffs, N.J.: Prentice-Hall, 1967); Silbey, "The Civil War Synthesis in American Political History," *Civil War History, 10* (1964), 130–140; Paul Kleppner, *The Cross of Culture: A Social Analysis of Midwestern Politics, 1850-1900* (New York: The Free Press, 1970); William E. Gienapp, "The Transformation of Cincinnati Politics, 1852-1860" (seminar paper, Yale University, 1969); Michael F. Holt, *Forging a Majority: The Formation of the Republican Party in Pittsburgh, 1848-1860* (New Haven: Yale University Press, 1969); and Ronald P. Formisano, *The Birth of Mass Political Parties: Michigan, 1827-1861* (Princeton: Princeton University Press, 1971). Formisano's study is especially noteworthy because he is one of the few historians to recognize that the Second Party System collapsed in 1853, *before* the introduction of the Kansas-Nebraska Act. His analysis of the role of the Know Nothings and the nature of Republican ideology also parallels that found here. Finally, my own previous articles on the Know Nothings point out the rise of antiparty sentiment in the early 1850s, but they provide a different explanation for it than the one presented in this book. See Michael F. Holt, "The Politics of Impatience: The Origins of Know Nothingism," *Journal of American History, 60* (1973), 309–331, and "The Antimasonic and Know Nothing Parties," cited above.

For quantitative evidence of voting trends in the 1850s, both as to turnout rates and patterns of realignment, I have relied on a number of sources aside from my own calculations. They include: Brian G.

Walton, "The Second Party System in Tennessee," *East Tennessee Historical Society Publications, 43* (1971), 18–33; the Evitts, Formisano, and Holt books and the Sweeney article listed above; Peyton McCrary, Clark Miller, and Dale Baum, "Class and Party in the Secession Crisis: Voting Behavior in the Deep South," forthcoming in *The Journal of Interdisciplinary History,* cited with permission; Dale Baum, "The Political Realignment of the 1850s: Know Nothingism and the Republican Majority in Massachusetts," forthcoming in *The Journal of American History,* cited with permission; William E. Gienapp, "The New York Know Nothings" (seminar paper, University of California at Berkeley, 1971); and David M. Mandel, "Party Transformation in Worcester County, Massachusetts, 1848-1860" (seminar paper, Yale College, 1972).

In addition to the works listed above, which reflect an ethnocultural interpretation of the voter realignment of the 1850s, I have used the following for information on the Know Nothing party: Ray A. Billington, *The Protestant Crusade, 1800-1860: A Study in the Origins of American Nativism* (Chicago: Quadrangle Books, 1964); Oscar Handlin, *Boston's Immigrants: A Study in Acculturation* (New York: Atheneum, 1968); George H. Haynes, "A Chapter from the Local History of Know Nothingism," *The New England Magazine, 21* (1896-97), 82–96; Seymour Martin Lipset and Earl Raab, *The Politics of Unreason: Right-Wing Extremism in America* (New York: Harper & Row, 1970); W. Darrell Overdyke, *The Know-Nothing Party in the South* (Baton Rouge: Louisiana State University Press, 1950); and Leon Cyprian Soule, *The Know Nothing Party in New Orleans* (New Orleans: The Louisiana Historical Association, 1961). The general relationship between economic change and the intensification of ethnic animosities, of which Know Nothingism was a manifestation, is discussed in Herbert G. Gutman, "Work, Culture, and Society in Industrializing America, 1815-1919," *American Historical Review, 78* (1973), 531–588, and Lee Benson, "Group Cohesion and Social and Ideological Conflict: A Critique of Some Marxian and Tocquevillian Theories," *American Behavioral Scientist, 16* (1973), 741–767.

For the political background and the framing of the Kansas-Nebraska Act, I have relied on Roy F. Nichols, "The Kansas-Nebraska Act: A Century of Historiography," *Mississippi Valley Historical Review, 43* (1956), 187–212; Roy F. Nichols, *Franklin Pierce: Young Hickory of the Granite Hills* (2nd. ed. rev.; Philadelphia: University of Pennsylvania Press, 1958); Glyndon G. Van Deusen, *William Henry*

Seward (New York: Oxford University Press, 1967); and especially Johannsen's biography of Douglas, which presents a masterly account of the framing of the act. None of these authors stresses as much as I do the purpose of Douglas and Seward to rekindle old party loyalties with the bill. Gerald W. Wolff, "Party and Section: The Senate and the Kansas-Nebraska Bill," *Civil War History, 18* (1972), 293–331, stresses Southern antipathy to the Missouri Compromise prohibition of slavery north of 36°30'.

The turmoil in Kansas Territory is described in Nevins, Potter, Berwanger, and Craven as well as in Paul W. Gates, *Fifty Million Acres: Conflicts over Kansas Land Policy, 1854-1890* (Ithaca: Cornell University Press, 1954); and James A. Rawley, *Race and Politics: "Bleeding Kansas" and the Coming of the Civil War* (Philadelphia: J.B. Lippincott, 1969). David Donald, *Charles Sumner and the Coming of the Civil War* (New York: Alfred A. Knopf, 1960), the definitive biography of Sumner, contains a stirring account of his caning and its consequences.

The critical years between 1854 and 1856, when Northern voters realigned and both the Know Nothing and Republican parties formed, are treated in a number of the general and specialized works listed above. In addition one can consult: Mark L. Berger, *The Revolution in the New York Party Systems, 1840-1860* (Port Washington, N.Y.: The Kennikat Press, 1973), which though misnamed and flawed by a lack of systematic voting analysis, gives an adequate account of those three years in the Empire State; Andrew Wallace Crandall, *The Early History of the Republican Party 1854-1856* (Boston: Gorham Press, 1930), which focuses on the formation of the national organization; Jeter A. Isely, *Horace Greeley and the Republican Party, 1853-1861: A Study of the New York Tribune* (Princeton: Princeton University Press, 1947); Fred H. Harrington, *Fighting Politician: Major General N.P. Banks* (Philadelphia: University of Pennsylvania Press, 1948); Roy F. Nichols, "Some Problems of the First Republican Presidential Campaign," *American Historical Review, 28* (1923), 492–496; and Hans L. Trefousse, "The Republican Party, 1854-1864," in Schlesinger, *History of U.S. Political Parties,* Vol. II, pp. 1141–1277. The central argument among historians about this period is whether nativism, anti-Catholicism, and prohibitionism on the one hand or antislavery and anti-Southern sentiment on the other was the major force causing the voter realignment.

That debate is also reflected in conflicting interpretations of the nature and appeal of the Republican party in the 1850s, a dispute that is further complicated by disagreements over the extent to which racism influenced Republican opposition to slavery expansion. Dwight L. Dumond, *Antislavery Origins of the Civil War in the Unites States* (Ann Arbor: University of Michigan Press, 1939), argues that Republicans were abolitionists, while Don E. Fehrenbacher, "The Republican Decision at Chicago," in Norman A. Graebner, ed., *Politics and the Crisis of 1860* (Urbana: University of Illinois Press, 1961), insists that moral antipathy to slavery constituted the core of Republicanism and was responsible for the party's triumph in 1860. The case that sincere moral outrage at black slavery motivated most Republicans has been forcefully reargued recently in Richard H. Sewell, *Ballots for Freedom: Antislavery Politics in the United States, 1837-1860* (New York: Oxford University Press, 1976). Like Eric Foner in *Free Soil, Free Labor, Free Men,* Sewell also tries to defend the Republicans from the charge that racist desires to keep all blacks, both free and slave, out of the territories motivated them. Those charges appear in Bernard Mandel, *Labor: Free and Slave, Workingmen and the Anti-Slavery Movement in the United States* (New York: The Associated Authors, 1955) and James M. McPherson, *The Struggle for Equality: Abolitionists and the Negro in the Civil War and Reconstruction* (Princeton: Princeton University Press, 1964), but they form the central theme of: Berwanger, *The Frontier against Slavery;* V. Jacques Voegeli, *Free But Not Equal: The Midwest and the Negro During the Civil War* (Chicago: University of Chicago Press, 1967); and C. Vann Woodward, "The Northern Crusade against Slavery," in his *American Counterpoint: Slavery and Racism in the North-South Dialogue* (Boston: Little, Brown, and Company, 1971).

Scholars like Silbey, Formisano, and myself also point out the racist component of Republican ideology, but our major argument with the idea that moral antipathy to black slavery constituted the core of Republicanism is that it exaggerates the importance of the sectional issue to Northern voters and overlooks their genuine concern with matters such as anti-Catholicism and temperance. Thus proponents of the ethnocultural interpretation argue that the Republican party was as much a vehicle for ethnic and religious resentments as it was for antislavery and anti-Southern feeling. In part this dispute stems from different definitions of what constituted the Republican party. Those who stress the slavery issue tend to focus on nationally oriented leaders; those who argue that Republicans were moved by a combination of sectional and ethnocultural grievances include local leaders and grass-roots voters in their conception of the Republican party.

Eric Foner, *Free Soil, Free Labor, Free Men* is easily the most complete and most influential analysis of Republican ideology. He argues forcefully that free-soilism instead of abolitionism or moral antipathy to black slavery formed the core of Republicanism, and he emphasizes hostility to the Slave Power and especially the desire to protect and expand the free labor system as the basis of free-soilism. In a more recent article, however, Foner seems to put more stress, correctly I believe, on negative opposition to the Slave Power than on a positive affirmation of the free labor system. See Eric Foner, "Politics, Ideology, and the Origins of the American Civil War," in George Fredrickson, ed., *A Nation Divided: Problems and Issues of the Civil War and Reconstruction* (Minneapolis: Burgess Publishing Company, 1975), pp. 15–34. In his book, Foner insists that Republicans absorbed Northern Know Nothings without making any concessions to their nativist principles and that once men voted Republican their former nativism had little political relevance. Foner will receive strong support for this contention in Dale Baum's forthcoming article on Massachusetts politics, to be published in *The Journal of American History*. In my judgment, both draw too sharp a distinction between nativism as a political force—when men voted Know Nothing—and nativism as a cultural force—when they voted Republican—on the one hand, while they underestimate the critical distinction between antiforeignism and anti-Catholicism on the other. Men did not have to vote Know Nothing to express their resentment against Catholics as long as they regarded the Republican party as more anti-Catholic than the Democratic party—and they did.

My argument that the essence of the Republican appeal was its charge that the Slave Power conspiracy, aided and abetted by the Democratic party, threatened to subvert the republic is based largely on my own reading of the primary sources. But the pervasiveness of conspiratorial thinking and the parallels among various countersubversive crusades in the Middle Period are suggested in David Davis, "Some Themes of Counter-Subversion: An Analysis of Anti-Masonic, Anti-Catholic, and Anti-Mormon Literature," *Mississippi Valley Historical Review, 47* (1960), 205–224, and Davis, *The Slave Power Conspiracy and the Paranoid Style* (Baton Rouge: Louisiana State University Press, 1969). Instead of the paranoia of such crusades against anti-republican monsters, I would stress that they had formed the essence of American political conflict since at least the 1820s.

William G. Shade, *Banks or No Banks* and Bruce W. Collins, "The Politics of Particularism: Economic Issues in the Major Northern States of the USA, 1857-1858" (Ph.D. dissertation, Cambridge University, 1975) provide useful information on the political impact of the Panic of 1857.

The classic account of the Buchanan administration is Roy F. Nichols, *Disruption of American Democracy* (New York: Collier Books, 1962), which contains the best single analysis of how the fight over the Lecompton constitution and subsequent events ruptured the Democratic party. For the Lecompton fiasco, I have also relied heavily on the superb chapter in Potter and Johannsen's biography of Douglas. Johannsen also presents an excellent account of the famous Lincoln-Douglas debates of 1858. Lincoln's political need to differentiate himself from Douglas in the Illinois election of that year is brilliantly developed in Don E. Fehrenbacher, *Prelude to Greatness: Lincoln in the 1850s* (Stanford: Stanford University Press, 1962). Fehrenbacher, however, stresses Lincoln's introduction of the moral question as his main tactic in this regard, as does Foner in *Free Soil, Free Labor, Free Men.* David Potter correctly identified the resurrection of the conspiracy thesis against the South as Lincoln's main weapon, although he seems to miss the distinction between that and his overall argument that moral antagonism to black slavery motivated Northerners. Aside from these works, able treatments of the 1858 congressional elections can be found in David E. Meerse, "The Northern Democratic Party and the Congressional Elections of 1858," *Civil War History, 19* (1973), 119–137, which argues persuasively that the Lecompton issue was not responsible for Democratic defeats, and Don E. Fehrenbacher, "Comments on Why the Republican Party Came to Power," in George H. Knoles, ed., *The Crisis of the Union* (Baton Rouge: Louisiana State University Press, 1965), pp. 21–29, which points out how important the Republican gains of 1858 were to the Republican victory in 1860.

For the political strife over personal liberty laws in the late 1850s, see Foner, *Free Soil, Free Labor, Free Men;* Thomas D. Morris, *Free Men All: The Personal Liberty Laws of the North, 1780-1861;* Stanley W. Campbell, *The Slave Catchers: Enforcement of the Fugitive Slave Law, 1850-1860* (Chapel Hill: University of North Carolina Press, 1968); and Norman L. Rosenberg, "Personal Liberty Laws and Sectional Crisis: 1850-61," *Civil War History, 17* (1971), 25–44.

The importance of corruption in the Buchanan administration as a political issue in the late 1850s and 1860 merits further study. See, however, Nichols, *Disruption of American Democracy;* David E. Meerse, "Buchanan, Corruption, and the Election of 1860," *Civil War History, 12* (1966), 116-131; and C. Vann Woodward, ed., *Responses of the Presidents to Charges of Misconduct* (New York: Dell Books, 1974).

The literature on the Southern movement toward secession is extensive, and I will not attempt to review all of it here. I would urge interested students to begin on this, as on so many other topics, with Potter, *The Impending Crisis.* Dwight L. Dumond, ed., *Southern Editorials on Secession* (New York: American Historical Association, 1931) is a useful collection that allows one to see the different responses to Lincoln's election in the upper and lower South. George H. Reese, ed., *Proceedings of the Virginia State Convention of 1861* (4 vols.; Richmond: Virginia State Library, 1965), provides the fascinating Virginia debates on secession in a convenient form, but one should see the suggestive essay review of those volumes, William W. Freehling, "The Editorial Revolution, Virginia, and the Coming of the Civil War: A Review Essay," *Civil War History, 16* (1970), 64-72.

In general, historians of secession have been less concerned with the specific question of why the upper and lower South responded differently to Lincoln's election than with the general problem of why Southerners seceded. Here they have disagreed about which groups effected secession and precisely what motivated them. Stephen A. Channing, *Crisis of Fear: Secession in South Carolina* (New York: W. W. Norton, 1974) argues that the racial fears of all whites in that state about the consequences of abolition or slave insurrection impelled them to secede. Otto H. Olsen, "Historians and the Extent of Slave Ownership in the Southern United States," *Civil War History, 18* (1972), 101-116, points out that slaveholding was especially widespread among whites in the lower South and implies they seceded to avoid the economic loss inherent in abolition. Eugene Genovese, *The Political Economy of Slavery,* on the other hand, argues that it was the Republicans' threat to slave extension instead of the prospect of abolition that caused the planter elite to resort to secession. William L. Barney, in *The Road to Secession* and *The Secessionist Impulse,* also insists that the demand for slavery expansion was the root of secession, but to the economic needs of planters he adds the racial fears of nonslaveholders who wanted expansion to disperse a growing black population.

Barney's two books also present the only sustained attempt to account for the different behavior of planters in regard to secession.

Briefly, he posits a generational difference between young and ambitious planters who favored secession and old and contented planters who opposed it. I have stated my reservations about this approach elsewhere: Michael F. Holt, "Two Roads to Sumter," *Reviews in American History, 3* (1975), 221–228.

My own interpretation of the secessionist impulse has been influenced most heavily by Thornton's study of Alabama. In effect, I have tried to extend his ideas to the rest of the South. I have also found useful Avery O. Craven, "Why the Southern States Seceded," in Knoles, ed., *The Crisis of the Union,* and J. Holt Merchant, Jr., "Lawrence M. Keitt: South Carolina Fire Eater" (Ph.D. dissertation, University of Virginia, 1976).

On the other hand, my attempt to locate the reasons for the different responses of the upper and lower South to Lincoln's election in their different political experiences during the 1850s is entirely my own. But even here I have been helped enormously by the unpublished papers of former students. Two papers in an undergraduate seminar on secession at the University of Virginia are especially noteworthy: Margaret Cooper, "Memminger and the Virginia Politicians" (seminar paper, University of Virginia, 1975), and particularly, Andrew R. L. Cayton, "Political Rhetoric and the Secession Crisis in North Carolina" (seminar paper, University of Virginia, 1975). I have also had the benefit of reading the chapter on secession from Marc W. Kruman's forthcoming dissertation at Yale University, "Parties and Politics in North Carolina, 1846-1865." Kruman, who was a former graduate student of mine and who now teaches at Wayne State University, arrived quite independently at the conclusion that North Carolina did not secede immediately because of the vitality of the two-party system there.

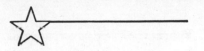

FOOTNOTES

CHAPTER ONE

[1] Eugene Genovese, *The Political Economy of Slavery* (New York: Pantheon Books, 1965); Eric Foner, *Free Soil, Free Labor, Free Men: The Ideology of the Republican Party before the Civil War* (New York: Oxford University Press, 1970).

[2] Mary P. Ryan, "Party Formation in the United States Congress, 1789-1796: A Quantitative Analysis," *William & Mary Quarterly,* Ser. 3, *28* (1971), 523-542; H James Henderson, "Quantitative Approaches to Party Formation in the United States Congress: A Comment," ibid., Ser. 3, *30* (April 1973), 307-324.

[3] James Sterling Young, *The Washington Community* (New York: Columbia University Press, 1966).

[4] Martin Van Buren to Thomas Ritchie, January 13, 1827, copy, Martin Van Buren MSS (Library of Congress); Richard H. Brown, "The Missouri Crisis, Slavery, and the Politics of Jacksonianism," *South Atlantic Quarterly, 65* (1966), 52-72.

[5] James Banner, "The Problem of South Carolina," in Stanley Elkins and Eric McKitrick, eds., *The Hofstadter Aegis: A Memorial* (New York: Alfred A. Knopf, 1974), pp. 60-93.

[6] Eric Foner, "Politics, Ideology, and the Origins of the American Civil War," in George Fredrickson, ed., *A Nation Divided: Problems and Issues of the Civil War and Reconstruction* (Minneapolis: Burgess Publishing Company, 1975), p. 16.

[7] Thomas Jefferson to John Taylor, June 1, 1793, quoted in Henderson, "Quantitative Approaches," pp. 322–323.

[8] Albany *Argus,* April 9, March 5, 1824, quoted in Michael Wallace, "Changing Concepts of Party in the United States: New York, 1815-1828," *American Historical Review, 74* (December 1968), 476. See also pp. 482-83.

[9] Sydney Nathans, *Daniel Webster and Jacksonian Democracy* (Baltimore: The Johns Hopkins University Press, 1973), pp. 30–36, 45, 212 and passim.

[10] Nathaniel Terry to Arthur P. Bagby, September 19, 1840, quoted in Jonathan Mills Thornton III, "Politics and Power in a Slave Society: Alabama 1806-1860" (Ph.D. dissertation, Yale University, 1974), p. 136. Philip Phillips to John Bragg, February 8, 1852, John Bragg MSS (Southern Historical Collection, University of North Carolina Library).

CHAPTER TWO

[1] Alexis de Tocqueville, *Democracy in America,* ed. by Phillips Bradley (2 vols.; New York: Vintage Books, 1945), Vol. II, pp. 99–103, 144–47, 259, 306–313.

[2] Much of the analysis in this and the following paragraph is based on Richard H. Brown, "The Missouri Crisis, Slavery, and the Politics of Jacksonianism," *South Atlantic Quarterly, 65* (1966), 52–72; see also Glover Moore, *The Missouri Controversy, 1819-1821* (Lexington: University of Kentucky Press, 1953).

[3] Martin Van Buren to Thomas Ritchie, January 13, 1827, Martin Van Buren MSS (Library of Congress).

[4] Lee Benson, *The Concept of Jacksonian Democracy: New York as a Test Case* (Princeton: Princeton University Press, 1961), pp. 11–63 and passim; Michael F. Holt, "The Antimasonic and Know Nothing Parties" in Arthur M. Schlesinger, Jr., ed., *History of U.S. Political Parties* (4 vols.; New York: Chelsea House, 1973), Vol. I, pp. 575–592.

[5] Bertram Wyatt-Brown, "Prelude to Abolitionism: Sabbatarian Politics and the Rise of the Second Party System," *Journal of American History, 58* (1971), 316–341.

[6] Wiley P. Harris, "Autobiography of Wiley P. Harris," in Dunbar Rowland, ed., *Courts, Judges, and Lawyers in Mississippi, 1789-1835* (Jackson, Miss, 1936), p. 287. I am deeply indebted to Professor William J. Cooper, Jr. of Louisiana State University for this quotation, which appears in a draft of his forthcoming study of the Second Party System in the South.

[7] Henry Clay to John M. Clayton, April 16, 1847, John M. Clayton MSS (Library of Congress).

[8] David J. Russo, "The Major Political Issues of the Jacksonian Period and the Development of Party Loyalty in Congress, 1830-1840," *Transactions of the American Philosophical Society, 62* (1975), 6, 26 and passim.

[9] Edward Pessen, *Jacksonian America: Society, Personality, and Politics* (Homewood, Ill.: Dorsey Press, 1969), pp. 233–247; Herbert Ershkowitz and William Shade, "Consensus or Conflict? Political Behavior in the State Legislatures during the Jacksonian Era," *Journal of American History, 58* (1971), 591–622.

[10] On the Democratic divisions, see Arthur M. Schlesinger, Jr., *The Age of Jackson* (Boston: Little-Brown, 1945), pp. 128-31, 171-76, 190-209; James Roger Sharp, *The Jacksonians versus the Banks: Politics in the States after the Panic of 1837* (New York: Columbia University Press, 1970), pp. 3-14; James C. Curtis, *The Fox at Bay: Martin Van Buren and the Presidency, 1837-1841* (Lexington: University Press of Kentucky, 1970), pp. 64-68.

[11] Joel H. Silbey, "The Election of 1836," in Arthur M. Schlesinger, Jr. and Fred Israel, eds., *History of American Presidential Elections* (4 vols.; New York: Chelsea House, 1971), Vol. I, pp. 577-600.

[12] Alexander Porter to Jesse Burton Harrison, January 12, 1836, and the Raleigh (North Carolina) *Register,* December 22, 1835, quoted in William J. Cooper, Jr., "The Politics of Sectionalism: Some Thoughts on the Second Party System in the South," (seminar paper, The Institute of Southern History, The Johns Hopkins University, 1972), pp. 20-21.

[13] Thomas Alexander, *Sectional Stress and Party Strength: A Computer Analysis of Roll-Call Voting Patterns in the United States House*

of Representatives, 1836-1860 (Nashville: Vanderbilt University Press, 1967), pp. 11-13 and passim.

[14] Thomas Ritchie to Francis P. Blair, March 27, 1835, quoted in Cooper, "Politics of Sectionalism," p. 23.

[15] William W. Freehling, *Prelude to Civil War: The Nullification Controversy in South Carolina, 1816-1836* (New York: Harper & Row, 1965), pp. 350-351; Curtis, *The Fox at Bay*, pp. 47-48; Leonard Richards, *Gentlemen of Property and Standing: Anti-Abolitionist Mobs in Jacksonian America* (New York: Oxford University Press, 1970), p. 92; Silbey, "Election of 1836," p. 590.

[16] The three were James M. Wayne of Georgia, Roger B. Taney of Maryland, and Philip P. Barbour of Virginia.

[17] Glyndon G. Van Deusen, "The Whig Party," in Schlesinger, ed., *History of U.S. Political Parties,* Vol. I, pp. 341; Alexander, *Sectional Stress and Party Strength,* pp. 11-13, 26-27, 31-33 and passim; Ershkowitz and Shade, "Consensus or Conflict," pp. 611-612.

[18] Albany *Argus,* April 9, 1824, quoted in Michael Wallace, "Changing Concepts of Party in the United States: New York, 1815-1828," *American Historical Review, 74* (December 1968), 476.

[19] James D. Richardson (ed.), *A Compilation of the Messages and Papers of the Presidents, 1789-1897* (10 vols.; Washington: Government Printing Office, 1896-1899), Vol. III, pp. 324-346. Throughout the remainder of this book this source will be cited as Richardson, *Messages and Papers of the Presidents.*

[20] For the differences between the parties at the national level, see Alexander, *Sectional Stress and Party Strength* and Joel H. Silbey, *The Shrine of Party: Congressional Voting Behavior, 1841-1852* (Pittsburgh: University of Pittsburgh Press, 1967). For the state level, see Ershkowitz and Shade, "Consensus or Conflict?" and Peter Levine, "State Legislative Parties in the Jacksonian Era: New Jersey, 1829-1844," *Journal of American History, 62* (1975), 591-608.

[21] Wiley P. Harris to John F. H. Claiborne, August 30, 1855, John F. H. Claiborne MSS (Mississippi Department of Archives and History); Felix K. Zollicoffer to William B. Campbell, July 14, 1851, Campbell Family Papers (Perkins Library, Duke University); Alexander H. Stephens to James Thomas, July 16, 1844, in Ulrich B. Phillips, ed., *The Correspondence of Robert Toombs, Alexander H. Stephens, and Howell Cobb* in *The Annual Report of the American Historical Asso-*

ciation for the Year 1911 (Washington, 1913), Vol. II, pp. 59–60. (Hereafter this will be cited as Phillips, *Correspondence.*)

[22] William G. Brownlow to Alexander Williams, October 18, 1841, Alexander Williams MSS (Perkins Library, Duke University).

[23] James Graham to William A. Graham, April 21, 1850, in J. G. de Roulhac Hamilton, ed., *The Papers of William Alexander Graham* (5 vols.; Raleigh: North Carolina Department of Archives, 1957-1973), Vol. III, p. 320.

[24] Pennsylvania, General Assembly, *Journal of the Fifty-Sixth House of Representatives of the Commonwealth of Pennsylvania* (Harrisburg, 1846), pp. 10–11.

[25] Jonathan Mills Thornton III, "Politics and Power in a Slave Society: Alabama 1806-1860" (Ph.D. dissertation, Yale University, 1974), pp. 135-138.

[26] Yancey is quoted in Chaplain W. Morrison, *Democratic Politics and Sectionalism: The Wilmot Proviso Controversy* (Chapel Hill: University of North Carolina Press, 1967), p. 50.

[27] Quoted in Thornton, "Politics and Power in a Slave Society," pp. 41, 180.

[28] Little Rock *Arkansas Banner,* January 30, 1844: Jackson *Mississippian,* September 5, 1851; and the *Richmond Whig,* November 21, 1845, quoted in a draft of William J. Cooper's *Politics of Slavery* that is to be published by the Louisiana State University Press.

CHAPTER THREE

[1] James C. N. Paul, *Rift in the Democracy* (New York: A. S. Barnes & Company, 1961); Charles G. Sellers, *James K. Polk: Continentalist, 1843-1846* (Princeton: Princeton University Press, 1966), pp. 15–55.

[2] Frederick Merk, *Slavery and the Annexation of Texas* (New York: Alfred A. Knopf, 1972), p. 9.

[3] Thomas Ritchie to Howell Cobb, May 16, 1844 in Phillips, *Correspondence,* p. 56.

[4] *Ohio State Journal,* November 5, 1842, quoted in Norman E. Tutorow, "Whigs in the Old Northwest and the Mexican War" (unpublished Ph.D. dissertation, Stanford University, 1967), pp. 69–70.

For the *Richmond Whig* and other evidence of Whig opposition to Texas annexation before 1844, see ibid., pp. 36, 44, 68, 75, 83.

[5] Frederick Merk, *Manifest Destiny and Mission in American History* (New York: Vintage Books, 1963), pp. 34–44. For party divisions in the Northwest, see Tutorow, "Whigs in the Old Northwest," pp. 73–93. In a vote in the Indiana assembly in December 1843, for example, 87 percent of the Whigs voted against annexation, while 86 percent of the Democrats favored it. On general voting patterns in Congress, see Thomas Alexander, *Sectional Stress and Party Strength: A Computer Analysis of Roll-Call Voting Patterns in the United States House of Representatives, 1836-1860* (Nashville: Vanderbilt University Press, 1967), pp. 51–54. On the Senate ratification votes, see Merk, *Slavery and the Annexation of Texas,* p. 81. Twenty-seven of 28 Whig senators opposed the treaty, while only one from Mississippi supported it.

[6] For the negative views of an influential Georgia Whig on Tyler's treaty, see Alexander H. Stephens to James Thomas, May 17, 1844, in Phillips, *Correspondence,* pp. 57–58. See also Paul Murray, *The Whig Party in Georgia, 1825-1853* (Chapell Hill: University of North Carolina Press, 1948), pp. 107–109. On three votes in the Mississippi legislature in early 1844 on annexation, an average of 98 percent of the Democrats voted in favor, while 64 percent of the Whigs voted in opposition for an average disagreement index of 62. M. Philip Lucas, "The Second Party System in Mississippi, 1836-1844" (unpublished seminar paper, University of Virginia, 1975), pp. 25–26. On Northern Democratic support even in Massachusetts, see Robert Rantoul to N.P. Banks, August 9, 1844, N. P. Banks MSS (Illinois State Historical Library).

[7] Lee Benson, *The Concept of Jacksonian Democracy: New York as a Test Case* (Princeton: Princeton University Press, 1961), pp. 254–269; Sellers, *Polk,* pp. 108–160.

[8] Merk, *Slavery and the Annexation of Texas,* pp. 158–159. The parties continued to be sharply divided by the Texas issue in Northeastern states during 1845 as well. On New Hampshire, see William Plumer to Charles Francis Adams, et al., July 2, 1845, Adams Family Papers (Massachusetts Historical Society, microfilm edition). On Connecticut, William W. Ellsworth to Charles Francis Adams, July 2, 1845, ibid. On New York, see New York *Tribune,* February 6, March 13, 1845.

[9] Merk, *Slavery and the Annexation of Texas,* pp. 117–135.

[10] James L. Sundquist, *Dynamics of the Party System: Alignment and Realignment of Political Parties in the United States* (Washington: The Brookings Institution, 1973), pp. 32, 304.

[11] Ellsworth to Adams, July 2, 1845 and Lemoyne to Adams, July 22, 1845, Adams Family Papers.

[12] Alexander, *Sectional Stress and Party Strength,* pp. 57–69, 188–190; Joel H. Silbey, *The Shrine of Party: Congressional Voting Behavior, 1843-1852* (Pittsburgh: University of Pittsburgh Press, 1967), pp. 67–97; Merk, *Manifest Destiny and Mission,* pp. 29, 46, 62–64; Richardson, *Messages and Papers of the Presidents,* Vol. IV, pp. 392–398; Sellers, *Polk,* pp. 336–339.

[13] New York *Tribune,* November 9, 16, December 13, 23, 1844; James Bowen to Thurlow Weed, July 21, 1846, Thurlow Weed MSS (Rush Rhees Library, Rochester University); John B. Lamar to Howell Cobb, June 24, 1846, in Phillips, *Correspondence,* pp. 82–84.

[14] Murray, *The Whig Party in Georgia,* pp. 127–130; Tutorow, "Whigs in the Old Northwest," pp. 214–287; on Massachusetts, see Boston *Daily Advertiser,* January 1, June 15, July 18, September 14, 1848; on Connecticut, see John Huntington to Gideon Welles, January 29, 1847, and John M. Niles to Welles, April 11, 1847, Gideon Welles MSS (New York Public Library) and Mark Howard to James M. Barnard, April 5, 1848, Mark Howard MSS (Connecticut Historical Society); and on New Jersey, see William Sharp, "The Collapse of the Whig Party in New Jersey" (unpublished seminar paper, Yale College, 1973), pp. 14–15.

[15] Samuel Sample to Schuyler Colfax, December 1, 1844, Schuyler Colfax MSS (Northern Indiana Historical Society); Godlove Orth to Schuyler Colfax, January 27, 1846, in J. Herman Schauinger, "The Letters of Godlove S. Orth: Hoosier Whig," *Indiana Magazine of History, 39* (1943), 378–380; T. H. Nelson to Richard W. Thompson, July 5, 1847, Richard W. Thompson MSS (Indiana State Library).

[16] *Pennsylvania Telegraph* (Harrisburg), January 7, 1846. Of all the substantive issues voted on in the 1846 session of the Pennsylvania house, Oregon produced the sharpest interparty conflict. The average party disagreement score on six roll calls on the Oregon issue was 62. The average disagreement score for all 326 roll calls in that session, in contrast, was only 37.5. For the disagreement in state party platforms over expansion and the Mexican War, see Michael F. Holt, *Forging a*

Majority: The Formation of the Republican Party in Pittsburgh, 1848-1860 (New Haven: Yale University Press, 1969), pp. 54–61.

[17] Letter of D. W. Foster in New York *Tribune,* August 14, 1845.

[18] *Pennsylvania Telegraph,* January 10, 1846; Pennsylvania, General Assembly, *Journal of the 56th House of Representatives of the Commonwealth of Pennsylvania, 1846* (Harrisburg, 1846), pp. 182–184. The Democrats were initially divided 25 to 36 against resolutions opposing revision of the Tariff of 1842, but once hard money amendments were added, they supported resolutions favoring tariff reduction 57 to 2, while the Whigs were unanimously opposed.

[19] *Richmond Enquirer,* October 20, 1846.

[20] *Pennsylvania Telegraph,* January 12, 13, 19, February 6, 10, 19, 1847; Holt, *Forging a Majority,* pp. 49–53.

The impact of congressional action on the Tariff and Independent Treasury with its hard-money implications on party lines in the Pennsylvania legislature is dramatically shown in the following table, which compares the internal cohesion for both parties and the disagreement indexes in the house for 1846, before national legislation was passed, and for 1847 after it was passed.

	Number of Roll-Calls	Average Rice Index of Democratic Cohesion	Average Rice Index of Whig Cohesion	Average Disagreement Index
TARIFF				
1846	12	45.7	80	43.5
1847	7	91	98.8	94.9
BANKING AND CURRENCY				
1846	34	41.8	56.6	34
1847	17	78.8	92.5	85.7
OTHER BUSINESS INCORPORATIONS				
1846	12	22.6	67.7	42.5
1847	29	80	89	84.4
ALL VOTES DURING ENTIRE SESSION				
1846	326	33.5	45.3	37.5
1847	201	67.2	69.9	57.7

These last figures for 1847 indicate that on average, 83 percent of the Democrats and 85 percent of the Whigs voted together and that over four-fifths of the Democrats opposed over four-fifths of the Whigs on the vast majority of roll-calls. Given the wide diversity of bills and motions legislators voted on, including a number of private petitions for divorces, motions to adjourn, and so on, this was a remarkably partisan performance. The parties were clearly much more united internally and polarized against each other in 1847 than in 1846, and the clarification of national party lines In 1846 together with the Democratic responsibility for specific legislation was largely responsible.

[21] David Wilmot to Franklin Pierce, July 13, 1852, Franklin Pierce MSS (New Hampshire Historical Society, microfilm copy); William H. Howe to Roger Sherman Baldwin, Jr., July 25, 1848, Baldwin Family Papers (Yale University Library). Aside from my own researches, this general analysis of free-soil sentiment is indebted to Chaplain W. Morrison, *Democratic Politics and Sectionalism: The Wilmot Proviso Controversy* (Chapel Hill: The University of North Carolina Press, 1967), pp. 52–74, and Eric Foner, *Free Soil, Free Labor, Free Men: The Ideology of the Republican Party before the Civil War* (New York: Oxford University Press, 1970).

[22] William J. Cooper, Jr., "The Cotton Crisis in the Antebellum South: Another Look," *Agricultural History, 49* (April 1975), 381–391; and Robert Fogel and Stanley Engerman, *Time on the Cross,* (Boston: Little, Brown, & Company, 1974), Vol. I, pp. 103–105.

[23] Henry Benning to Howell Cobb, February 23, 1848, in Phillips, *Correspondence*, pp. 97–103; Morrison, *Democratic Politics and Sectionalism*, pp. 27, 58.

[24] Peter V. Daniel to Martin Van Buren, quoted in Morrison, *Democratic Politics and Sectionalism*, p. 65; the Calhoun resolutions are quoted, ibid., pp. 34–35; Alexander H. Stephens to the Milledgeville (Georgia) *Federal Union*, August 30, 1848 in Phillips, *Correspondence*, pp. 117–124.

[25] *Richmond Whig*, March 6, 1840; Milledgeville *Federal Union*, August 18, 1840; the Mississippi platform is quoted in Morrison, *Democratic Politics and Sectionalism*, p. 47. I am indebted to Professor William J. Cooper, Jr. of Louisiana State University for the newspaper quotations.

[26] George Fredrickson, *The Black Image in the White Mind: The Debate on Afro-American Character and Destiny, 1817-1914* (New York: Harper & Row, 1971), pp. 61–70.

[27] William T. Minor to George S. Houston, January 12, 1849, George S. Houston MSS (Perkins Library, Duke University); *Advertiser,* June 25, 1851, quoted in J. Mills Thornton, III, "Politics and Power in a Slave Society: Alabama, 1806-1860" (unpublished Ph.D. dissertation, Yale University, 1974), pp. 78–79; Charleston *Courier,* September 25, 1856. For this last citation, I am indebted to Professor Holt Merchant of Washington and Lee College, whose dissertation on Keitt I read in preliminary draft form.

[28] Robert C. Winthrop to John P. Kennedy, January 24, 1848, copy, Robert C. Winthrop MSS (Massachusetts Historical Society, microfilm).

[29] Silbey, *The Shrine of Party,* pp. 90–97.

[30] Morrison, *Democratic Politics and Sectionalism,* pp. 33–51, 83, 93–120; Tutorow, "Whigs in the Old Northwest," pp. 275–365, 457.

[31] Isaac E. Holmes to Howell Cobb, August 21, 1847 in Phillips, *Correspondence,* p. 88; Morrison, *Democratic Politics and Sectionalism,* pp. 38–51; Silbey, *The Shrine of Party,* pp. 98–106.

[32] Speech of Howell Cobb, July 1, 1848, *Congressional Globe,* 30th Cong.; 1st Sess., Appendix, pp. 775–777, reprinted in Joel H. Silbey, *The Transformation of American Politics, 1840-1860* (Englewood Cliffs, N.J.: Prentice-Hall, 1967), pp. 40–42; Howell Cobb to a Committee of Citizens in Charleston, S. C., November 4, 1848, in Phillips, *Correspondence,* pp. 133–135.

[33] Washington Hunt to Thurlow Weed, March 19, 1848, Thurlow Weed MSS.

[34] Holman Hamilton, *Zachary Taylor: Soldier in the White House* (Indianapolis: The Bobbs-Merrill Co., 1951), p. 44; George R. Poage, *Henry Clay and the Whig Party* (Chapel Hill: University of North Carolina Press, 1936), pp. 154–159; Joseph G. Rayback, *Free Soil: The Election of 1848* (Lexington: University Press of Kentucky, 1970), pp. 33–54.

[35] Hunt to Weed, March 19, 1848, Weed MSS.

[36] John A. Watkins to Leslie Combs, May 15, 1848, Daniel Ullmann MSS (New York Historical Society).

[37] *Daily National Intelligencer,* July 7, 1848; John McLean to John Teesdale, December 10, 1848, John McLean MSS (Ohio Historical Society); the Massachusetts Whig State Platform and Address to the Voters, Boston *Daily Advertiser,* September 14, 15, 1848; Pennsylvania Whig State Platform, Pittsburgh *Daily Commercial Journal,* September 6, 1848; Thornton, "Politics and Power in a Slave Society," pp. 232–240; Rayback, *Free Soil,* pp. 241–242.

[38] Holt, *Forging a Majority,* pp. 48–53; Boston *Daily Advertiser,* July 18, August 11, October 16, 25, 28, 1848; S. C. Phillips to Salmon P. Chase, October 19, 1848, Salmon P. Chase MSS (Library of Congress).

[39] John H. Clifford to Robert C. Winthrop, November 19, 1848, Robert C. Winthrop MSS.

[40] Comparing party percentages of the vote instead of absolute totals as I have, Rayback, *Free Soil,* p. 288, estimates that Cass held 81 percent of the Democratic vote in the North and 94 percent in the South, while Taylor retained 95 percent in the North and increased it in the South. A recent, more sophisticated statistical analysis of voting in Alabama, Mississippi, and Louisiana estimates that 9.5 percent of those who voted Democratic in 1844 switched to Taylor in 1848, but at the same time 13.3 percent of those who voted Whig in 1844 switched to the Democratic column in 1848. Peyton McCrary, Clark Miller, and Dale Baum, "Class and Party in the Secession Crisis: Voting Behavior in the Deep South, 1856-1861," forthcoming in *The Journal of Interdisciplinary History,* Table I, cited with permission of the authors.

[41] New York *Tribune,* November 11, 26, 1844, January 7, 9, 1845; Boston *Courier,* quoted in the *Pennsylvania Telegraph,* October 29, 1845; Benson, *The Concept of Jacksonian Democracy,* pp. 165–207 and passim; Holt, *Forging a Majority,* pp. 40–83; Ronald P. Formisano, *The Birth of Mass Political Parties: Michigan, 1837-1861* (Princeton: Princeton University Press, 1971).

CHAPTER FOUR

[1] The Southern Address can be found in Richard Crallé, ed., *The Works of John C. Calhoun* (6 vols.; New York: D. Appleton & Company, 1854-1855), Vol. VI, pp. 285–313.

[2] *Mercury,* January 22, 1849, quoted in Joel H. Silbey, *The Shrine*

of Party: Congressional Voting Behavior, 1841-1852 (Pittsburgh: University of Pittsburgh Press, 1967), p. 261, n. 64.

[3] Robert Toombs to John J. Crittenden, December 3, 1848, George Badger to Crittenden, January 3, 1849, John J. Crittenden MSS (Library of Congress); Toombs to Crittenden, January 22, 1849 in Phillips, *Correspondence,* pp. 140–42.

[4] Quoted in Holman Hamilton, *Zachary Taylor: Soldier in the White House* (reprint ed.; Hamden, Conn.: Archon Books, 1966), p. 225.

[5] For evidence that Southern Whigs blamed their defeat in part on the Democratic exploitation of the slavery issue, see Washington Barrow to John M. Clayton, Nashville, August 5, 1849, and William J. Ward to Clayton, Greensburg, Ky., August 17, 1849, John M. Clayton MSS (Library of Congress); David Gordon to Thomas Ewing, Jackson, Miss., November 9, 1849, Ewing Family Papers (Library of Congress).

[6] This composite of Taylor's thinking is based on the following: Zachary Taylor to Crittenden, September 15, 1847, March 25, 1848, Crittenden MSS; Taylor to ?, August 16, 1847, draft, Taylor to ?, December 16, 1847, draft, Taylor to Joseph P. Taylor, January 1, 1848, Zachary Taylor MSS (Library of Congress).

[7] After talking with Taylor in December 1848, Crittenden reported that Taylor would build a nonpartisan administration that would offend "men devoted to party" but one that would pursue *"republican"* policy. Crittenden to John M. Clayton, December 19, 1848, Clayton MSS.

[8] A. C. Bullitt to Crittenden, December 3, 1848, Albert T. Burnley to Crittenden, January 12, 1849, Crittenden MSS.

[9] Clayton to Crittenden, December 13, 1848, ibid.

[10] William Henry Seward to Thurlow Weed, December 3, 1848, Thurlow Weed MSS (Rush Rhees Library, University of Rochester).

[11] John. M. Clayton to J. J. Crittenden, November 8, December 13, 1848, January 23, 1849, Crittenden MSS; Morton McMichael, n. d., and Robert Bird, n. d., to John M. Clayton, Clayton MSS; Reverdy Johnson to Crittenden, December 12, 1849, Crittenden MSS.

[12] Burnley to Crittenden, January 12, July 22, 1849, Crittenden MSS.

[13] Hamilton, *Zachary Taylor,* pp. 239-244; Orlando Brown to Crittenden, June 27, July 10, 1849, Toombs to Crittenden, April 23, 1850, Crittenden MSS.

[14] Henry Clay to Thomas B. Stevenson, April 21, 1849, Thomas B. Stevenson MSS (Indiana Historical Society Library).

[15] Numerous examples of these complaints can be found in the correspondence of Crittenden, Thomas Ewing, Meredith, and Clayton. I have also relied on Jonathan Fanton, "The Politics of Compromise" (unpublished seminar paper, Yale University, 1973).

[16] Crittenden to Clayton, July 8, 1849, J. W. White to Clayton, April 30, 1849, Clayton MSS; Richardson, *Messages and Papers of the Presidents,* Vol. V, pp. 4-6.

[17] Taylor to ?, August 16, 1847, draft, Zachary Taylor MSS.

[18] Crittenden to Clayton, December 19, 1848, Clayton MSS.

[19] Clayton to Crittenden, April 18, 1849, Crittenden MSS; Richardson, *Messages and Papers,* Vol. V, p. 19.

[20] E. D. Baker to Clayton, March 20, 1849, Clayton MSS.

[21] Quoted in Hamilton, *Zachary Taylor,* p. 225.

[22] Clay to Thomas B. Stevenson, December 21, 1849, Stevenson MSS; on the entanglement of patronage and reaction to the Taylor plan, see William H. Seward to Thurlow Weed, April 30, 1850, John L. Schoolcraft to Weed, August 30, 1850, and Philo Shenton to Weed, May 9, 1850, Weed MSS; Fanton, "The Politics of Compromise."

[23] William H. Bissell to William Martin, February 5, 1850, William H. Bissell MSS (Chicago Historical Society); David H. Abell to Thurlow Weed, February 15, 20, 1850, Weed MSS.

[24] Holman Hamilton, *Prologue to Conflict: The Crisis and Compromise of 1850* (New York: W. W. Norton and Company, 1966), pp. 53-83; Crittenden to Clayton, February 18, 1850, Clayton MSS; Robert F. Dalzell, Jr., *Daniel Webster and the Trial of American Nationalism* (Boston: Houghton-Mifflin Co., 1973), pp. 175-176.

[25] George Rawlins Poage, *Henry Clay and the Whig Party* (Chapel Hill: University of North Carolina Press, 1936), p. 199; Fanton, "Politics of Compromise," pp. 19-23.

[26] Dalzell, *Daniel Webster,* pp. 157-195; William D. Lewis to John

M. Clayton, December 6, 1849, Clayton MSS; George W. South to Zachary Taylor, April 22, 1849, Townsend Haines to William M. Meredith, March 17, 1849; Thomas Ewing to Meredith, April 25, 1849, Meredith Family Papers (Historical Society of Pennsylvania); W. H. Seward to Thurlow Weed, March 11, 15, 1850, Weed MSS.

[27] Quoted in Robert W. Johannsen, *Stephen A. Douglas,* (New York: Oxford University Press, 1973), p. 271.

[28] John L. Schoolcraft to Thurlow Weed, August 30, 1850, Weed MSS; Robert Rantoul to Stephen A. Douglas, August 30, 1850, and C. J. Ingersoll to Douglas, September 7, 1850, Stephen A. Douglas MSS (University of Chicago).

[29] This table is based on the extraordinary scalogram in Thomas B. Alexander, *Sectional Stress and Party Strength* (Nashville: Vanderbilt University Press, 1967), p. 72 and on the tables listed in Hamilton, *Prologue to Conflict,* pp. 112, 191–200. In the House, for example, the proportions of the delegates voting "yea" on the Texas-New Mexico bill were:

	Whig, percent	Democratic, percent
North	35	71
South	93	47

[30] Boston *Daily Advertiser,* October 1, 2, 1850; C. R. Ingersoll to Thomas Seymour, March 26, 1851, Thomas Seymour MSS (Connecticut Historical Society); Simeon Draper to Thurlow Weed, October 2, 1850, Weed MSS; Ronald P. Formisano, *The Birth of Mass Political Parties: Michigan, 1837-1861* (Princeton: Princeton University Press, 1971), pp. 205–212.

[31] The average index of party disagreement in the Pennsylvania House of Representatives on 17 roll-call votes on the fugitive slave issue in 1851 was 77.8; in 1852 the average on 13 roll calls was 72.7. On average, that is, about 87 percent of the Whigs opposed 87 percent of the Democrats. For party disputes in the South, see Arthur C. Cole, *The Whig Party in the South* (reprint edition; Gloucester, Mass.: Peter Smith, 1962), pp. 174–94.

[32] Richardson, *Messages and Papers,* Vol. V. p. 93.

[33] Seward to Weed, July 28, 1850, Weed MSS.

[34] Joshua R. Giddings to Milton R. Sutliffe, December 30, 1850, Milton R. Sutliffe MSS (Western Reserve Historical Society); Cole, *Whig Party in the South*, p. 182; Webster to Peter Harvey, October 2, 1850, quoted in Dalzell, *Daniel Webster*, p. 21; see ibid., pp. 230-237.

[35] I have not considered South Carolina, where a similar battle raged, because the Second Party System never really existed there to be replaced.

[36] The relevant sections of the Georgia Platform may be found in David M. Potter, *The Impending Crisis, 1848-1861* (New York: Harper & Row, 1976), p. 128.

[37] On Mississippi, see Cole, *Whig Party in the South*, p. 186. On Georgia, see Horace Montgomery, *Cracker Parties* (Baton Rouge: Louisiana State University Press, 1950), pp. 17-37; Howell Cobb to James Buchanan, June 2, 17, 1849, John Burke to Howell Cobb, March 22, 1849, John Lumpkin to Cobb, July 21, 1850, and William Woods to Cobb, September 15, 1850, in Phillips, *Correspondence*, pp. 157-159, 163-164, 206-208, 212-213. On Alabama, see J. Mills Thornton, III, "Politics and Power in Slave Society: Alabama, 1806-1860" (unpublished Ph.D. dissertation, Yale University, 1974), pp. 229-259 and passim.

[38] Paul Murray, *The Whig Party in Georgia, 1825-1853* (Chapel Hill: University of North Carolina Press, 1948), pp. 145-146. For voting trends and other information on the Georgia situation, I have relied on Daniel J. Hoisington, "From Whig to Union: The Whig Party in Georgia, 1849-1853" (unpublished seminar paper, University of Virginia, 1975). Hoisington has discovered that Murray erred when he asserted that the Democratic plan for legislative reapportionment failed.

[39] Johannsen, *Stephen A. Douglas*, p. 340; Washington *Union*, January 2, 3, 29, 1851.

[40] Samuel P. Lyman to Simeon Draper, January 20, 1851, E. G. Spaulding to Thurlow Weed, January 20, 1851, and William A. Sackett to Weed, January 22, 1851, Weed MSS.

[41] Webster to Peter Harvey, October 2, 1850, quoted in Dalzell, *Daniel Webster*, p. 214 and in Allan Nevins, *Ordeal of the Union: Fruits of Manifest Destiny, 1847-1852* (New York: Charles Scribner's Sons, 1947), p. 350.

[42] Washington Hunt to Thurlow Weed, March 19, 1848, Weed MSS.

[43] Dalzell, *Daniel Webster,* pp. 196–258; William A. Graham to James Graham, March 12, 1851, in J. G. deRoulhac Hamilton, ed., *The Papers of William Alexander Graham* (5 vols.; Raleigh: State Department of Archives and History, 1957-1973), Vol. IV, p. 52; E. D. Barber to Salmon P. Chase, February 24, 1851, Salmon P. Chase MSS (Library of Congress); Philip Greely to Thurlow Weed, September 4, 1850, Weed MSS; Charles Upham to Henry L. Dawes, September 14, November 20, 1850, Henry L. Dawes MSS (Library of Congress); Robert C. Winthrop to Roger Sherman Baldwin, July 11, 1851, Baldwin Family Papers (Yale University Library); and Edward McPherson to John B. McPherson, October 16, 1851, Edward McPherson MSS (Library of Congress).

[44] Rutland (Vermont) *Herald,* April 10, 1851 quoted in Peter Olberg, "Coalition Politics: Party Formation in Vermont, 1845-1855" (unpublished seminar paper, Yale College, 1972), p. 11; Philo S. Shenton to Thurlow Weed, November 20, 1850, Weed MSS; Meredith P. Gentry to William B. Campbell, December 27, 1851, Campbell Family Papers (Duke).

[45] Alexander, *Sectional Stress and Party Strength,* p. 218, Vote No. 30.

CHAPTER FIVE

[1] George Julian to F. W. Bird, et al., April 29, 1853, quoted in Richard H. Sewell, *Ballots for Freedom: Antislavery Politics in the United States, 1837-1860* (New York: Oxford University Press, 1976), p. 250.

[2] New Orleans *Bee,* March 23, 1848; John A. Calhoun to Joseph White Lesne, July 10, 1848, quoted in J. Mills Thornton, III, "Politics and Power in a Slave Society: Alabama, 1806-1860," (unpublished Ph.D. dissertation, Yale University, 1974), p. 233. I am indebted to Professor William J. Cooper of Louisiana State University for the citation from the *Bee.*

[3] A. F. Perry to Thomas Corwin, March 23, 1852, Thomas Corwin MSS (Library of Congress); Ralph A. Wooster, *Politicians, Planters, and Plain Folk: Courthouse and Statehouse in the Upper South, 1850-*

1860 (Knoxville: University of Tennessee Press, 1975), pp. 56–60, 98–109.

[4] John S. Davis to David F. Caldwell, February 19, 1852, David F. Caldwell MSS (Southern Historical Collection, University of North Carolina Library).

[5] These generalizations are based on Wooster, *Politicians, Planters, and Plain Folk;* William G. Shade, *Banks or No Banks: The Money Issue in Western Politics, 1832-1865* (Detroit: Wayne State University Press, 1972), pp. 112–144; Fletcher M. Green, *Constitutional Development in the South Atlantic States: A Study in the Evolution of Democracy* (New York: W. W. Norton, 1966), pp. 254–296: Robert Hampel, "The Ohio Whig Party, 1848-1854" (unpublished senior thesis, Yale College, 1972), p. 36 and Table 17; Robert Hampel, "Constitution-Making at Mid-Century: Indiana, 1850-1852" (unpublished seminar paper, Cornell University, 1973); and Stephen Green, "The Collapse of the Whig Party in Maryland" (unpublished seminar paper, Yale College, 1973), pp. 9–13.

[6] Baltimore *Sun,* June 6, July 4, 1851, quoted in Green, "The Collapse of the Whig Party in Maryland," pp. 11–12. This account rests heavily on Green's excellent seminar paper; Douglas Bowers, "Ideology and Political Parties in Maryland, 1851-1856," *Maryland Historical Magazine, 64* (1969), 197–217; and Wooster, *Politicians, Planters, and Plain Folk,* pp. 56–57. Table 3 presents roll-call voting patterns in the Maryland legislature. See also William J. Evitts, *A Matter of Allegiances: Maryland, 1850-1861* (Baltimore: The Johns Hopkins University Press, 1974), pp. 23, 31–41.

[7] Thomas D. Willett, "International Specie Flows and American Monetary Stability, 1834-1860," *Journal of Economic History, 28* (1968), 28–50; Jeffrey G. Williamson, *American Growth and the Balance of Payments, 1820-1913* (Chapel Hill: University of North Carolina Press, 1964), p. 111.

[8] See the William Bigler MSS (Historical Society of Pennsylvania) for 1852 and 1853. George D. Green notes in his study of Louisiana banking that by 1852 popular demand for more banks and railroad charters forced Democrats to jettison their traditional opposition to both and to accept the 1852 constitution, which allowed both. Following the mandate of that constitution, the Louisiana legislature

then passed a free banking act in 1853. Green, *Finance and Economic Development in the Old South: Louisiana Banking, 1804-1861* (Stanford: Stanford University Press, 1972), pp. 132–135.

[9] Shade, *Banks or No Banks,* pp. 145–188.

[10] Joseph Grinnell to John J. Crittenden, January 31, 1849, John J. Crittenden MSS (Library of Congress); Robert C. Winthrop to John P. Kennedy, December 24, 1851, copy, Robert C. Winthrop MSS (Massachusetts Historical Society). The proportion of roll-call votes concerning the tariff in the Pennsylvania legislature fell from 12 of 326 in 1846, 7 of 201 in 1847, and 15 of 277 in 1851 to 2 of 433 in 1852, 0 of 363 in 1853, and 0 of 411 in 1854. On state Whig platforms and the reactions of Pennsylvania's Democrats to the Whigs' national platform in 1852, see Michael F. Holt, *Forging a Majority: The Formation of the Republican Party in Pittsburgh, 1848-1860* (New Haven: Yale University Press, 1969), pp. 101–104. For the national platforms, see Kirk H. Porter and Donald B. Johnson, eds., *National Party Platforms, 1840-1964* (Urbana: University of Illinois Press, 1966), pp. 16–21.

[11] Thomas B. Alexander, *Sectional Stress and Party Srength,* pp. 110–113; George H. Paul to James R. Doolittle, September 19, 1853, James R. Doolittle MSS (State Historical Society of Wisconsin); Isaac R. Diller to Stephen A. Douglas, February 2, 1853, Stephen A. Douglas MSS (University of Chicago).

[12] Out of 326 roll calls in the 1846 session, 66 (20.2 percent) concerned railroads. The average index of party disagreement on those votes was 23.2 compared to an average of 37.5 for all votes. There were 27 votes on the Baltimore and Ohio, the Pennsylvania, or both. On those, the average index of party disagreement was only 12.7. On the other hand, the average disagreement between eastern and western Pennsylvania, as divided very crudely by the Susquehanna River, was 61.2. In all the years for which I have thus far obtained indexes for Pennsylvania—1846 to 1854—the level of party disagreement on railroad legislation was well below the average level on all votes except for 1850 and 1852.

[13] Charles Barringer to Daniel M. Barringer, February 4, 1853, Daniel M. Barringer MSS (Southern Historical Collection, University of North Carolina Library).

[14] William A. Graham to James Graham, January 6, 1851, in J. G. deRoulhac Hamilton, ed., *The Papers of William Alexander Graham*

(5 vols.; Raleigh, 1957-73), Vol. IV, p. 3; Washington *Union,* January 24, 1851; Benjamin F. Wade to Milton R. Sutliffe, January 2, 1852, Milton R. Sutliffe MSS (Western Reserve Historical Society); Joel H. Silbey, *The Shrine of Party,* pp. 121–136; Alexander, *Sectional Stress and Party Strength,* pp. 77–84.

[15] Hampel, "The Ohio Whig Party"; Green, "The Collapse of the Whig Party in Maryland"; Alexander Deland, "Rum, Romanism, Regionalism, and Slavery: Requiem for a Whig Party in Connecticut, 1848-1855" (unpublished senior thesis, Yale College, 1972); Peter Olberg, "Coalition Politics: Party Formation in Vermont, 1845-1855" (unpublished seminar paper, Yale College, 1972); and Thomas Bright, "The Anti-Nebraska Coalition and the Emergence of the Republican Party in New Hampshire: 1853-1857" (unpublished seminar paper, Yale College, 1972). Because Bright's study of New Hampshire begins its analysis with 1853, I have not included his figures in Table 3. But the average index of disagreement on four banking bills in 1853 was 45, and on five votes in 1854 it was 35. Compare these with the New Hampshire banking indexes listed in Table 1.

[16] I hope to analyze the complicated voting patterns in the Pennsylvania legislature in a future article.

[17] William L. Marcy to Andrew Jackson Donelson, May 7, 1851, Andrew Jackson Donelson MSS (Library of Congress); William Cullen Bryant to Salmon P. Chase, May 12, 1851, Salmon P. Chase MSS (Historical Society of Pennsylvania); William H. Seward to Thurlow Weed, June 3, 1851, Thurlow Weed MSS (Rush Rhees Library, University of Rochester).

[18] On Mississippi, see James Roger Sharp, *The Jacksonians versus the Banks: Politics in the States after the Panic of 1837* (New York: Columbia University Press, 1970), p. 87; on Georgia, Paul Murray, *The Whig Party in Georgia, 1825-1853,* pp. 31–140; on Alabama, Thornton, "Politics and Power in a Slave Society," pp. 64, 240-264, 352-431.

[19] Diary entry for September 24, 1852, in Charles R. Williams, ed., *Diary and Letters of Rutherford B. Hayes* (5 vols.; Columbus: The Ohio State Archaeological and Historical Society, 1972), Vol. I, pp. 421-422.

[20] Robert C. Winthrop to John H. Clifford, October 26, 1851, copy, Winthrop MSS.

[21] On the opposition of farmers to temperance, see John F. Kienly to William L. Bigler, March 22, 1852, Bigler MSS, and Roger Sherman Baldwin to Emily Baldwin, April 10, 1852, Baldwin Family Papers (Yale University Library). On the internal divisions in both parties, see, for Maine, C. N. Bodfish to Franklin Pierce, June 8, 12, 1852, Franklin Pierce MSS (New Hampshire Historical Society, microfilm); for Massachusetts, Edward Hamilton to Benjamin Butler, August 28, 1852, Benjamin Butler MSS (Library of Congress), George Colley to Caleb Cushing, November 17, 1852, Caleb Cushing MSS (Library of Congress), and R. T. Paine to Roger Sherman Baldwin, November 17, December 31, 1852, Baldwin Family Papers; and for Pennsylvania, William J. Rogers to William L. Bigler, October 4, 1852, Bigler MSS. On Whig reluctance to use the temperance issue in New York, see Robert H. Morris to Hamilton Fish, February 10, 1852, Fish MSS. On the negative impact for Whigs in Connecticut, see Roger Sherman Baldwin to Roger Sherman Baldwin, Jr., March 19, 1852, and to Emily Baldwin, April 15, 1850, March 13, 1852, and April 10, 1852, Baldwin Family Papers.

[22] Washington Hunt to Thurlow Weed, May 19, June 4, 1848, Weed MSS; George W. Knight to Millard Fillmore, April 17, 1852, Thomas Corwin MSS: Robert L. Martin to James Watson Webb, March 12, 1852, James Watson Webb MSS (Yale University Library); Caleb Cushing to Stephen A. Douglas, February 1, 1852, copy, Cushing MSS; and George F. Emery to Franklin Pierce, June 11, 1852, Pierce MSS.

[23] Philadelphia *Public Ledger,* quoted in John Brodhead to Franklin Pierce, June 7, 1852, Pierce MSS. On Illinois, see S. Francis to Richard Yates, May 10, 1852, Richard Yates MSS (Illinois State Historical Library); on Pennsylvania, see J. C. Van Dyke to James Buchanan, October 18, 1851, and George F. Lehman to Buchanan, October 30, 1851, James Buchanan MSS (Historical Society of Pennsylvania); James Macmanus to William L. Bigler, October 23, 1851, Bigler MSS; and Isaac McKinley to Franklin Pierce, June 7, 9, 1852, Pierce MSS. The quotation is from C. L. Ward to Pierce, June 21, 1852, ibid. On Massachusetts, see Kevin Sweeney, "Rum, Romanism, Railroads, and Reform: The Twilight of the Second Party System in Massachusetts, 1849-1854" (unpublished seminar paper, Yale University, 1973).

[24] Truman Smith to Thurlow Weed, September 19, 1852, Weed MSS.

[25] Horace Greeley to Schuyler Colfax, September 3, 1852, Greeley-Colfax MSS (New York Public Library); Neal Dow to Seward, Septem-

ber 25, 1852, Weed MSS; Pittsburgh *Gazette,* October 14, 15, 1852; Sweeney, "The Twilight of the Second Party System in Massachusetts," pp. 19–21.

[26] J. Teesdale to John McLean, November 19, 1852, John McLean MSS (Library of Congress).

[27] Robert L. Martin to James Watson Webb, March 12, 1852, J. W. Webb MSS; S. C. Stearns to John McLean, April 19, 1852, McLean MSS; John McKeen to Franklin Pierce, September 28, 1852, Pierce MSS; Lewis C. Levin to William L. Marcy, October 5, 31, 1852, Marcy MSS; John H. Brinton to Pierce, October 6, 1852, and John Davis to Pierce, October 18, 25, 1852, Pierce MSS; E. A. Penniman to William L. Bigler, October 13, 15, 1852, Bigler MSS; Enoch Hale to Caleb Cushing, October 13, 1852, Cushing MSS; and James Johnston to Edward McPherson, December 3, 1852, Edward McPherson MSS (Library of Congress).

[28] Andrew Johnson to Sam Milligan, December 28, 1852, in Leroy P. Graf and Ralph W. Haskins, eds., *The Papers of Andrew Johnson, Volume 2, 1852-1857* (Knoxville: University of Tennessee Press, 1970), p. 102; the Cincinnati Whig, quoted in Sewell, *Ballots for Freedom,* p. 249; Baltimore *Sun,* October 4, 6, 1852, quoted in Stephen Green, "The Election of 1852 in Maryland" (unpublished seminar paper, Yale College, 1972), pp. 1–2; *Baltimore County Advocate,* September 4, 1852, quoted in Evitts, *A Matter of Allegiances,* p. 49.

[29] B. B. French to Franklin Pierce, June 27, 1852, Pierce MSS.

[30] I calculated most of the percentages in the preceding paragraphs from voting returns listed in the *Tribune Almanac.* The rates for Maryland are given in Evitts, *A Matter of Allegiances,* p. 48, and the estimates of participation in Tennessee can be found in Brian G. Walton, "The Second Party System in Tennessee," *East Tennessee Historical Society Publications, 43* (1971), 19. The regression estimates for the Deep South can be found in Peyton McCrary, Clark Miller, and Dale Baum, "Class and Party in the Secession Crisis: Voting Behavior in the Deep South," forthcoming in *The Journal of Interdisciplinary History.* I have cited these figures with the permission of the authors as I have those for Massachusetts in Dale Baum, "The Political Realignment of the 1850s: Know Nothingism and the Republican Majority in Massachusetts" (unpublished paper, University of Minnesota, 1976). Dale Baum also generously sent to me the estimates for the five North-

western states that are based on data originally gathered by Professor Philip Shively and are deposited in the Political Science Data Archives of the University of Minnesota.

[31] Samuel Bowles to Henry L. Dawes, May 13, 1853, Henry L. Dawes MSS (Library of Congress); Charles W. March to Caleb Cushing, October 14, 1853, Cushing MSS; Emily Baldwin to Roger Sherman Baldwin, Jr., April 4, 1853, Baldwin Family Papers; J. C. Comstock to Thomas Seymour, March 23, 1853, Thomas Seymour MSS (Connecticut Historical Society); Pittsburgh *Gazette,* March 28, May 17, 25, 1853.

[32] Alex Brooks to Benedict Lewis, August 22, 1852, Daniel Ullmann MSS (New York Historical Society); Thomas Macdowell to Simon Cameron, September 13, 1853, Simon Cameron MSS (Dauphin County Historical Society); James L. Reynolds to James Buchanan, September 20, 1853, Buchanan MSS (Historical Society of Pennsylvania); G. G. Wescott to William Bigler, October 10, 1853, Bigler MSS. The quotation is from William Rice to Bigler, October 11, 1853, ibid. On Michigan, see Ronald P. Formisano, *The Birth of Mass Political Parties: Michigan, 1827-1861,* pp. 229–238.

[33] Deland, "Requiem for a Whig Party in Connecticut," pp. 14–19. In Ohio the Free Soil share of the vote rose from 6 percent in the gubernatorial election of 1851 to 17.7 percent in 1853 while the Whigs' share plummeted in those years from 42 to 30.2 percent. On the Free-Soilers' unreserved and unrivaled endorsement of temperance in 1853, see Hampel, "The Ohio Whig Party," pp. 43–44. In Wisconsin, the protemperance candidate had the endorsement of most Whigs and Free-Soilers, although a regular Whig ticket was also in the field. He won 39.3 percent of the vote in 1853 as compared to 11.9 percent for the Free Soil gubernatorial candidate in 1849. In Maine, the major parties' share of the vote fell from 91 percent in the gubernatorial election of 1850 to 76 percent in the 1853 election. The temperance issue cut both ways in Maine, however. In 1852, for example, an independent anti-Maine Law candidate received 23 percent of the popular vote. For background on Maine political developments, I have used Mark W. Summers, "The Rise of the Republican Party in Democratic Maine, 1850-1858" (unpublished seminar paper, Yale College, 1972).

[34] Holt, *Forging a Majority,* pp. 109–116; Formisano, *Birth of Mass Political Parties,* pp. 215–229; William Gienapp, "The Transformation

of Cincinnati Politics, 1852-1860" (unpublished seminar paper, Yale University, 1969), pp. 24–42.

[35] Robert McLane to Caleb Cushing, October 14, 1853, Cushing MSS; W. H. Butler to William L. Bigler, October 16, 1853, Bigler MSS; William Pettit to John M. Niles, December 8, 1853, Gideon Welles MSS (Library of Congress).

[36] *Baltimore Clipper,* January 6, 1851, quoted in Evitts, *A Matter of Allegiances,* p. 45; William E. Russell to Thomas Corwin, December 1, 1851, Corwin MSS.

[37] *Cleveland Plain Dealer,* February 27, 1850 and *Galena Jeffersonian,* n. d., quoted in Shade, *Banks or No Banks,* pp. 118, 157.

[38] Thomas J. McGarry to Thomas Corwin, November 4, 1852, Corwin MSS; Francis P. Blair to Franklin Pierce, November 25, 1852, Blair Family Papers (Library of Congress); "Truth" to Corwin, September, 1850, Corwin MSS; St. Louis *Daily Democrat,* September 8, 1853, clipping in Caleb Cushing MSS; William Mason to Corwin, May 27, 1851, Corwin MSS; C. F. Cleveland to Gideon Welles, July 22, 1854 and draft of a letter by Welles, March 1855, Gideon Welles MSS (Library of Congress); Arthur Cole, *The Whig Party in the South* (Gloucester, Mass.: Peter Smith, 1962), p. 280; Andrew Johnson to Albert G. Graham, December 10, 1852, in Graf and Haskins, *Papers of Andrew Johnson, Volume 2,* pp. 96–97.

CHAPTER SIX

[1] Andrew Johnson to Sam Milligan, December 28, 1852, in Leroy P. Graf and Richard Haskins, eds., *The Papers of Andrew Johnson, Vol. 2, 1852-1857* (Knoxville: University of Tennessee Press, 1970), p. 102; Horace Greeley to Schuyler Colfax, January 18, 1853, Greeley-Colfax MSS (New York Public Library); Washington Hunt to Thurlow Weed, November 3, 1853, Thurlow Weed MSS (Rush Rhees Library, Rochester University).

[2] James D. Richardson, ed., *Messages and Papers of the Presidents,* Vol. IV, p. 198.

[3] Charles Shaler to Caleb Cushing, July 21, 1853, Caleb Cushing MSS (Library of Congress); Samuel Treat to Stephen A. Douglas, December 18, 1853, Stephen A. Douglas MSS (University of Chicago).

[4] Robert W. Johannsen, *Stephen A. Douglas* (New York: Oxford University Press, 1973), pp. 395–400. The following account of the framing of the Kansas-Nebraska Act is based largely on Professor Johannsen's book and on Roy F. Nichols, "The Kansas-Nebraska Act: A Century of Historiography," *Mississippi Valley Historical Review, 43* (1956), 187–212.

[5] Douglas to Charles H. Lanphier, November 11, 1853, Charles H. Lanphier MSS (Illinois State Historical Library).

[6] Douglas to Cobb, April 2, 1854, in Phillips, *Correspondence,* p. 343; Douglas to Lanphier, February 13, 1854, Lanphier MSS.

[7] Edmund Burke to Douglas, January 9, 1854, quoted in Johannsen, *Douglas,* p. 409; J. J. Jones to William L. Marcy, February 7, 1854, William L. Marcy MSS (Library of Congress).

[8] Nichols, "The Kansas-Nebraska Act," p. 205; Glyndon G. Van Deusen, *William Henry Seward* (New York: Oxford University Press, 1967), p. 150.

[9] Louisville *Daily Journal,* March 20, 1855. I am indebted to Mr. Harry Volz III of the University of Virginia for bringing this issue of the *Journal* to my attention.

[10] William Larimer to James Pollock, quoted in Pittsburgh *Gazette,* May 3, 1854; T. M. Parmalee to Caleb Cushing, February 15, 1854, and William E. Cramer to Cushing, January 26, 1854, Cushing MSS; J. J. Jones to William L. Marcy, March 21, 1854, Marcy MSS; George W. Patterson to Thurlow Weed, March 16, 1854, Philo Shenton to Weed, June 6, 1854, Weed MSS; B. Thompson to Daniel Ullmann, May 16, 1854, Daniel Ullmann MSS (New York Historical Society).

[11] John S. Bryan to Simon Cameron, September 4, 1854, Simon Cameron MSS (Dauphin County Historical Society); Samuel Lewis to Salmon P. Chase, April 17, 1854, Salmon P. Chase MSS (Historical Society of Pennsylvania).

[12] John Law to William L. Marcy, September 25, 1854, Marcy MSS.

[13] In a four-way race in Maine, the Whigs polled only 15.5 percent of the vote, compared to 49.5 percent for the new Republican party. In New Hampshire, Whigs and Free-Soilers continued to divide the anti-Democratic vote. In the Connecticut gubernatorial election, the Whig received only a third of the vote in a four-way race, although he was

later elected by the legislature. In a four-way race in Massachusetts, neither the Whigs with 21 percent nor the Free-Soilers with a meager 5 percent prevailed. The New York Whig gubernatorial candidate won in a four-way race with only 33 percent of the vote. The Whigs also won the Pennsylvania gubernatorial election in 1854, but they had help from the Know Nothings. A three-way race for a lesser state office showed that the Whig party itself could attract only 21 percent of the popular vote, while the Know Nothings won 33 percent.

[14] I have relied on the extracts of the "Appeal" printed in Johannsen, *Douglas,* pp. 418–419 and in Hans L. Trefousse, "The Republican Party, 1854-1864," in Arthur M. Schlesinger, Jr., ed., *History of U.S. Political Parties* (4 vols.; New York: Chelsea House and R. W. Bowker, 1973), Vol. II, pp. 1175–1180. I have rearranged the order of individual statements and hence have not relied on a single indented quotation.

[15] The *National Era* (Washington), May 22, 1854, is quoted in Mark L. Berger, *The Revolution in the New York Party Systems, 1840-1860* (Port Washington, N.Y.: The Kennikat Press, 1973), p. 36. The Michigan Republican platform is printed in Trefousse, "The Republican Party," pp. 1185-1188.

[16] Buffalo *Commercial Advertiser,* November 6, 1854, quoted in William E. Gienapp, "The New York Know Nothings" (unpublished seminar paper, The University of California at Berkeley, 1971), p. 23.

[17] Samuel J. Mills to the New York Central Whig Association, August 12, 1854, Daniel Ullmann MSS.

[18] This summary of the New York situation is based on extensive manuscript correspondence. An adequate secondary account is Berger, *Revolution in the New York Party Systems.*

[19] John Lorain to William Bigler, January 10, 1854, William Bigler MSS (Historical Society of Pennsylvania); Daniel S. Jenks to James Buchanan, October 3, 1854, James Buchanan MSS (Historical Society of Pennsylvania); Harry Hunter to Caleb Cushing, March 25, 1854, Caleb Cushing MSS (Library of Congress); John J. Bowen to Stephen Sammons, October 30, 1854, A. J. Calhoun to Marcellus Ells, August 9, 1854, Daniel Ullmann MSS; Jonas McClintock to Simon Cameron, September 16, 1854, Cameron MSS; B. Thompson to Daniel Ullmann, May 16, 1854, Ullmann MSS; Washington Hunt to Thurlow Weed, October 21, 1854, Weed MSS.

[20] James W. Taylor to Hamilton Fish, November 11, 1854, Hamil-

ton Fish MSS (Library of Congress); Edward L. Pierce to Salmon P. Chase, November 9, 1855, Salmon P. Chase MSS (Library of Congress); E. A. Penniman to William Bigler, June 8, 1854, Bigler MSS; Rutherford B. Hayes to Charles Birchard, October 13, 1854, in Charles R. Williams, ed., *Diary and Letters of Rutherford Birchard Hayes, Nineteenth President of the United States* (5 vols.; Columbus: The Ohio State Archaeological and Historical Society, 1922). Vol. I, p. 470; Robert J. Arundel to John McLean, October 14, 1854, John McLean MSS (Library of Congress); Isaac O. Barnes to Caleb Cushing, November 4, 1854, Cushing MSS.

[21] This and subsequent paragraphs on the sources of Know Nothingism are condensations of more complete accounts I have presented elsewhere. See Michael F. Holt, "The Antimasonic and Know Nothing Parties" in Schlesinger, *History of U.S. Political Parties,* Vol. I, pp. 593–620, and "The Politics of Impatience: The Origins of Know Nothingism," *Journal of American History, 60* (1973), 309–331. Documentation can be found in the latter. I should note that the overall interpretation of Know Nothingism given here differs slightly from that in my earlier articles.

[22] George W. Morton to Hamilton Fish, February 27, 1854, Fish MSS. For the general relationship between economic change and the intensification of ethnic identity, see Herbert G. Gutman, "Work, Culture, and Society in Industrializing America, 1815-1919," *American Historical Review, 78* (1973), 531-588, and Lee Benson, "Group Cohesion and Social and Ideological Conflict: A Critique of Some Marxian and Tocquevillian Theories," *American Behavioral Scientist, 16* (1973), 741–767.

[23] Peter Wager to Bigler, June 17, 1853, Bigler MSS.

[24] This composite of Know Nothing rhetoric is based on the sections of Thomas R. Whitney, *A Defence of the American Policy* (New York, 1856), reproduced in Holt, "The Antimasonic and Know Nothing Parties," pp. 680–698; The Protest of the Northern Bolters from the American Convention, June 14, 1855, ibid, pp. 706–707; Protest of the First Presbyterian Church of Detroit, quoted in Ronald P. Formisano, *The Birth of Mass Political Parties: Michigan 1837-1861* (Princeton: Princeton University Press, 1971), p. 224; and Charles G. Irish to Daniel Ullmann, March 1855, Ullmann MSS.

[25] Lynde Eliot to William Bigler, September 20, 1852, Bigler MSS;

Charles Shaler to William L. Marcy, January 7, 1854, Marcy MSS; William G. Brownlow, *Americanism Contrasted with Foreignism, Romanism, and Bogus Democracy,* excerpts reproduced in Joel H. Silbey, *The Transformation of American Politics, 1840-1860* (Englewood Cliffs, N.J.: Prentice-Hall, 1967), pp. 53-57; Ross Wilkins to John McLean, January 11, 1855, McLean MSS (Library of Congress).

[26] Gideon Welles to ?, n. d. (1856 folder), draft, and draft article, October 1859, Gideon Welles MSS (Connecticut Historical Society); Charles Sumner to Hamilton Fish, November 15, 1854, Fish MSS; Livingston *Republican,* October 11, 1855, quoted in Gienapp, "The New York Know Nothings," p. 39; Pittsburgh *Daily Dispatch,* September 5, 1855; Donald McLeod to John McLean, March 1, 1855, McLean MSS (Library of Congress).

[27] D. W. Owen to Charles D. Fontaine, May 30, 1855, Charles D. Fontaine MSS (Mississippi Department of Archives and History); J. H. Shirrard to William C. Rives, December 21, 1854, William C. Rives MSS (Library of Congress); John M. Patton to David Campbell, May 3, 1855, Campbell Family Papers (Duke University); Louisville *Daily Journal,* March 20, 1855.

[28] Wiley P. Harris to John F. H. Claiborne, October 8, 1855, John F. H. Claiborne MSS (Mississippi Department of Archives and History), J. J. Henry to Daniel Ullmann, October 10, 1854, James R. Thompson to Ullmann March 24, 1855, Ullmann MSS; Horace Greeley to Schuyler Colfax, August 24, 1854, Greeley-Colfax MSS; American Platform, reprinted in Holt, "The Antimasonic and Know Nothing Parties," pp. 701–705.

[29] Moses Kimball to Henry L. Dawes, August 28, 1854, Henry L. Dawes MSS (Library of Congress); Pittsburgh *Gazette,* February 24, 1855; F. S. Edwards to Ullmann, December 6, 1854, Ullmann MSS; John McLean to Hector Orr, November 25, 1854, McLean MSS (Library of Congress).

[30] Holt, "Politics of Impatience," p. 319; William J. Evitts, A Matter of Allegiances: Maryland from 1850 to 1861 (Baltimore: The Johns Hopkins University Press, 1974), pp. 81–82; Emily Baldwin to Roger Sherman Baldwin, Jr., March 17, April 11, 1855, Baldwin Family Papers (Yale).

[31] See footnote 20.

[32] Henry Gardner to Samuel Bowles, August 17, 1855, Samuel Bowles II MSS (Yale University Library); Charles English to Gideon Welles, May 8, 1856, Welles MSS (Library of Congress).

[33] John Boyd to Gideon Welles, March 23, 1855, Welles MSS (Library of Congress); Gideon Welles to James F. Babcock, February 18, 1856, copy, Welles MSS (New York Public Library); Michael F. Holt, *Forging a Majority: The Formation of the Republican Party in Pittsburgh,* pp. 149-164; Thomas Shankland to Gideon Welles, January 1, 1855, Welles MSS (Library of Congress).

[34] Eric Foner, *Free Soil, Free Labor, Free Men: The Ideology of the Republican Party before the Civil War* (New York: Oxford University Press, 1970), pp. 226-260, and passim.

[35] George H. Haynes, "A Chapter from the Local History of Know Nothingism," *The New England Magazine, 21* (1896-97), 82-96; Gienapp, "The New York Know Nothings"; David M. Mandel, "Party Transformation in Worcester County, Massachusetts, 1848-1860" (unpublished seminar paper, Yale College, 1972); John M. Bradford to Hamilton Fish, November 8, 1855, Fish MSS; A. J. Parker to William L. Marcy, November 10, 1855, Marcy MSS.

[36] John M. Clayton to Daniel Ullmann, June 26, 1855, B. Thompson to Ullmann, July 6, 1855, Ullmann MSS; James Dean to Simon Cameron, June 22, 1855, Simon Cameron MSS (Library of Congress).

[37] The two quotations are from Kenneth Rayner to Daniel Ullmann, June 2, 1856 and n. d. (1856 folder), Ullmann MSS. For warnings about alliances with the Silver Grays, see Darius Perrin to Ullmann, November 13, 1854, F. S. Edwards to Ullmann, December 6, 1854, L. C. Pratt to Ullmann, October 19, 1854, ibid; on Pennsylvania, see Holt, *Forging a Majority,* p. 165.

[38] Jacob Heaton to Salmon P. Chase, February 25, 1856, Chase MSS (Library of Congress).

[39] Thomas J. Marsh to N. P. Banks, March 19, 1856, David R. Hitchcock to Banks, March 28, 1856, and George White to Banks, June 10, 1856, N. P. Banks MSS (Library of Congress); draft editorial 1856, Gideon Welles MSS (Connecticut Historical Society).

[40] Stephen Molitor to Salmon P. Chase, March 27, 1856, Chase MSS (Library of Congress); E. Peck to Lyman Trumbull, February

24, 1856, Trumbull Family Papers (Illinois State Historical Library); J. S. Morrison to Stephen A. Douglas, April 16, 1856, Douglas MSS.

[41] Holt, *Forging a Majority,* pp. 207–208; Silbey, *The Transformation of American Politics,* p. 66; and Formisano, *The Birth of Mass Political Parties,* pp. 271–272. For evidence that previously naturalized immigrants favored reforms to prevent abuses of the naturalization laws, see F. Hassaurek to Salmon P. Chase, April 11, 1857, Chase MSS (Historical Society of Pennsylvania). Such immigrants, however, vehemently opposed discrimination against previously naturalized citizens.

[42] Edwin D. Morgan to Thurlow Weed, October 4, 1856, Morgan to Allen Monroe, October 9, 1856, and Morgan to Charles M. Dudley, September 5, 1856, copies, E. D. Morgan MSS (New York State Library); the Republican platform can be found in Porter and Johnson, eds., *National Party Platforms,* pp. 27–28.

[43] James Walker to Salmon P. Chase, October 4, 1856, Chase MSS (Library of Congress); Thaddeus Stevens to E. D. Gazzam, August 24, 1856, Edward McPherson MSS (Library of Congress); R. M. Corwine to Chase, December 8, 1856, Chase MSS (Historical Society of Pennsylvania). For other examples of the Republicans' use of anti-Catholic appeals, see William Gienapp, "The Transformation of Cincinnati Politics, 1852-1860" (unpublished seminar paper, Yale University, 1969), pp. 85–124; Formisano, *The Birth of Mass Political Parties,* pp. 271–272; and Holt, *Forging a Majority,* pp. 206–209, 243–44, 259–261, 286–288.

CHAPTER SEVEN

[1] For a discussion of radical motivations and intentions, see Eric Foner, *Free Soil, Free Labor, Free Men: The Ideology of the Republican Party before the Civil War* (New York: Oxford University Press, 1970), pp. 103–148, and Richard H. Sewell, *Ballots for Freedom: Antislavery Politics in the United States, 1837-1860* (New York: Oxford University Press, 1976), pp. 292–320 and passim.

[2] Pittsburgh *Morning Post,* March 18, July 28, August 11, 18, October 16, 1856.

[3] Dwight L. Dumond, *Antislavery Origins of the Civil War in the*

United States (Ann Arbor: University of Michigan Press, 1939); Don E. Fehrenbacher, "The Republican Decision at Chicago" in Norman A. Graebner, ed., *Politics and the Crisis of 1860* (Urbana: University of Illinois Press, 1961), p. 36.

[4] The Illinois banner and 1860 speech of Seward are quoted in James M. McPherson, *The Struggle for Equality: Abolitionists and the Negro in the Civil War and Reconstruction* (Princeton: Princeton University Press, 1964), pp. 24–25; the Hartford *Courant* is quoted in Bernard Mandel, *Labor: Free and Slave, Workingmen and the Anti-Slavery Movement in the United States* (New York: The Associated Authors, 1955), p. 12; Pittsburgh *Daily Gazette,* July 26, 1856, September 8, 1855. The speaker in Pittsburgh was Thomas Williams, who would later serve as one of the House prosecutors in the impeachment trial of Andrew Johnson. Eugene Berwanger, *The Frontier against Slavery: Western Anti-Negro Prejudice and the Slavery Extension Controversy* (Urbana: University of Illinois Press, 1967) argues that racism was a major component of Republican free-soilism.

[5] Both Foner and Sewell attempt to defend the Republicans from charges of racism. Foner, *Free Labor,* pp. 261–300 and Sewell, *Ballots for Freedom,* pp. 321–342. Foner's book presents the most forceful case that free-soilism constituted the core of Republicanism, especially the desire to protect and expand the free labor system.

[6] Charles Sumner to Henry J. Raymond, March 2, 1856, Henry J. Raymond MSS (New York Public Library).

[7] N. Field to George W. Julian, September 19, 1856, quoted in Foner, *Free Soil,* p. 59; Henry Bennett, quoted in Sewell, *Ballots for Freedom,* p. 305.

[8] Moses M. Davis to John Fox Potter, October 25, 1857, John Fox Potter MSS (State Historical Society of Wisconsin); Speech by John Farnsworth, *Congressional Globe,* 38th Cong., 1st Sess., 2979 (I am indebted to Dr. Gary Lee Cardwell of Ferrum College for this quotation); Douglass is quoted in Eric Foner, "Politics, Ideology, and the Origins of the American Civil War," in George M. Fredrickson, ed., *A Nation Divided: Problems and Issues of the Civil War and Reconstruction* (Minneapolis: Burgess Publishing Company, 1975), p. 30.

[9] For this insight and the figures, I am indebted to David Potter, *The Impending Crisis,* 1848-1861 (New York: Harper & Row, 1976), pp. 175–176.

[10] Thomas J. McCormack, ed., *Memoirs of Gustave Koerner, 1809-1896* (2 vols.; Cedar Rapids, 1909), Vol. II, p. 3; Foner, *Free Soil,* p. 162.

[11] My account of Kansas is based primarily on Berwanger, *The Frontier against Slavery,* pp. 97-114, and Potter, *The Impending Crisis,* pp. 199-224.

[12] Andrew Reeder, quoted in Potter, *The Impending Crisis,* p. 205.

[13] New York *Tribune,* May 28, 1856, quoted ibid., p. 220; Seward's speech is summarized in Roy F. Nichols, *Franklin Pierce: Young Hickory of the Granite Hills* (2nd. ed. rev.; Philadelphia: University of Pennsylvania Press, 1958), p. 448.

[14] Springfield *Republican,* quoted in David Donald, *Charles Sumner and the Coming of the Civil War* (New York: Alfred A. Knopf, 1960), p. 302.

[15] James E. Harvey to John McLean, May 30, 1856, John McLean MSS (Library of Congress); Russell Sage to Nathaniel P. Banks, May 31, 1856, N. P. Banks MSS (Library of Congress); Lyman Trumbull to Abraham Lincoln, June 15, 1856, Trumbull Family Papers (Illinois State Historical Library); T. M. Monroe to Daniel Ullmann, June 13, 1856, Daniel Ullmann MSS (New York Historical Society).

[16] Schuyler Colfax to Charles Heaton, May 21, 1856, Schuyler Colfax MSS (Northern Indiana Historical Society); James Kendall to John Fox Potter, July 8, 1856, Potter MSS; V. Wales to N. P. Banks, July 21, 1856, Banks MSS (Library of Congress); Kirk H. Porter and Donald B. Johnson, eds., *National Party Platforms, 1840-1964* (Urbana: University of Illinois Press, 1966), pp. 27-28.

[17] Francis P. Blair to Montgomery Blair, September 21, 1856, Blair Family Papers (Library of Congress); Seward is quoted in Mandel, *Labor: Free and Slave,* p. 162; notice of the Buffalo meeting in E. G. Spaulding to Hamilton Fish, May 29, 1856, Hamilton Fish MSS (Library of Congress); notice of the Hartford meeting, February 11, 1856 in Baldwin Family Papers (Yale University Library).

[18] Pittsburgh *Gazette,* June 5, 1856, November 18, 1859; E. B. Long, ed., *Personal Memoirs of U. S. Grant* (New York: Universal Library, 1962, p. 209).

[19] In a previously published essay I incorrectly include Alabama and Arkansas in this list and erroneously assert that a shift of 10,500

votes out of 440,000 cast in those six states would have given them to Fillmore. Michael F. Holt, "The Antimasonic and Know Nothing Parties," in Arthur M. Schlesinger, Jr., ed., *History of U. S. Political Parties* (4 vols.; New York: Chelsea House and R. W. Bowker, 1973), Vol. I, p. 616.

[20] For the much neglected political impact of the Panic of 1857 at the state level, I have relied on William G. Shade, *Banks or No Banks: The Money Issue in Western Politics, 1832-1865* (Detroit: Wayne State University Press, 1972), pp. 199–223, and Bruce W. Collins, "Economic Issues in American Politics following the Panic of 1857," a preliminary draft of a dissertation in my personal possession. This has subsequently been revised and retitled: Bruce W. Collins, "The Politics of Particularism: Economic Issues in the Major Northern States of the USA, 1857-1858" (Ph.D. dissertation, Cambridge University, 1975). See also Foner, *Free Soil,* p. 171, and Michael F. Holt, *Forging a Majority: The Formation of the Republican Party in Pittsburgh, 1848-1860* (New Haven: Yale University Press, 1969), pp. 220–262.

[21] F. S. Rutherford to Lyman Trumbull, December 7, 1857, quoted in Larry Gara, "Slavery and the Slave Power: A Crucial Distinction," *Civil War History, 15* (1969), 14; Seward is quoted in Potter, *The Impending Crisis,* p. 288.

[22] Washington Hunt to J. J. Crittenden, March 18, 1858, John C. Lemon to Crittenden, April 15, 1858, S. B. Benton to Crittenden, March 27, 1858, M. C. Johnson to Crittenden, March 22, 1858, John J. Crittenden MSS (Library of Congress). For the enthusiasm of other Northerners about a conservative revival, see Sewell, *Ballots for Freedom,* pp. 349–360 and Foner, *Free Soil,* pp. 202–205.

[23] Benjamin D. Pettengill to Edwin D. Morgan, May 16, 1859, Edwin D. Morgan MSS (New York State Library); James Ashley to Salmon P. Chase, November 28, 1858, W. H. P. Denny to Chase, September 4, 1858, Horace Greeley to Chase, September 28, 1858, and R. C. Parsons to Chase, July 10, 1859, Salmon P. Chase MSS (Library of Congress); Joshua R. Giddings to Chase, June 7, 1859, Salmon P. Chase MSS (Historical Society of Pennsylvania).

[24] Circular dated May 25, 1859 in Morgan MSS.

[25] The House Divided speech can be found in Roy P. Basler, et al., eds., *The Collected Works of Abraham Lincoln* (9 vols.; New Bruns-

wick: Rutgers University Press, 1953), Vol. II, pp. 461–469. Lincoln's political need to differentiate himself from Douglas is brilliantly developed in Don E. Fehrenbacher, *Prelude to Greatness: Lincoln in the 1850s* (Stanford: Stanford University Press, 1962) and Potter, *The Impending Crisis,* pp. 328–355.

[26] The Irrepressible Conflict speech is reprinted in Hans Trefousse, "The Republican Party, 1854-1864," in Schlesinger, ed., *History of U. S. Political Parties,* Vol. II, pp. 1229–1238; William Seward to James Watson Webb, December 6, 1858, James Watson Webb MSS (Yale).

[27] Charles S. Spencer, quoted in Thomas D. Morris, *Free Men All: The Personal Liberty Laws of the North, 1780-1861* (Baltimore: The Johns Hopkins University Press, 1974), p. 191. On the strife over personal liberty laws after 1857, see ibid., pp. 186–201; Norman L. Rosenberg, "Personal Liberty Laws and Sectional Crisis: 1850-1861," *Civil War History, 17* (1971), 25–44; and Foner, *Free Soil,* pp. 133–138.

[28] The quotation is from the Pennsylvania People's Party state platform, Pittsburgh *Daily Gazette,* July 17, 1858; on Indiana, see Foner, *Free Soil,* p. 204; on Massachusetts I have relied on Collins, "Economic Issues," Chapter IV and Dale Baum, "The Political Realignment of the 1850s: Know Nothingism and the Republican Majority in Massachusetts" (unpublished paper, University of Minnesota, 1976) cited with the author's permission; for Ohio and New York see J. H. Barrett to Chase, August 22, 1859, Chase MSS (Library of Congress) and John A. King to Morgan, October 30, 1858, Russell Sage to Morgan, October 30, 1858, Morgan MSS.

[29] Preston King to Salmon P. Chase, January 11, 1859, Chase MSS (Historical Society of Pennsylvania). The closest analysis of the Democratic defeats in the congressional elections of 1858 is David E. Meerse, "The Northern Democratic Party and the Congressional Elections of 1858," *Civil War History, 19* (1973), 119–137. The importance of Republican gains in 1858 to Republican victory in 1860 is argued in Don E. Fehrenbacher, "Comment on Why the Republican Party Came to Power," in George H. Knoles, ed., *The Crisis of the Union* (Baton Rouge: Louisiana State University Press, 1965), pp. 21-29. The Republican percentage in Illinois rose from 40.2 in 1856 to 50.8 in 1858; in Indiana it increased from 40.1 to 49.4. Foner, *Free Soil,* p. 218.

[30] Abraham Lincoln to Nathan Sargent, June 23, 1859, Basler, *Collected Works,* Vol. III, pp. 387-388; Foner, *Free Soil,* p. 147.

[31] I have summarized the Democratic record under Buchanan at greater length elsewhere. See C. Vann Woodward, ed., *Responses of the Presidents to Charges of Misconduct* (New York: Dell Books, 1974), pp. 85-96.

[32] Ralston Skinner to Salmon P. Chase, June 7, 1860, Chase MSS (Library of Congress).

[33] D. F. Williams to Simon Cameron, September 24, 1856, Simon Cameron MSS (Dauphin County Historical Society); Seward is quoted in Foner, *Free Soil,* p. 140. On November 7, 1860, immediately after Lincoln's election, Charles Francis Adams wrote in his diary, "There is now scarcely a shadow of a doubt that the great revolution has actually taken place, and that the country has once and for all thrown off the domination of the Slaveholders." Quoted ibid., p. 223.

CHAPTER EIGHT

[1] See, for example, William L. Barney, *The Road to Secession: A New Perspective on the Old South* (New York: Praeger Publishers, 1972), pp. 188-189.

[2] The portrait of the secession movement presented in this and the following paragraphs is based primarily on ibid., William L. Barney, *The Secessionist Impulse: Alabama and Mississippi in 1860* (Princeton: Princeton University Press, 1974); Stephen A. Channing, *Crisis of Fear: Secession in South Carolina* (New York: W. W. Norton & Company, 1974); and David M. Potter, *The Impending Crisis 1848-1861,* completed and edited by Don E. Fehrenbacher (New York: Harper & Row, 1976), pp. 485-513.

[3] Foes of immediate secession explicitly made this argument. See the Louisville *Daily Journal,* November 8, 1860, the Wilmington (North Carolina) *Daily Herald,* November 9, 1860, the *Kentucky Statesman,* November 20, 1860, and the Charlottesville (Virginia) *Review,* November 23, 1860 in Dwight L. Dumond, ed., *Southern Editorials on Secession* (New York: American Historical Association, 1931), pp. 218-263.

[4] On Southern control of the Democratic congressional party, see David M. Potter, *The South and the Concurrent Majority* (Baton Rouge: Louisiana State University Press, 1972).

[5] Yancey is quoted in Potter, *Impending Crisis,* p. 465; Rhett to William Porcher Miles, January 29, 1860, quoted in Channing, *Crisis of Fear,* p. 153; Keitt, Public Letter, August 3, 1857 quoted in J. Holt Merchant, Jr., "Lawrence M. Keitt: South Carolina Fire Eater" (Ph.D. dissertation, University of Virginia, 1976), p. 158; Barney, *Road to Secession,* pp. 162-163; Barney, *Secessionist Impulse,* pp. 195-196, 251; Channing, *Crisis of Fear,* pp. 242-243.

[6] Barney, *Secessionist Impulse,* p. 23, and passim; Eugene Genovese, *The Political Economy of Slavery* (New York: Vintage Books, 1965), pp. 3-10, 243-270.

[7] The *Mercury* and *Constitutionalist* are quoted in Barney, *Road to Secession,* p. 202; on the internal contradictions in Southern arguments, the opposition of Bell men to expansion, and Yancey, see Barney, *Secessionist Impulse,* p. 315, footnote 74, and passim; on the planters' economic optimism in the 1850s, see above, Chapter III, footnote 22.

[8] George H. Reese, ed., *Proceedings of the Virginia State Convention of 1861* (4 vols.; Richmond: Virginia State Library, 1965), Vol I, pp. 53-62; Otto H. Olsen, "Historians and the Extent of Slave Ownership in the Southern United States," *Civil War History, 18* (1972), 101-116; Channing, *Crisis of Fear,* passim.

[9] Potter, *Impending Crisis,* p. 455; Toombs's speech of November 13, 1860 is quoted in N. B. Beck, "The Secession Debate in Georgia, November 1860-January 1861," in J. J. Auer, ed., *Antislavery and Disunion, 1858-1861* (New York: Harper & Row, 1963), p. 340.

[10] "Python" and Christopher Memminger to James H. Hammond, quoted in Barney, *Road to Secession,* pp. 40, 36; Robert Toombs to Alexander H. Stephens, February 10, 1860, in Phillips, *Correspondence,* p. 462.

[11] Barney, *The Secessionist Impulse,* provides the most thorough study of the local leadership of the two sides. My generalizations on voting support are based on the study of Alabama, Mississippi, and Louisiana by Peyton McCrary, Clark Miller, and Dale Baum, "Class and Party in the Secession Crisis: Voting Behavior in the Deep South, 1856-1861," forthcoming in the *Journal of Interdisciplinary History.* I have cited this with the permission of the authors. Alabama is a significant exception to this generalization of party continuity in voting on secession. There almost half the Breckinridge voters, pri-

marily nonslaveholders from north Alabama, supported Cooperationists instead of Immediatists. This ostensible anomaly will be examined below.

[12] North Carolina, *Standard,* November 14, 1860. I am indebted to Marc Kruman of Wayne State University for this citation.

[13] Lawrence Keitt to William P. Miles, October 3, 1860, quoted in Channing, *Crisis of Fear,* p. 244; Charleston *Mercury,* January 22, 1849, quoted in Joel H. Silbey, *The Shrine of Party: Congressional Voting Behavior, 1841-1852* (Pittsburgh: University of Pittsburgh Press, 1967), p. 261, footnote 64.

[14] I have not counted the few Free-Soil votes cast in 1848 and 1852.

[15] The races in Florida in 1858 and in Arkansas in 1860 were also between two Democrats instead of two parties. On the Georgia election of 1859, see Horace Montgomery, *Cracker Parties* (Baton Rouge: Louisiana State University Press, 1950), pp. 227–230.

[16] Barney, *Road to Secession,* pp. 178–179.

[17] William C. Rives to W. M. Burwell, March 19, 1855, copy, William C. Rives MSS (Library of Congress); Montgomery, *Cracker Parties,* p. 188.

[18] J. L. M. Curry to Clement Claiborne Clay, June 30, 1854, C. C. Clay Family Papers (Duke University); Albert Gallatin Brown to John F. H. Claiborne, December 17, 1854, John F. H. Claiborne MSS (Mississippi Department of Archives and History).

[19] Augusta *Chronicle and Sentinel,* quoted in Barney, *Road to Secession,* pp. 138–139.

[20] Andrew Jackson Donelson, quoted ibid., p. 57; Charter of the "Minute Men for the Defence of Southern Rights," quoted in Channing, *Crisis of Fear,* p. 269; Simms to John Jacob Bockee, December 12, 1860, in Mary C. Simms Oliphant, et al., eds., *Collected Letters of William Gilmore Simms* (5 vols.; Columbia: University of South Carolina Press, 1952-1956), Vol. II, p. 288.

[21] Andrew Pickens Butler, quoted in Gerald W. Wolff, "Party and Section: The Senate and the Kansas-Nebraska Bill," *Civil War History, 18* (1972), 297; Simms to Bockee, December 12, 1860, loc. cit., p. 287; Avery O. Craven, "Why the Southern States Seceded" in George

H. Knoles, ed., *The Crisis of the Union* (Baton Rouge: Louisiana State University Press, 1965), p. 62.

[22] Dunbar Rowland, ed., *Jefferson Davis, Constitutionalist: His Letters, Papers, and Speeches* (10 vols.; Jackson: Mississippi Department of Archives, 1923), Vol. V, pp. 198–203; Keitt quoted in Holt Merchant, "Lawrence M. Keitt," p. 131; Edgefield, South Carolina *Advertiser,* October 31, 1860, quoted in Channing, *Crisis of Fear,* p. 270; Fitzhugh, quoted in Barney, *Road to Secession,* p. 203; Edmund Ruffin, *Anticipation of the Future* (Richmond, 1860), p. viii, quoted in Margaret Cooper, "Memminger and the Virginia Politicians" (seminar paper, University of Virginia, 1975), p. 7.

[23] Rowland, ed., *Jefferson Davis,* Vol. V, p. 202.

[24] This generalization about economic issues is based on J. Mills Thornton III, "Politics and Power in a Slave Society: Alabama 1806-1860" (Ph.D. dissertation, Yale University, 1974), and Bruce W. Collins, "Economic Issues in American Politics Following the Panic of 1857" (draft copy of a dissertation in my possession).

[25] Montgomery, *Cracker Parties,* pp. 154, 205–221; Thornton, "Politics and Power in a Slave Society," pp. 325–442.

[26] William J. Evitts, *A Matter of Allegiances: Maryland from 1850 to 1861* (Baltimore: The Johns Hopkins University Press, 1974).

[27] The indexes of party disagreement on roll-call votes concerning banking in the Kentucky legislature, for example, were 52 and 48.7 in 1858 and 1860, respectively, whereas they had been 31 and 35.7 in 1851 and 1852. In Georgia, on the other hand, roll calls on banking in 1858-1859 produced a disagreement index of only 25.7. The Kentucky figures are based on all banking roll calls in each session and were calculated by Harry A. Volz III of the University of Virginia. I calculated the indexes for Georgia. They are based on six roll calls selected by Bruce W. Collins in his "Economic Issues in American Politics." Here as elsewhere I do not give specific page citations from Collins's study; I have used a personal copy of a preliminary draft instead of the final version, which has been revised and retitled as "The Politics of Particularism: Economic Issues in the Major Northern States of the USA, 1857-1858" (Ph.D. dissertation Cambridge University, 1975).

[28] Waynesboro *Argus,* May 12, 1859, (I am indebted to Marc

Kruman for this citation and others for which specific sources are not listed); Raleigh *Register,* June 4, 1856, June 20, 1859, January 4, 1860, and the Asheville *News,* February 24, 1859, all quoted in Andrew R. L. Cayton, "Political Rhetoric and the Secession Crisis in North Carolina" (unpublished seminar paper, University of Virginia, 1975), pp. 9-21. My portrait of North Carolina is based on this paper and on Kruman's draft chapter on secession in North Carolina for his Yale University Ph.D. dissertation, to be called "Parties and Politics in North Carolina, 1846-1865."

[29] Whig platform, quoted in Cayton, "Political Rhetoric," p. 20.

[30] Oliver H. Dockery to Edward Hale, August 11, 1860, quoted by Kruman.

[31] Augusta *Daily Constitutionalist,* November 16, 1860, and the New Orleans *Bee,* November 19, 1860, in Dumond, *Southern Editorials on Secession,* pp. 242-250.

[32] This interpretation, which is at odds with standard accounts, is based wholly on Thornton, "Politics and Power in a Slave Society," pp. 443-545.

[33] Charlottesville *Review,* November 23, 1860, in Dumond, *Southern Editorials on Secession,* pp. 261-263; *Greensborough Patriot,* October 4, 1860, quoted by Kruman.

[34] *Daily Nashville Patriot,* November 19, 1860, in Dumond, *Southern Editorials on Secession,* pp. 250-252; see also the *North Carolina Standard,* March 9, 1861, ibid., pp. 476-479; Leroy P. Graf and Ralph W. Haskins, eds., *The Papers of Andrew Johnson, Volume 4, 1860-1861* (Knoxville: University of Tennessee Press, 1976), p. 43.

[35] Return J. Meigs to Andrew Johnson, December 23, 1860, in Graf and Haskins, *Papers of Andrew Johnson, Volume 4,* p. 78; *Herald,* November 9, 1860, in Dumond, *Southern Editorials on Secession,* pp. 225-228; C. C. Jones to Zebulon Vance, February 4, 1861, quoted in Cayton, "Political Rhetoric," p. 26.

[36] Speech of George Badger to the North Carolina secession convention, May 10, 1861, quoted in Cayton, "Political Rhetoric," p. 28.

[37] Richardson, *Messages and Papers of the Presidents,* Vol. VI, p. 9; Worthington to Benjamin Wade, January 12, 1862, quoted in William G. Shade, *Banks or No Banks: The Money Issue in Western Politics, 1832-1865* (Detroit: Wayne State University Press, 1972), p. 244.

Index

Abolitionism, as cause of Civil War, 2
  as cause of secession, 223-225
  and election of 1836, 28
  free-soilism distinguished from, 52
  in Kansas, 193
  nonimpact of, 39
  Republicans accused of, 186-187,
    224-225
  Southern fear of, 55, 69, 223-225
Adams, Charles Francis, 44, 62
Adams, John Quincy, 20, 22
Alabama, legislative tactics in, 36
  reaction to Compromise of 1850,
    92-94
  and secession, 253-54
Albany Regency, 12-13, 22, 31
Alexander, Thomas, 43
American System, 18
Anti-Catholicism, antislavery com-
    pared to, 159
  as cause of realignment, 11, 180

and elections of 1853, 131-132
  and Know Nothingism, 156, 161-
    62, 174, 185
  as menace to republic, 6, 171
  as problem for Whigs, 121-123, 126
  and Republican party, 176-180, 215
Antimasonry, 21-22, 171, 173
Antiparty sentiment, and collapse of
    Second Party System, 4-5, 130-
    138, 165
  and Know Nothingism, 163-169
  and republicanism, 4-4, 133-138
  and Republican party, 172, 175-76
  and secession, 37, 220-222, 230,
    240
Appeal of Independent Democrats in
    Congress, 151-153
Asheville *News*, 250
Association of 1860, 219
Atchison, David R., 142, 193
Augusta *Constitutionalist*, 223

Baldwin, Roger Sherman, 96
Baltimore County Advocate, 127
Baltimore and Ohio Railroad, 109, 112
Baltimore *Sun,* 109, 127
Banking issue, and Democratic party
    before 1837, 24
  in 1820s, 18
  and Jackson, Andrew, 19, 22
  and new money supply, 110-11, 114
  and Panic of 1857, 199-201, 245,
    249
  and state constitutional revision,
    108-109
Banks, Nathaniel P., 175-177, 212-
  213
Barker, James, 157, 178
Barker, Joe, 132
Barnburners, 59-60, 129, 141
Bedini, Gaetano, 162, 164
Bell, John, 148, 207, 223, 227-228,
  233, 248-249
Benning, Henry L., 224
Berrien, John M., 57
Bigler, William L., 110, 133, 150, 162
Blair, Francis P., 137, 197
"Bleeding Kansas," *see* Kansas
"Bleeding Sumner," *see* Sumner,
  Charles
Border Ruffians, 193-194
Bowles, Samuel, 130, 140
Breckinridge, John C., 198, 206, 219,
  227, 249
Breckinridge Democrats, 219, 227
Brooks, Preston S., 195
Brown, Albert G., 206
Brown, John, 194, 214, 224-225, 228
Brown, Joseph, 246
Brownlow, William G. (Parson), 164
Buchanan, James, corruption of ad-
  ministration, 214, 240, 255
  as Democratic presidential candi-
    date, 175-176, 186
  and Dred Scott decision, 202-203
  and Lecompton constitution, 203-
    204
  and Panic of 1857, 199-200
  vote for, 198
Burnley, Albert T., 74

Butler, Andrew Pickens, 142, 195

Cabell, Edward C., 79
Calhoun, John C., antipartyism of, 37
  as opponent of Clay plan, 85
  as opponent of Jackson, 23
  as opponent of Van Buren, 41
  and Resolutions of 1847, 54
  and slavery expansion issue, 53
  and Southern Address, 69, 230
  and Southern Rights party, 59, 61
California, admission applied for, 77
  admission opposed, 71, 79-80
  gold rush in, 68, 110
  Polk's designs on, 46
  Southern interest in, 53
  Taylor plan for, 76-77
Cameron, Simon, 173-174
Campbell, James, 124, 141, 162
Cass, Lewis, 57, 60, 70
Catholic Church, comparison with
  Slave Power, 159, 162
  and Democratic party, 155, 162,
    215-216
  nativist fears of, 121, 156, 161-164,
    174, 185
  and public schools, 132
  and Republican party, 176-180, 215
  as subverter of republic, 5, 162-164
  and Whig party, 101, 121-126, 164
Charleston *Mercury,* 69, 223, 230
Chase, Salmon P., 72, 152, 170, 177,
  179, 209
Civil War, interpretations of, 1-2, 9-11
  and political system, 8-11, 16, 184,
    258-259
  sectional conflict as cause of, 1-2,
    16, 183, 217, 258-259
  timing of, 2-3, 16
Clay, Henry, and American system,
  18
  and Compromise of 1850, 81-84,
    86, 89
  foe of Jackson, 23
  foe of Old Republicans, 20
  foe of Tyler, 40
  interpretation of defeat, 46
  rivalry with Taylor, 73, 75, 79, 84

and Texas annexation, 43
and Union party movement, 91, 94-
95
and Whig nomination of 1848, 62-
63
Clayton, John M., 74, 76-77, 81, 96
Clemens, Jeremiah, 94
Cleveland Plaindealer, 135
Cobb. Howell, and Compromise of
1850, 86
and deficit financing, 201
and election of 1848, 61-62
election as Speaker of House, 79
and Kansas-Nebraska Act, 145
and Southern Address, 70
and Union party movement, 92-94
warning on tariff issue, 47
Colfax, Schuyler, 124
Compromise of 1850, as basis for new
parties, 91-94, 118
components of, 86-87
distinction from Clay's proposals,
82-84
distinction from Taylor plan, 82-83
and election of 1852, 97-98, 106,
119
impact on Second Party System, 68
as model for Kansas-Nebraska Act,
145
party positions on, 87-98
Pierce's views on, 140
political determinants of, 67
and sectional conflict interpretation,
102
Confederate States of America, 2,
219, 257
Connecticut, election of 1853 in, 130-
131
impact of Kansas-Nebraska Act in,
114, 155
prohibition issue in, 114, 123, 155
Conscience Whigs, 44, 59
Constitutional Union party, 215, 228
Cooper, James, 84, 95
Cooperationists, 220, 227, 253-254
Corruption, Democrats charges with,
134, 208, 214, 250-251, 253, 255
and Know Nothingism, 165-167

and republicanism, 134, 137, 165
Corwin, Thomas, 62, 209, 215
Covode Committee, 214
Crawford, George W., 75, 77
Crittenden, John J., as advisor of
Taylor administration, 73-77
and new Opposition party, 207-209,
212, 248-249
prominence in upper South, 228
Cushing, Caleb, 141, 143

Dallas, George M., 57
Davis, Jefferson, and federal slave
code, 206
inaugural address as Confederate
president, 242-243
opponent of Compromise of 1850,
82, 85
opponent of immediate secession,
222
in Pierce cabinet, 141
rival of Henry S. Foote, 86, 92
DeBow's Review, 225
Deep South, collapse of Whig party
in, 93, 118-119, 231
concentration of slaveholders in,
228-229, 244-245
contrasted to upper South, 2-3, 6-9,
14, 226-227, 229-231, 243-244,
252-257
and Democratic party, 236, 244-
248
political developments in during
1850s, 244-248
and republicanism, 243-244
and Republican party, 237, 240-
243, 246
secession movement in, 2, 219, 220
slavery issue in, 233, 236, 244-248
stake in black slavery, 228-229
Union party movement in, 13, 91-
94, 97-98, 118, 141
weakness of two-party system in,
230-237
Democratic party, coalition with Free
Soilers, 72, 141
and Compromise of 1850, 87-98
and economic issues, 24-25, 31-33,

110-112, 199-201
and election of 1836, 25-29
and election of 1844, 41-44
and election of 1848, 60-61, 64-65
and election of 1852, 106, 119,
127-130
and election of 1856, 186-187, 198
and election of 1858, 213
and election of 1860, 205-206, 216
factionalism during Pierce Administration, 140-143
fate in 1850s compared to Whigs',
103-104
final disruption of, 205-206
formation of, 18-21
impact of Kansas-Nebraska Act on,
150-151, 154
and Jackson, Andrew, 22-28
and Know Nothings, 157, 177, 186,
198, 239-240
and Lecompton constitution, 204-
206, 213
and negative state, 32-33
and Panic of 1837, 31-33
and Panic of 1857, 199-201
and personal liberty laws, 211-212
as pro-Southern party, 183, 191-
192
racist appeals of, 187
response to Clay plan, 85-86
response to Taylor plan, 79-81
and secession, 227, 230
secessionists' distrust of, 220-222
and slavery issue, 29-31, 70-72, 79-
98, 141, 150-151, 154, 204-206,
211-213, 244-248
in South in 1850s, 244-248
and Southern Address, 70-71
as surrogate for Catholic conspiracy,
215
as surrogate for Slave Power, 191-
192, 211, 214-215
and Van Buren, Martin, 7, 20-21,
25-29, 31-33, 41-42, 60
Democratic Review, 46
Dickinson, Daniel S., 57, 80, 142
Dix, John A., 142
Dixon, Archibald, 146-147

Douglas, Stephen A., and Compromise
of 1850, 85-87
as Democratic presidential candidate,
206
and Dred Scott decision, 205
and Kansas-Nebraska Act, 143-147,
149, 184
and Lecompton constitution, 204-
205
opponent of Union party movement,
94, 99, 113
and popular sovereignty, 145, 154
and Preston bill, 78
Republican support of, 206
voting support in 1860, 228, 237
Douglas Democrats, 227
Dow, Neal, 125
Dred Scott decision, 201-203, 205

Economic issues, before 1837, 17-19
as bulwark of Second Party System,
31-35, 40, 101, 109-110, 115,
134-136
and constitutional revision, 107-109
disappearance in Deep South, 118
disappearance of party lines on, 107-
115, 118, 245-247
impact of economic boom on, 107-
115
and Panic of 1857, 199-201, 245
and republicanism, 110, 134-136
Republican party exploits, 212, 215
Election of 1836, 25-31
Election of 1844, 41-44
Election of 1848, 59-65
Election of 1852, 96-98, 119-130
Election of 1856, 175-179, 185-199
Election of 1858, 213
Election of 1860, 215-216
Eliot, Samuel, 95
Ellsworth, William, 45
Erie Canal issue, 115-118, 128
Erie Railroad, 112
Ethnocultural issues, and Democratic
party, 33-34, 123-128, 186
and election of 1848, 66
importance of anti-Nebraskaism
compared to, 155-159

and realignment of 1850s, 11, 155-159, 176-177, 186
and Republican voters, 179-180
and Second Party System, 34, 101-102, 120-125, 131-132
and Whig party in 1852, 120-125

Federal system, and election of 1836, 30-31
and election of 1848, 60-64
and Second Party System, 12, 14-16, 30-31, 60-64, 95-97, 104-105, 115-119
and slavery issue, 14-16, 30-31, 60-64, 95-97
and Whig party, 30-31, 95-97, 115-119
Federalist party, 7, 12
Fillmore, Millard, and Compromise of 1850, 81, 87, 89-90, 94-95
impact on Republican vote in 1856, 179, 198
as Know Nothing presidential candidate, 171, 174-176, 185, 187, 245
rivalry with Seward, 75, 80, 87, 96
vote for in 1856, 198
and Whig convention of 1852, 97
Fitzhugh, George, 242
Fitzpatrick, Benjamin, 222
Foner, Eric, 2, 9
Foote, Henry S., 82, 86, 92-94
Fort Sumter, 2, 257
Freeport Doctrine, 206
Free-soilism, abolitionism distinguished from, 52
and anti-Nebraska parties, 151-152
as cause of secession, 222-223
and Know Nothings, 174
Northern motivations for, 50-52
and racism, 52
and republicanism, 51-52
and Republican party, 188-189
and Slave Power, 51
Free Soil party, coalition with Democrats, 68, 72, 89
and Compromise of 1850, 87
and economic issues, 105
formation of, 60-61

and prohibition, 124, 131
and Taylor patronage, 75
and Taylor plan, 78
vote for in 1848, 64
vote for in 1852, 129
Frémont, John C., as antiparty candidate, 176
charge of Catholicism against, 179, 186
contrast to Buchanan and Fillmore, 176
and North Americans, 171, 177-178
vote for, 198, 237
F Street Mess, 142, 145, 147
Fugitive Slave Act, 89-90, 97-98, 153, 211-212

Gadsden, James, 140
Gag Rule, 29, 39
Gardner, Henry, 170, 174
Genovese, Eugene, 2
Georgia, and Georgia Platform, 92
reaction to Compromise of 1850, 92-94
secession in, 224
Whigs and Walker Tariff in, 47
Germans, alienation from Republicans, 179
in Republican party, 178
opponents of nativism, 177
opponents of prohibition, 121-122, 177
Protestant-Catholic division in, 176
support for Pierce, 126
Giddings, Joshua R., 91
Graham, William A., 113
Grant, Ulysses S., 197
Greeley, Horace, 46, 167
Guadeloupe-Hidalgo, 50, 58
Gwin, William, 94

Hale, John P., 174
Hall, Nathan K., 95
Hammond, James H., 222
Harper's Ferry, 214, 224
Harrison, William Henry, 25, 40
Hartford Courant, 188
Hayes, Rutherford B., 120, 169

Hilliard, Henry, 79
Hughes, Archbishop John, 162
Hunt, Washington, 208
Hunter, Robert M. T., 142, 252

Immigrants, and Democratic party,
    155, 177, 198, 216
  fear of, contrasted to anti-Nebraska-
    ism, 159-161
  in South, 239, 248
  nativist fears of, 121
  as threat to Whig party, 120-121,
    123
  vote suppressed by Know Nothings,
    173-174
Independent Treasury, 32, 34, 46
Indiana, reaction to Polk administra-
    tion, 47-48
Irish, and prohibition, 121-122
  Protestant-Catholic rivalries among,
    176
  and Protestant Democrats, 162
  support for Pierce, 126

Jackson, Andrew, and formation of
    Second Party System, 22-25
  hard money policies of, 24-25
  impact of retirement of, 25, 28, 31,
    40
  and Nullification, 7
  proslavery position of, 22, 29
  and Texas annexation, 41
Jefferson, Thomas, 12
Jeffersonian party, 7, 12, 20
Johnson, Andrew, 127, 137, 140,
    252, 255
Johnson, Reverdy, 74, 77
Johnson, Richard M., 22
Johnston, William F., 85, 89-90, 95-
    96
Julian, George W., 103

Kansas, death as issue, 205-207, 211
  and Lecompton constitution, 203-
    204
  Republican concentration on, 189,
    194-196
  Southern refusal to go to, 53

strife in, 192-193
Kansas-Nebraska Act, as attempt to
    save Second Party System, 147-
    148, 184
  and Democratic party, 145-146,
    186
  framing of, 145-147
  impact of, 114, 148-152, 181, 184,
    186
  and sectional conflict interpreta-
    tion, 102
Keitt, Lawrence M., 56, 222, 230,
    242
Kentucky, political patterns in 1850s,
    249
King, Thomas Butler, 77
Know Nothing party, and antiparty
    sentiment, 163-169
  appeal of, 162-169
  as base for Opposition party, 199
  and campaign of 1856, 185-186
  and collapse of Second Party Sys-
    tem, 164-166, 169, 180
  disillusionment with, 172-175, 195
  emergence of, 156-159
  as menace to republic, 186, 239-
    240
  merger with Republicans, 158, 162-
    165, 172
  and realignment of 1850s, 180
  and republicanism, 156, 162-165,
    172
  as rival of Republican party, 156-
    157, 159, 162-163, 169-171, 179,
    186, 198-199
  as rival of Whig party, 156-157, 159
  secession compared to, 221
  and slavery issue, 171-173
  sources of, 159-169
  in South, 165-167, 198, 231, 233,
    239-240, 245, 249
  strength of, 158, 170-171

Lawrence, Abbott, 111
Lawrence, the Sack of, 194-195
Lecompton constitution, and Demo-
    cratic party, 204-206, 247
  and Douglas, 204-205

and new Opposition party, 207-209, 248

and Republican party, 204-209

and Southern Democrats, 247

Lemoyne, Julius, 45

Letcher, John P., 252

Levin, Lewis, C., 126

Liberty party, 44-45, 59

Lincoln, Abraham, and call for troops, 2, 257

election of, 152

election of as cause of secession, 219, 222, 227, 242, 252-253, 255, 257

and Know Nothings, 170

reaction to Kansas-Nebraska Act, 149

and Republican party, 214-215

and Slave Power conspiracy, 210-211

vote for in 1860, 215-216, 237

Whig party abandoned by, 159

Lincoln-Douglas debates, 206, 210-211

Lower South, see Deep South

McLean, John, 23, 164, 168

Maine Law, 121, 130-131

Manifest Destiny, 46, 106, 145

Marcy, William L., 29, 115, 126, 141-142, 146

Maryland, banking issue in, 114

collapse of Second Party System in, 108-109

politics of 1850s in, 248-249

realignment in, 158

turnout in 1852 in, 129

Mason, James M., 142

Massachusetts, ethnocultural issues in, 124

Whig collapse in, 130

Whig divisions in, 44, 59

Meredith, William M., 74, 84

Mexican Cession, Clay plan for, 83-84

Southern interest in, 53, 59

and slavery extension issue, 40, 49

Taylor plan for, 68, 72, 76-78

Mexican War, 46-47

Mississippi, reaction to Compromise of 1850 in, 92-94

Missouri Compromise, 7, 19-20, 69, 144-146, 202

Molitor, Stephen, 177

Montgomery Advertiser, 56

Morgan, Edwin D., 178, 209

Nashville Convention, 71, 83, 88

National Intelligencer, 63

National Republicans, 21

Native American party, 62, 66, 74-75, 101, 126

Nativism, as cause of realignment of 1850s, 11, 155, 180

and Know Nothingism, 156-157

political versus cultural, as spurious distinction, 179

as problem for Whigs in 1852, 121-123, 126

and Republican party, 178

and Whig vote in 1848, 66

New England Emigrant Aid Company, 192

New Mexico, 53, 76-77, 78, 83

New Orleans Bee, 105

New York, antiabolitionism in, 29

Democratic factionalism in, 72, 115, 141-142

election of 1854 in, 155-156

Erie Canal issue in, 115-116

Whig factionalism in, 91, 115

vote in 1848 in, 65

New York Central Railroad, 112

New York Tribune, 46

Nonslaveholders, and Democratic party, 237-238, 244-245

political proclivities of, 237-238, 244-246

and political strategies in South, 244-245

as potential recruits for Republican party, 225-226, 237

racism of, 223-224

as rivals of planters, 225-226, 237, 249-251, 253-254, 256

role in secession, 222-223, 224, 226-227, 230, 237-238, 243-

244, 253-257
role in Union party movement, 93
and Second Party System, 238
stake in slavery extension issue, 52-
56
North American party, 171, 176-177
North Carolina, political developments
in 1850s in, 249-251
suffrage reform as issue in, 119
"No-Territory," 57-58
Nullification, 7, 23, 28

Ohio State Journal, 43
Omnibus Bill, 86-87
Opposition party, and Lecompton
issue, 207-209
as rival of Republicans, 208-214
in South, 220, 249-250, 252
Order of Star Spangled Banner, 156
Order of United Americans, 126
Oregon, 42, 46, 53, 59

Palfrey, John Gorham, 64
Panic, of 1819, 17-19
Panic of 1837, 31-32
Panic of 1857, 199-201, 245, 249
Pennsylvania, and Catholic issue, 124,
126
and Fugitive Slave Act, 90
impact of Polk administration on,
47-48
legislative voting in, 36, 112, 114-
115
and Taylor Republican movement,
74
Whig bankruptcy in, 130
Pennsylvania Mainline Canal System,
114-115, 128
Pennsylvania Railroad, 112, 114-115
People's Party, 137, 150, 167-168,
175, 212-213
Pierce, Franklin, and Catholic issue,
123-125
and Democratic factionalism, 140-
143, 246
as Democratic presidential candidate, 98, 119
and Kansas-Nebraska Act, 147, 149

support for Lecompton government,
194
vote for in 1852, 127-130
Pittsburgh *Gazette,* 125
Political Crisis of 1850s, causes of, 9-
16
and collapse of Second Party System, 130-138
definition of, 3-5
distinction between political reorganization and realignment in, 4,
11
phases of, 9-11
and reaction to Kansas-Nebraska
Act, 151-154
and republicanism, 5-9
and secession, 6, 240
Polk, James K., 42, 46-49, 101
Popular Sovereignty, and Compromise
of 1850, 78, 80, 85, 89
and Democratic party, 57, 72, 80,
85, 186, 192
and election of 1848, 61-64
endorsement by Republicans, 212
faith of Douglas in, 145, 154, 192
interpretations of, 147
in Kansas, 193, 203-204
and Kansas-Nebraska Act, 144-147
and republicanism, 145
Pottawatomie Massacre, 194
Preston, William Ballard, 74, 77
Prohibitionism, as cause of realignment of 1850s, 11, 155
and collapse of Second Party System, 131
party positions on in 1830s and
1840s, 33-34
and Republican party, 178
in state politics in early 1850s, 114
and Whig party in 1852, 121-123,
125
Public school issue, 132, 162-163,
178-179

Raleigh *Register,* 250
Raymond, Henry J., 189
Realignment of 1850s, 4, 11, 102,
158-159

Reemelin, Charles, 175
Republicanism, and American political system, 4-6, 8, 16-17, 184
and Antimasonry, 21-22
and anti-Nebraska sentiment, 151-154
and antiparty sentiment, 133-138, 238-240
definition of, 5, 17
and economic issues, 18, 22-23, 33-35, 110, 134-136
and Free-soilism, 51-52
and Know Nothingism, 156, 162-165, 172
and popular sovereignty, 145
and Republican party, 172, 175-176, 189-199, 257-258
and secession, 6, 238-244, 252-254
and Second Party System, 37-38, 134-138
and slavery issue, 6, 37-38, 55-56, 134-135
Southern devotion to, 6, 37-38, 54-56, 238-240, 241-259
Republican party, and abolitionism, 187-189, 224-225
and anti-Catholicism, 176-180, 215
and antiparty sentiment, 172, 175-176
and black slavery, 185, 187-189, 216
challenge from new Opposition party, 208-214
and Dred Scott decision, 202-203, 206
and election of 1856, 171, 175-181, 187-199
and election of 1858, 208-213
and election of 1860, 214-217
and Fugitive Slave Act, 153, 211-212
and Lecompton constitution, 204-209, 212
and majority rule, 197-198, 257
merger with Know Nothings, 171-180, 212-213
Michigan platform of 1854, 153-154
nomination of Frémont, 171, 176-177
and Panic of 1857, 200-201
persuasion of, 180-181, 184-185, 187-198
potential in South, 225-226, 236-237
potential weaknesses after 1860, 220-221
and prohibitionism, 155, 178
and racism, 187-189
and republicanism, 172, 175-176, 189-199, 214, 216, 226, 257-258
rise of, 9, 150, 154
rival of Know Nothings, 156-157, 159, 162-163, 169-171, 180, 185, 198-199
secession compared to, 221, 238, 240
and sectional conflict, 10, 180-181
and Slave Power conspiracy, 181, 184-185, 189-191, 197, 209-211, 214-215, 257-258
and slavery extension, 188-189, 208
Southern fear of, 224-227, 240-243
triumph of, 4, 183, 216-217
Rhett, Robert Barnwell, 222-223
Richmond *Enquirer,* 48
Richmond Whig, 38, 43
Ritchie, Thomas, 20-21, 42
Rives, William C., 239
Round Robin, 94-95
Ruffin, Edmund, 242

Sanford, John A., 201
Scott, Dred, *see* Dred Scott decision
Scott, Winfield, 62, 96-97, 119, 123-130
Secession, abolitionism as cause of, 223-225
as antiparty movement, 220-222, 230, 240
difference between upper and lower South, 2-3, 6-9, 14, 226-231, 243-244, 252-257
explanations of, 222-227
and fear of Southern Republican

party, 225-226, 236-237
fear of white enslavement as cause
of, 240-243
internal divisions over, 226-227
movement for in Deep South, 219-
220
persuasion of, 238-244, 252-257
as reform movement, 6, 238, 243
and republicanism, 238-244, 252-
254
role of Democrats in, 227, 230
similarity to Republican party, 221,
238, 240
threat of, in 1850, 92-93
two-party system as deterrent to,
6-9, 37-38, 69, 230-231, 236-237,
254-257
Second American Party System, as
bulwark of republicanism, 8, 37-
38, 135, 238, 258-259
and causes of Civil War, 3, 13, 258-
259
collapse in North, 151-159
collapse in South, 92, 238-239
and Compromise of 1850, 87-90,
98
and disappearance of ethnocultural
issues, 125-126
dynamics of, 3, 11-13, 35-38, 103,
135-136
and economic issues, 17-19, 31-35,
40, 101, 107-115, 118, 135-136
and election of 1848, 60-66
and election of 1852, 98-99
failure of, 3-4, 9-14, 92, 102-105,
128-139, 151-169, 238-239
formation of, 17, 20, 22-25, 28-31
impact of economic boom on, 107-
115
and Kansas-Nebraska Act, 147-148,
184
and Panic of 1837, 32-35
and Polk Administration, 45-49
and sectional conflict, 3, 9-11, 37-
38, 40, 49, 102, 138, 181-183,
258-259
and slavery issue, 9-11, 20, 28-31,
40, 43-45, 49, 57-66, 68, 87-90,

98, 147-148
and state constitutional revision,
106-109
survival in New York, 118
and Taylor, Zachary, 73
and Texas issue, 43-45
and threat of new parties in 1850-
51, 91-94
Sectional Conflict, as cause of Civil
War, 1-3, 16, 183, 258-259
impact in 1850s assessed, 181, 183-
184
Negro slavery as source of, 1-3, 9-11,
258-259
and politics in Deep South, 245-248
and republicanism, 151-154
and Second Party System, 3, 9-11,
22-25, 28, 31, 37-38, 49, 102,
138, 181, 183, 258-259
Seward, William Henry, and Compromise of 1850, 80, 85, 90-91
and Erie Canal issue, 115-118
and Kansas-Nebraska Act, 146-147,
149, 184
and Know Nothings, 167, 171, 215
and nativists, 155
and pro-Catholic strategy, 123
and prohibition issue, 125, 156
and Republican nomination, 215
and Republican persuasion, 188,
194, 197, 203, 211, 216-217
and Winfield Scott, 96, 119, 123
and Taylor Republican movement,
74
Whig party abandoned by, 159
Silvery Grays, 91, 95-96, 115, 149,
174
Simms, William Gilmore, 241-242
Slave Power, and anti-Nebraska sentiment, 149, 151-154
definition of, 51
Democratic party as surrogate for,
191-198, 211, 214-215
and Dred Scott decision, 202-203
as menace to republic, 89, 151-154,
202-203, 240, 257-258
as target of Republican party, 170,
181, 184-185, 190, 197, 202-

203, 209, 257-258

Slavery, as basis of republican society, 241

as cause of Civil War, 1-2, 258-259

and Deep South politics, 223, 246-248

and formation of Democratic party, 20-21, 28-29

and formation of Whig party, 28-30

importance of issue contrasted to republicanism, 238, 258

and Know Nothings, 171-173

political impact of, 10-11, 14, 20-21, 28-30, 39-45, 49, 60-67, 70-72, 95-98, 148-152, 159, 183-184, 187-189, 190, 223, 246-248, 258-259

and Republican party, 187-189, 190

and secession, 222-223

stake of upper and lower South in, 228-229

and Whig party, 28-30, 70-72, 95-98, 148-152

white status distinguished from black institution, 55-56, 134-135, 152, 190-191, 217, 240-243, 258-259

Slavery Extension Issue, as cause of secession, 222-223, 241

and disruption of Democracy, 206

in Kansas, 192-193

Northern interest in, 50-52

and Oregon, 53

and Second Party System, 39-45, 50-66

settlement of, 206-208

Southern interest in, 52-56, 222-223, 238, 241

Smith, Truman, 63, 124-125

Soulé, Pierre, 141

Southern Address, 69-71, 230

Southern Rights, 53-56, 63, 146, 220

Southern Rights party, 59, 61, 92-94, 105, 118, 141

Springfield *Republican,* 130

Stephens, Alexander H., 36, 54, 57, 62, 79, 86, 92-94, 148, 222

Sumner, Charles, 64, 152, 165, 189, 194-196

Sundquist, James L., 44

Taney, Roger B., 202-203

Tariff Issue, 47-49, 74, 111, 201, 208

Taylor, John, 12

Taylor, Zachary, attacks from Southern Democrats on, 71

comparison with Pierce, 143

confidence of Southern Whigs in, 70

death of, 87

disillusionment of Southern Whigs with, 71-72

embrace of Native Americans, 101, 122

and No-Party strategy, 62, 67-68, 72-76, 105, 134

patronage policy of, 74-76

policy for Mexican Cession, 68, 72, 76-78

response of Congress to, 79-81

rivalry with Clay, 84

speech at Mercer, Pennsylvania, 71, 78

Taylor Republican party, 74-75, 121

Tennessee, turnout in 1852, 129

Texas, 40-45, 78, 83

Tocqueville, Alexis de, 18

Toombs, Robert, 57, 62, 70, 75, 77, 79, 86, 225

and Union party movement, 92-94

Tyler, John, 40-44

Ullmann, Daniel, 174, 215

Union party, 13, 91-94, 97-98, 118, 141

Upper South, contrast to Deep South, 2-3, 6-9, 14, 226-231, 243-244, 252-257

and political developments of 1850s, 248-252

and republicanism, 243-244, 248-249, 255

and Republican party, 237, 255

secession movement in, 227, 257

stake in black slavery, 228-229

two-party system in, 230-237, 248-252

Van Buren, Martin, and election of 1844, 41-42
  as founder of Democratic party, 7, 20-21
  as Free Soil candidate, 60, 64
  and New York factionalism, 60, 141
  and Panic of 1837, 31-33
  as proponent of party conflict, 7, 31, 37
  and presidential campaign of 1836, 25-29
  pro-Southern actions of, 29, 31
Virginia, and secession, 252
  Whig losses in, in 1849, 71, 75

Walker, Robert J., 41-43, 53, 203, 247
Walker Tariff, 47-49, 74, 111
Washington *Republic,* 74
Washington *Union,* 85, 113
Webster, Daniel, and Compromise of 1850, 81, 84
  in Fillmore administration, 87, 94-95
  rivalry with Seward, 85, 96
  rivalry with Taylor, 73, 75
  and Second Party System, 13, 25
  and Union party movement, 91
  and Whig convention of 1852, 97
Weed, Thurlow, 61, 80, 115-118, 124-125, 156, 159, 167, 171
Welles, Gideon, 165
Whig party, and California, 78
  collapse of, 10-11, 14, 93, 118-119, 148-159, 163-169, 231, 238-239
  collapse in Deep South, 93, 118-119, 231, 238-239
  collapse in North, 151-159, 163-169
  and Compromise of 1850, 87-98
  and economic issues, 34-36, 109-112, 117-120
  and election of 1836, 25-30
  and election of 1844, 41-44
  and election of 1848, 61-66
  and election of 1852, 97-98, 119-130
  and ethnocultural issues, 120-125, 155-159
  and expansionism, 106
  fate in 1850s contrasted to Democrats', 103, 119
  formation of, 22-23
  impact of Know Nothingism on, 156-159, 163-169
  and Kansas-Nebraska Act, 146-155
  and loss of flexibility on slavery issue, 95-98
  and Pierce administration, 140
  and pro-Catholic strategy, 123-126
  revival of promoted, 199, 207-209, 250-251
  and secession, 227-228
  and Southern Address, 70-72
  and Taylor plan, 79-81
White, Hugh Lawson, 25, 28-29
Wide Awake Clubs, 176, 215
Wilmington *Herald,* 256
Wilmot, David, 49, 51
Wilmot Proviso, alternatives to, 56-58
  and election of 1848, 59-64
  impact on Second Party System, 58, 61, 72, 102, 141
  introduction of, 50
  Northern support for, 50-52
  and Republican party, 209
  and sectional conflict interpretation, 102
  Southern opposition to, 52-56
Wilson, Henry, 174
Winston, George, 246
Winthrop, Robert C., 57, 79, 96, 122
Wise, Henry A., 40, 252
Wright, Silas, 29

Yancey, William Lowndes, 37, 60, 92, 221, 223, 231, 254

NINETEENTH AND TWENTIETH CENTURY
AMERICAN HISTORY IN NORTON PAPERBACK

Burton Bledstein   *The Culture of Professionalism: The Middle Class and the Development of Higher Education in America*   N891

Fawn Brodie   *Thaddeus Stevens*   N331

Roger H. Brown   *The Republic in Peril: 1812*   N578

John D. Buenker   *Urban Liberalism and Progressive Reform*   N880

David Burner   *The Politics of Provincialism: The Democratic Party in Transition. 1918–1932*   N792

Stanley W. Campbell   *The Slave Catchers: Enforcement of the Fugitive Slave Law. 1850–1860*   N626

Steven A. Channing   *Crisis of Fear: Secession in South Carolina*   N730

Dudley T. Cornish   *The Sable Arm: Negro Troops in the Union Army, 1861–1865*   N334

Robert F. Dalzell, Jr.   *Daniel Webster and the Trial of American Nationalism, 1843–1852*   N782

Merton L. Dillon   *The Abolitionists: The Growth of a Dissenting Minority*   N957

Robert J. Donovan   *Conflict and Crisis: The Presidency of Harry S Truman, 1945–1948*   N924

Dwight Lowell Dumond   *Antislavery*   N370

Richard E. Ellis   *The Jeffersonian Crisis: Courts and Politics in the Young Republic*   N729

W. McKee Evans   *Ballots and Fence Rails: Reconstruction on the Lower Cape Fear*   N711

Federal Writers' Project   *These Are Our Lives*   N763

Herbert Feis   *Three International Episodes: Seen from E.A.*   N351

Robert H. Ferrell   *Peace in Their Time: The Origins of Kellogg-Brand Pact*   N491

George B. Forgie   *Patricide in the House Divided: A Psychological Interpretation of Lincoln and His Age*   N035

John Hope Franklin   *The Free Negro in North Carolina, 1790–1860*   N579

Margaret Fuller   *Woman in the Nineteenth Century*   N615

William H. Goetzmann   *Exploration and Empire: The Explorer and the Scientist in the Winning of the American West*   N881

Margaret Jarman Hagood   *Mothers of the South: Portraiture of the White Tenant Farm Woman*   N816

John S. Haller and Robin M. Haller   *The Physician and Sexuality in Victorian America*   N845

Holman Hamilton *Prologue to Conflict: The Crisis and Compromise of 1850* N345

Pendleton Herring *The Politics of Democracy* N306

Francis Jennings *The Invasion of America: Indians, Colonialism and the Cant of Conquest* N830

George F. Kennan *Realities of American Foreign Policy* N320

Gabriel Kolko *Railroads and Regulation, 1877–1916* N531

Stanley I. Kutler *Privilege and Creative Destruction: The Charles River Bridge Case* N885

Howard Roberts Lamar *The Far Southwest, 1846–1912: A Territorial History* N522

Peggy Lamson *The Glorious Failure: Black Congressman Robert Brown Elliott and the Reconstruction in South Carolina* N733

Richard P. McCormick *The Second American Party System: Party Formation in the Jacksonian Era* N680

Robert C. McMath, Jr. *Populist Vanguard: A History of the Southern Farmers' Alliance* N869

Donald R. Matthews *U.S. Senators and Their World* (Rev. Ed.) N679

Herbert S. Mitgang *The Man Who Rode the Tiger: The Life and Times of Judge Samuel Seabury* N922

Burl Noggle *Teapot Dome* N297

Douglass C. North *The Economic Growth of the United States, 1790–1860* N346

Arnold A. Offner *American Appeasement: United States Foreign Policy and Germany. 1933–1938* N801

Nell Irvin Painter *Exodusters: Black Migration to Kansas After Reconstruction* N951

Robert E. Quirk *An Affair of Honor: Woodrow Wilson and the Occupation of Veracruz* N390

James L. Roark *Masters Without Slaves: Southern Planters in the Civil War and Reconstruction* N901

Richard H. Sewell *Ballots for Freedom: Antislavery Politics in the U.S.* N966

Bernard W. Sheehan *Seeds of Extinction: Jeffersonian Philanthropy and the American Indian* N715

Kathryn Kish Sklar *Catharine Beecher: A Study in American Domesticity* N812

John W. Spanier *The Truman-MacArthur Controversy and the Korean War* N279

Sarah Stage *Female Complaints: Lydia Pinkham and the Business of Women's Medicine* N038

Ralph Stone *The Irreconcilables: The Fight Against the League of Nations* N671

Ida M. Tarbell *History of the Standard Oil Company* (David Chalmers, Ed.) N496

Tom E. Terrill and Jerrold Hirsch, Eds. *Such As Us: Southern Voices of the Thirties* N927

George Brown Tindall *The Disruption of the Solid South* N663

Frederick Jackson Turner *The United States 1830–1850* N308

Richard W. Van Alstyne *The Rising American Empire* N750

Thomas L. Webber *Deep Like the Rivers: Education in the Slave Quarter Community, 1831–1865* N998

Joel Williamson *After Slavery: The Negro in South Carolina During Reconstruction, 1861–1877* N759